TOWARD A GLOBAL

EASY STREET

SUCCESS AND FAILURE
IN THE SEARCH FOR PROSPERITY

TOWARD A GLOBAL

EASY STREET

SUCCESS AND FAILURE
IN THE SEARCH FOR PROSPERITY

From the Editors of Insight

Insight
books

First edition, 1990

Published in the United States by
Insight Books
3600 New York Avenue, N.E.
Washington D.C. 20002

ISBN 0-9627798-0-6
Printed in the United States of America

TABLE OF CONTENTS

THE UNITED STATES

PART 1

NO PLACE LIKE HOME

PART 2

EXPENSIVE CONGRESSIONAL TASTES

PART 3

UP FROM THE BOTTOM OF THE HEAP

THE VISUAL TALE

PART 4

IMAGES OF RICH AND POOR

117

THE WORLD

PART 5

OLD FRIENDS

PART 6

AN EMPIRE'S END

PART 7

ENIGMAS OF THE EAST

PART 8

LATIN LABYRINTHS

PART 9

AFRICAN QUAGMIRES

PART 10

ROADS TO RUIN

INDEX

FOREWORD

If there is nothing so old as yesterday's newspaper, it probably has less to do with the intrinsic limitations of journalism than with the way all too many journalists practice their craft. Their imperative, which is a natural consequence of competition between media outlets, is to be the first with the news. The danger reporters face, which has grown more pronounced in a media age dominated by television, is that the rush of events will sweep the reporters along with it. When the practice of journalism becomes little more than the recitation of the latest fact in a perpetually flowing stream of facts, it is no wonder that the result does not age well. Journalism has been called a first draft of history, but as it is now commonly practiced, it is a bizarre form of history writing indeed — one that is indifferent to the past and uncertain about the future in spinning a tale that has no beginning or end, only a perpetual middle. It is history as shaggy dog story.

This book is a collection of journalism of a different kind. The virtue of journalism in general is that it is firmly grounded in time (which is the near-present) and place (which can be anywhere). The here and now has to be conveyed vividly, but this is only a starting point. To avoid the danger of becoming transfixed by the latest fact, the perpetual middle, reporters have to get beyond the news. Those latest facts do not pop up out of nowhere. They do not necessarily have significance all by themselves. By providing context, even by offering a little historical perspective, however, reporters can let larger issues — the things that usually get lost — see the light of day.

This book is about some of those larger issues, specifically those concerning the basic question of why some people are well-off in material terms and others are not. There is more to a full life than prosperity, of course, and a depressingly large number of people prosper only to find themselves spiritually and intellectually empty. Some even see material privation as a necessary route to spiritual fulfillment. But most people do not, and their aspirations are what concern us here.

This is the story of the way people live their lives and the story of how governments let them live those lives. It is the story of what people want and what they can get. It is the story of what a single person can and cannot do and what a government, whether it means well or ill, can and cannot do.

For more than 40 years, the salient point on this as on so many other issues was the ideological conflict between West and East — between liberal, democratic capitalism and the command economies of communism. The broad contour of the postwar era was a Western world growing richer and richer and a communist world (though many in the West would not admit it) slipping farther and farther behind. That crisis for the East came to a head in 1989-1990, and it is fair to say that for most of the people of Eastern Europe, the single greatest obstacle to prosperity — rule according to principles laid down in Moscow — was gone at last. As the rulers of the East lost faith in the command economy or gave way to people who did not share that faith, so too did the Soviet "model" of development lose credence in the Third World as any sort of road map for economic growth (though it remained in many places a useful model for political subjugation).

But this, of course, barely begins to tell the story. In the West, some countries did very well for themselves, others less so. Some started out brilliantly and declined, others skidded badly and then recovered. Within each country, some people did well and others did not. The question that lies just beyond the description of the here and now is: Why?

In the Third World, countries that appear on the map cheek by jowl have often exhibited even greater disparities of fortune. Some built industries rapidly while life in others remained in 1990 as it had been in 1890 or 1790. Some had only recently become independent nations and had to cope with the cast-away baggage of empires that had gone home.

In the formerly communist world, decades of centrally planned economic misery had exacted a ferocious toll, and concrete plans for how to undo the mess lagged far behind people's aspirations for freedom. Groping for new ways began at once, but results promised to be a long way off.

Since **Insight** began publishing in 1985, the magazine has made no secret of its anticommunist, pro-market orientation, but in a sense, this puts the matter too abstractly. For many people around the world, the day-in, day-out struggle is simply for the possibility of living a normal life: to be safe in one's home with one's family; to be treated fairly by others; to do better today than yesterday, better tomorrow than today; to live the joys and pains of a full life and to die with the expectation that one's children will be able to do the same. For some, prosperity in this sense is a relatively simple thing to come by, and Easy Street is an address on a local map. For others, prosperity is a matter of life and death, and the chance of achieving it is grim. At both extremes, however, the fundamental aspiration is the same. In the end, this volume is about ordinary people, whose aspirations the editors of **Insight** by and large share and, moreover, believe to be just.

The journalism compiled here is drawn from the first five years of **Insight**'s publication. It is presented as it was originally published, with the exception of some trivial trimming in the interest of space. The editors and writers involved in these articles had no ambition to produce material for the ages, but they were confident that in describing the here and now adequately, they would also be raising issues of enduring significance. Success on the latter front is what has made this volume possible.

Insight's Editor-in-Chief is Arnaud de Borchgrave. Its Managing Editor is Kirk E. Oberfeld, and its Deputy Managing Editor is Tod Lindberg. News editors who have been involved in the articles collected herein are: Charlotte Low Allen, David Brock, Stephen Brookes, Glenn Emery, John Holmes, Elizabeth Kristol, Deborah Papier, John Podhoretz and Richard Starr. Executive Editor Linda Moore Navas coordinated the production of this volume.

Washington, D.C.
August 7, 1990

PART 1

NO PLACE LIKE HOME

CHAPTER 1

It's an interesting paradox of modern urban life: Some cities are alive and full of energy, while others all but roll up the sidewalks when the office workers leave at five o'clock. This article, which was originally published August 14, 1989, found an explanation. The rash of "urban redevelopment" projects since World War II often promoted a grand aesthetic vision of a city at the expense of the human activities that go on in one. Fortunately, some architects and urban planners later began to rediscover that human scale.

THE DULL LEGACY OF URBAN PLANNING

Directly across Independence Avenue from the Victorian castle that is the headquarters of the Smithsonian Institution, whose museums are some of Washington's favorite tourist attractions, is a vacant concrete expanse called L'Enfant Plaza (designed by I. M. Pei, the man who put the glass pyramid in the Louvre courtyard), named after the French architect Pierre Charles L'Enfant, who designed the District of Columbia's street grid. Surrounding the plaza is a cluster of concrete-and-glass government office buildings, architectural monuments of the Sixties. What a contrast: the fussy, turreted, fanciful Smithsonian with its tapestry of carpet-bedded flower gardens, abuzz with visitors and Washington residents alike, and the stark, gray, dull and empty plaza, visited by few.

L'Enfant Plaza is a product of an ambitious government-financed experiment in changing the face of the urban landscape. It began in 1945 with a federal statute designed just for the District, then spread to almost every major city after Congress passed Title 1 of the 1949 Housing Act, promising to pay two-thirds the cost of every city's urban renewal program.

All the programs were similar: The government — or its authorized redevelopment authority — took over the land from private owners using its eminent domain powers, razed all existing structures, then sold the land to private developers at cut-rate, write-down prices in return for the developer's promise to rebuild in accordance with a master plan concocted by the local redevelopment agency and approved in Washington. The experiment petered out during the Sixties and formally ended in 1974, when Congress substituted a revenue sharing block grant program for community redevelopment. By then, the consensus was that large-scale urban renewal was out-of-date. It regularly proved to be a poor investment for cities, because it produced large tracts of land that would be off the tax rolls for decades between the bulldozing and the construction of anything new. Meanwhile, the municipality and its taxpayers had to eat the difference between the market price paid for acquiring the property and the write-down it got from the developer.

Urban residents began complaining that their downtowns were being not so much renewed as ruined. They started to miss the buildings that had gone down: the Victorian houses deemed hopelessly old-fashioned by the master planners, the little neighborhood retail stores. Critics on both the left and the right had even less kind words for urban renewal, which typically involved bulldozing low-end housing to build property tax-generating upper-middle-class apartment and office buildings. "Socialism for the rich, laissez-faire for the poor," is the way Gideon Kanner, a real estate law professor at Loyola Marymount University in Los Angeles, expresses it. Over the years, Kanner has represented numerous small businesses that happened to be in the way when urban renewal came to their block. The renewers' message to small businesses: Drop dead.

Many of the developments failed to pay off in the form of the higher tax revenues their proponents had touted. But close — and, to many, objectionable — government intertwinement with the rebuilding of cities, in the form of federal block grants, tax-exempt bond financing, write-down sales of government-acquired property, tax abatements, zoning concessions and low-rent leasing deals, continues to this day, if on a reduced scale. The major difference: A few cities and city planners have lately learned how to do it better, to design projects with a little more respect for the human scale and the older fabric of the cities surrounding the brand-new architecture. There are fewer L'Enfant Plazas going up today, more developments with some kinship to the Smithsonian.

Washington's urban renewal experiment was one of the nation's most ambitious. It involved almost the entire Southwest quadrant of the city, from Independence Avenue along the Washington Mall, down along the Potomac waterfront to the juncture of the Potomac and Anacostia rivers. Large parts of Southwest are within walking distance of the U.S. Capitol. During the Forties, some 23,000 people lived in the quadrant. By the late Fifties, almost every one of them was gone, forcibly removed by government fiat (the typical method: a notice telling them their homes would be torn down to make way for "modern apartments and stores and playgrounds." By then, Southwest resembled a ghost town, in the words of one former Washington resident, a war zone, in the words of another former resident. Blocks of cleared, empty lots stretched as far as the eye could see, their occupants scattered elsewhere.

Before urban renewal, Southwest Washington was a very poor, 80 percent black district. Many of the 5,600 or so houses dated back to the 19th and even 18th centuries: small wooden buildings on tiny lots with stoops in front and back. More than 43 percent of the houses lacked indoor toilets and 70 percent lacked central heating. A large portion of the quadrant was a slum by any standard, but life was not all bad compared with today's underclass life. Of the families with children, two-thirds had both parents living at home. Incomes were low, but fewer than one-fourth of the households collected welfare payments. More than 60 percent of the residents had lived there for more than a decade. "A lot of people didn't realize the extent to which this slum was actually home to the people who lived there," says Daniel Thursz, president of the National Council on the Aging. In 1966, when Thursz was a professor of social work at the University of Maryland, he published a study of displaced Southwest residents called "Where Are They Now?" Says Thursz: "We say, 'My God! How could they stand living in a house with an outdoor privy?' But there was a very complicated, well-established social fabric in those neighborhoods."

Parts of Southwest were not a slum at all, but a tidy if run-down row house neighborhood, dotted with handsome redbrick Victorian churches. Journalist Ernie Pyle had lived there. Part of the area had once been a Jewish neighborhood where Al Jolson grew up. By 1950 most of the Jews had left, but there were still a number of small Jewish-owned stores. Down at the waterfront, a bar called Harrington's was a favorite with Washington's bohemian crowd, and several family-owned fish restaurants served family-style meals.

When the renewal plans were drawn up, almost everything was slated for demolition: wooden shacks, row houses, restaurants, bars, churches and businesses. Several of the stores sued the government

to save themselves from the wrecking ball. Under the Fifth Amendment, the government can use its eminent domain powers to seize
private property only if it is for "public use." While slum clearance
may indeed by a salutary public use, the stores argued, they were
hardly slum buildings. The case went to the Supreme Court. In a
unanimous 1954 ruling, the liberal Justice William O. Douglas said
a public use was essentially whatever the legislature said it was. "If
those who govern the District of Columbia decide that the national
capital shall be beautiful as well as sanitary, there is nothing in the
Fifth Amendment that stands in the way," he wrote.

That decision, Berman vs. Parker, was the great legal green light,
not just for urban renewal but for every manner of government
seizure of property that might seem to benefit private interests more
than the public interest. In 1984, for example, the Supreme Court
approved a land redistribution scheme in Hawaii that broke up large
holdings and turned the plots over to tenants. The giant World Trade
Center in New York is an urban renewal project, opened in 1970 by
a joint New York-New Jersey agency that acquired the land for the
office buildings by seizing going businesses in Lower Manhattan, all
with court approval. The shopping malls in several California cities
are 1970s urban renewal projects, the Glendale Galleria and Culver
City's Fox Hills Mall to name two. "New shopping centers were being
built in the suburbs back then on cheap land," explains Murray
Kane, a lawyer who represented both cities in their redevelopment
transactions. "There was a flight from the cities to the suburbs, so
there had to be some incentive to make inner cities competitive."

The Fifth Amendment requires governments to pay "just compensation" to owners when they take property by eminent domain.
The rub is that the courts have interpreted just compensation to
mean strictly the value of the real estate, not the goodwill that attach-
es to a going business at a particular location. To the owner of the
hardware store, drugstore or luncheonette standing in the way of
progress, that means not enough money to buy a new business elsewhere, and to an elderly owner, it means a penurious forced retirement. Property owners have started to fight back in recent years,
learning how to use the courts to tie up development projects. Laws
now usually require substantial relocation payments for evicted tenants.

The notion that the new, redeveloped Southwest Washington
would be an improvement over the old stemmed from fashionable
notions of what a city ought to look like. For more than a half-cen-
tury before Douglas wrote his opinion, traditional notions of urban

life — that it was by its very nature crowded, noisy, dense, variegated and seemingly disorderly — had been under attack among intellectuals. At the turn of the century flourished the Garden City movement, suggesting that the ideal city was a country village (minus the manor house and the parish church) carefully laid out in a large green park, with houses facing away from main streets and commercial uses carefully segregated from residential. Numerous U.S. and English suburbs and "new towns" consciously patterned themselves on the Garden City model, and it remains to this day the model for the tract house, town house, condominium and senior citizens developments that cover America's suburban landscape.

Next to come along was the vastly influential architect Le Corbusier, who adapted the Garden City model to more heavily populated urban areas. During the 1930s he devised the Radiant City, a utopian cluster of gleaming skyscrapers, some office buildings, some universities, hospitals, residences and administrative centers — all also sitting in a green park. Le Corbusier was a leading practitioner of the International style of architecture, the Bauhaus-inspired movement that favored unadorned boxlike buildings with ultraclean lines — in short, the dominant style of architecture for most of this century until the Postmodern movement of the Eighties.

Complementing the Garden City and Radiant City movements were the writings of the prolific (21 books) urban philosopher Lewis Mumford. Mumford hated most cities, and the city he hated most was New York, which struck him as vulgar, chaotic, overcrowded, full of "wasteful streets," as he called them, and lacking sufficient light and air. Mumford urged comprehensive urban planning as a cure for all of this — an analogue to the comprehensive economic planning of socialism that he and other intellectuals of the Thirties believed ought to replace the chaos of capitalism. The philosopher boldly urged cities to raze their "blighted" areas and start anew. "No urban community can afford the costly luxury of uncoordinated and insecure private enterprise," he wrote in his 1938 book, "The Culture of Cities." The kind of residential urban construction Mumford liked most was the high-rise, multibuilding, architecturally uniform housing project.

One cannot underestimate the influence of the architectural ideas of Le Corbusier and the philosophical ideas of Mumford; they still persist. To drive around Southwest Washington today, a melancholy journey, is to see the results of planning — when the planning, like the rest of the best-laid plans of mice and men, has gone agley.

L'Enfant Plaza, for example, was not meant to be quite so barren.

Pei's original layout called for it to reflect L'Enfant's original design; it was to be a tree-lined promenade flanked by federal buildings in an area that would also contain numerous private office buildings and a street-level hotel. A series of compromises with Congress and the District of Columbia planted a large federal government office complex, the Forrestal Building, at the end of the promenade, and the trees never got planted. Plans are afoot at the National Capital Planning commission to landscape and otherwise try to rehabilitate the plaza.

One of the aims of the renewal effort was to ease perceived over-crowding. The means in Southwest was deliberate depopulation by building only about half as many housing units. Another was to ensure architectural compatibility by permitting only a handful of architects to design the new quadrant. But it took years, in some cases as many as 20, before the last new developments were finished. The idle land went off the tax rolls, defeating another goal of urban renewal districts: raising the property tax base.

A large portion of the new Southwest is taken up by the blocklike office headquarters of Great Society government agencies (the biggest and ugliest building belongs, ironically, to the Department of Housing and Urban Development, designed by Bauhaus alumnus Marcel Breuer), whose workers chronically complain of a lack of cheap nearby restaurants. A shopping center designed to coordinate all the area's retail activity has never proved profitable. An office building is empty. On Fourth Street, where the little cluster of stores that unsuccessfully fought the bulldozers once stood, is a block-size, 10-story, late-Sixties apartment house of no particular architectural distinction. Another large apartment complex was turned into the Environmental Protection Agency's headquarters. There are some genuinely handsome town houses and multifamily buildings here and there, such as the Tiber Island complex on the Potomac water-front.

The raffish Harrington's is gone, and the fish restaurants negoti-ated barnlike new structures for themselves along the waterfront that are today corporate-owned and considered strictly for tourists. Of all the Southwest churches, only one remains from the past: St. Dominic's, a rusticated stone Roman Catholic edifice whose green-shingled steeple rises bravely above the glass and concrete. The area's other churches were rebuilt in the airport-hangar style of Fifties religious buildings. One of the vaunted features of the devel-opment was supposed to be brand-new low-income housing, but rel-atively few units were built. Though constructed in the most enlightened mode of their era — row houses — the public housing went the way of most housing projects, turning into another slum within a few years.

A new elementary school was set up as one of the nation's first magnet schools, a model of integrated, high-quality education. A desegregation lawsuit ended its magnet status, and all families with school-age children who could afford to fled Southwest. Here and there are a few attractive features: a cluster of houseboats on the Potomac where some Washingtonians live year-round and a tatty open-air fish market that somehow escaped demolition and is now one of the city's liveliest spots.

"The waterfront was butchered; it's a horror, and the whole area is totally barren at night," says sculptor Theodore Fields, a longtime Washington resident. "The city had too much power, and it used it." The area contrasts dramatically with Capitol Hill, another run-down district of row houses, small stores and churches. Starting in the late Sixties, the area was gradually regentrified, entirely by private owners, and it is now one of Washington's most fashionable neighborhoods, all without losing a shred of its architectural integrity.

The Southwest debacle has parallels in many other areas. One was Los Angeles's Bunker Hill section. Unlike Southwest Washington, this downtown neighborhood of once-elegant Victorian houses could not have been called a slum; it was merely shabby. Here is how Raymond Chandler described it: "You could find anything there from down-at-the-heels ex-Greenwich-villagers to crooks on the lam, from ladies of anybody's evening to County Relief clients brawling with haggard landladies in grand old houses with scrolled porches, parquetry floors and immense sweeping bannisters of white oak, mahogany and Circassian walnut." The hill even had its own funicular railroad called the Angels' Flight. It is not hard to imagine that it would have been eventually regentrified by private owners, as has an adjacent turn-of-the-century neighborhood, Angeleno Heights.

Starting in the late Fifties, Bunker Hill was bulldozed with the help of Title I funds, to be replaced with residential high rises (none of which has been an economic success) and office and civic buildings. Boston's West End met the same fate, and the city's North End was supposed to be next to go, when city officials finally decided it would be wrong to tear down that colorful Italian neighborhood. Books like Thursz's appeared, delineating the grief and sense of dislocation poor people feel when wrenched from their neighborhoods.

During the Seventies, there was a good deal of retrenching and rethinking on urban redevelopment. Giant public housing projects, the kind Mumford liked, were abandoned when it became apparent that tenants felt stigmatized living there, and elevators, walkways and hallways became centers of crime. The 1972 demolition of the award-winning 1955 Pruitt-Igoe project in St. Louis was a milestone in this trend. The Department of Housing and Urban Development was marked by funding-corruption scandals — typically involving cozy relationships with builders — that prefigured this year's $2 billion contretemps.

The demise of bulldozer-style urban renewal did not mean the end of ways for governments to go on subsidizing land development projects that theoretically improved the appearance of cities. California pioneered a device called tax increment financing that has been widely copied. In such a system, the redevelopment agency has the authority to issue tax-exempt bonds to pay for a project — effectively, a low-interest loan to the developer. On the parcel in question, two tax valuations are calculated, one (called the frozen valuation) on what the property was worth before the development, the other at its current value.

The taxes on that difference go to pay off the bonds and other projects, such as low-income housing, that the redevelopment agency cares to fund. And because the bonds in California are not secured by general treasury revenues, they need no voter approval, putting the whole project outside voter scrutiny. The tax increment system has been criticized because of the likelihood that at least some of the increased value can be traced to other factors besides the redevelopment. Increment-financed projects tend to starve local tax rolls, meaning reduced revenues for other city services, critics say. Increment financing has gone to pay for industrial parks and for downtown shopping malls designed to compete with suburban malls — often with disastrous results for the life of the city. A blank-walled, fortresslike shopping center adds nothing to the vitality of a downtown, charge critics, and residents sometimes go to the suburbs for shopping anyway, leaving the inner-city mall to flounder.

The increment system, ensuring huge revenue increases for the redevelopment agencies whenever property values go up, is so popular that most localities now use federal block grants only for public buildings and other structures that cannot go onto the tax rolls. Government-subsidized projects keep alive a whole segment of the development industry. Atlanta architect John Portman's development firm is part of that industry. Many of the monumental "trademark" Seventies-era Portman hotels found in almost every major city that feature stadium-sized atria festooned with hanging philodendrons are there because a local government helped pay for them. The Rouse Co., famous for its festive port and downtown revitalization projects (Underground Atlanta, which reopened July 15, is the latest of these), is another company that lives mostly off the government.

Trying to compete with the suburban malls has been the kiss of death for many cities. A 1969 book by Bernard Rudofsky, "Streets for People," touted the narrow lanes, paseos and pedestrian-only plazas that give many European cities their charm. If ideas have consequences, poorly understood ideas have disastrous consequences. Many a U.S. city tried to turn its fading Main Street into Perugia by shutting it off to automobile traffic and installing dozens of oversize brass street lamps. Cities did not realize that pedestrian-only streets work well abroad because people live on them and they abound with sidewalk cafes and pushcart vendors. Blocked-off U.S. streets tended to kill what was left of downtown retail business because people missed the hum and honks of automobiles and they felt cut off from the rest of life.

The Le Corbusier-Mumford philosophic axis has also proved an urban bane. The loveliest product of the International style is the bronze-on-bronze Seagram building on New York's Park Avenue. Designed with Philip Johnson by Ludwig Mies van der Rohe in 1958 and sitting gracefully in the middle of a little plaza with a fountain in front whose ledge was ideal for sitting and people-watching, it draws the variegated crowds that make urban life endlessly interesting. In 1961 New York revamped its 1916 zoning ordinance, a simple affair whose height and air limits were responsible for the city's many wedding-cake-shaped Art Deco apartment buildings and skinny skyscrapers like the Chrysler and Empire State buildings.

The new law allowed bulkier buildings, but it also offered what are called incentive bonuses that allowed developers to add more floors than the height limits permitted — in effect, a subsidy — in return for Seagram-like plazas. The result: Every new office building in New York came with a plaza. The problems: The oversize structures were not so nice as the Seagram building and they all looked alike. The worst excess was the west side of Sixth Avenue, once an interesting row of little coffee shops, Irish bars and delicatessens. During the Sixties and Seventies, due to the bonuses, it turned into a monotonous row of hulking Mies-on-the-cheap high rises.

Nonetheless, Sixth Avenue is not such a bad place to be these days. The office buildings are just as homely, but the trees in many of the plazas have grown tall, and the ledges in front draw the sitters, the lunch-eaters and the people-watchers. Pushcarts, some legal, some not, hawking every sort of food from hot dogs to shish kebab, and street vendors of books, earrings, Islamic literature and incense dot the avenue. The 47th Street diamond district is nearby, mingling Hasidic Jews in black coats with the shirt-and-tie crowd from several publishing houses along Sixth Avenue and ethnics of every variety. "It's the revenge of the streets," says urbanologist William H. Whyte, whose 1988 book, "City: Rediscovering the Center," hectors against blank walls at street level, big empty spaces, inward-facing buildings and other leftovers from Radiant City theory.

The heavy hand of the recent past, and even of the present, is hard to fight. For the past three decades, the chief nightmare of cities has been abandonment — that businesses, residents, retail customers and, worst of all, developers would just light out for the suburbs and beyond. This has made it easy for developers to "bribe" city officials via campaign contributions (a California court recently ruled that Los Angeles City Council members were not illegally influenced in a land use decision by contributions because every single member got a donation). But even more prevalent has been reverse bribery: subsidies and tax breaks of every sort for developers.

In 1982 New York again revamped its zoning law to cut back on wheeling-and-dealing, plaza-and-atrium trade-offs, downzone some areas such as the Upper East Side and set standards that allow developers to build without negotiating first as long as they are willing to stay within strict limits. But "land in New York is so heavily taxed that if you want to build something, you have to take the government as a senior partner; you have to make a deal," says urbanologist William Tucker.

Most current Washington redevelopment is at a discount, via tax abatements and write-downs on city land sales. One new Washington office and shopping complex was assessed no taxes last year even though it was open for business; a legal loophole regards a building as not completed if its roof is not finished.

Some cities will put anything a developer wants in their downtowns just to get the new buildings and the business they are expected to bring. Big, self-contained megastructures such as the Portman-designed Detroit Renaissance Center have been favorites, although the urban fortresses have turned out to do nothing to bring life back to inner cities. In 1978, during New York's darkest financial hours, a desperate Mayor Edward I. Koch made a deal with Portman to build a hotel in Times Square in an effort to help clean up that porn-

shop-afflicted area. The agreement included about $100 million
worth of government sweeteners for Portman: a $21.5 million fed-
eral urban development action grant under a 1977 law that hands
out money for projects involving some private investment, 10 years'
worth of low-interest loans, a $33 million tax abatement, a $15 million sales tax exemption for construction products, and seven rent-
free years on land acquired via eminent domain by the New York
State Urban Development Corp., plus reduced rent after that.

Portman also got to pick the site he wanted, which also happened
to be the site of four historic Broadway theaters, of which two, the
Helen Hayes and the Morosco, were known for perfect acoustics and
lush, classic theater design. Preservationists and an array of actors
ranging from Charlton Heston on the political right to Susan Saran-
don on the left battled for four years to save the theaters. Both won
temporary landmark status from the U.S. Interior Department, but
the presidentially appointed Advisory Council on Historic Preser-
vation approved the demolition. In 1982 the theaters went down,
and in 1985, Portman's 48-story Marriott Marquis Hotel opened. By
this time, the Portman high-rise atrium concept, which seemed fun
in the early Seventies, looked tired and dated.

Landmark designation, like so many land use issues, is basically a
political question. Two historic theaters could not be saved. Washington's concrete Convention Center is built over the ruins of Victorian residences whose landmark status was overruled by a mayoral
decree that the center would serve the public interest. Yet neighbors
recently secured provisional landmark status (since rescinded) as a
"cultural institution" for a Los Angeles car wash from the 1950s.
Observers say the problem is few governments are willing to pay for
historic designations or to give tax concessions to owners. Land use
battles can turn conservatives into socialists, liberals into free market enthusiasts. "If private industry had just given itself the responsibility for dealing with Times Square redevelopment from the
beginning, this wouldn't have happened," says Barbara Handman,
a community board member for the area who helped spearhead the
fight against Portman project.

Fortunately, localities have learned a lot from 40 years of urban
development mistakes. New York's new Battery Park City, built on
publicly created landfill next to the Hudson River, is filled with architectural variety, street-level stores, a street grid that matches the rest
of Lower Manhattan and genuine city-style sidewalks, sidewalk
cafes, miniparks, benches, whimsical sculptures and a lengthy, popular esplanade with a breathtaking view of the Statue of Liberty,

Staten Island and New Jersey. The condominium and apartment buildings started out Radiant City in design in the early Eighties but lately have moved toward real city. It is not perfect; it tends to be a "thirtysomething" age-and-income ghetto for Wall Street professionals, and too much of it is physically cut off from the rest of Lower Manhattan by an expressway. "It's like a suburb in a city," says a youthful female resident; sad to say, it is.

Rouse redevelopment projects, with their emphasis on small non-chain shops, some as tiny as pushcarts that rent for a couple of hundred dollars a month, and a bountiful variety of food and merchandise offerings (Boston's Quincy Market, New York's South Street Seaport and Baltimore's Harborplace), also have a pleasant, bustling flavor that draws crowds. A midweek visit to the brand-new Underground Atlanta reveals the place to be packed with people, in contrast to the rest of that city's sagging, underpopulated downtown.

Underground Atlanta, an indoor-outdoor revival of a below-the-railroad jazz district that succumbed to drug traffic and vacant storefronts during the early Eighties, is not perfect, either. Washington architect Sanford Nelson tried to bind a new multilevel mall with existing street-level retail structures, but with little else on the street outside, shop owners have already closed off their street-level doors to the public, making it mostly pure shopping center. There is not enough outdoor eating. In fact, not enough eating, period. A few too many chain stores: Oh, no, not another Ann Taylor, Eddie Bauer and Victoria's Secret. And Rouse projects themselves, for all their charm, are starting to look alike.

These are all faults that can be corrected, though. The burgeoning crowds reveal an Atlanta public that is starved for real urban life, and the Underground crowds are already starting to spill out onto this tired end of Peachtree Street. In fact, many people are starved for genuine urban life. Regentrification is likely to be the dominant development mode of the Nineties, with city after city coming back. "When a man is tired of London he is tired of life," said Samuel Johnson. The reign of the Radiant City may at last be over.

Charlotte Low Allen

CHAPTER 2

The Ozzie and Harriet type of life that attracted millions to suburbia has vanished. Originally published May 30, 1988, this article described how once quiet and uncluttered communities became noisy and congested. Cheaper land and lower rents than the city centers had to offer made the suburbs magnets for industry. Industry brought revenue and revenue brought services. And the entire process of development brought the overcrowding that suburbanites hoped to avoid. Some suburbs and activists worked to slow down the overbuilding, but eager developers were ready to do battle.

BURBS OF PARADISE CALL TO THE MASSES

Northwest of Atlanta, along U.S. Route 41, all the necessities of life are lined up like dishes on a sideboard. The cars that residents buy from dealers on the strip between the Chattahoochee River and Marietta can be washed, gassed up, repaired and resold without leaving the road. Locals can buy groceries and eat in or they can dine out in the vast array of restaurants in the corridor known as Cobb Parkway. They can charge clothes and household furnishings at the Cumberland Mall, work in the Galleria office center, bowl or catch a movie. They can live in deluxe apartments amid well-groomed complexes that front on the roadway or in large, detached single-family homes on landscaped lots a mere block from it. They never have to leave Route 41. Eternity is there at the Georgia Memorial Park cemetery.

As noon approaches and workers spill from the offices and retail stores in quest of repast, autos, vans and trucks slow to a crawl at numerous points. Heavy traffic, the kind that induces stomachs to churn, is the most visible evidence that the suburbia in which many Americans grew up is vanishing. A transplanted Chicagoan who moved to the Atlanta suburbs five years ago recognized the end of the traditional suburban experience when she timed an increasingly routine traffic delay: a mile in 17 minutes. "Our image of suburbia is at odds with what suburbia is today. So many of the people who live in suburbs want this old suburb, this quiet residential Ozzie and Harriet suburb that no longer exists," says sociologist Mark Baldassare, author of "Trouble in Paradise."

Once the urban fringes to which workers retired at the end of a busy day in the city, suburbs have been transformed into places where Americans live, shop, work and play. Condominiums and town houses are plotted on land that in years past would have yielded a single home on a lush and stately lawn or several tract houses of nearly identical exterior.

Geographer Truman A. Hartshorn of Georgia State University refers to the evolving suburbs as suburban downtowns, natural progressions of a form that had its origin in the bedroom communities that sprang up in the first half of the century. While the United States was caught up with the Vietnam War and the counterculture movement of the Sixties and early Seventies, the suburbs were quietly undergoing their own revolution. Typically preceded by the arrival of a regional shopping mall to capture the middle- and upper-class markets, massive employment opportunities migrated out of town. By 1973, according to Hartshorn, there were more jobs in the suburbs than in the central, and oftentimes decaying, cities.

Only since the beginning of this decade, as Hartshorn and Peter O. Muller of the University of Miami describe it in a study of suburban downtowns, have these areas gained a prominence that may eventually transcend the central city from which they were spawned. In two suburban nodes in the Atlanta region, Cumberland-Galleria and Perimeter Center-Georgia 400, for instance, the average rents surpass those in downtown Atlanta. Higher rents for prestigious high-rise office and high-tech buildings are likely to become ubiquitous as developers offer amenity packages often unavailable from the downtown landlord: free parking, exquisite landscaping and health clubs.

Baldassare, a professor at the University of California at Irvine, dubs the new form "disurbia": dense, industrial, self-contained urban regions. Within disurbia, minicenters arise, serving as magnets for commerce, culture, entertainment, the arts, major shopping areas and high rises. "No one center by itself is a [traditional] downtown," he says. Taken together, though, the minicenters enable regions to break their ties to the central city.

Historian Robert Fishman of Rutgers, the State University of New Jersey, calls them technoburbs or technocities in his recent study of the evolution of suburbia. They differ from the suburbs of the past in their linkage of the work site and the dwelling place. Suburbia originated as a place to escape the city, to shield women and children from the evils of urban society and to ensconce the family unit in a privacy and intimacy that the city could not offer. "Every true suburb is the outcome of two opposing forces, an attraction toward the opportunities of the great city and a simultaneous repulsion against urban life," Fishman writes in "Bourgeois Utopias: The Rise and Fall of Suburbia."

The great attraction of the suburbs confounds stalwart city dwellers. Yet more than four in 10 Americans now live in the burbs, more than the number living in cities. Their reasons are plentiful and illustrate the dichotomy Fishman addresses. Schools generally are better, housing is cheaper and crimes are fewer. Suburbs have also served as a buffer between the haves and the have-nots and lent credence to a middle-class family's upward mobility. Perhaps most important, they signified the United States' pioneering spirit represented by that piece of earth Americans could call their own.

These new suburban forms have not emerged everywhere, but they are represented in many regions of the country. In Schaumburg, outside Chicago; in the City Post Oak section of Houston; along the U.S. Route 1 corridor near Princeton, N.J.; and in Orange County, southeast of Los Angeles.

Among the first of the new suburbs was Perimeter Center, in De Kalb County north of Atlanta. Nestled among the trees and shrubs in the campuslike setting are office buildings (the creations of renowned architects), restaurants, hotels and a shopping mall. From the streets, many of these structures are partially obscured by mature trees in bloom. Plants and flowers flourish on manicured medians.

In the late Sixties the Atlanta development firm of Taylor & Mathis Inc. acquired 550 acres north of Atlanta where De Kalb and Fulton counties converge at Interstate 285, the Perimeter Highway. Pioneers of the suburban office park concept, the developers had learned from a prior venture the importance of controlling their surroundings. Their leases gave them control over signs, landscaping, curb cuts and other design elements. "We wouldn't be infiltrated with the fast foods, the filling stations, car washes, with those parasite type of uses that would spawn off of the population that we created," says James D. Fluker, Jr., executive vice president.

The company also practiced a low-rise, low-density philosophy during the early years of the project to minimize residential impact. Building height was kept to 10 stories and density to 12,000 square feet of building per acre. "We felt we were invading suburbia with office developments. We were going into people's backyards. We were moving an office element into a residential environment," says Fluker.

Five years ago, two Texas developers outbid Taylor & Mathis on the two remaining tracts. Two 18-story buildings at 45,000 square feet per acre have been constructed on one of the parcels. A 45-story tower is planned nearby. Skyscrapers rise out of the foliage in plain view of the traffic on Perimeter Highway. Taylor & Mathis never intended to recreate downtown Atlanta, says Fluker. "That concept, though, is growing in the mind of other developers."

Along the stretch of highway between Perimeter Center and the community of Buford in Gwinnett County, northeast of Atlanta, a solitary 65 mph speed limit sign is posted in a tiny patch of a nearby county. How can the higher speed, which Congress allows only in rural areas, be permitted? The rural definition, explains Johnny Isakson, minority leader of the Georgia House of Representatives, is based on the 1980 census; when the 1990 census results are in, no place in the seven-county region will be able to claim rural status.

The population of the Atlanta region has exploded to 2.56 million, its newfound economic vitality attracting entrepreneurs and regional companies as well as those of the Fortune 500. Only Dallas-Fort Worth and Phoenix, among large metropolitan areas, registered population rate gains larger than Atlanta's 19.8 percent from 1980 to 1986, according to Census Bureau estimates. Gwinnett County has its own distinction: Its rate of growth is the fastest among urban counties in the United States, having added an estimated 312 percent, 225,000 people, from 1970 to 1987.

"Growth can be a win-win situation," says Isakson, a Republican. He also acknowledges that the unbridled growth has its drawbacks. "Services are always chasing development. That is where the major problem comes."

Three times Gwinnett County has forbidden new tie-ins to the sewer system. Millions of dollars in road improvements need to be made. The county is under court order to build a jail, and eight new libraries (at long last, in the view of many residents) are in the works. The county was about 1,900 acres behind the standard set for recreational use by the National Recreation and Park Association. "During the time when Gwinnett's growth was really gearing up, there were no infrastructure improvements made. All the water system plans, all the road system plans, nothing was done," says Helen Preston Tapp, executive director of the Council for Quality Growth, a broad-based industry group.

Newspapers are filled with articles, editorials and letters about the problems associated with growth. When the county alerted residents about plans to close off some streets to "thru traffic," Deborah M. Donaldson of Norcross decried the dangerous precedent she feared would be set. "The problem is not being solved, it is just being shifted to someone else," she wrote to the Gwinnett Daily News. "I'm sure that with the uncontrolled growth of our county there are numerous other subdivisions [that] would like their roads closed to through traffic. But where does it end?"

Where, indeed? In Manassas, Va., a far-western suburb of Washington, D.C., developers have broken ground on a regional mall at the site of a Civil War battleground. While the National Park Service seeks a compromise, Congress is attempting to block the development altogether. At times it seems as though all of suburbia is being converted into concrete, glass and steel.

The Council for Quality Growth found surprising results in a survey of residents. Those who had lived in the area the longest were the least concerned about growth; short-term residents were more upset, says Tapp. "One of the problems is unrealistic expectations. People come out here and expect, when they buy a house in a subdivision that looks at a farm, that farm will be there in five years or 10 years. When that rezoning sign goes up, they go crazy."

Nowhere are the infrastructure shortcomings more pronounced than on the roads and highways. Some 20 miles from downtown Atlanta on Interstate 85, two lanes of exiting traffic back up onto the freeway during the curiously named evening rush hour. Turning onto the interstate from such arterial routes as Pleasant Hill Road — which is anything but pleasant in the morning rush — is also a waiting game.

The Gwinnett scene is replayed twice daily in suburban growth centers nationwide. The Southern California Association of Governments warned recently that average commuter speeds on the nation's most famous freeways will plummet to 11 mph by 2010 unless drastic measures are taken. At 3:30 in the afternoon traffic has backed up on the Los Angeles freeways as basketball fans try to make their way to the Forum in suburban Inglewood for a 7:30 Lakers game. It's not just the highways; local roads are ill-equipped to absorb the growing traffic. And it's not just during rush hour.

Already the traffic in Orange County is making an impact on how business is conducted and where and how people live. Breakfast meetings beginning at 7 to 7:30 are becoming fashionable because traffic dooms luncheon meetings — a cruel blow to the image of laid-back Southern Californians. Orange Countians postpone visiting friends, change their choice of restaurants and movies and, if they can afford to, move closer to their places of employment.

"If you're not here by 10, forget it," says a teenager at Sand Creek Park on the Coast Highway. Then there is no place to park his pastel-decorated white van at the beach.

Although Baldassare lives near the Irvine campus, he regularly visits the Los Angeles Times and San Francisco Chronicle, for which he conducts survey research. Yet the flight to San Francisco is often less time-consuming than the 40-mile drive from Irvine to the Times. John Wayne Airport is within minutes of the university, and the 430-mile trip to San Francisco is less than an hour. "It can take me two hours to get to Los Angeles."

Other physical limitations have surfaced as development has outpaced services and improvements. Overburdened water and sewage systems, dwindling farmland and crowded schools add to the frustrations.

In Atlanta, the problem of diminishing water supply is exacerbated by regional growth. Harry West, executive director of the Atlanta Regional Commission, is cautiously optimistic: "We aren't going to run out of water anytime soon if we are able to implement the management techniques that we know work and are available." A proposed dam would alleviate the region's water shortage until 2010.

Gwinnett schools are not alone in feeling the crush of a surging student body. The county's public school system enrolls about 4,000 new students a year. "We have 90 more than last week, 18 more than yesterday," says Superintendent Alton Crews. By 1990 he expects the total number of students to have doubled during the decade.

"We are very crowded. We are jammed into buildings, but our pupil-to-teacher ratio [20-to-1] has not gone up. We do not stack more kids in a room." Auxiliary facilities — cafeterias, libraries and so on — bulge. Lunch is served in shifts from 10:30 to 1:30 to accommodate all the students. What the school district has done to alleviate the crowding is embark on an aggressive construction program and ring its schools with 325 portable classrooms. During the past decade it has built an average of 100 classrooms annually and anticipates doubling that in the next five years. "That will not catch us up," says Crews.

In spite of the crowding, the school system consistently ranks at the top of the academic achievement ladder in the state. Crews believes the degree of growth has been advantageous in some respects. A greater variety of classes can be offered. The district's reputation attracts a rich supply of teachers from around the nation, and students are exposed to people of many nationalities as employment opportunities draw a worldwide pool of workers.

Gwinnett County residents have been willing to support the massive construction program that requires a bond issue every other year. Gwinnett also has the good fortune of a tax base that has expanded along with the need for additional revenue.

Similar financial support, however, is not always achievable in many high-growth areas. John Erskine, executive director of the Building Industry Association of Orange County, faults the public for rejecting in 1984 a 1-cent sales tax earmarked for road improvements. He also blames local governments for not finding ways to solve the problems. In his role as mayor of Huntington Beach, though, he concedes that certain kinds of development may have to be curbed. "We probably have approved too much commercial and industrial development," he says, explaining that such buildings, which are operating at about a 25 percent vacancy rate, generate a lot more traffic than housing.

Irvine Mayor Larry Agran, who is on the opposite side of the development debate in Orange County, holds a similar view on taxation. Since California voters approved Proposition 13 in 1978, which severely restricts property taxes, elected officials have interpreted that as a signal that the public will not tolerate any new taxes. "You can play that game for just so long," says Agran, before building to expand the tax base overburdens the infrastructure.

How localities would apply new taxes to solve the problems associated with rapid growth is a problem in itself. Mass transportation systems were planned to bring the masses from the suburbs into the central city; most do not operate well in reverse. Outbound commuters are dumped at large parking lots or rail stations from which they have to figure out ways to reach their workplaces. Rarely are mass transit systems set up to convey passengers from one suburb to another. And cars add to the congestion on suburban roads.

Lower-income workers are the big losers, as more jobs become physically inaccessible. One Southern Californian tells of a former coworker who left for work at 5 a.m. and got home at 8 p.m. because she had to take three buses in each direction. "The large disadvantaged populations of the inner central cities can be expected to experience further erosion of their already weak economic-geographical position vis a vis the metropolitan labor market," Hartshorn and Muller say in their study. One category of workers, however, has profited: those from rural areas who lived far away from central business districts.

Housing is too expensive in many of these thriving suburban areas for clerical and retail workers and other support staff. Average prices last year for houses in southern Orange County ranged from $545,000 in Newport Beach to $139,987 in El Toro, according to a report in the Orange County Register.

The six-city area of Santa Clara County known as the Golden Triangle is experiencing severe housing and job mismatches. Not only is housing far removed from employment centers, but numerous workers must be imported from elsewhere. In 1980, 170,000 workers made the daily commute to the area, southeast of San Francisco on the bay. The Golden Triangle will need an estimated 48,000 to 67,000 new housing units merely to keep commuter congestion from getting any worse. Aggravating the situation, building houses where land is available would worsen congestion because the sites are not near employment centers.

Some people fear that the independence of the suburbs is leading toward a more isolated society. Everyone gets in cars to drive — to work, to lunch, to the grocery, to home. Fewer people walk down the city streets. They go home to communities built behind gates and fences. "The suburbs do seem to breed a kind of insularity through a lack of community," says Baldassare. "A greater social separation of groups occurs than has ever existed before."

Belinda Blacketer, an attorney who helped draft a "balanced growth" initiative for Orange County, theorizes that the rapid transformation of suburbia has stripped people of their sense of community, identity and social responsibility. The county, she notes, ranks lowest nationwide in proportion of income given to charity. "It's hard to have a sense of community in Orange County. You spend all your time driving from one place to another. We don't design places for people anymore. We design monuments."

In his book, Fishman notes that many planners condemn the new suburban form on two fronts. "First, decentralization has been a social and economic disaster for the old city and for the poor, who have been increasingly relegated to its crowded, decayed zones. It has resegregated American society into an affluent outer city and an indigent inner city, while erecting higher barriers that prevent the poor from sharing in the jobs and housing of the technoburbs. Second, decentralization has been seen as a cultural disaster." Despite all the amenities that are being brought to the suburbs, their cultural richness will never replace that of the old urban core. Fishman buys into that argument, but he also believes that while the form is still evolving, progress cannot be ruled out.

Local officials sometimes are the targets of a suspicious public. Voters in Fairfax County, Va., last fall ousted their longtime county chairman because of traffic and development. Tom Rogers, a former Orange County Republican chairman and a founder of the initiative movement, has called for the recall of two county supervisors. "The people have to be brought back into the loop of decision making," he says.

Some of the criticism seems justifiable. In Gwinnett County, $1.16 million in federal and state money was spent to build a park-and-ride lot off Interstate 85 at the Indian Trail-Lilburn Road exit. Opened in 1984, the 506 space lot is about 90 percent empty at midday because there is no transit system to take drivers anywhere.

As the rural gives way to the suburban, not everyone has been locked out of the sylvan setting, at least not yet. But "only the wealthy are going to be able to live in suburbs that are not at all commercial or industrial," says Baldassare.

Hartshorn adds another likely place where suburbs will persist in the old mold: "You'll probably find [traditional suburbs] where there's a dying economy, where no one would want to be." He believes people will be happy in the new suburbs, once the kinks from rapid growth are straightened out. "I think all these people who have been negative about it are missing the point. For most Americans, I would think it's more important to have a job and have access than it is to live that myth."

Karen Diegmueller

CHAPTER 3

The small town eludes precise definition. It is the subject of romance — in literature, even in rock and roll songs — and often the subject of derision. But, as shown in this August 24, 1987, article, the people who inhabit small towns, by and large, would not live anywhere else. It's a feeling of community, that everybody knows you. Although sometimes faced with economic hardship, small towns have preserved the rootstock of America.

SMALL-TOWN LIFE IS THE HEART OF THE LAND

Byron Farwell, former mayor of Hillsboro, Va., (population 114) has a scheme to keep the city folk at bay. "People are like rats; they follow sewerage," Farwell advises readers of Small Town magazine. "City folk do not understand septic systems. If you have sewers, my best advice to you is to blow them up."

Throw a dart at a map of the United States and you are likely to hit Farwell's small-town America. Partake of popular culture and you won't be able to miss it. The small town is everywhere: on the radio, in the movies, on the bookshelf and by the side of the road. Rural routes spring eternal from the American highway system, disappearing over hills and under bridges, becoming little roads used only by the locals.

Woe betide the outsider who becomes lost on such a road. If he finds someone to help steer him out of his vertigo, he is likely to become even more confused — small-towners are partial to the old ways and may not remember to say that Johnson Road, at which the crucial turn must be made, is now known as Route 12.

Small-town America offers plenty of chances for locals to tweak the outsiders. Of the 39,527 general-purpose governments below the state level in the United States, about 72 percent (28,484) serve populations of less then 3,000. Half serve populations under 1,000. "It takes a heck of a lot of those little towns to make New York City," says Beverly Nykwest, staff associate with the National Association of Towns and Townships in Washington, D.C. Small-town and rural route dwellers make up 37 percent of the U.S. population, living on 94 percent of the populated land. "The small town literally dominates the U.S." But even the experts hedge if pressed to define a small town. "I purposely don't have an answer," says Kenneth Munsell, director of the Small Towns Institute in Ellensburg, Wash. Munsell is also editor of the institute's bimonthly magazine, Small Town. "There is no lower population limit, except how many people it takes to form a sense of community."

States have the power to define a town. In Iowa a town cannot incorporate without at least 250 people; Virginia requires 1,000. In some less populous states, entire counties contain fewer people than the small towns of larger states. White Pine County, Nev., has about 8,000 people, roughly one per square mile. The county's big city is Ely, population 4,882.

If a concrete definition of a small town is hard to come by, a single qualitative definition simply does not exist. Consider the experience of a California couple on vacation in 1982. The Los Angelenos' closet brush with small-town America was reading "Harvest Home," Thomas Tryon's novel of ritual murder and torture in a small New England town. Their car broke down outside rural Winters, Calif., population 2,650, which has its fair share of homegrown mechanics. But rather than risk an unhappy run-in with the locals a la "Harvest Home," the couple arranged to have their vehicle towed more than 10 miles to higher-priced Vacaville, which has a population of 43,370.

Theirs is a funny story, particularly in comparison to the sad one told by one displaced New Yorker. Her closest contact with small-town American was also through literature — but this was through romantic sagas such as the writings of Sherwood Anderson. She labored long and hard to find a teaching job in a small Montana community, where she hoped to live and raise a family. But at age 26, she had entered the local marriage pool way too late. "People here have their futures planned by the time they leave high school," she laments. "My options are to marry an older widower, wait for an outsider to show up or leave town."

The popular imagination has designated small-town America a place of extremes, where you find Utopia — or the Twilight Zone. The extreme images come not from the mysterious nature of isolated little towns, says one specialist in rural sociology, but from Americans' continuing search for identity. The literature is self-examining, and the examination table is set firmly in the heartland.

"Most of us have roots in rural America," says Robert Bealer, professor of rural sociology at Pennsylvania State University. "There is a huge territory where we can reach back to. It's a fascinating place because maybe Americans are suffering from rootlessness. We've always been on the go. There is a tremendous concern for asking, where do we come from?"

We come from little places named Jonesville, Smithtown and Greenfield, wrote W. Lloyd Warner in his 1949 work, "Democracy in Jonesville": "No two American habitations are identical, but all of them, big or little, bear the strong family resemblance of the same parentage."

Nearly 40 years after the appearance of "Democracy in Jonesville," the family resemblance among small towns is hard to ignore. They nearly always have a dominant industry. Most small towns are in farming areas, says Munsell; but towns have also developed around lumber mills, manufacturing, mining and fishing.

No matter what their economic character, though, the same kinds of things tend to happen in them. The children join the 4-H Club. The local service clubs invent an endless cycle of events designed to boost hometown pride. Local power structures are solidly defined. High school football scores are the biggest news in town.

Small-town papers, usually weeklies, contain similar items. the Pocahontas (Iowa, population 2,350) Record-Democrat devoted 6 inches to Minnie Johnson's 85th birthday party. The bulk of the article was a guest list. There is bad news, too. Shain, Shad and Shay Shimic took out an ad in the Torrington (Wyo., population 5,440) Telegram: "Whoever took the butterfly off the tree in Grandma's yard in Torrington — PLEASE leave it at Long Branch in Hawk Springs. It was a Christmas present from us. No questions asked." On a more serious note, the Apache Junction Independent in Arizona reports that two local families are suing a business they believe improperly stored and destroyed chemical pesticide barrels. The litigants fear contamination of an underground water supply.

Small-town economics are not on a par with those in the big city. Unemployment is nearly twice the national average, Beverly Nykwest says. Small towns are really suffering in the western plains and Cornbelt states, says Gene Summers, professor of rural sociology at the University of Wisconsin in Madison. "These are areas where, historically, the economy has been heavily dependent on agriculture. There is a bit of concern in the timber regions of the Northwest, but they're coming back somewhat. In other parts of the country, small towns are doing reasonably well."

But perhaps the most common feature of small-town America is that it wants to stay that way. Town councils agonize over growth. Residents often complain of the need to revitalize the town, says Munsell, but most are willing to endure economic problems in exchange for the benefits of small-town life. "Even people who have grown up there and consider themselves stuck would feel that way deep down."

Small town residents represent a passing era in U.S. politics, says Rep. Vic Fazio. The California Democrat's 4th District includes several small towns. "People in small towns tend to vote for the man. They have a clear sense of leadership; they have a sense of direction." People in large cities can be frustrating, he says. "How do you get to them? They don't go to church, they don't have faith in government. They are rudderless. In small towns, you can reach them through schools, church, any institution they believe in."

The best and worst of small-town America is the same thing, says Munsell: Everybody knows you. "What drives people away, what has been described by 20th century authors who didn't like small towns, is that they can be very oppressive. A little more privacy and anonymity would be a lot nicer. but if you're in trouble, if you need the safety net, all these people will help you out."

Susan Katz Keating

PART 2

EXPENSIVE
CONGRESSIONAL
TASTES

CHAPTER 4

Much of U.S. farming has grown from self-sufficient roots into a highly dependent commercial enterprise surviving at the federal trough. How this happened is a story of government intervention, as those meaning to help farmers sought price supports and stymied the basic rules of supply and demand. This December 7, 1987, article looked at how massive subsidies came to dominate the system and why many think farmers must be weaned from them. More recent developments have brought little change. The 1990 farm bill went further, extending subsidies to additional agricultural products as well as perpetuating the basic support structure that Washington erected as a response to the Great Depression.

HELP THAT CAME TO RULE THE FARM

Chuck Merja's farm stretches for 10,000 acres into the vastness of Montana's Golden Triangle, a wheatland that spreads northward from Great Falls to the Canadian border. The Merjas — Chuck, brothers Patrick and Elliot, and their father — farm the early 1900s homestead of the boys' great-grandfather, a desolate and harsh place made bountiful, a symbol of the American family farm and its heritage of independence and free enterprise.

Last year the Merjas received checks totaling nearly $200,000 — almost half the farm's gross income — from the Agricultural Stabilization and Conservation Service of the Department of Agriculture. The checks were a drop in a $26 billion ocean of federal subsidies to farmers last year.

Net farm income is at near-record highs — not because crop

prices improved but because Washington is shoveling in subsidies. More than 95 percent of Montana's wheat growers receive federal farm supports. They get as much money from the U.S. treasury as they earn selling wheat. The story is much the same across America for a range of commodities, as farm payments balloon to record levels. A record 84 percent of all eligible cropland is enrolled in federal programs, and subsidies account for about 35 percent of net farm income. By the end of next year, total subsidies paid since 1980 will top $110 billion.

Without that money, Merja would probably go bankrupt. But even with that money, many of his neighbors already have. "I can understand the outrage that people have about farms that get millions of dollars from the government," says Merja. "I share that outrage." If his statement seems a contradiction, it is but one of thousands in the Byzantine world of U.S. farm policy. To point a finger at Chuck Merja is to miss by 2,000 miles. If agriculture policy has gone astray, the blame lies not in the wheat fields of Montana, any more than in the irrigated valleys of California, the dairy barns of Pennsylvania or the cornlands of Iowa. It lies in Washington, D.C.

From there have come policies, dating back to at least 1933, that have so distorted American agriculture that farmers today plant crops not by what a bushel of wheat will bring at the local grain elevator but by what it will yield in government payments. The overriding object of many farming decisions is clear: maximize subsidies. "You tell me what the government program is, and I'll tell you what I'm going to do next year," says David Buck, who raises corn just outside Connersville, Ind.

As a result, U.S. policy has gutted export sales, swamped grain markets, angered allies, raised consumer prices, ripped up fragile land and made independent farmers wards of the state. Inequities abound. Some prosperous farmers bathe in subsidies while indebted ones face bankruptcy. Only $1 out of every $4 in government payments goes to those in financial trouble. Yet $2.2 million went to a Texas farming operation in which Prince Hans Adam of Liechtenstein is partner. Citizens whose median household net worth is $32,667 subsidize farmers with a median net worth of $189,542, according to the Agriculture Department's Economic Research Service.

After decades of congressional attempts to protect farmers, government's presence in the farm economy has become overpowering. Yet with every good intention has come a nasty side effect. "They see a problem in agriculture, so they put a box around it," says Buck.

"And it causes another problem, so they put another box on the side of this box to take care of that problem. That creates another problem, and so they put another box on. First thing you know, the architecture of the problem is completely gone. There's no design that anybody would try to build to start off with."

In a policy fraught with contradictions, maybe the most startling irony is that the flood of tax money is spent largely in vain. In many ways, subsidies may be the undoing of the very farmers Congress says it is trying to help. "It's like a drink of liquor," says Don Paarlberg, professor emeritus of economics at Purdue University. "One drink can give some exhilaration, but if you take repeated drinks, you slide under the table. And we have been taking these repeated drinks now for 55 years."

How the great American farm machine landed in such a state is a tale of politics and rural mythology, misfired intentions and costly outcomes for farmers and taxpayers alike. Their fate is unfolding in a Washington policy debate now under way, heated by an approaching presidential election. The once-independent American farmer, tiller of the soil and backbone of the nation, has got the jitters.

BELIEFS BOUND TO THE LAND

Not since 1933, when Franklin Delano Roosevelt was president and the New Deal was doctrine, has the American public's view of farming or U.S. farm policy changed significantly. The federal government has tried to protect the family farm, to stabilize the farm economy, to ensure an abundant food supply, to conserve resources and, above all, to raise farmers' incomes.

Behind these policies has stood the broad support of the American public. The symbol of the family farm, bastion of Jeffersonian democracy, is deeply embedded in the American consciousness. A nationwide survey published in June by Luther Tweeten, a regent's professor at Oklahoma State University, found that farm fundamentalism permeates every social stratum. "The family farm must be preserved because it is a vital part of our heritage," agreed more than 80 percent of those surveyed. Some 70 percent think most farmers today are in financial trouble and that "government should have a special policy to ensure that family farms survive."

The roots of such beliefs and the policies that spring from them go back to the origins of the nation. Government nurtured agriculture long before the 1862 Homestead Act opened the West in plots of 160 acres. But boom and bust cycles plagued grain growers, who are more dependent on exports than others. Export swings and monetary contractions fueled agrarian uprisings in the Great Plains. Unable to influence prices, farmers tried to form cooperatives to gain market power but failed.

Prairie populism still flourishes. The farmer's 19th century complaint echoes today from Stan DeBoer's corn fields near Bertrand, Neb. "Prices are not high enough to deliver to the average American farmer the standard of living that he's entitled to," he says.

The golden age of agriculture arrived in the decade after 1910, a boom with many parallels to the farm expansion in the 1970s. A burgeoning population and World War I sent demand up 2 1/2 times faster than farm output. As prices rose, farm populism faded. Farmers expanded production and debt and bid up land prices. Then in June 1920, commodity prices collapsed.

In 1929, the entire country entered the Depression. Farm prices skidded 50 percent from 1929 to 1932, but production kept flowing. Farmers were trapped on the farm. The cities offered no jobs. People went hungry in New York while wheat was left uncut in Montana fields. On one day in April 1932, a quarter of the state of Mississippi went into foreclosure.

In 1933, under Roosevelt's guidance, Congress for the first time intervened directly in the farm economy. It passed the landmark Agricultural Adjustment Act, described by one New Dealer as "the greatest single experiment in economic planning under capitalist conditions ever attempted by a democracy in times of peace."

To boost prices, the government paid farmers to cut acreage on six commodities: corn, wheat, cotton, tobacco, rice and peanuts. To this day the programs remain, affecting half of U.S. farmers, who produce these and a handful of other commodities. Southerner William Faulkner wrote afterward: "Our economy is not agricultural any longer. Out economy is the federal government. We no longer farm in Mississippi cotton fields. We farm now in Washington corridors and congressional committee rooms."

By the 1940s, American agriculture had begun a robust recovery. It was not, however, the New Deal that saved farmers, historians say, but the timely conspiracy of drought and war. The Dust Bowl years beginning in 1934 slashed production. World War II swelled demand and drew marginal farmers to city jobs.

The New Deal policies remain today, adjusted but never fundamentally changed for 55 years — 55 years in which American agriculture has been through nothing short of a revolution. The number of farms hit its high-water mark at 6.8 million in 1935, when a quarter of Americans worked in agriculture. Since then, a massive exodus has been under way, through good times as well as bad.

During the booming 1940s, 600,000 farms disappeared; in the 1950s, 1.5 million. In the next decade, another million farms dropped out; in the next, a half-million. So far in the 1980s, nearly 40,000 farms have vanished each year. Today the total stands at 2.2 million, the number of farmers at about 2 percent of the population. Some 25 million fewer people live on farms than did in the 1930s, despite federal farm programs. During this severe contraction in numbers, the adoption of new technologies by those remaining in agriculture sent output soaring. The tractor alone switched 90 million acres from horse and mule feed to human food production. Hybrid seeds and cheap fertilizers multiplied yields.

Farms swelled in size; farmers left, but land remained in production. Capital replaced labor, slashing costs. Driven by technology, productivity has risen, resulting in a tidal wave of abundant, cheap food. Higher productivity freed labor from the farm. People left for jobs outside of agriculture to produce cars and computers — industrial and service goods — generating a huge increase in the standard of living.

The exodus from obsolete farm jobs has often been painful and frightening. Don Paarlberg of Purdue University compares it to the displacement of cottage weavers by textile mills. "People didn't understand it. They found all kinds of villains who were perpetrating this great problem. But gradually the change was made. The new system was more efficient than the old, and we got an abundance of products, low in cost, and we were all eventually better-off.

"Grandfather's farm is the equivalent of the cottage industry. It can't compete, except at a very low level of living. It's got to modernize. That process is going on. It's painful, and people don't understand it. There are all kinds of alleged villains. But as a result of all this, we are producing an abundance of food at a low cost, and we are better-off."

The numbers paint a startling picture. Of the 2.2 million operations counted as farms, the great majority — about 1.6 million, or 73 percent — are in fact owned by hobbyists, who earn most of their income outside the farm. They produce just one-tenth of farm output and receive 18 percent of all government agricultural subsidies. About 27 percent of farms, just 599,000 in all, produce nearly 90 percent of total output. These are the commercial farms. They receive 82 percent of federal farm subsidies.

Of these, farms with annual sales of $100,000 to $499,999, just

12.5 percent of all farms, produce 41 percent of total cash receipts. They receive 47 percent of the subsidies. Their owners have average household incomes of nearly $120,000 and average net worths of $665,000 to nearly $1.16 million. The largest farms, with annual sales of $500,000 or more — only 1.3 percent — produce about one-third of all output. They get 9 percent of the subsidies. Average household income is $723,315, average net worth more than $2.18 million.

These farms are businesses. Commercial farmers are as sophisticated in financing and marketing their crops as they are in growing them. Their budgets can run into millions of dollars. They are not self-sufficient. They specialize in one or two commodities, and they are highly integrated with the industrial economy and international markets. These commercial operations are also overwhelmingly family farms, owned and operated by a family. But families today can farm thousands of acres. The family farm of 1987 is not grandpa's farm of 1940: hogs, chickens and a few acres of corn. Farmers are not poor. The average net worth and income of today's farmer are several times higher than the U.S. average.

"We have a farming structure as different from that in 1935 as day is from night," says Willard Cochrane, who was a farm policy adviser in the Kennedy administration.

But the fact that policies have not changed means that 82 percent of the $26 billion in crop subsidies goes to about 599,000 commercial farms whose owners are far wealthier than the average citizen. Government programs do not rescue the small family farmer. If anything, they may hasten his demise by putting vast sums of money into the hands of aggressive farmers who buy out less successful neighbors.

Hugh Pinkerton, 65, farms 360 acres near Liberty, Ind., that have been in the family for five generations. He has watched federal agricultural programs operate since the 1930s. "A lot of these big farms have been buying a farm every year or every other year with the government payments," he says. "Personally, that's not my way of thinking. I wasn't brought up that way."

Cochrane, who fully supported federal farm subsidies when he worked with President Kennedy, has "become so disenchanted" with farm programs that he is "now convinced that we should do away with these programs completely. In fact, they should be eliminated immediately."

The American public is "horribly uninformed" about agriculture, says Tweeten of Oklahoma State. Yet it is public support that remains "the principal reason that we have farm commodity programs that can't be justified on any kind of rational basis. That farmers are poor, that they could not survive without government programs, that food supplies would be inadequate without the programs, that corporations would take over farming without the programs, that the family farm has got to be preserved because it's essential for democracy, or that programs are essential to preserve the rural community: All of these things, all of it is myth. All myth."

A BOUNTY OF SURPLUSES

Economist Lester Thurow of the Massachusetts Institute of Technology once characterized U.S. farm policy for Newsweek as an excellent model for government economic planning. The 1983 article was titled "Farms: A Policy Success."

Farmer Paul McDivitt, of Glenwood, Ind., has a different view. "Sitting here on the farm and knowing the money being spent on the farm programs," he says, "I think if people understood it more and knew they were paying that kind of price, there'd be an uprising."

Since the first "temporary" farm bill of 1933, each Congress has attempted to correct the problems caused by the preceding bill, without substantially changing the basic thrust of policy. Over the years congressional tinkering has created a mind-boggling profusion of programs, each one causing another new problem, which led to more corrections and more problems.

Problems consistently reappear — and grow — because the structure of the subsidy programs is in fundamental internal conflict: The government tells farmers to cut production and at the same time tells them to increase production. People say it's like driving a car with one foot holding down the accelerator and the other holding down the brake.

"It's a mess," says Gene McKeever, who farms near Fort Benton, Mont. "It's so unpredictable. Nothing stays the same. If they tell you one thing one minute, they have to rescind it the next."

It's also very expensive.

Congress's overriding goal is to raise farm incomes. The big subsidy programs — those funded directly by the treasury — apply only to about half of U.S. agriculture, primarily wheat, corn and other feed grains, and rice and cotton. A few other crops get government aid as well, but the costs are hidden. Government-enforced monopolies, for example, assist a few fruit and vegetable growers. Import quotas protect sugar producers. Dairy farmers get a combination of quotas, subsidies and monopoly-marketing schemes.

Livestock producers and most fruit and vegetable growers operate in a relatively free market. They receive no subsidies. Yet they are often hit by the effects of programs ricocheting off other commodities. As government moves corn prices up or down, it hurts or helps livestock producers. When government tells cotton growers to cut back acreage, they start growing vegetables and glut those markets. All farmers feel these spillover effects.

The subsidy programs operate primarily through price manipulation — they attempt to raise farm income by boosting crop prices. The government uses three basic tools: price supports, income supports and acreage controls. Price supports set a guaranteed floor on crop prices. They work through loans. The government makes a loan to a farmer, using his harvested crop as collateral. The loan amount depends on the loan rate set by Congress. The loan rate is a fixed amount per bushel, say $2 per bushel of corn. A 500-acre corn farm, with a yield of 100 bushels per acre, or 50,000 bushels, could get a loan for $100,000.

If market prices rise above $2, the grower will sell his corn and pay back the loan with interest. If market prices fall below $2, he can forfeit his corn and the loan will be considered paid in full. The $2 loan rate thus becomes a price floor. The farmer can always "sell," or forfeit, his crop to the government for at least $2 a bushel. When the loan rate is set above market prices, the government finds itself buying crops and collecting surpluses, which it pays growers and commercial elevators to store.

Surpluses are common, because Congress frequently sets the loan rate above market prices. At the end of last year the government owned nearly a year's supply of wheat and about eight months' supply of corn. The mere existence of these surpluses can depress market prices, causing more grain to be forfeited to the government and the surpluses to grow larger.

Because the United States is the world's largest agricultural producer and exporter, the U.S. price floor becomes the world price. If it is high, it encourages farmers abroad to increase their production, which competes with U.S. crops. It also causes U.S. farmers to forfeit their crops to the government instead of selling them on the world market. Foreign producers can then undercut the U.S. price and capture export sales, as they did from 1981 to 1986, when U.S. farm exports fell from more than $43 billion to $26 billion annually.

Income supports are the accelerator part of the programs. They work through what is called the target price. Congress sets the target price according to what it feels farmers should get for their crops. This price is always higher than the loan rate. The government pays farmers the difference between the target price and either the market price or the loan rate, whichever is higher. The amount paid depends on the farmer's "base," which is the number of acres he planted of a government program crop over the past five years, and on his bushel yield per acre.

Say the target price for corn is $3 per bushel. The loan rate is $2. So the government pays the farmer $1 per bushel on his base acres. That amount is called a deficiency payment. The more bushels he produces, the higher his payment. If the market price rises above the target price, he receives no deficiency payment.

This year, the target price for corn is $3.03 per bushel; the loan rate is $1.82. So the farmer gets a deficiency payment of $1.21 per bushel. A corn farmer with 500 acres of base and proven yields of 100 bushels per acre would get, for his 50,000 bushels, $60,500 from the government in deficiency payments — except that because deficiency payments were skyrocketing, Congress capped them at $50,000 per farmer. The farmer also received a loan for $100,000, which is income if he forfeits his crop. The loan plus the deficiency payment comes to $150,000.

Market corn prices went as high as $1.69 on average this summer. If the grower did not take part in the government program and instead sold his corn at the peak market price, he would have earned $84,500 for his crop — and taken a big gamble on lower market prices.

Farmers often complain about low market prices. But it is the target price, not the market price, that a farmer looks at when he decides how much corn, wheat, cotton or rice to plant. The target price determines his income. "We've got $3 corn," says David Buck, a corn and hog farmer near Connersville, Ind. "Don't let anybody tell you we've got $1.25 corn [the market price] and say, 'Boy, we can't make it on $1.25 corn.' Who's growing $1.25 corn?"

In fact, a rise in market prices can be bad news for a farmer because it lowers his deficiency payment. "Everybody who's celebrating the price increase in wheat is fooling themselves," says one farmer. "The worst thing that could happen would be for wheat to go up $2 a bushel." A grower would have to sell at peak market prices to recapture in full the loss of his deficiency payment. A government check is much more certain.

Until 1985 the target price induced farmers to get their yields as high as possible. The higher the yield, the higher the deficiency payment. Farmers poured on fertilizers, pesticides and herbicides. In 1985 Congress froze yields at each farmer's average from 1981 to

1985, with the high and low years thrown out. Freezing yields made some farmers lucky, others unlucky, depending on how good or bad their weather was from 1981 to 1985. Some wheat farmers have 47 bushels of proven yield per acre; others have 26. The lucky ones get much higher deficiency payments.

Target prices still induce farmers to plant the program crops because they guarantee an above-market price. So farmers plant a lot of corn, wheat, sorghum, barley, oats, rye, rice and cotton. (Soybeans have a loan rate, but no deficiency payment.)

Acreage controls are the brake part of the program. Because the target prices are telling farmers to plant more program crops and the loan program is adding millions of bushels to government-owned surpluses, Congress tries to cut back production. It could do this by lowering the target price but instead it makes growers reduce acreage.

To qualify for a deficiency payment, a farmer has to agree not to plant a certain percentage of his base acreage. This is called diverting, or setting aside, acreage. For corn this year the acreage set-aside was 20 percent; for wheat, 27.5 percent. This land becomes part of the Acreage Conservation Reserve. More than 50 million of the nation's 421 million acres of cropland have been idled this way. Most farmers set aside their poorest-yielding acres and keep planting the best land. So when the government tries to reduce acreage 20 percent, it may get only a 5 percent reduction in output. That's called slippage.

On top of the acreage controls, the government operates a "paid diversion" program. It pays farmers $2 a bushel on average to take additional cornland out of production. Moreover, in 1985 the government established the Conservation Reserve Program to take up to 45 million acres of land prone to erosion out of production. It pays farmers an average of $48 an acre for 10 years if they agree to plant the land with grass or some noncrop cover. The government pays half the costs of two grass seedings. The payment limit for the reserve program is $50,000 per year per farmer, which does not include the additional $50,000 he can get in deficiency payments. The cost of this program is expected to reach $1.4 billion next year.

The House of Representatives has just passed a provision called 0-92 aimed at taking more land out of production. It is an expansion of the 50-92 provision now in effect. If a farmer plants zero acres of his crop base, he will receive deficiency payments on 92 percent of that base. He cannot plant the acres with any other crop.

Marketing loans were instituted by Congress in 1985 for rice and cotton, because very high loan rates had cut deeply into export sales and government surpluses were building rapidly. With a marketing loan, the farmer does not have to repay his government loan or forfeit his crop. Instead, if market prices fall below the loan rate, he can pay back his loan at the lower market price (as low as half the loan rate) and keep the difference.

This year rice farmers received price support loans at $6.84 per hundredweight. But they could repay those loans in June, say, for $3.53, the average market price at the time. The government loses the $3.31 difference. Moreover, the target price on rice is $11.66. The difference between the target price and the loan rate is an additional $4.82, so the total subsidy is $8.13 per hundredweight. With marketing loans, U.S. farmers can undercut foreign growers. It is a form of government-financed dumping. The government pays farmers twice the market price for rice but allows them to sell it at a huge loss on the world market.

This year, the program cost the government about $900 million. Marketing loans for rice and cotton are exempt from the payment limitation of $50,000. Soybean and wheat growers want the government to extend marketing loans to their crops.

Import quotas and tariffs protect several commodities that fall somewhat outside the major subsidy programs. These include sugar, honey, tobacco, peanuts and wool. Sugar has a price support of 18 cents a pound. But producers usually do not forfeit their loans because import quotas keep out foreign sugar costing 6 cents a pound and force U.S. sugar prices up to about 22 cents a pound. Consumers, rather than taxpayers, pay for the program. It does not show up on the federal budget.

Peanut farmers get quota allotments, first assigned in the 1930s. These are like a license to sell peanuts in the U.S. market. The quotas restrict supplies, forcing prices up. Farmers who do not have a quota can buy or rent one from whoever has one available. Import restrictions keep out cheaper peanuts; exported peanuts are sold at market prices. Peanut farmers also get price support loans. Consumer costs run up to $300 million a year, with the benefit going to about 23,000 growers, mainly in Georgia, Alabama and Florida. Tobacco farmers operate under a similar program.

Honey producers get price supports and import restrictions. About 2,100 professional beekeepers received most of the $89 million in government subsidies last year. Consumers pay 23 cents a pound extra for honey as a consequence of import quotas, and the government owns 22 million pounds in surplus.

Betty McDivitt of Glenwood, Ind., started raising honeybees as a hobby. She entered the government honey program last year because the loan rate was higher than the wholesale market price. Like many producers, she forfeits her poor-quality honey to the government and retails the good honey. "You feel a little bit of guilt doing it," she says, "but yet the program's available. It's there."

About 120,000 wool producers get $100 million a year in "incentive payments" financed through an import tariff. Congress sets an "incentive level" at what it "deems a fair price for wool," according to Daniel Murphy of the National Wool Growers Association. This year the incentive price is $1.81 per pound, while the market price is about 90 cents.

Export subsidies help dispose of government surpluses. The Food for Peace program, which gives away food for famine relief or sells it overseas at long-term subsidized interest rates, has been a major outlet for federal stockpiles since 1954. In 1985 Congress set up the export enhancement program to move more stockpiles and subsidize export sales. This program gives government grain to U.S. exporters who are competing with subsidized sales from other countries. The exporter will mix the free wheat with his own wheat, thus lowering the total price to his customer. Numerous other subsidized credit arrangements or guarantees help move farm exports, at a total estimated cost this year of $7 billion.

Marketing orders grant a few fruit, nut and vegetable growers a government-enforced cartel, a group of producers who band together to limit competition. (Farmers are exempt from antitrust laws.) Not all marketing orders restrict competition; often they merely allow growers to jointly promote their crops. But in some cases, the grower cartel, or cooperative, restricts output in order to raise prices. The Department of Agriculture enforces the rules. Consumers, not taxpayers, bear the cost.

Growers of any commodity can vote to organize a cooperative. Monopolistic marketing orders are more common in such specialty crops as oranges or spearmint oil, because the fewer the producers, the easier it is to organize and police the group. (Sunkist Growers Inc. is a huge citrus cooperative in Arizona and California that dominates the Western citrus market.)

If a specified majority agrees to the order, Agriculture determines whether the marketing of the crop has been "chaotic," that is, too many lemons coming on the market at one time, causing prices to fall sharply. Marketing orders have been justified on these grounds for almond growers, yet pecan growers operate without them. California oranges were found to require supply controls, but Florida oranges were not.

Some of the 48 marketing orders have been operating since the 1930s, though many operate mainly as promotion groups. A few growers — of cherries in the upper Midwest, hops in California and grapefruit in Florida — have dissolved them. Some growers say they lose money because they are forced to let fruit rot in the field. In 1937 Congress prohibited the Office of Management and Budget from studying marketing orders; in 1983 an amendment in Congress to strike the law was defeated.

Farm credit programs subsidize farmers' borrowing. In the 1920s Congress set up the Farm Credit System, a farmer-owned bank cooperative. The system paid back the original federal funding but has always enjoyed an implicit federal guarantee on the bonds it sells to raise funds. Indeed, because the system has sustained heavy losses on farm real estate loans, Congress will probably approve a rescue.

In the 1930s the government began to make subsidized loans through an agency that became the Farmers Home Administration. Originally it provided technical assistance and loans to sharecroppers. Today Farmers Home acts as the grower's lender of last resort for operating expenses and land acquisition. It also lends for water and sewer systems, recreation facilities, housing and businesses in rural areas. Clifton Luttrell, an economist formerly with the Federal Reserve Bank of St. Louis, said Farmers Home lending has "been broadened to the extent that subsidized loans are available for almost any purpose if the borrower lives outside a major metropolitan area."

Last year the agency's loan volume reached $7 billion, $4.4 billion of which went to farmers. Outstanding loans and loan guarantees totaled $70 billion; 43 percent, or $12 billion, of its farm loans are delinquent, many for several years. The government estimates that it will incur costs of $3.6 billion in 1988 for subsidy, loan write-offs and other losses. Total spending this year on Farmers Home will be $7.6 billion.

Other farm subsidies include the research performed by land grant colleges that is disseminated through county extension offices; crop insurance, a subsidized insurance fund for crop losses, which this year cost taxpayers $1.3 billion; and irrigation subsidies, which a House subcommittee estimated run to as much as $376 million annually.

In 1981, after a long inflationary period when crop prices had been rising, Congress froze target prices in the major subsidy programs at their highest levels ever. Soon after, the bottom dropped out of the world commodity markets. After a long, heated debate, in which the Reagan administration tried to cut subsidies, Congress passed the 1985 Food Security Act. It was a response to a dramatic loss in U.S. exports.

The 1985 bill dropped the loan rates sharply, moving them to a formula that would keep them at below-market prices. This way the loan rate would become a "safety net" in case of a sharp price drop, instead of a hammock. Congress insisted that loan rates drop by no more than 25 percent in the first year and then 5 percent in every year thereafter. Congress also instituted marketing loans for rice and cotton and the Payment-in-Kind program. But Congress left target prices frozen for two years. They will begin falling slightly only next year — on wheat, for example, from $4.38 to $4. By leaving target prices high while dropping the loan rate, Congress ensured an explosion in deficiency payments.

BOOM TO BUST TO BAILOUT

As an Iowa high school student in the 1970s, Craig Hill saw farmers become millionaires. "I admired those farmers," he recalls. "And those farmers made their net worth not from milking cows or feeding the pigs. They had bought land in 1967 for $250 an acre and now that land was worth $2,500 an acre."

Hill went on to study agriculture at Iowa State University. He remembers a professor "standing up there and saying, 'You guys are going to feed the world. Plant fencerow to fencerow and go, go, go.'"

During the summers Hill baled hay for a neighbor, an older man who had farmed through the Depression and kept telling him not to mortgage anything. "And I said, 'You've been preaching this for five years, and we haven't had a depression yet. You've been wrong every year.'" So Hill sank $40,000 as down payment into an 80-acre farm. He paid $2,600 an acre, or $208,000. He borrowed another $165,000 to buy another farm. "There were people running around the country preaching that land was going to continue to inflate," recalls Hill. He added machinery and operating loans. "That sounds like too much debt, but at the time I thought I could service it. Then the thing just crashed."

The great farm bust of the 1980s had begun.

A peculiar confluence of world events fed the boom. Droughts hit large parts of the world. August bodies predicted widespread famine.

The Soviets bought grain. food demand rose sharply, prices followed and shoppers boycotted supermarkets. The dollar fell, making U.S. farm goods cheaper for foreigners. Third World governments borrowed heavily and spent freely on U.S. farm products. Exports surged.

An inflationary spiral set in. Farm earnings and land prices began to escalate. Not only was land a hedge against inflation; land grew food, and food prices were exploding. An asset that produces something rising in value itself becomes more valuable. People bid up the price of farmland to capture its income potential. Land values were going up so fast that a farmer could borrow to buy land, wait, and the land would be worth more. It would be worth so much more that banks encouraged farmers to use it as collateral for more borrowing.

Some went deeply into debt buying land, even when the cost of planting the crop and servicing the debt was more than the crop was worth. In farm jargon, the land didn't cash flow. But they believed that continued capital gains would make up for income losses. Will Rogers's famous line about land, "They don't make any more of it," became farmer wisdom. Farmers bought new equipment to boost production. Their debt rose from $53 billion in 1972 to $200 billion by 1984. Still, half kept their debt manageable or stayed debt-free. All of them saw their real estate wealth soar. Capital gains, in 1986 dollars, hit $500 billion in the 1970s. Farm assets hit $1 trillion.

In 1976 the government raised the loan rates and the target prices in the big farm programs. In 1981 Congress set those prices into law at their highest level in history, sending a powerful signal to produce more food. World economic and political forces were coming together in a big wave, and farmers were riding on its crest. Suddenly, in the early 1980s, everything reversed course. The Federal Reserve Board tightened the money supply to squelch inflation. The dollar rose. Strapped Third World countries stopped buying food. President Carter embargoed grain sales to the Soviet Union. Foreign countries moved in on sales. Exports plummeted. Interest rates skyrocketed. Food prices fell, dashing expectations of rising earnings.

The bottom fell out of the land market. Values everywhere plummeted. An acre of grape land in the San Joaquin Valley of California that sold for $15,000 fell to $3,000. Land that Hill had bought for $2,600 an acre fell to $800. "All of a sudden," he says, "I was in a world of trouble."

A farmer owning debt-free land pays only the cost of raising his crop. If Hill hadn't had to pay interest, "I could have lived well and survived the storm." But when a couple of droughts hit, operating losses began piling up. The drop in land values had wiped out his equity: his down payment and the value of his assets. He and thousands of other farmers were left without any equity cushion. Those whose land was worth less than their debt were bankrupt. Those whose crops did not generate enough cash to service their debts when interest rates were low and food prices were high faced bankruptcy. In spring 1985 Hill's bank cut off his operating loans, warning of liquidation in the fall.

Lenders were caught too. About 200, or 4 percent, of the commercial agricultural banks have failed. The Farm Credit System, a farmer-owned bank cooperative, might fail unless Congress approves a bailout. Some 43 percent of the outstanding farm loans at the Farmers Home Administration, a government agency, are delinquent. From a Department of Agriculture survey, Emanuel Melichar of the Federal Reserve Board estimates that in January 1986, when total farm debt was $188 billion, problem loans totaled $60 billion and potential lender losses stood at $16 billion. Since 1980 capital losses from falling land prices, in 1986 dollars, have reached $450 billion, nearly as high as the $500 billion capital gain during the 1970s.

The worst is probably over. Land values have stopped falling nearly everywhere except Texas; delinquencies and loan write-offs are dropping off. Whereas early statistics in 1984 showed one-third of all farmers might fail, a later comprehensive survey showed that many of those were squeaking by. By January this year 12 percent of commercial farmers were in the financially "vulnerable" or "stressed" categories. Farm debt has fallen nearly 25 percent since its 1984 peak, partly through foreclosures and loan write-offs. Many farmers paid off debt and cut back operating costs. The largest drop in farm expenses in more than 30 years is helping increase profits.

Most farmers were never heavily indebted. While they lost the real estate wealth they had accumulated during the boom, their average net income did not drop and they were not financially threatened. These farmers, Melichar writes, "are financially distressed only in comparison with what was or what might have been."

Clearly, both boom and bust centered on land values. Farming itself "has remained a profitable activity," according to John Lee, administrator of the Agriculture Department's Economic Research Service. In fact, by almost any measure, farm income is at or near the record levels of the 1970s. Much of this income is from government payments. Yet only $1 out of every $4 in federal deficiency payments — justified by Congress on the grounds of the farm financial crisis brought about by a drop in real estate values — is going to farmers experiencing severe financial stress.

Congress, debating other ways to help farmers, heard testimony from Jessica Lange and Sissy Spacek, the heroines of two farm-crisis movies, and Jane Fonda. Last year Congress passed the Chapter 12 bankruptcy law, requiring lenders to reduce a farmer's real estate debt to the land's current value if his debts are under $1.5 million. For example, if a farmer cannot service his debt on $3,000-an-acre land, it will be reduced to $1,000 an acre, if that is the land's market value. Many states have also placed moratoriums on foreclosures.

But the idea of such assistance rankles many farmers. "My neighbor over there, who went and bought a piece of land at the same time I did—he just has to pay half price for it and me not?" says Kenneth Hood, a Mississippi cotton farmer. Says Indiana corn farmer David Buck, "Here's the rest of the guys sitting out here that didn't make those kinds of mistakes. And [Congress is] saying, 'Look, we're going to forgive you at $2,000 an acre times however many acres you bought. Go and sin no more.' And that's not right."

Chapter 12 has made it harder for many farmers to get credit. "What Chapter 12 did for us was it scared the hell out of banks, and they just tightened up tighter than they ever were before." says A. J. Yates, a California cotton and sugar beet grower.

"If you're going to gamble to make money," says Bob Schoonover, who farms near Loma, Mont., you "gotta be able to lose money and accept the responsibility."

Many farmers find that renting land is better than borrowing to buy it. In the past, farming was financed almost exclusively with debt, a much riskier form of investment than equity, in which an investor puts money in a business in the hope of receiving dividends. Unlike interest, dividends are paid only when profits justify them. Leasing land is a way to get equity financing in farming, says economists. The landlord becomes the investor; the farmer's land rental is the dividend, which fluctuates with farm profits. The landowner then assumes some of the risk. Farmers don't have to invest millions in land, and in the 1980s some of the most successful aren't.

Hill sold his farms and machinery and got a loan from Farmers Home; he survived. Now he rents equipment and land. "I look back," he says, "and it was a good lesson. Now I look at investments differently. I want more security and less faith."

The Push-Pull of Programs

Pity, say farmers, the government workers at the Agricultural Stabilization and Conservation Service, the arm of the U.S. Department of Agriculture that reaches into every county in the nation to administer the farm programs. "They're the ones who take all the punishment," says Rick Bailey, a Montana farmer. "The people that are writing [the rules] back in Washington don't get too much flak, but you go in and see the ladies in the office in Fort Benton after they've been there all day." Administration of the programs has become a nightmare, rules upon rules upon rules in constant flux. Complexity reigns. What begins as a general decree becomes an intricate web of regulations to distinguish subtleties and correct accidents.

When Congress removed farmers from the market, it linked their prosperity and even their survival to government programs. As a result, manipulating the programs has become a high art. Farmers hire consultants and lawyers to stay on top of the latest nuances. Congress and the federal bureaucracy counter with new rules.

The primary objective of any farmer in the program is to maximize subsidies, which is done by planting program crops — whether anyone wants them or not. "It's the only parade going through town," says Tom Towers, an Iowa corn grower. That's because program crops have high target prices. When farmers decide to plant, they look at target prices, not market prices. They may sell their goods on the market, but it is the target price that determines their income, in the form of a government deficiency payment.

To maximize deficiency payments, they plant as much of the program crops as the government allows. "I dig out my sheets from the ASCS office," says Mark Sather, who grows corn and raises hogs near Hanska, Minn. His sheets tell him how many acres of corn he can plant. He plants all of those acres to produce the maximum number of bushels at the target price. "I don't care what the market price is. If I looked at the market price of corn, I'd cut my production in half."

On land left over, a farmer sows a market crop, basing his decision on market prices and costs. "After I've maximized government payments," says wheat grower Chuck Merja, "then I look at how I can produce the crop I plant for the least amount of dollars to get the most return, which is what I should be doing all the time."

Ed Bumgarner, one of the few wheat farmers in Montana who plans not to be in the wheat program next year, explains the difference between planting for the government and planting for the market. With a market crop he asks, "What is my profit line? What does it cost me to actually raise a bushel of wheat? If that price is lower than what I can get in the market, I'm going to make money. But if that price is higher than I can get in the market, I've got to go back and find out how I can raise it cheaper. But you see, with the government program, nobody thinks about that."

James Wood, a Montanan in the program, says, "We have no telling what our profit margin is. When you dedicate yourself to farming, you just dedicate yourself. That is the last thing we would ever stop to figure out, what our margin of profit was."

When farmers maximize program crop yields, grotesque distortions develop. They grow huge surpluses because the crops are linked not to market supply and demand but to subsidies. "I've got half my 1984 crop in an elevator in town," says Sather, who weathered a Chapter 11 bankruptcy recently. "I've got my 1985 crop sitting in my machine shed. I've still got some of my '86 crop at home, and the '87 crop has nowhere to go. I produce crops for food, not to put in my granary. That's disgusting. That's the wrong result. And that's the problem when we get the wrong signals."

Tom Glau, a vegetable grower near San Ardo, at the tail end of California's Salinas Valley, doesn't have guarantees: "If you guaranteed me that I'd have a certain price on my broccoli, the government would have all the cold storage rooms in the United States full of broccoli or it would be rotting away fresh."

Farmers keep planting program crops year after year for fear of losing their base, the number of acres on which the government allows them to collect subsidies. The base is determined by planting history. So even when the government allows farmers to cut back on program crops and still receive subsidies, they continue planting them. They never know when the government might change its mind, reducing their base if they had cut back acreage that year.

When the government collects surpluses, it usually gets the worst quality raised that year. Premium grains are sold on the market. Ray Jergeson of Computer Information and Marketing Systems, a Great Falls, Mont., farm consulting firm, says the government owns 660 million bushels of wheat unfit for milling. Because it holds mammoth crop stockpiles, the government requires and pays farmers to restrict, or set aside, some of the land that might be planted with program crops. Usually farmers set aside their least productive land, often acres they plowed up in the first place only to increase their base. The government then finds that the reductions hardly make a dent in the surpluses.

The Agricultural Stabilization and Conservation Service must limit what can be sown on the set-asides or else the programs spill over into other crops. When the government chose to further cut back on cotton acreage, for example, cotton growers in California's San Joaquin Valley began raising lima beans on their set-asides. Their output glutted the market, causing losses among unsubsidized lima bean growers.

Farmers also have trouble with the 1985 Conservation Reserve Program. Funded by the Agriculture Department, it pays growers not to cultivate fragile soil. The 10-year program, run by the agricultural service, is scheduled to idle up to 45 million acres. "Have you seen the ground that's gone into the CRP?" asks Virginia Bailey, Rick's mother. "It's nothing but tumbleweeds."

"The weeds are all going to go to seed, although they're supposed to be sprayed," says Bumgarner. "But who's going to administer that? How are they going to come out and look at 45 million acres and make sure every farmer does what he's supposed to do? So here I am, downwind from all these weeds, and now I've got to go out and spend all kinds of money on chemicals to kill them. I just don't know."

One reason Washington pays farmers to put land in the reserve is that it is, at the same time, paying them to plant crops. Many plowed up erodible land at least in part to get subsidies, a practice known as sodbusting and swampbusting. "There's been a lot of bad farming done because of programs in agriculture," Pam Schoonover says. She and her husband, Bob, farm in Montana, where sodbusters plowed up thousands of acres, turning prairies into sand dunes. "All the ground that was broken up, they never should have broken it up in the first place," she says. "And now they're going to get paid to put it back."

One farmer says he could sell his land for about $300 an acre, but the government will in effect lease it for $45 an acre for 10 years, and he gets the land back. By February, the Conservation Reserve will be the biggest "crop" in Montana. Almost a quarter of northeastern Missouri is now reserve program land. To prevent further erosion, the government in 1990 will begin requiring every farmer in any federal program to follow a detailed conservation plan individually approved and policed by Agricultural Stabilization and Conservation.

When Congress became alarmed at ballooning federal deficiency payments going out to farmers, it limited them to one $50,000 deficiency payment each, and up to $250,000 each for all programs.

Farmers responded with the "Mississippi Christmas tree," named after the state whose farmers have had the greatest success and the longest history skirting the limitation.

The General Accounting Office found that several thousand "new" farms sprang up after the payment limits went into effect. Farmers simply broke their land into smaller units. "The son gets a piece, the daughter gets a piece, and some farmers get so desperate even mother-in-law gets a piece," observes Earl L. Butz, secretary of agriculture under Presidents Nixon and Ford. If current trends continue, the office estimates that about 31,000 "new farmers" will have appeared by 1989 as a result of such reorganizations, at a cumulative cost of $1.23 billion.

The Agriculture Department may try to close loopholes with the latest, 2-inch-thick book of payment limitation rules, but as long as conflicts remain, farmers will find ways around them. "You've got a bunch of people in Washington writing a program, and then you've got all these farmers looking for holes in it, and they find them," says A. J. Yates, a San Joaquin Valley cotton and sugar beet grower. "Let's face it. You can't write a perfect program."

Farmers of all stripes, whether they favor subsidies or want to do away with them, often recall the government's $2.3 trillion debt and wonder how long the spending will — or can — continue.

"With so much publicity about all these farmers getting $50,000, it's bound to end up no good," speculates one. "How in blazes can they afford to be paying out money to people when we're that far in debt?" wonders a neighbor. "It just is scary." And from another: "We have such a huge level of government cash coming into this operation, we shake every time we get a letter from the post office."

THE HIDDEN ADDICTION TO AID

Throughout farm country, the phrase "cheap food policy" rings over and over. "You either pay for it at the Safeway or at the Internal Revenue Service" is the retort to anyone questioning the high cost of farm subsidies.

Farmers say the government holds commodity prices down and then covers farmers' production costs with tax dollars. Therefore Americans spend less of their income on food than people anywhere else. "The ultimate subsidy is to the consumer," asserts cotton and sugar beet farmer A. J. Yates. "You've got the cheapest food in the world. You never go into a grocery store and want."

"Rural mythology," counters Robert Thompson, dean of agriculture at Purdue University. If anything, say economists, U.S. policy aims at raising food prices. Price supports are just that: They hold prices up, guaranteeing farmers more money for their crops than the market would deliver. Competition in the unsubsidized broiler industry, for example, has driven chicken prices down almost one-third in the past two decades. In the highly subsidized dairy industry, by contrast, cheese and milk prices have risen.

High U.S. incomes are why consumers spend a lower percentage of their income on food than do poorer people in poorer nations, say economists. In absolute terms, Americans spend more on food than almost anyone. Comparisons with food prices in Western Europe and Japan are misleading because prices there are exorbitant as a result of farm protection. Last year a pound of steak cost $30 in Japan, for example: a melon, $25.

Farmers also argue that they cannot compete with farmers from less-developed countries, where wages are far lower. "If the people in the U.S. would be willing to accept the standard of living that the Thai farmers live under, we could produce the product as cheap as they do," says David Hillman, a rice farmer near Almyra, Ark. "But we're not going to accept that and we shouldn't accept that."

But in low-wage nations farming is labor-intensive. Rice beds are planted and harvested by hand because labor is cheap. U.S. farming is capital-intensive. Planting and reaping are done by machine, because capital is comparatively cheap. "What matters," says Thompson, "is the total cost of producing the commodity, not the cost of any individual input." To say the Arkansas farmer cannot compete against the Thai farmer is the equivalent of the Thai farmer's saying he cannot compete with the Arkansas farmer because machinery is so costly.

Most growers maintain that subsidies ensure that no food shortages develop. "We don't want welfare," maintains Iowa corn farmer Craig Hill, "but farm programs are necessary in agriculture, necessary to the government and the people, because you always want an abundant supply of food." Yet there are no meat, fruit or vegetable shortages, even though growers of those foods get no subsidies.

What farm programs have done, say economists, is to suffuse U.S. agriculture to the extent that without them, many farmers would probably go broke. "You pretty much have to work with Uncle Sam to make a go of it," says one. "We will not survive without them," says another.

Farmers of program crops are thoroughly addicted to subsidies. Given their sheer size ($26 billion last year) and the way they operate, sudden government withdrawal would be catastrophic, not only to farmers but to anyone who owns land, labor or capital that is tied to farming. In the sense that the government collects surplus commodities, its policies depress market prices; they also then force growers to rely on subsidies for their income.

The purpose of guaranteeing prices to farmers was to raise their incomes. While the intention sounds laudable, the deed has colossal repercussions. When Congress artificially inflates the price of corn, the value of land that produces corn also rises: It is worth more because it now produces a higher income. And as the price of corn-growing acreage rises, the rate of return on investment in such land falls back to its earlier level. The subsidy shows up not only as higher corn income but as a potential capital gain to the person who owns cornland when Congress raises corn prices.

It is the land market, not Congress, that determines the total rate of return from farm investment. Every time Congress raises subsidies and hence farm income, land values adjust upward, and the rate of return on farm investment stays the same. When farmers see their land costs rising and their returns retreating to market levels, they tell their congressmen that growing corn is not profitable. If Congress raises the subsidies again the cycle repeats itself.

Evidence of this process abounds. British farmland values doubled within a year after the nation joined the Common Market's farm subsidy program. In Japan, where rice farmers are heavily subsidized, rice land sold last year at $45,500 an acre on average. The World Bank found that in the United States, farm subsidies had "no effect on the rate of return to investment in farming. . . . Overall, the rate of return in agriculture tended to follow the general rate of return in the economy and was not affected by agricultural policies."

Removing subsidies would lower land prices. Landowners become "vitally interested in the price support programs," says Clifton B. Luttrell, an economist formerly with the Federal Reserve Bank of St. Louis. Subsidies also induce farmers to pour on fertilizers to increase output at the subsidized price and so raise their income. "If my crop is subsidized at $3 a bushel," explains Mark Sather, a Hanska, Minn., corn and hog farmer, "my production costs expand to the point where I use up that $3 a bushel. The machinery dealers love it, the chemical companies love it, but my net return is the same. With any subsidy program, your input costs adjust. And you come out with about the same net."

The existence of subsidies also makes it nearly impossible for many farmers to stay out of the programs. When the government pays farmers $3 to raise corn that sells for $1.50 on the market, the subsidized farmer has a huge advantage. In fact, many banks require participation in government programs before they lend a grower money.

Ed Bumgarner does not own any land, but the land he rents and farms — 2,500 acres of wheat spreading below the mountains near Highwood, Mont. — will not be part of the government program next year. He thinks federal programs deprive the farmer of his free will. "The farmer can't go out and say, 'By golly, by good hard work and by trust in God above I can plant this crop and know that I'll try to get something.' I really think that it should be that if I can raise my wheat for $2 and get [a market price of] $2.25, I'll be in business. If it costs me $3 to raise my wheat, I won't." he says. "The same way with someone who has a dress shop in Great Falls. If they buy their dresses for $15 and sell them for $14, they're not going to be there very long.

"We can't have the government come along and say, 'Oh you poor farmers, we're going to bail you out.' What's going to happen when the dress people come along and say, 'Hey, we aren't making any money, we have to have a deficiency payment on dresses,' for Pete's sake?"

The Farmers Home Administration acts as the lender of last resort to farmers who have been rejected elsewhere. These loans, just as other subsidies do, prevent marginal growers from going out of business. In 1978, Congress intensified this effect with the Economic Emergency Credit Act, which appropriated $6.6 billion to FmHA. The money refinanced the loans of those farmers who could demonstrate an economic emergency.

"A few years ago, anybody who walked into Farmers Home could get money," recalls a farm consultant in Fort Benton, Mont. "The more broke you were, the better chance you had to get it. Those people years ago were insolvent in the worst way. And of course Farmers Home was terribly generous and naive or whatever, and it kept them on. That's why there's a big crisis."

Insolvent farmers were strung along, says Sheila Macdonald of the National Taxpayers Union, a Washington, D.C., lobbying group. Their added production deepened the 1980s price collapse, leading to failures among stronger farmers. "It spread misery up the ladder," she maintains.

Mississippi cotton grower Kenneth Hood agrees. Higher surpluses, which may trigger increased required set-asides, are partly the result of production from "people that the [FmHA] has put in business to compete directly against me," he says. "We're competing against the federal government. It's just not fair. And it's not fair to them. The [FmHA] did them an injustice, it really did, because they should never have been farming, and they got all this debt load on them and had to take bankruptcy. That five to seven years that they were actually in there farming, that was seven years they could have been progressing in another job somewhere else."

Congress dropped Economic Emergency lending in 1982 and charged the disaster loan program. But the agency still carries many long-delinquent borrowers.

Carolyn Lochhead

CHAPTER 5

*When the government began making
loans to farmers, students, home buyers
and small businessmen, it intended to
make money. But a spate of nonpayments,
together with congressional shackling of
debt-collection efforts, left a huge deficit in
the government's loan portfolio. While
banks have written off some debt,
taxpayers, as explained in this January
30, 1989, article, were likely to be stuck
with the burden of defaults.*

UNCLE SAM'S
PROFLIGATE LENDING

One of Congress's dirty little habits is finally getting an overdue public airing. For the past 20 years, legislators have been handing out government loans to everybody and his brother. Now taxpayers are beginning to find that these reputedly cost-free goodies are anything but cheap.

Just before Christmas, it was revealed that the Farmers Home Administration, which lends for rural housing and agriculture, had losses of $36 billion in its $90 billion loan portfolio. Nobody knows for certain how much of the rest of Uncle Sam's $771.9 billion in outstanding loans will ultimately prove uncollectible. Sooner or later, though, the losses will have to be made good out of the public purse.

These loans-cum-giveaways account for a big chunk of what are known as the middle-class entitlements. Many of the beneficiaries are farmers, students, home buyers and small-business men, not the hungry, homeless and unemployed. If the estimates are right, many of the recipients are also deadbeats. For example, 15 percent of the students who receive federally guaranteed loans and college loans, which already come with subsidies of nearly 50 percent, may never pay them back, says the Education Department. Federal loans and guarantees "often amount to direct grants," writes economist Dennis Ippolito.

When the federal government first got into big-time lending, during the early days of the Great Depression, losing money was not part of the plan. By charging fees to cover their operating costs and spreading their risks over a large pool of borrowers, the New Dealers showed that making loans to homeowners and small farmers could be profitable. Today's multibillion-dollar mortgage banking industry is the result.

The erosion of bankerly standards has gone hand in hand with a dramatic expansion in federal lending. Since 1972, the government's portfolio of outstanding loans and guarantees has quadrupled. By one count, there are 422 separate credit programs being administered by agencies from the Pentagon to the Small Business Administration. One of every five dollars lent in U.S. credit markets has federal fingerprints on it.

The aroma of pork is everywhere. Loans for small businesses, shipbuilders, students and disaster victims have always operated as giveaways disguised as loans. Others, such as the Rural Electrification Administration and the various farm agencies, began as self-financing programs but degenerated into handouts. Thanks to the development of interstate banking and various modern financing techniques, many of these programs can no longer even claim to fill holes in the marketplace. Some, like the farm credit programs, probably left their clients worse off than before, encouraging them to load up on debt just in time for the collapse of commodity prices.

"There are way too many programs, many of them created to appeal to individual little constituencies," says Barry Bosworth, a senior fellow at the Brookings Institution. "They were not justified in the beginning and are certainly not justified now."

The way they survive is by masquerading as cheap. New loans are recorded as direct outlays, just like any other expenditure. But offsetting them are the repayments trickling in from loans made in previous years. Thus, even though a loan program may be losing gobs of money over time, the annual budget snapshot makes it look like the program is paying its own way. For proponents of truth in accounting, however, the most damnable trend is the government-wide mania for guaranteeing loans made by commercial bankers. When an agency issues a guarantee, it promises to repay the loan itself if the borrower defaults. Guarantees make up about 70 percent, or $550 billion, of the federal credit portfolio, up from $159 billion in 1972. The fad has taken government credit shops far afield from their traditional rural focus by making it easier politically to dish out cheap financing to all and sundry. Noteworthy recipients have included Lockheed Corp., Chrysler Corp., New York City, Conrail, Amtrak, the synthetic fuels program, rich resort towns, and foreigners who buy U.S.-made military hardware and other big-ticket exports.

There is nothing mysterious about the popularity of guarantees with bureaucrats and legislators. Under the government's accounting rules, the guarantees add nary a cent to the budget totals when issued. The real cost does not appear until Uncle Sam is called upon to shell out to compensate lenders for defaults down the road. In practice, when they go sour, guaranteed loans often end up on the books of federal agencies as direct loans. And, like the government's other bum loans, they are seldom written down to reflect the fact that they will most likely never be collected.

Judging by what is written in the federal budget, then, the loan and guarantee programs are miraculous cases of getting something for nothing. Not only can deficit-haunted legislators authorize them without having to steer funding away from other programs, but their actions are easily overlooked in the crush of media attention focused on the budget itself.

In the coming weeks, the General Accounting Office, the green-eyeshade arm of Congress, will try to put that right by issuing a special report on the programs. "The basic theme is going to be that we have a lot more in guarantees out there than anybody realizes," says Frederick D. Wolf, director of the agency's accounting and financial management division. "The cost of guarantees has gone up substantially, and we don't have very good control."

Presidents from Lyndon Johnson to Ronald Reagan have repeatedly lobbied in favor of making loan-program accounting more candid, but Congress has either demurred or watered down the medicine to the point of ineffectiveness. In 1980 the Carter administration made headway by introducing a separate budget for federal lending agencies. But the accounting method still conceals the true cost of the programs. President George Bush has yet to weigh in on the side of the reformers.

Proposals to shed more light on what goes on inside the credit agencies provoke a pack of lobbyists. Howls are elicited not just from housing groups, veterans organizations, university administrations and various industries but also from banks, which profit handsomely from making riskless loans. Nevertheless, credit reform remains a perennial agenda item for good-government types, who argue that enlightened policy-making is not served by hiding from taxpayers how much the programs cost.

Fear of offending the powerful constituencies also explains the kid-gloved treatment meted out to overdue borrowers. Even with the get-tough measures adopted in the early Reagan years — turning deadbeats over to private collection agents, trashing their credit ratings, etc. — Forbes magazine could still call Uncle Sam "tough as marshmallows." The softheartedness begins with Congress. When establishing many of the programs, it put tight limits on how hard bureaucrats may squeeze borrowers. As far as the direct lending programs are concerned, there is little incentive for Congress to do anything but let bum loans pile up on agency books indefinitely. The only budgetary impact is the loss of revenues as borrowers skip payments. On the other hand, mounting defaults in the guarantee programs are harder to ignore, and Congress is under pressure to set aside precious funds as a backstop against future losses.

The reason is that some experts have begun sounding the tocsin about a wave of loan defaults in the next economic downturn. If so, the government could be forced to spend billions paying off private lenders, leaving Congress with the unpalatable choice of diverting money from other programs, raising taxes or throwing deficit reduction to the winds. On the other hand, setting aside money before a crisis hits, while a laudable precaution, would absorb scarce funds lawmakers would rather spend for more vote-winning purposes.

How much should lawmakers appropriate for future defaults? Nobody will really know until the General Accounting Office completes its first audit of federal lending programs. Wolf reckons that at least $3 billion a year will be needed. Such a sum, if approved by Congress, would quickly disabuse members of the notion that loan guarantees are cost-free. Bosworth, a persistent advocate of reform, argues that in many cases it would be cheaper and more effective simply to write the beneficiaries a check and be done with it. That might also have the healthy effect of persuading legislators to curb programs that shower federal aid on the unneedy.

A root-and-branch paring of the loan programs probably would be good economic medicine too. By steering money toward high-risk borrowers and less attractive projects, such as farming and dubious trade schools, the programs divert funds from more promising enterprises or at least drive up the interest rate that more creditworthy borrowers have to pay.

Holman Jenkins Jr.

CHAPTER 6

In 1990 the nation's disabled got their own civil rights law. The Americans with Disabilities Act banned bias and exclusion by any business, requiring accommodation on all goods, services and facilities. Critics, as explained in this article published October 30, 1989, pointed to the cost of complying with the measure. Supporters said opponents were using scare tactics. The Congress and President Bush agreed with supporters and the bill became law.

FINANCIAL HANDICAPS IN CIVIL RIGHTS BILL

D isabled Americans may soon celebrate passage of a sweeping new civil rights law that supporters say will achieve for the disabled what the landmark Civil Rights Act of 1964 achieved for racial minorities. The Americans with Disabilities Act, now before various House committees, has already breezed through the Senate with the Bush administration's support.

The new legislation promises equal employment opportunity to the disabled and "full and equal enjoyment" of all goods, services, facilities and privileges. It would ban discrimination by any firm that sells to the public. If the bill becomes law, it will touch virtually every retail business, from corner grocery stores to telephone companies to motels to law firms, encompassing some 3.9 million businesses in all.

Critics of the bill invariably describe it as well-intended. What they fear, especially the business community, is the cost of complying with the new law. The intercity bus industry, for example, which faces specific mandates, predicts disaster. Others worry about language that, depending on how it is interpreted by regulators and courts, could spell staggering cost and liabilities. "There can be no doubt about what is ahead for us," Fred Currey, chairman of Greyhound Lines Inc., told a House subcommittee. If the bill requires, as current versions do, that all new motor coaches be equipped with wheelchair lifts, he says, Greyhound will pull out of the smallest 5,000 of the 10,000 communities it serves and terminate some 10,000 workers.

Christopher Hoey, assistant general counsel for the F. W. Woolworth Co., which operates 5,700 stores, told another House subcommittee that if the law means all aisles and shelves must be accessible to a person in a wheelchair, the loss of display room would be "drastic, and in some cases ruinous." Retailers, he said, could lose one-third to three-fifths of productive space, "the functional equivalent — in lost sales and employment — of closing a substantial fraction of the nation's stores, or even outlawing some types of stores."

The bill's promoters call such talk scare tactics. Says Michael Auberger, cofounder of American Disabled for Accessible Public Transportation in Denver, "They're playing real heavy-handed. What we're seeing with their overstatements is that business doesn't like to be told what to do. That's typical of the business sector, that they prefer not to have government interference." Justin Dart, chairman of the Task Force on the Rights and Empowerment of Americans with Disabilities, asks, "Would this assertion [that the act is too costly] be made about the rights of black, Hispanic or Jewish people? The very existence of the assertion reveals the insidious assumption of inequality."

In any event, Dart maintains, the cost of the legislation is "negligible and painless" relative to the cost of discrimination, which he says keeps many disabled people unemployed and dependent on taxpayers. Congressional estimates place the size of the disabled population at 43 million, or about one of every six Americans. The bill's principal Senate sponsor, Democrat Tom Harkin of Iowa, has argued that "costs do not provide a basis for exemption from the basic principles of a civil rights statute."

Unlike the 1964 Civil Rights Act, however, the disabilities bill not only bans discrimination and exclusion, it requires accommodation, and thus imposes costs, which are unknown. No one has attempted a total estimate, because the act does not specify the type and extent of required accommodation, only that it be "reasonable" and not impose an "undue burden." (Intercity buses are an exception.) Moreover, says the National Federation of Independent Business, a lobby for small businesses, the bill may encompass as many as 900 types of disabilities.

Many business owners do not know what they will have to do to avoid charges of discrimination, says Duane A. Rasmussen, president of Sell Publishing Co., a newspaper publisher in Forest Lake,

Minn. "They're using general terms to describe what is expected of a small-business man without any clear definitions," he says.

Some of the necessary accommodations could be relatively inexpensive, such as adding braille instructions in elevators or amplifiers on telephones. Others, such as altering store formats, could be quite costly. Just how costly is an important question, say business owners. "They're quick to jump on us, saying we're against any improvements, but we're not," says Rasmussen. "The proponents and even the authors of the bill indicated that money was no object, that it's important enough to do these things. But then they don't suggest providing any money."

Although the bill will be in flux until the House and Senate agree on a final version, several sections mandate heavy spending. New city buses must have wheelchair lifts; cities must provide transportation for those who cannot use the lifts. Public phone systems must offer access to the deaf, usually through a special operator. American Telephone & Telegraph Co. estimates the cost at about $300 million a year.

All new private intercity buses must be equipped with a lift. This applies to large companies like Greyhound as well as charter and tour operators, and would take effect six or seven years from the enactment, depending on company size. Airlines, hotel shuttles, school buses and Amtrak, by contrast, would have to provide access only on a portion of their fleets or cars. Lifts costing about $35,000 each are currently used on intercity coaches in Massachusetts (which are structurally different from city transit buses) as part of a program funded by the state to promote intercity bus transportation. All buses used in the program must be wheelchair accessible.

One wheelchair rider takes the space of six seats. Lift equipment eats up half the space normally used for baggage and package express, the latter of which is an important revenue source for Greyhound. If the bill means that bus rest rooms must also be accessible, those must be enlarged and the aisles widened. Such alterations would reduce package space, seating and revenue so much that "there just isn't any industry anymore," says Peter Picknelly Sr., chairman of Peter Pan Bus Lines Inc., a regular-route service out of Springfield, Mass.

Although disability rights groups argue that there is significant pent-up demand for wheelchair-accessible intercity buses, Picknelly notes that since 1985, his accessible buses, now numbering seven out of a fleet of 150, have been used only once every two months on average, despite company and state advertising.

Bus owners argue that given 24 hours' notice, they could provide a wheelchair-accessible bus to anyone who wanted it, as airlines do, at far less cost than making all new buses accessible. (People in wheelchairs can ride buses now, but they must be lifted into the seat.) Proponents argue, however, that requiring the disabled to give notice fails to constitute equal access.

"We're not facing a transportation question," says Steven Sprague of the United Bus Owners of America. "We're facing a civil rights question. That's pounded into us every day. We say if it were a transportation issue, we are answering your needs. If it's a matter of going from point A to point B, we'll get you there."

The bill's proponents charge that Greyhound is a monopolist that has found money to modernize terminals, so it can find money for equal access. The industry "proposes Jim Crow service and Jim Crow citizenship, to millions," Marca Bristo, past president of the National Council on Independent Living, has said. Greyhound responds that the cost of complying with the new bill will total $40 million a year; the company expects to earn about $8.5 million this year after posting a $17 million loss last year. Chairman Currey says Greyhound cannot absorb such costs, that it faces heavy competition from rail and air travel, and that capital improvements are crucial to rebuilding the business.

On average, the intercity bus industry operates on a 3 percent profit margin; its passengers are heavily rural and poor. "We have been lectured repeatedly that costs don't count and can't be considered in matters of this type," Currey told Congress. "That is easy to say for someone who is spending other people's money." Greyhound's compliance with the new bill "will not be paid by American taxpayers," he said. "It will be paid by our customers, who are the least able to afford higher fares. It is nothing less than a regressive tax."

As originally introduced, the bill's employment provisions also drew fire. The current Senate version would require all employers of 15 or more workers to make "reasonable accommodation" of all disabled employees, unless such actions pose "undue hardship." In its original form, the bill would have enabled prospective job applicants to sue if they thought they were "about to be" discriminated against. It also would have protected, as disabled, employees abusing alcohol or drugs. And the bill would have allowed employees to sue for punitive damages, a remedy not sanctioned under other civil rights laws. The Senate removed these provisions.

What remains of most concern to businesses are passages regarding discrimination against disabled customers, clients or visitors of privately owned "public accommodations." They apply to any firm that sells goods or services to the public. Although the bill states that accommodation of disabled customers must be "readily achievable" without placing an "undue burden" on a firm, it will require some retrofitting of buildings. At what point cost becomes an undue burden worries many owners. Such language "may just create a heyday for lawyers to try out different theories about what's required and what's not," says Albert A. Foer, chairman of Melart Jewelers Inc., a Maryland-based chain. "The cost of defending a lawsuit and the cost of bad publicity are very important leverage points. We would prefer not to be in the position of having the law tested and refined against small businesses who are least able to defend themselves."

Attorney General Dick Thornburgh, expressing the view of the White House, argues that a similar disability statute has governed federal contractors and federal grant recipients since 1973 without causing a litigation explosion or imposing unreasonable costs. But business groups say that some key language differs and that the 1973 law was never applied to retailing. Some businessmen say they may not be able to pass costs along as readily as do the large federal contractors or universities covered by the older law.

Woolworth's Hoey noted in his testimony that the Senate report cites such "modest adjustments" as lowering telephones or adding grab bars; but the report also suggests moving restaurant tables and department store display racks. While such accommodations may sound minor, he said that rearranging merchandise in even a small store could cost a retailer $25,000. Calculating profit margins among mass merchants at about 2 percent, offsetting an added $25,000 expense would require generating $1.25 million in sales. Far more important, if the law requires wheelchair access throughout a store, it could entail widening aisles, moving display cases and lowering shelves. Such space reductions in a retail store would mean substantial sales losses. "Most stores pay very high square-foot rents to be in shopping malls and shopping centers," he says, "and every square foot that has to be reduced and taken out of productive use is expensive."

It is unclear whether the bill mandates actual physical access to "every nook and cranny of the store," says Morrison Cain of the International Mass Retail Association, which represents general merchandisers. "We're saying: Make the building accessible," but once a person is inside, stores should be allowed the flexibility to determine how best to make goods accessible — using sales clerks to assist the disabled, as one example, Cain says. Retailers say they believe this is Congress's intent but that the bill remains unclear.

The disabled community says such arguments grossly overstate what businesses will be required to do. They charge that opponents attack the bill with bizarre illustrations. Some opponents have said, for instance, that the bill extends civil rights protection to pyromaniacs. Or that people with back injuries might sue restaurants for failing to provide orthopedic chairs.

"That's just carrying absurdity to the max," insists Auberger of American Disabled for Accessible Public Transportation. "That's not why the bill was written and that's not who is going to ask to have that bill mandated. That's not who has made this bill happen. It's not pyromaniacs. It's mobility-impaired, it's visually impaired, it's deaf people who want to be part of, instead of separate from."

Business groups worry, though, that while Congress and the measure's promoters may have one idea of what is a reasonable accommodation or an undue burden, a regulator may have another, and a judge still another. "Anyone who's been in this town for even a few years knows" that the enforcement of legislation usually does not take into account clarifications in floor debates or in report language, says Susan Loomis, executive director of congressional relations for the Associated General Contractors of America. "This is not a simple bill, as many have portrayed it to be. And the way regulations regularly go and enforcement is generally done, you can't leave anything to chance."

Carolyn Lochhead

PART 3

UP FROM
THE BOTTOM
OF THE HEAP

CHAPTER 7

Whatever the origins of their poverty, it is an impoverishment deep, broad and apparently abiding. They are the underclass, a sliver at the bottom of the segment labeled poor, and their lives were examined in this April 3, 1989, article. They lack means more than financial, their lives tightly defined by patterns of idleness, illiteracy, illegitimacy. They live in small towns as well as large, but members of the underclass are concentrated more and more in major cities. Their growing number disturbs policy analysts, who worry about costs that are more than economic.

NO WAY OUT OF POVERTY'S CLUTCHES

A schoolteacher, who grew up with nine brothers and sisters in the inner-city neighborhood where she now teaches, surveys the broken lives of children living there today. She thinks back to her own childhood home — poor and crowded, yes, but somehow very different. She keeps telling her students, "You can do it, you can do it, you can do it," she says. "I remind them, 'I was born in this neighborhood. Hey look, I went to school here. I made it.' But then — " She pauses. "It's not there."

Somewhere along the line, many of the poor of that neighborhood and thousands like it lost something that earlier generations, despite their condition, had been able to cling to: a sense of hope, possibility and shared values with America's mainstream.

Their poverty has assumed a new and forbidding shape, and they, a new name — the underclass, a term that describes a deficit more behavioral than financial and a poverty more permanent than was ever thought possible in America. Mired at the bottom of society, these poor people have few prospects and few hopes. However young and able-bodied, they seem to lack the means to escape to a better life. Their neighborhoods, located mostly in the rapidly decaying inner cities and wracked by violence, mirror a poverty more bleak and insidious than in years past.

The underclass is growing rapidly, despite the billions taxpayers spend each year on antipoverty programs and income transfers. Its source, say many experts, can be traced to the social and political upheaval of the Sixties, the full consequences of which are only now unfolding.

Analysts define the underclass less by income than by such behavioral attributes as idleness, drug use, illiteracy, illegitimacy and chronic welfare dependence. Estimates of its size range from 2 million to 8 million, the lower figures based on a tight geographic definition, the higher on long-term welfare use. However measured, nearly all believe, the underclass is growing rapidly. It probably more than doubled from 1970 to 1980, according to Isabel Sawhill of the Urban Institute, and there is little doubt that it has grown since the 1980 census. Its concentration in large cities is increasing rapidly. And, although most poor Americans are white, the underclass is composed primarily, but by no means exclusively, of black and Hispanic people.

The data are often misinterpreted: Contrary to common misconceptions, most black and Hispanic Americans are not poor. And the underclass, Sawhill figures, comprises less than 6 percent of all black Americans, the vast majority of whom belong to the burgeoning black middle class.

Moreover, a significant white underclass exists. Like other poor white people, those in the underclass are more dispersed across rural areas, but their numbers are rising visibly. A visit to any small town reveals the typical behavior patterns: idleness of young males, illegitimacy, alcoholism, drug abuse, criminality, illiteracy.

Despite its growth, the underclass remains but a small fraction, probably less than one-tenth by the lower estimates, of the 32.5 million Americans listed as officially poor by the Census Bureau. Not only are most poor people not in the underclass, but the official figure, say many experts, grossly overstates the true incidence of poverty. While the release of the census number draws headlines each year, the measure ignores such things as food stamps and home ownership. These shortcomings and others lead many analysts to believe that the measure seriously exaggerates the number of poor people in the United States.

Nonetheless, the rapid growth of the underclass is deeply troubling to social policy analysts. Its youth are a growing percentage of new potential workers. It forms the locus of explosive growth in drug use and violence in cities. It consumes far more than its share of welfare and criminal justice expenditures. Taxpayers spend $100,000 to support over her life each mother who joins the welfare system as a teenager, about $17 billion a year all told. To keep a man in prison costs more than $20,000 a year.

Worse, the existence of an underclass corrodes the foundations of a free society, says a bipartisan consensus of researchers drawn together by the American Enterprise Institute; its pathologies "are today so at odds with what this country stands for, and so damaging to the citizens caught up in them, that a common assault on them is absolutely indispensable."

NEIGHBORHOODS IN DECAY

At small outposts in a ravaged land, good people are battling a deepening social disintegration. The decay shocks those who remember these neighborhoods in an earlier era — one of civility and vitality, of strong families, respectable neighbors and busy shops at places like 119th Street and Second Avenue in New York's Harlem. Places where now, every afternoon, a line forms 20 or more deep to buy crack from a van pulled up to the sidewalk. "My worst dreams, my worst, were nowhere near this," says Shakoor Aljuwani, project director of the Youth Action Construction Training Program, a community group that works with Harlem teenagers. "I never thought it could ever have gotten this bad."

Or places like Newark, where one day some men in a car carried away a 13-year-old schoolgirl as she walked from the back door of her home and raped her. "Those are the kinds of things we deal with around here," says James Wallace, founder of the International Youth Organization, where he and his wife, Carolyn, work with local youngsters. "It's a long way from peaches and cream. This a war zone. And that's what we do. We're fighting a war."

The war is on the streets — and in the home. Teachers at urban schools speak of chaotic, scattered families, of gross parental irresponsibility, of small schoolchildren who witness open sexual activity at home. The cycle perpetuates itself across generations: a teenage mother, abused as a child, cannot read, write, add or subtract. She is pregnant with her third child and living on welfare. She has zero skills, zero work habits, zero future. Work at a fast food restaurant seems beyond her capacity. She is neglecting her 3-year-old, who is often sick and ill-fed. She shunts the child off to relatives as often as she can.

These poor neighborhoods and families are radically different from their counterparts of two decades ago. People talk now of an inability to cope with life's most rudimentary demands, such simple things as getting up in the morning to go to work. Idleness and irresponsibility pave a tragic road to self-destruction; teenage pregnancy, long-term welfare dependence, drugs, crime, prison and death. A black male has a 1-in-21 chance of being murdered before he reaches the age of 25.

Not all who grow up in the poor city neighborhoods become trapped there, nor is their route out any mystery. Three accomplishments, in the view of social policy analysts, almost guarantee escape from poverty; completing high school; working consistently at a job, even a low-wage job; and getting married and staying married. But it is precisely these three pillars of life — education, work and marriage — that have collapsed among the underclass.

The single mother dominates the poverty statistics, heading nearly half of all poor families. In the inner city, she stands out in vivid relief: There, 74 percent of blacks, 55 percent of Hispanics and 41 percent of whites live in single-mother families, according to 1980 census figures. "No other major demographic group is so poor, and none stays poor longer," write Irwin Garfinkel and Sara McLanahan of the University of Wisconsin in the book "Single Mothers and Their Children." By contrast, 94 percent of husband-wife families are not poor. In 1985, black families where a husband and wife were present had a median income of $24,570; black single-mother families had a median income of $9,305. Poverty has become largely a function of family structure. When the family breaks down, individuals and communities break down too. As Daniel P. Moynihan, a New York Democrat, wrote in a 1965 report on the decline of the black family: "The stability and quality of family life is a prime determinant of individual and group achievement."

For a long time, the subject of black family breakdown was taboo, until trends became norms and like patterns emerged among whites. The change has been astonishing: In 1950, only 9 percent of black homes were headed by one parent; in 1965, 28 percent; in 1970, 33.3 percent. Today, half of all black families with children are headed by a single parent and some 60 percent of black births are out of wedlock.

While starting from a proportionally lower base, the white underclass is following a like trend. Illegitimate births rose from 2.3 percent of all white births in 1960 to 12.8 percent in 1983; even these numbers obscure the fact that for whites, as for other groups, illegitimacy is much higher among the poor. In some areas it has reached the level where black rates stood in 1965, when Moynihan, then assistant secretary of labor, wrote of the disintegration of the black family.

White or black, with few exceptions, out-of-wedlock teenage pregnancy dooms both mother and child to lives of dependency. American teenagers have the highest pregnancy and abortion rates in the West; in 1983, 86 percent of black and nearly 40 percent of white babies born to girls under 19 were illegitimate. These "children of children" show high rates of infant mortality; they are more often neglected or abused; they typically do poorly in school and frequently wind up as teenage mothers themselves. "It multiplies," says a teacher at an inner-city school. "We have children living in chaos and they grow up and have children living in chaos."

If single mothers bestow trouble on their daughters, Moynihan pointed out the consequences for their sons 24 years ago: "There is one unmistakable lesson in American history: A community that allows a large number of young men to grow up in broken families, dominated by women, never acquiring any stable relationship to male authority, never acquiring any set of rational expectations about the future — that community asks for and gets chaos. Crime, violence, unrest, disorder . . . are very near to inevitable".

A New York schoolteacher, who grew up in the poor neighborhood where she now teaches, plugs "responsibility, dignity, self-pride — those values that help you conduct yourself through hard times." she says. "The kids can mouth the words, but if it's not reinforced at home, it's hard." The "back and forth connection" between parents and school "is wearing thin," she says.

Many poor, single mothers raise their children successfully, but the odds are against them. The Rev. Harold Simmons, a Baptist pastor who counsels youngsters at the Wallaces' International Youth Organization in Newark, says that while people may argue about the validity of various family structures, "when we look around, we can find a whole lot of structures that don't work, because they produce the kinds of degeneracy that we see now."

There is a 10-year-old boy in Newark who should be in the fifth grade; he is in third and still is not reading. His mother had the first of her four children at age 15, each of them by a different father. Her sister moved into the house with her five children, three of whom have drug habits. Confusion reigns at home. "Now under those particular circumstances, what do you think this child is going to accomplish in the evenings?" asks Carolyn Wallace.

His mother "has no knowledge of what she should be doing with the child. She just feels that you go to school to learn, and at her age, that's probably what I thought too," says Wallace. "He went to school prepared. He'd go to school with his notebook, book bag, pencils. He was the most prepared child I've seen in my life — erasers, little scissors. Prepared. Waiting for a miracle. Here this child was every day, 10 years old, stayed back two times, every day prepared, sitting in place. Waiting for a miracle. Can you imagine? Can you imagine what that feels like?"

As families were falling apart, public schools began failing, failing those who most depend on them. Undoubtedly there are many urban teachers and administrators committed to education; but undoubtedly there are many who are not or who are unable to cope. Says a Newark dropout, "Nothing was being taught. The teachers were too busy trying to stop the fighting."

"Most of the time and energy is devoted just to maintaining order," confirms a New York teacher. "Simple order. We hardly get down to the business of education." Of students, he says, "Nothing much is expected." The results are predictable. More than half of all teenagers drop out of high school in Newark; in parts of Chicago it is more than 60 percent. Many of those who do graduate can barely read.

Peer group values mirror community and family indifference. Achievement at school carries no status, says the New York teacher. "If a child is smart and does well, he or she is not set up as someone you might aspire to be like. It's simply not valued. If you do well, so what? Nobody's going anywhere. It's be hip and fashionable today. There's no long range." Many youngsters, lacking a solid foundation at home and without any sense of a higher purpose in life, "can't see the reason for even being bothered" with trying to accomplish more, says Simmons. Instant gratification is the order of the day, many counselors point out.

"Everything on television is instant," says Wallace. Good things are supposed to happen as if by magic, effortlessly. "It's Bill Cosby and 'Facts of Life' all lumped into 'As the World Turns,' " she says. "It's all fantasy, and they live that fantasy. That's the bad part. They live it without doing it."

Joblessness among underclass youths is rampant and peculiar in several ways. Like the single-mother home, it is a distinct departure from the past, having developed only over the past two decades. In 1954, equal percentages of black and white youths were employed. In the Sixties, black youths began dropping out of the labor force in large numbers.

Despite a narrowing of black-white wage differentials, nearly 40 percent of poor black males 22 to 34 were not working or looking for work in 1986, up from 12 percent in 1970, according to Census Bureau figures. In 1984, nearly half of black males 16 to 24 had no work experience. Harvard University economist Richard Freeman has called unemployment levels of young black men catastrophic.

Work attitudes among poor youths have changed, says Wallace. "The old feeling of get a job, no matter what it is, is dead," she says. "That's another era."

The schoolteacher who grew up in Harlem remembers when her older sister, at 16, "got a job sticking pins in shirts in some store. Then from there she went to a special high school for the fashion industry, and from there she got a job at Ohrbach's. Now that was real high class for an 18-year-old from East Harlem, a kid from Puerto Rico. And we knew. Even when I was 5 years old, I knew that my sister had a job somewhere else, at a fancy store called Ohrbach's.

"We didn't sit around and talk about a better life," she says. "It was just something we knew we had to do. And we knew we had to go to school. We did not have an alternative to that. We didn't know you could go out and sell drugs or just hang on the corner. We didn't know that was available. We stayed on track because that's what you had to do. You had to go to school so you could get a fancy job somewhere downtown and then bring home money and make life easier."

As work levels have declined, crime has risen as a scourge of poor neighborhoods, where residents are victims of burglaries, muggings, rape and murder more often than any other group. Crime seriously undermines efforts to escape poverty by lowering property values, chasing away small businesses and sharply raising prices to poor consumers.

In 1980, 95 percent of those who committed crimes against blacks were themselves black, and most of the criminals were under the age of 24. Their victims are primarily black women over 25, black men age 50 to 64, and black youngsters of 12 to 15. Says Robert L. Woodson, president of the National Center for Neighborhood Enterprise in Washington, a self-help organization, "A civil war is raging within the black community."

James Wallace says working people in Newark stay in their homes. "They're living in a prison around here," he says. Residents are

aware of criminal activity but do not report it for fear that the criminals will "come back and burn up their house."

Drug warfare marked by daily gun battles has become commonplace. Last year, 201 murders were committed in New York housing
projects. Said the New York Daily News, "The greensward at the
Unity Plaza housing project in Brooklyn is stained red with blood
so regularly that people call it Dead Man's Park." One resident told
the paper, "They just blow people away. There are wide-open gun-
fights here all the time."

"What frightens me is the family," says Simmons in Newark.
"Kids are not getting any kind of direction. I'm concerned about
where we're going as a people, as a city, as a nation — this generation
in particular. What are they going to do going into adulthood? In the
21st century, we're looking at adults who grew up in this era.

"I pray a lot," he says.

THE RADICAL ERA'S LEGACY

As he launched the War on Poverty in 1964, President Lyndon
Johnson predicted that the "days of the dole are numbered."

Johnson's optimism, naive in retrospect, was widely shared at the
time. "We believed that our rich country had both the material
resources and the intelligence to eliminate poverty," writes Nathan
Glazer, a member of the Kennedy administration, now a Harvard
University professor. Some 25 years and hundreds of billions of dollars later, life for the poor in the cities is markedly worse. Something
had gone wrong. "We seemed," Glazer writes, "to be creating as
many problems as we were solving."

It is more than a coincidence, many experts say, that the problems
the War on Poverty attacked — welfare dependence, poor education, juvenile delinquency, unemployment — are the very problems
that a generation later have assumed horrific dimensions in the
cities. That connection was drawn most forcefully in 1984 by Charles
Murray in "Losing Ground," an emperor-has-no-clothes book that
has recast the poverty debate. Murray argued that the Sixties revolution in social policy, regarding welfare, education and criminal
punishment in particular, backfired; instead of eliminating the
underclass, policies adopted in the Sixties expanded it. Opponents
attacked his statistics, but Murray stood his ground. Others joined
him and today experts across the political spectrum adopt parts of
his argument.

Still others have enlarged it: Hand in hand with this revolution in

social policy, they maintain, came a cultural upheaval whose consequences are only now becoming plain. Wisdom born of the Sixties
reshaped ancient values and beliefs about the family, about sex,
about religion and about personal behavior. Among intellectual
elites, the nuclear family was derided as stifling and obsolete; God
was declared dead; drugs would free the soul.

For the privileged and educated who originated them, many of
these ideas proved to be a passing fancy, and the consequences of following them were usually not severe. Safety nets provided sufficient
cushion. But nowhere did such notions take root with greater
vengeance or extract a higher price than among the poor, for whom
the margin for error in life is painfully slim. Today, illegitimacy and
drug addiction are hallmarks of the underclass. Those who work
with poor youths speak of battling instant gratification and of trying
to replant such quaint ideas as accountability, responsibility and
morals.

"You're seeing the results now" of Sixties counterculture, says
Carolyn Wallace, whose husband, James, founded the International Youth Organization, a community group in Newark. "It's 'I want
what I want when I want it.' It's that permissiveness, that total lack
of morals, that Sixties stuff about Woodstock and free love and all
that craziness."

Michael Novak, a welfare scholar at the American Enterprise
Institute, describes a shift in values "from self-control and self-mas-
tery to self-expression and doing what one pleases." The first set of
values helps people break free from poverty. Impulse release, on the
other hand, "may be pleasant to the children of the well-off, who
after experimenting with it and finding it wanting, nonetheless often
have a second or even a third chance. But it's terribly destructive to
the poor."

These new cultural beliefs fueled and magnified a radical change
in government policy toward the poor. Remarkably, the poverty
"issue" lay undiscovered until the Sixties, when the Kennedy White
House was searching for reelection campaign themes; the government did not even measure poverty until President Johnson
declared war on it in 1964. There was no popular clamor for action;
on the contrary, as Sen. Daniel P. Moynihan later noted, the attack
on poverty "was from the first an affair of scholars and bureaucrats."

Johnson's original intent was to give the poor "a hand, not a hand-
out." But when the quick results expected by the poverty warriors
failed to arrive, intellectuals soon altered their views of the poor.

From ordinary citizens who needed a temporary helping hand, the poor were transformed, en masse, into victims of "structural poverty" arising out of the unfair capitalist economic system. As victims of economic failures over which they could not possibly have control, the poor could not be held responsible for their condition. To do so would be to blame the victim.

"There was a mind-set in the 1960s," Murray says, "that could best be summarized as, 'It's not your fault.' If you don't study, it's not your fault. If you don't get a job, it's not your fault. If you commit a crime, it's not your fault. If you have a baby, it's not your fault. There was a message being sent out to disadvantaged, and especially young disadvantaged, and most especially poor young disadvantaged people: 'You have been wronged, it's not your fault, and it's somebody else's job to make things right.' "

The race riots of the late Sixties, which provoked a sudden torrent of white guilt about the nation's mistreatment of blacks, buttressed these ideas, helping to create a "reparations idea of welfare," says Stuart Butler, coauthor of "Out of the Poverty Trap." Ordinary people were still expected to be self-sufficient and independent, free to succeed or to fail. The poor, by contrast, would rely on the state for their needs. Butler describes the dual standard as "capitalism for the rich and socialism for the poor."

The change came swiftly. In 1965, the federal government embarked upon a massive income redistribution "tantamount to a revolution," according to Robert H. Haveman, an economist at the Institute for Research on Poverty at the University of Wisconsin. From 1965 to 1985, federal spending on cash income transfers increased more than tenfold; spending on health, education, training, housing and social services rose thirtyfold. Antipoverty programs "were America's main growth industry during this period," he writes.

Transfers to the poor climbed from $16.2 billion in 1960 to more than $100 billion in 1984, adjusted for inflation. These included Aid to Families with Dependent Children, the basic welfare program for single mothers, which is jointly funded by the state and federal governments and is administered by the states; food stamps and child nutrition programs; and Medicaid. The government spent billions more on economic development and urban programs.

Swept aside in this rush to end poverty was a centuries-old dilemma: how to help the poor without encouraging behavior that produces poverty. As David T. Ellwood, a liberal poverty expert at Harvard's Kennedy School of Government, has put it, "When you give people money, food or housing, you reduce pressure on them to work and care for themselves." That proposition, recognized since at least the 16th century, "no one seriously disputes."

If money alone could eradicate poverty, it would have vanished long ago. About $48 billion — far less than the government spends annually on antipoverty programs — would provide sufficient income to raise everyone above the government's official poverty line.

Back in the Sixties, however, advocates argued that welfare was not a last resort but a civil right. Eligibility rules were loosened. Government agencies encouraged people to sign up. As the rolls expanded, welfare's stigma eroded within poor communities. State budgets began to sink under the cost of Aid to Families; by the late Seventies, states had backed off on spending and caseloads stabilized. There are now about 10.8 million recipients; more than 7 million are children. Food stamps and Medicaid usually accompany AFDC receipt; in several states, the value of this package exceeds what recipients could earn from a minimum-wage job.

AFDC itself originated with the New Deal; it was intended to assist widows and orphans until the Social Security system came into full operation, at which time it was expected to disappear. By the early 1950s, however, it was obvious that the program was used not so much by widows as by the mothers of illegitimate children. And the rolls were growing, not declining. Today, about half of the children on the rolls are illegitimate; 2 percent are orphans.

Many women — about half — who collect the aid are off the rolls within a couple of years; generally, they are divorced and past their early 20s. By contrast, 70 percent of the women who have been on the rolls for at least five years were younger than 25 when they first received welfare; more than one-third collect welfare for at least a decade. These women are often high school dropouts, never married, with little if any work experience. Almost two-thirds of AFDC spending goes to these long-term dependents.

Economists agree that rising benefit levels attracted people to welfare. Similar work disincentives have been demonstrated in the Social Security and disability insurance programs, for example. But while spending on Social Security, mainly a middle-class entitlement, is much higher than welfare spending, it has not radically altered behavior, because eligibility is beyond the recipient's control. A person cannot change his age to collect Social Security. And Social Security did sharply reduce poverty among the elderly.

AFDC, on the other hand, can provide an alternative to marriage or work among the young and able-bodied. As Murray has put it, "Welfare does not bribe poor women to have babies; it enables them to do so. For the young woman who is not pregnant, enabling means that she does not ask, 'Do I want a welfare check badly enough to get pregnant?' but rather, 'If I happen to get pregnant, will the consequences really be so bad?'" The aid package, experts agree, is enough to allow pregnant teenagers to set up their own households; it also lets fathers leave their responsibilities with taxpayers.

Maria Motta, who works with Youth Action Program, a Harlem community group, was once on welfare herself. She calls it a trap. "They paid my rent, I got food stamps and stuff and I wasn't asked to do anything," she says. "So I ended up staying home and watching TV — becoming a bathrobe person, not doing anything and feeling sorry for myself."

Welfare encourages passivity, say Shakoor Aljuwani, a project director at Youth Action. "You go and you pick up the check and you're told to go here, you're told to go there. You're totally powerless . . . . So then you pick up a tendency to sit home and pick up that check. Something will come in on a monthly basis, and you have to do nothing to provide it. It's not a decent life. It's hell. But you can eke it out and make it through."

Work levels among the poor have been dropping since the Sixties, most sharply among young men. By 1984, nearly half of black males in the 16-21 age group had no work experience at all. A similar trend, though not as severe, has appeared among young white males: By 1980, one out of 10 white men of 18 to 24 was neither working nor in school.

Some scholars, notably William Julius Wilson at the University of Chicago, argue that the able-bodied urban poor cannot find work because jobs have moved to the inaccessible suburbs; because underclass youths lack basic skills; and because racial discrimination remains serious, particularly in retailing. Furthermore, many add, minority youths face tough job competition from the (mainly white) baby boom generation and women.

Some of the best evidence on the joblessness of the urban poor comes from a 1979-1980 survey of young men in Boston, Philadelphia and Chicago directed by Richard B. Freeman, a Harvard University economist. Among the findings: A strong economy did boost employment among minority youths, and women did compete with young black men for jobs. But job location had little effect on work.

Moreover, when out of work, the typical youth was likely to spend his time just hanging out. One in four had been fired, mainly because of absenteeism. Of those not in school or working, 71 percent said they could easily obtain a minimum-wage job. Nearly one-third believed "the street" offered greater earnings; one-quarter of the income reported by those surveyed came from crime.

Church attendance, career aspirations and high school graduation all had strong positive influences on work. Youths were also more likely to hold jobs when other members of their family were employed. By contrast, living in a welfare home or in public housing had a strong negative effect: The unemployment rate among those 19 to 24 who lived in nonwelfare homes was 28 percent; among those whose families were on welfare, unemployment rose to nearly 44 percent; if their families were on welfare and living in public housing, unemployment was 52 percent.

The no-jobs argument is wearing thin, Murray says. Since 1982 the economy has produced 18.5 million jobs. He maintains that many cities, particularly on the East Coast, many with excellent public transportation, have had extremely tight labor markets for several years, with negligible effect on the work efforts of the urban poor. "Simply putting jobs out there is not going to get rid of the underclass," he says. Moreover, many argue, cities have been absorbing — and employing — a flood of immigrants, many of them nonwhite. Black-white wage differentials also have narrowed sharply in the past 20 years. Annual earnings of middle-aged black men rose from less than two-fifths to more than three-quarters of white men's earnings at each educational level. Black women have almost entirely caught up with white women in earnings.

In reality, Murray says, work is just one of many options for the urban poor. Lack of job skills and job readiness — the ability to get to work on time, get along with supervisors and so forth — is a problem for many a young man. Yet "if tomorrow his choice were between starving and taking that job paying $5.50 an hour, I suspect that at that point, lo and behold, the behavioral change would occur quite rapidly. But the fact is, he isn't facing that choice." Living with a woman who collects welfare, selling drugs, street crime, hustling or other such alternatives offer a way to survive, he says, other than by working at a menial job.

While scholars debate the role of welfare, many youths speak frankly. A young man who graduated from high school in Harlem describes the attitudes of some of his classmates: " 'High school, yeah, so what? If I pass, I pass. If I don't, I don't.' And if they're going to have children, then, 'It's OK, I can always get on welfare,' or 'It's OK, my boyfriend will provide for me.' But yet, what does the boyfriend do? In most cases, the boyfriend has the same problems she has. He doesn't care about anything, but he's a man. A good number either have children or are working on children. And they all believe that welfare is going to stand there and back them up."

In Maria Motta's neighborhood, she says, "they're not all on welfare, but the majority are on welfare. The majority are baby factories, they're addicted to drugs, they don't have high school diplomas. They don't want to leave their community. They don't want to leave their block. For them to leave their block is a major thing. For them to go to Midtown [for a job] would be like another world to them.

"I'm not making excuses. I believe that these people should get off their rear ends and go down there. As long as we have welfare supporting them and they keep having children and not being accountable for their money, then they're going to stay home. They're not going to do anything. They're not encouraged to do anything. The welfare system says, 'OK, well you have a 3-year-old and you've got a 5-year-old, so OK, your rent is paid for, we'll give you food stamps, we'll give you your Medicaid.' So everything they need is there."

If welfare isolates the underclass from the mainstream, crime and drugs drive in the wedge. A teenager can stand on the corner and make hundreds, possibly thousands, of dollars selling drugs. "You're a chump if you're working for five, six bucks and hour," says a New York schoolteacher.

From 1963 to 1980, robbery and rape rates quadrupled, burglary and assault rates tripled, and the murder rate doubled. Fewer than one-third of those convicted of a serious crime go to prison, yet the prisons are overflowing. The police, says Carolyn Wallace, "have such restrictions now: They can't do this , they can't do that. They lock up somebody, and 30 minutes later [he's] out on the corner."

Without question, drugs magnify the problem. "I have colleagues who say you can't blame everything on drugs," says another teacher. "But I'm going to blame drugs. I know it's drugs. It's the drugs that prevent people from holding down a job. It's the drugs that take away motivation to get a job. It's the drugs that are causing the crimes against people. It's the drugs that are causing the neglect. It's the drugs that are causing the breakup of families."

The one public institution that could stanch the decay, that has proved it can lift millions of poor Americans into the mainstream — the public school — also fell to newer wisdom. Strict authority in the classroom was called oppressive. Academic standards, said to discriminate against the disadvantaged, collapsed. Politicians took over school boards.

Disruptive students, no longer expelled or suspended, took over classrooms. Today teachers say 10-year-old pupils advise them of their civil rights. Many schools use metal detectors to check students for weapons. "Years ago," says Leon Moore, a private school director who graduated from Newark's public system, "they had all the desks lined up in a row, and they bolted them to the floor. They never thought that maybe they could move the chairs around. Well, schools in those days worked. I don't know of anybody who went through school with me who could not read."

In 1969, Moore helped to found an elementary school for students from some of Newark's worst neighborhoods, because, he says, the public schools had started "taking a nosedive." It is precisely when home life becomes horrendous, he believes, that school becomes critical in a child's life. "When you have nothing, if your home life is chaos, and the street is chaos and the school — if that is chaos, too — then all dreams become nightmares. But if one of those things is very positive, then you can hold on. And I believe that many children have the strength and they have the courage to hold on. And they choose the right way. And I think if the public schools accepted that, and set up an environment for the children, instead of just saying, 'The mother's a junkie, the father's in prison, what the hell can we do?' " schools could make a difference.

Elites hatched Sixties notions about values, welfare, crime and education, but it was the poor, Charles Murray and others argue, who paid the price. When all the poor were treated as victims, when it became unfashionable to speak of the "deserving poor" because all the poor were deserving, those who stuck by the older conventions — marrying before having children, working at menial jobs, going to school, obeying the law — were robbed of their dignity and respect. Yet it is the older conventions — working hard, studying hard, staying out of trouble — that have led and still do lead millions out of poverty.

When the system became nonjudgmental, stigma disappeared along with status. Instead of expelling pregnant teenagers, enlightened school administrators looked on benignly. Today, pregnancy is a rite of adolescent passage in poor neighborhoods. Walter E. Williams, a professor of economics at George Mason University in Virginia, says, "There's probably a very good reason to have strong social sanctions against having babies when you're 15 or 16. But these sanctions are gone now. They're virtually absent. And these are the kinds of things that used to hold families together and make people do the right thing."

The philosophy of public assistance "became focused on holding people harmless for their misdeeds and became very reluctant to punish or disapprove of their behavior," says Harvard economist Glenn Loury. "A relativism came into the thinking, where it was inappropriate to impose 'middle-class values' on poor people." Politicians and administrators withdrew support for the old-line view, he says, which often "was being espoused by people right in those communities who were themselves poor, who were distraught about the way youngsters were behaving or who didn't want newfangled ideas brought into the schools."

For the poor, and only the poor, society began to reward what used to be seen as failure. "If you are poor and you are pregnant, there's a program for you," says Robert L. Woodson, president of the National Center for Neighborhood Enterprise, a self-help group. "If you are poor and you are a drug addict, there's a program for you. If you're a truant, there's a program. But you name the programs that are in place for families living in low-income communities where the kids are not exhibiting any pathology. What is there for those kids? There's not even recognition. There's an old adage that you get more of what you reward and less of what you punish. As long as we keep rewarding pathological behavior, we will get more of it."

Escape from poverty requires painful sacrifices — far greater than those needed to remain in the middle class. To save when barely scraping by, to work long hours at a dirty job, to struggle through school, to overcome all the disadvantages of being poor, require a strength and determination that society must celebrate and encourage, says Woodson, not punish and demean.

Many still maintain that holding the poor accountable for themselves is blaming the victim. "That expression," retorts Williams, "is probably one of the most vacuous and inane phrases that has ever come up. Having illegitimate children is not an act of God. People are killing and mugging, and they're calling the perpetrator the victim. That's a strong twist of the English language. What that says is that people don't have any control over themselves . . . in terms of having a baby, in terms of destroying property, in terms of going to school and trying to get educated, in terms of robbing and raping people. The blaming-the-victim argument says that these people don't have any control over that. It's society that makes them do it."

One must question, he says, the social policies that follow. "In saying people do this because they are victims of racist society, are you then saying that blacks, particularly blacks, should continue to be afraid to walk the streets, to shudder in fear in their homes until white people decide to act nicely? That's the policy recommendation. You just allow this rape, murder, property destruction, arson to go on until, someday, we get white people to act nice. I mean, people could be waiting a long time."

Glazer now says that social policy, however well-intentioned, has inherent limits: When government tries to help, it assumes, at least in part, the traditional role of the family, the church, the neighborhood. It weakens those institutions and encourages people to depend on government for help. When help came from the outside, the poor surrendered control over their communities. A common element in many of the reforms of the Sixties and Seventies, says William Barclay Allen, chairman of the U.S. Commission on Civil Rights, was that these reforms wound up "taking more and more control over [poor people's] own lives out of the hands of poor people."

"If you keep being told by your own leaders that you really just can't hack it without special assistance, that you're just sort of naturally in poverty unless the federal government does something to help you — what a suffocating, undercutting, demoralizing image to give to people," says Butler, the coauthor of "Poverty Trap." "If you keep telling people that there's no point in trying because everybody's against you, not to bother staying in school because you're going to drop out and if you do drop out it's not your fault, it's somebody else's fault, all the time you're reinforcing negative behavior in people. It's a great tragedy."

STRIPPING BONDS OF FAILURE

Many people wonder whether conditions in the inner cities have spun out of control. Positive examples have become the exception and negatives the norm, to the point, they say, that there has emerged a self-perpetuating cycle of child abuse, drug addiction, illiteracy, unwed teenage motherhood, indolence and crime. A child growing up in such a world adopts its standards, and so it continues and grows, generation upon generation.

It is time, counters Michael Novak of the American Enterprise Institute, to stop examining failures and start studying successes. Millions still escape from poverty, he insists, just as millions escaped it before, and the way out is no mystery: getting a good education, working hard, even at a low-wage job, and building the strong two-parent family that provides financial and spiritual sustenance. "For 20 years or more we've neglected the fundamentals," he says. They still work. Thousands of inner-city teenagers stay in school and get jobs. They do not make headlines, but they prove that not every poor inner-city youth is a drug addict or a dropout.

The question, Novak says, is how to inspire and to help those poor who are not achieving independence to do so. Analysts from across the political spectrum agree that there are things government can do and things society can do. And there is much that is being done today, in the streets of Harlem and Newark, in the housing projects of St. Louis, Chicago and Washington, in the neighborhoods of cities everywhere. Robert L. Woodson, president of the National Center for Neighborhood Enterprise, a self-help organization, call these local citizens groups "community antibodies."

Their bywords are empowerment and independence. Youngsters who come to the Youth Action Program in Harlem have been told all their lives that they are failures, says director Sonia Bu. All their lives they have been treated as clients of this or that agency that does things for them and gives them things. "We reverse that process," she says, "by acknowledging first of all that they are intelligent and that they have ideas" about how to improve themselves and their communities. Youngsters learn how to carry out those ideas. They also learn the responsibility that accompanies citizenship.

Youth Action erased "client" from its vocabulary, says Bu. "The minute you treat people as clients, you begin to give them a passive role in the whole relationship. Here it's reversed. 'No, we're not going to give you anything. We're going to give you opportunity and support, but you're going to get it yourself.' Our ultimate goal is to make that person self-sufficient."

For many youths, this is a startling change, says Shakoor Aljuwani, director of the organization's construction training program, in which youths renovate abandoned buildings. "They've been through so many different programs before, sometimes a youth who is only 21, 22 years old can list a whole resume full of programs that he's passed through. And all these programs are never really calling on them, showing them that the solution to their problems is within themselves, that they have to figure out how to bring that forward and deal with whatever conditions they face. . . . A lot of the programs are not set up for them to stand on their own two feet."

When youngsters who have been told they would never accomplish anything, and who never have, see a floor that they have laid in a building or the walls they have raised, says Aljuwani, "that's a big step in that person's reconstruction. They begin to see they're capable of doing a great thing if they believe in themselves."

James Wallace founded the International Youth Organization in

Newark because, he says, "a man saved me when I was young, about 17. And ever since then it's been my life." He works with youngsters others have given up on, taking them "by the hand, step-by-step, until they can walk on their own," he says. "We must go back to our basics, back to things that really work, and teach these kids how to respect themselves. Once they respect themselves, they're going to respect other people, and then they want to do something with their lives."

What youngsters lack most, says his wife, Carolyn, is "knowledge that they have the power to overcome all this." What she and her husband try to do, she says, "is be the hand that they need to help them over, pumping into their heads that Jesus is able to restore all that you think you've lost, giving them a sense of responsibility and the motivation and the moral values that they need. That's the only way it can happen." Change has to come from inside a person, she says. "And what we try to do is develop a good, moral, spiritual inside."

These groups are battling titanic forces, and not least among them is the idea that poor people are somehow incompetent. "Confidence in people's ability to govern themselves is the most important gift we have to give to people," says William Barclay Allen, chairman of the U.S. Commission on Civil Rights. "Having been raised poor, and knowing something about it, I am very sensitive to the fact that nothing is so precious for a poor person as control over his own life."

People who are allowed to take control over their communities can change them, many say. About 12 years ago, a housing project on Duncan Avenue in Jersey City, N.J., was among the worst in the city, scheduled for demolition. Garbage filled the stairwells, drunks lay passed out in the hallways. Muggings were common. People had been murdered. Addicts had set up shooting galleries in vacant apartments. But a group of tenants had gathered together in one building, where they were trying to hang on. "It wasn't that we didn't want it changed," says the Rev. Robert Blount, the project's manager, "but we really had no control over it. It wasn't the tenants who would make the final decision, it was the bureaucrat."

Around that time, the director of the Jersey City Housing Authority heard of Bertha Gilkey, a woman who, with other tenants, had taken control of a similar housing project in St. Louis and accomplished a stunning turnaround. As a last resort, the housing authority offered management control to the residents of the Duncan Avenue project. Armed with the power to evict, the tenant board was able to confront parents of teenagers who had been mugging residents. The muggings stopped. Today the project is clean and safe.

Many inner-city residents refuse to allow teenage criminals to take control of their lives. "Not all of us believe that we have to cede our neighborhoods to these folks," says Leon Moore, director of an independent school in Newark. Police, politicians and communities capitulate to the criminals, he maintains. "They say, 'We can't handle this. It's too much for us.' Does that mean we don't have the sense or the guts to take control of small neighborhoods, small neighborhoods that make big neighborhoods, which make a town or a city? If we cede all of that, then we're going to live in fear the rest of our lives, and I refuse." When criminals kill policemen, says Moore, the police "track them down like the dogs that they are and lock them up." The police could do the same for ordinary citizens, he insists.

Communities have other weapons: status and stigma. According to Jewelle Taylor Gibbs, a clinical psychologist who teaches at the University of California at Berkeley's social welfare school, community groups and churches as well as national leaders can make it clear to boys that making babies without accepting responsibility for them requires no special talent and is no mark of manhood. They can help make dropping out of school unfashionable. They can help make criminals uncomfortable. Rather than tolerance and tacit acceptance, she says, "the message has to go out in the black community that we don't reward teenagers who go out and sell dope and wear gold chains, that we don't approve of these behaviors, and that these people need to be socially ostracized and weeded out of the black community."

The Family Assistance Act of 1988, a welfare reform law sponsored by Sen. Daniel P. Moynihan, a New York Democrat, reflects a major shift in thinking. It talks more of obligations than benefits. It calls for payroll withholding of child support from absentee fathers. It allows states to deny welfare benefits to teenage parents who set up their own households. It requires that states enroll at least some welfare recipients in work programs.

The federal government will chip in $3.34 billion over five years to pay the additional cost of new work incentives. These include job training and a year's worth of both Medicaid and subsidized day care for welfare recipients who take jobs. The loss of such valuable benefits by those who take jobs, experts believe, has kept many welfare recipients from working.

Many analysts, however, think the law will backfire. There is no way, they say, to make it easier to get off welfare without also making it more attractive to get on. Offering a year of free health insurance and day care to former welfare recipients automatically penalizes women who are already working at low wages and receiving no benefits. The new law will tempt these women, they say, to move onto the welfare rolls at least temporarily.

Many point out further that the government has created countless job training programs, not one of which has shown more than marginal success. "A mere roll call of the initials of different programs reduces one to dumbness," writes Harvard professor Nathan Glazer. "ARA, MDTA, JC, NYC, WIN, JOBS, CEP, PEP, CETA, PSE, STIP, HIRE, YEDPA, PSIP, PIC's, YCCIP, YIEPP. They all stand for something. . . . All once excited enthusiasm."

The taxpayer investment has been huge: The federal government spent what today would amount to $281 billion on education and training programs for the poor from 1963 to 1985, according to Isabel Sawhill of the Urban Institute, a Washington-based research organization.

The Rev. Harold Simmons, who works with the Wallaces' group in Newark, says many of the training programs he has seen produce "brats" instead of workers. The participants sign in at a job site, leave after a half-hour and get paid for doing nothing. That's what they learn. "Four years of that and it's a mind-set," he says.

Many failed programs continue year after year, Woodson of the National Center for Neighborhood Enterprise maintains, because they benefit not so much the poor, but the poverty industry, for whom the poor are what he calls a commodity. Social workers, counselors, doctors, lawyers and other professionals receive much of the money plowed into antipoverty programs, he says. "The worse poverty gets, the more money they get. They are not required to perform. There's just no relationship between expenditures and outcomes in terms of relieving poverty or dependency."

Many times, says Carolyn Wallace, government agencies "send in money, but they don't know where they're sending it, they don't know who they're sending it to, and then they pat themselves on the back when it does not work. . . . You can't change people with money. You can't just slap money on it." Although they now contract with government agencies, the Wallaces operated for 14 years without government funds, relying on volunteers and community donations. They and similar groups need money to operate and welcome the government help; they believe that help should go to groups with a proven track record.

Woodson says citizen groups all over the country have shown success reducing teenage pregnancy, school dropout rates and delinquency. "We should convene those people in communities who have demonstrated that they can achieve success in spite of poverty and bring them together, with the microphones turned on," he says. "We should begin to celebrate these achievements and confer authority and legitimacy on these efforts."

Taxpayer money can be used to "empower people, rather than injuring them," he says. The criteria for any program, he says, should be that it build self-esteem and independence, and provide choice. "There should be a kind of Hippocratic oath in social policy, to do no harm."

Carolyn Lochhead

CHAPTER 8

*The homeless seem to be everywhere. But
even so, some of the fundamental facts are
missing. How many are there? Answers
were speculative and vulnerable to
exaggeration, as this May 16, 1988, article
reported. The actual number was likely
but a fraction of the 2 million to 3 million
that had commonly been bandied about.
The absence of reliable data thwarted
efforts to address their varied and
sometimes painful situations. By 1990,
some cities were cutting back on
open-ended entitlements to shelter.*

NOWHERE TO GO, ALWAYS IN SIGHT

At 8 a.m. in New York's Port Authority bus terminal at Eighth Avenue and West 42nd Street, commuters step over bodies sprawled on the platforms. Maintenance crews have covered a pile of excrement. Crack addicts sleep in the stairwells. The police, abiding by a recent court ruling, do not arrest anyone for loitering. A well-dressed student, 18, stands on a bus platform. Two men lie on the seats. "I don't have anything against bums," she says, "but the ones that rob you or the ones that are nasty I'm really afraid of. Every morning I come here and they're sleeping all over the place. It makes me feel very uncomfortable."

Downstairs in the main terminal building is another young woman. She looks almost like a student, but her shoulders are slumped. She has been wandering through the terminal for six months. Approached, she hurries away. This woman, possibly mentally ill, is obviously homeless too. She shares the terminal and that catchall term with a wild mix of humanity. Penniless families, single mothers with children, the sick, the drunks, derelicts and addicts, the mentally ill, former foster-care children, people temporarily out of work, people who do not want to work, released convicts, the illiterate and unskilled, battered wives, veterans, transients and dangerous predators — these are the people who make up the homeless. And even these categories overlap. There are the mentally ill alcoholics, the drug-addicted single mothers.

Initially, the increases in the homeless population might have been explained by the recession of 1979 and the continued growth by the deeper 1981-82 recession. But now the numbers simply do not square with most economic measures. The economy is enjoying a record expansion. The 5.6 percent unemployment rate is a nine-year low. Some 15.5 million jobs have been created since 1983 — a quarter-million last month alone, and 84,000 of those were in the blue-collar mining, construction and manufacturing sectors. Housing vacancy rates are at a 20-year high. Poverty rates are falling. Yet the numbers of the homeless seem to have risen most rapidly since 1983.

Astonishingly little is known about the homeless, other than that their numbers have grown and that they are an extremely mixed lot. Even the most basic facts are clouded by political controversy.

Why are people homeless? Advocates such as Mitch Snyder, who runs a 900-bed shelter in Washington, D.C., contend that the homeless are victims of Reagan administration policies. Robert Hayes, counsel to the National Coalition for the Homeless, says, "The homeless are indeed the most egregious example of a cruel economy, an unresponsive government, a festering value system."

"Homelessness is primarily a housing problem to be addressed with more housing," says Maria Foscarinis of the National Coalition for the Homeless, reflecting the view of many advocates.

Advocates have launched a national campaign to get their views to the media. A coalition called the Campaign to End Hunger and Homelessness, for example, seeks to "propel the issues of hunger and homelessness to the forefront of political debate" during the 1988 election. The coalition is sending out media kits, organizing news conferences, preparing radio and television interviews, planning media events and directing reporters to the homeless. The campaign financed a poll that found hunger and homelessness to be second only to the federal budget deficit among the public's top concerns.

Outlining the campaign's strategy, James B. Chapin, chairman of World Hunger Year, warns advocates that while Americans want to help the deserving poor, they are hostile to those who make no effort to help themselves. "Therefore," he says, "it is most important that we make poor children the center of the campaign."

Some advocates seek to exploit public sympathies by using the homeless as a lever to increase spending on social welfare programs, cut the military budget and enact national health insurance. According to Chapin, government must finance "broad-based, mass programs. . . . We have to look at what government does well. What it does well is to issue checks." He tells advocates to "try to package our programs in a way designed to appeal to those who may not necessarily share our priorities."

Mike Elias, director of Christian Temporary Housing Facilities, Inc. in Orange, Calif., was once homeless himself and has worked with homeless people for 11 years. He is critical of these approaches. "What the advocates are doing is saying, 'We're going to put a massive shelter here and we're going to use you to make a point. We're going to embarrass the government.' Another thing they do is they make homeless people noble, as though it's noble to be homeless. It isn't noble to be homeless. They're not the magical, mythical underclass of America. There's nothing romantic about being homeless.

"I've never seen anybody say in the media, 'Homeless person, you are to blame.' I've never seen that. It's like they're innocent victims. Like there's a great power out there that's destroying these homeless people. I don't see the guy that's working in the newspaper. That's missing. The people who get the most coverage are the negative advocates or the negative people. Not the people looking after the dignity of the family or getting people on their feet. If you tell people to get a job, that's not newsworthy."

Perhaps nothing better illustrates what has assumed the shape of a propaganda war than the controversy over the size of the homeless population. Because the homeless are so difficult to count and define, no one knows for certain how many there are. Advocates say the population ranges from 2 million to 3 million, a number widely reported in the media. That is about 1 percent of the population, one out of every 100 people. Advocates also say the number will rise to 18 million by the end of the century. Only massive federal spending on housing and welfare will stem such appalling growth, they maintain.

By contrast, a 1984 study by the Department of Housing and Urban Development put the population at a drastically lower 250,000 to 350,000. The range came under loud attack by advocates, who said the administration was trying to dismiss the problem.

Both estimates are highly suspect, the HUD figure for its weak methodology, the advocates' number for its lack of any methodology. "The advocates made it up," says Anna Kondratas, administrator of the Food and Nutrition Service at the Department of Agriculture. "The idea of 2 to 3 million homeless is totally preposterous.

There is absolutely no data, no study, no report that would indicate anything of that magnitude." In fact, the estimate of 2 million to 3 million reflects mostly advocate guesses of the number of homeless in various cities. These numbers are often inflated by including such groups as "hidden homeless" who cannot be located or "borderline homeless" who are doubled up with relatives. Kondratas cites a tally for the District of Columbia that began with a physical count of about 2,500. Adding the "hidden homeless" factor eventually brought the number to 6,500, which is now a commonly cited figure. Advocate Snyder continues to use his own estimate of 10,000 to 15,000.

Recent studies by respected researchers indicate that the number of homeless is far below the advocates' estimates. Last year, Peter H. Rossi of the Social and Demographic Research Institute of the University of Massachusetts, himself an advocate for more public spending on homelessness, put the homeless population of Chicago on an average night at 2,722, a fraction of previous estimates of 12,000 to 25,000. "We have never been able to locate any data from which these numbers were derived," says Rossi's study. "There is no evidence that they are anything but guesses."

Richard Freeman, a Harvard economist with the National Bureau of Economic Research, in 1986 estimated the national homeless population to have been about 279,000 in 1983, the lower end of the much-maligned Housing and Urban Development range. By 1985, he estimated, the population had grown as high as 383,000. "While our figures are to be viewed as rough orders of magnitude only," Freeman wrote, "it is important to recognize that they are strongly inconsistent with the claim that 1 percent of Americans are homeless." He maintained that "high, undocumented claims" about the number of homeless have "had the unfortunate effect of making what should be seen as shockingly large numbers — over a quarter of a million Americans homeless in 1983 — seem moderate by contrast."

Exaggeration also can lead the private citizens and businesses on whom many shelter operators rely for financial support to throw up their hands. Martha Brown Hicks, who since its inception in 1978 has headed the Skid Row Development Corp., a not-for-profit shelter and development concern in Los Angeles, believes the estimate of 50,000 homeless there is "just crazy. I don't mean to underestimate the problem," she says. "We have to deal with homelessness every day. But I think the figures have really been blown out of proportion. If you're going to the private sector and saying, 'Here's a problem. Can you help us?' and they feel they can have some impact, you'll get help. But if they think it's an impossible situation, nobody wants to help."

Compassionate Americans have donated untold amounts of time and money to shelters for the homeless across the country. But a brush that paints all homeless people as innocent victims of a selfish, even ruthless, society can turn sympathy and generosity into anger and indignation. A New Jersey commuter who cleans homes for a living says that when he passes homeless panhandlers he feels little sympathy. "Here I am, cleaning people's apartments, and they're sitting there asking me for money."

A commuter at Grand Central Terminal, where large numbers of the homeless congregate, says she used to offer them food. "They didn't want that," she says. "They wanted money. Now I just walk over them. And that disturbs me."

"These people are filthy," says a Port Authority commuter. "They are urinating and defecating in the stairwells. It's horrendous. I know there are some cases where people need help, but I think the majority don't want to be helped or don't give a damn." She wants the homeless banned from public places, "regardless of what the civil liberty organizations say. Our civil liberties are being violated at this point."

John Stendaro, a Port Authority agent, says that his initial compassion toward the homeless has turned cold. "If you work here," he says, "you get hard to it. These people sit around here doing nothing, and I have to get up and go to work every day. My taxes are going up, and the bum population is going up." During rush hour, he says, panhandlers make as much as $80 an hour. "You'd be surprised. They have some pitiful rap they run. They stay in the same place every day. I talk to these people. They could work. But people drop $20 bills in their cups and then complain to the Port Authority. Between the people and the courts, it's a catch-22."

Many commuters are fearful, unable to distinguish between who is harmless and who is not. A city councilman in Secaucus, N.J., says some of his constituents quit their jobs in Manhattan because they fear for their safety in and around the terminal.

Ambivalence and hostility are not confined to New York. In the coastal communities of California, the appearance of the homeless has pitted residents who want to rid the cities of them against those who want to provide shelter. Many citizens feel particularly vulnerable to the transient homeless, and in fact large numbers of the California homeless are new arrivals. One shelter operator says some of the homeless call ahead from other towns to see what services are

available there. Residents fear a "mecca effect" that could draw
more transients to their communities.

In response, several cities have tried to obliterate homelessness or
deflect it elsewhere. Santa Barbara banned sleeping in parks. A local
uproar ensued, and the ordinance has since been lifted. It is still illegal to sleep on the Santa Barbara beach; the city recently bulldozed
a shantytown. Farther north, in small, picturesque San Luis Obispo,
the appearance of the homeless has shocked citizens accustomed to
manicured parks and storybook streets. At the behest of angry businessmen, city cleanup crews cleared the creek that runs through the
heart of the shopping district of shanties that had sprung up along
it. In response, equally angry citizens organized a shelter.

Says Betty Nielsen, president of the People's Kitchen and the People's Shelter in San Luis Obispo, "Locals think the homeless can't be
coming from here, that they must all be from Los Angeles, but that's
not true. We had the grandson of a former sheriff [in the shelter],
and that was a bitter pill for the locals to swallow — that these people could be from their town."

ALL ALONE, WITH NO HOME

Everything proceeds from why. Those who work with the homeless often find mental illness, loneliness, dependency, deep-rooted
isolation, alienation from society, self-destruction, drug and alcohol
abuse, and perhaps at the bottom of most of these things, the breakdown of the family.

Many of the young people who arrive at the People's Shelter in the
small California city of San Luis Obispo come from broken homes
— a 19 year-old, say, whose parents are divorced and who is welcome in neither household. Sometimes relatives live right in town. "I
hate to say it," says Betty Nielsen, president of the shelter, "but I
think they just don't want to be bothered. I don't want to believe that,
but I think it's true."

John Jamison, director for social services of the Salvation Army
in nearby Santa Barbara, says "this incredible increase in numbers"
of young homeless has "come from situations where there is no family role model." Mike Elias of Christian Temporary Housing Facilities Inc. in Orange, Calif., says one of his clients had been in 52 foster homes.

"The family structure that would have been traditional even 10
years ago is nonexistent," says Jamison. "There are large numbers
in the homeless population who if they died tomorrow, nobody

would care. And they know it. It's painful to them. There is no mother, there is no father, there is no sister, there is no brother they can turn to as you or I would. These ties have disintegrated, broken down."

Take the husband who leaves his family. The mother is now single, caring for her children. She finds a boyfriend. He is not interested in the children, and they know it. After a while, he leaves. The mother finds another boyfriend, perhaps the same or worse. She begins to see the children as a drag on her life. They feel the rejection, and by the time they become teenagers, they are in trouble. There are spoken and unspoken requests that they bug out of her life. Sometimes abuse develops. Such children, says Jamison, have no self-confidence, no feeling of self-worth, no motivation and no sense of caring about society, "because they don't care about themselves. Nobody else cares." He traces homelessness in part to the "1960s mentality that has affected all of society. It's basically a more self-centered stance, and that has not been good for society, for the family or for the individual." He says drug and alcohol abuse has taken an enormous toll. So has the waning of religious values.

Many of those who operate shelters say more cheap housing and higher welfare benefits would help many people, particularly families. But they also say that just providing a bed, a meal and a shower is in most cases no solution. Some even contend that such approaches can accelerate a homeless person's slide into dependency or attract those in marginal living arrangements to the shelters.

Advocates for homeless people often contend that most such folk are out on the streets because of a lost job, a low minimum wage and lack of housing — things over which they have no control. There are many such individual cases, particularly among those who are homeless for only a short spell. But the few reliable studies available do not support this assertion on any kind of broad scale. The homeless are not yeoman steelworkers laid off from high-paying jobs. Those not mentally ill often have histories of chronic unemployment, chronic poverty, family breakdown, illiteracy, welfare dependency and crime. The vast majority are single males. Among homeless families, most are headed by urban welfare recipients, predominantly single mothers. This profile indicates much deeper social ills, of the sort little affected by blunt economic measures or Great Society prescriptions.

One of the largest single categories of the homeless is made up of the mentally ill — somewhere between 30 and 40 percent, sometimes more, according to most serious studies. They are the people emp-

tied from the state mental hospitals in the nationwide wave of dein-
stitutionalization that began in the Sixties. They are also those who
reached adulthood since then and who have never been in a mental
institution. This is not the way it was supposed to work. The idea was
to free patients from the often wretched and abusive conditions of
the hospitals and treat them instead in the community. But community treatment, where it was thought out at all, never really materi-
alized.

Nonetheless, says Dr. Paul S. Appelbaum, director of the Law and
Psychiatry Program at the University of Massachusetts Medical
School, the move within the mental health professions to empty state
hospitals "took on the nature of an ideological crusade, a crusade
that said all patients can not only survive in the community but
would be better-off in the community." Civil libertarians joined in
with court victories that prohibited people from being involuntarily
committed unless they were found to be dangerous to themselves or
others. Finally, politicians saw great savings in closing down hugely
expensive state hospitals.

The fruits of this movement are visible everywhere. In San Luis
Obispo County, home of a state mental hospital in Atascadero, shelter operators say the hospital appears to be letting patients out into
the community. "Some people get out and don't know where they
are," says Capt. Dan L. Hughes of the San Luis Obispo Salvation
Army, whose shelter houses mentally ill homeless people. Hughes
says the patients may start out receiving Social Security assistance
and staying in a board-and-care home, but then they "have some
sort of deterioration, get off their medication and leave. For some of
them, their families just burn out."

Betty Nielsen, whose shelter is nearby, says the county mental
health clinic is swamped and furthermore cannot keep any patient
longer than 72 hours. "I've seen them put raving maniacs out on the
street with a bottle of pills," she says. "A national scandal," says Jamison. "Farm animals and pets live a better existence than many of the
homeless mentally ill." Many end up in jail. Nielsen says Vietnam veterans have told her that they merely wanted to talk to someone but
instead got "Hi, how are you? Here's some pills, good-bye."

Dr. H. Richard Lamb, a professor of psychiatry at the University
of Southern California, says that while they are eligible for Social
Security funds, chronically or severely mentally ill people often lose
touch with the system. Unable to deal with even ordinary landlord-
tenant matters, or sometimes the cause of disturbances, they are vulnerable to eviction, he says. Many tend to drift away from their fam-

ilies. Or their families, unable to cope with them any longer, turn them out. Many refuse medication and begin, in psychiatric jargon, to "self-medicate" themselves with alcohol and other drugs, magnifying their illness. "There are a lot of people who aren't objectively dangerous to themselves or others but who are leading miserable lives out there on the basis of psychotic decision making," says Appelbaum.

"The chronically and severely mentally ill are not homeless because they want to be or because of lack of housing or a lack of jobs," says Lamb. He calls for establishing intensive community mental health services, including individual case management, which means assigning a caseworker to each patient. Some change in the commitment laws is also necessary, he believes. Paul Appelbaum agrees.

Intensive community-based care could be extremely costly. "And that's something many people have not wanted to say," says Appelbaum, "because the public doesn't want to hear it. And there's a good deal of fear on the part of advocates that if it ever becomes clear just how costly the solutions are likely to be, the public will abandon all interest in helping the mentally ill."

Even simply providing shelter for the mentally ill and others is expensive. New York, the nation's homeless capital, has probably set up more shelters than any other city, housing more than 10,000 individuals and 5,000 families a night. Under court orders, the city has since 1979 provided emergency shelter to anyone who asks for it. Each time the city opens a new shelter, it fills up. New York's operating budget for the homeless has grown from $6.8 million in 1978 to $312 million this year. Nearby Westchester County, also obliged to provide shelter on demand, has seen its spending rise from $750,000 in 1983 to a projected $55.4 million this year. New York probably has more homeless families than any other city. It spends an average of $1,900 a month to put up a family of four in a welfare hotel. Half the money comes from the federal government.

Shelters may indeed be helping tens of thousands of the homeless, but the question to ask, says Christian Temporary Housing's Elias, is how many then return to independent living? Washington area advocate Mitch Snyder "shelters 900 people a night," Elias says. "So you've got 900 angry, frustrated, low self-esteem people. It's difficult if you have one. How can you change 900? If your goal is to give them a bed and throw them back on the street in the daytime, fine. But when those people go back for the next night of lodging, they're still angry. I don't think anything's changed."

Martha Brown Hicks, president of Skid Row Development Corp. in Los Angeles, says governments should examine which shelters are working best, not just keep building new ones, "I don't want to become the czar of homelessness," she says. "If I had all the money in the world, I wouldn't want to run another 1,000 beds. You'd have people coming from everywhere saying, 'Oh, in Los Angeles there's this wonderful place you can stay for free and if you want to work, fine. If you don't, fine.' I think the problems would simply escalate if you just keep putting up new buildings."

Carolyn Lochhead

CHAPTER 9

Man or woman, black or white,
opportunity in employment must be equal.
So says the law. Period. But the Supreme
Court, in two notable rulings described in
this April 27, 1987, article, gave policies
meant to dismiss workplace
discrimination a good shake. In fact, the
court seemed to be forging considerations
of race and sex into crucial tools for
molding a more proportional society. That
paradox, coupled with affirmative
actions's great reach, suggested the age of
grievances was far from over.

A GREEN LIGHT FOR HIRING BY THE NUMBERS

Using sex or race as a guide in hiring and promoting employees is suposed to violate both the Constitution, which requires "equal protection" under state and local law for everyone, and a host of federal civil rights laws. The best known of these, Title VII of the 1964 Civil Rights Act, specifically bans any sort of discrimination in employment on the basis of race or sex.

But in the past two months, in a pair of highly publicized decisions, the Supreme Court completely demolished the notions of color blindness and sex neutrality as legal standards. The court "deconstructed the statutes," charges Philip B. Kurland, a University of Chicago constitutional law professor.

The two rulings do have a distinctly utopian flavor. On March 25, in Johnson vs. Transportation Agency, Santa Clara County, six of the nine justices approved an affirmative action system for employees of the California county that allowed a woman to be promoted to crew dispatcher over a man who had more on-the-job experience and scored marginally higher in an oral interview.

In a similar ruling Feb. 25, the court voted 5-4 to approve a one-to-one promotion scheme for black and white Alabama State Police troopers briefly in operation under a 1983 U.S. District Court order. The situation in Alabama was somewhat different from that in California. Like other states, Alabama had for decades deliberately excluded blacks from state trooper positions. The 1983 order came in the wake of 11 years of bitterly contested litigation, during which time no blacks ever attained higher ranks and the state could justly be accused of foot-dragging.

Still, the order upheld in United States vs. Paradise had a troubling feature for the four dissenting justices: As issued by the lower court, it was to stay in effect until the number of promoted blacks equaled 25 percent, the percentage of blacks in Alabama's labor market as a whole (or until the state came up with its own policy that would give significant numbers of qualified blacks quick access to promotions).

The Supreme Court has for eight years approved race-conscious schemes for hirings and promotions but almost always as temporary remedies for past intentional discrimination and with an eye toward protecting the expectations of white workers. In May, for example, it struck down a clause in a collective bargaining agreement in Michigan that allowed some layoffs of white teachers so minority group teachers could keep their jobs. The Paradise ruling falls into this tradition.

In Johnson vs. Santa Clara, however, the high court ventured for the first time into approval of sex preferences for pure social engineering: getting more women into nontraditional jobs. "As long as there is a manifest imbalance" in the ethnic or sexual composition of a work force, wrote Justice William J. Brennan Jr. in the majority opinion, "an employer may adopt a plan even when the disparity is not so striking." The rulings in Johnson and Paradise both uphold the idea that a plan can stay in effect until the day arrives when the percentage of women or minority group members matches that in the labor market as a whole.

Unlike Alabama, Santa Clara County had no history of intentional discrimination. Nonetheless, in 1978 the transit district's Board of Supervisors adopted a long-range goal of having a work force whose proportions of women, members of minority groups and the handicapped at all job levels equaled those in the county's labor market. Women constituted 36.4 percent of that market at the time, but only 22.4 percent of the district's workers were female and they were clustered mostly in clerical jobs. There were only two road dispatcher positions in the entire agency.

Using a classification system developed by the Equal Employment

Opportunity Commission, the county lumped the dispatcher jobs, entailing responsibility for deploying crews and equipment, with 236 other jobs, mostly involving heavy equipment operation, and labeled them "skilled craft positions." No woman occupied any of the 238 jobs when Diane Joyce and Paul E. Johnson competed for a dispatcher opening in late 1979. Johnson did better on the test. Joyce talked to the union, which reminded the county of the long-range proportional goals. She got the job. Johnson sued.

The Johnson ruling drew a scorching dissent from Justice Antonin Scalia, who accused the majority of ignoring both the letter of the law and the sociology of the sexes: "It is absurd to think that the nationwide failure of road maintenance crews, for example, to achieve the agency's ambition of 36.4 percent female representation is attributable primarily, if even substantially, to systematic exclusion of women eager to shoulder pick and shovel."

Those legal thinkers, such as Scalia, who argue for a color-blind approach to the law and the Constitution are fighting a rearguard action these days. Although hard-and-fast racial quotas at a state-operated medical school were ruled illegal in the Supreme Court's famous University of California Regents vs. Bakke decision in 1978, softened versions in the form of goals and timetables are almost universal these days. They are distinctive features of hundreds of settlements and court orders in suits against governments, large corporations and universities and of many voluntary plans as well.

Business and government entities have learned to live with, even embrace, affirmative action. The U.S. Chamber of Commerce, whose 180,000 members include thousands of small businesses typically hostile to government regulation, took no position on the Santa Clara case. Many business organizations filed amicus curiae briefs supporting the program and praised the Supreme Court ruling. The reason for the business support is simple: A tough affirmative action program now can stave off expensive discrimination suits later. Sears, Roebuck & Co. has spent 15 years fighting charges by the Equal Employment Opportunity Commission, first in administrative proceedings, then in court. The trial alone lasted 10 months in 1984-85. The 806-store retailer refuses even to reveal how much it spent on lawyers, though it gives a hint: Expenses, including hiring statisticians, sociologists and other expert witnesses, came to $6.8 million, and one can guess fees to attorneys were probably at least twice that much.

Sears finally won at trial (the judgment is on appeal) against a charge that its female employees tend to be concentrated in lower-paying sales jobs than men because of discrimination. The company's chief litigator in the case, attorney Charles Morgan Jr. of Washington, specifically credits the court victory to a race- and sex-conscious hiring program Sears started in 1968 for its work force, now at 300,000. "They have the best," declares Morgan, "Out of every two job openings at Sears, they filled one with a black or a woman."

Governments, especially in large cities, similarly view affirmative action plans as a small price to pay for political harmony, particularly because minority groups taken together make up majorities in many urban areas. In 1984, the Justice Department sent letters to 51 state and local governments offering to help them overturn affirmative action consent decrees in court. All but one said "no thanks."

How did race- and sex-consciousness become institutionalized on the contemporary American scene? After all, a mere 33 years have elapsed since schools, buses and public accommodations were racially segregated by official fiat in many parts of the country. College quotas, often disguised as guidelines for geographic diversity, kept down enrollments of Jews at many schools.

Women were openly denied jobs on account of their sex almost everywhere. Justice Sandra Day O'Connor graduated third in her class from Stanford Law School, but a large Los Angeles law firm offered her only a secretarial job. The Rev. Martin Luther King Jr. talked of a society in which people would be judged not on the color of their skin but on the content of their character.

The civil rights legislation of the 1960s, banning discrimination in voting, housing, education and jobs, was also color-blind. Title VII, the employment statute, makes it unlawful to take any action that would "adversely affect" anyone's employment status on the basis of race, color, religion, sex or national origin.

In 1964, when Title VII was originally passed, some members of Congress expressed fear that it would be used to mandate quotas. Sen. Hubert H. Humphrey, one of the statute's architects, assured them this was just a bugaboo raised by bigots. Similarly, 1963's Equal Pay Act for women guaranteed just that, pay equal to men's for equal work — no more, no less.

But even as the ink was drying on these laws, activists were demanding and getting more. Colleges and professional schools began aggressive efforts to recruit minority students, often bending standards, as in the Bakke case, to make the numbers look better.

"There was an enormous amount of white guilt during the mid-1960s." says Charles Murray, a social analyst and author of "Losing Ground: American Social Policy, 1950-1980." "We were in the process of coming to terms with the degree to which we had discriminated in the past, so it was a very natural reaction to say we're going to make it up."

Blacks and other minority groups also saw a society that had moved far too slowly to honor their rights in the past. They wanted to make up for lost time — and lost jobs and income — more quickly than by simply waiting for effects of past roadblocks to wither away. "Affirmative action is a way to help people catch up with what they had lost by racial discrimination in the past," says Grover Hankins, general counsel for the National Association for the Advancement of Colored People, expressing the view of most black leaders.

This has left very few willing to play Roland at the Roncesvalles of a changing zeitgeist. Of this lonely bunch, many are in the Reagan administration. Two prominent administration figures, Justice Department spokesman Terry Eastland and Education Secretary William J. Bennett, are authors of "Counting by Race," a 1979 book that criticized the Supreme Court for capitulating to notions of "numerical equality" rather than "moral equality," as the two believed the Constitution and the law demanded. The court had just ruled, in United Steel Workers of America vs. Weber, against a blue-collar white man who challenged a one-to-one admissions policy for blacks and whites to an on-the-job training program at a Kaiser Aluminum & Chemical Corp. plant.

"We believe the correct principle is one of no discrimination whatsoever," Eastland says now. "Employment considerations should not be based on race or gender." Under William Bradford Reynolds, assistant attorney general for the civil rights division, the Justice Department has pursued a course of aggressive participation in virtually every affirmative action case before the Supreme Court and an argument that relief should be meted out only to actual victims of discrimination. In the Alabama case, for example, the department contended that fines and penalties, not a race-conscious hiring plan, were the way to deal with the recalcitrant state.

The high court has rebuffed Justice almost every time. Only in a couple of cases involving layoff priorities — where whites can be hurt most by race preferences — has it reined in an affirmative action policy. The Justice Department has even been rebuffed inside the administration. Its attempts to persuade President Reagan to rescind Lyndon Johnson's 1965 executive order authorizing a vaguely worded policy of "affirmative action" have been firmly and successfully opposed by Labor Secretary William E. Brock III, who is far less conservative than other administration figures on many issues.

Some observers have wondered: Has Justice pushed too far? Hankins accuses the department of trying to "turn back the clock" and of reneging on long-standing government commitments to civil rights. Reagan-appointed blacks (such as the Commission on Civil Rights chairman, Clarence M. Pendleton Jr.) who oppose affirmative action are themselves labeled racist or, at the very least, insensitive. "The department sometimes pushes the idea of a color-blind remedy to the extremity," notes an otherwise sympathetic administration observer. "When they sent those [51] letters to the states over the consent decrees, they were stepping into a very delicate political situation. Many suspected the department was not acting in good faith."

One agency, the Equal Employment Opportunity Commission, has managed to effect subtle but important policy changes. In the 1970s massive lawsuits such as the one against Sears, hitting large corporations and aiming for massive restructuring of employment practices, were the rule at the commission. Lately, its focus has turned away from affirmative action. In one 1983 settlement that the commission is particularly proud of, General Motors Corp. agreed to spend $42.5 million for on-the-job training, minority scholarships and resolving hundreds of individual complaints after the EEOC accused it of discriminating against blacks, Hispanics and women.

"These are the toughest remedies," says the commission's vice chairman, R. Gaull Silberman. "They act as deterrents for future conduct, and they make it expensive to discriminate." But there is a problem, she admits. Lawmakers who passed Title VII kept it "deliberately weak" in terms of monetary relief for victims. Those who prove discrimination claims under it can collect only lost pay and attorney fees, not punitive damages or compensation for emotional stress.

This view of money and injunctions as the best salve for the wounds of discrimination has yet to make much headway in either federal courtrooms or the offices of lawyers who file civil rights suits. There, race-based hiring goals and timetables have been the remedies of preference for almost two decades. This is largely because courts in the early 1970s began relaxing rules to allow more class action suits, says Ronald Rotunda, constitutional law professor at the University of Illinois. In such cases, the individual in whose name the suit is brought is typically insignificant; the focus is on group relief.

As for Title VII's apparent ban on race- or sex-based employment practices, the Supreme Court has virtually admitted it is ignoring the statute. In a concurring opinion in Johnson, Justice John Paul Stevens said Congress's intent was no longer relevant. "They are ignoring Congress," says Chicago's Kurland.

Obviously, individuals get hurt when affirmative action goals, not merit or seniority rules, decide who gets hired or promoted. More often than not, those individuals are men; white men, blue-collar men like Paul E. Johnson, seeking personal advancement of a kind that may appear trivial to judges deciding their cases or legal scholars reading the rulings. Scalia, in his dissent in the Johnson case, called them victims of "'injustice at the hands of a court fond of thinking itself the champion of the politically impotent."

To others, these hapless men are the eggs that must be broken to make the omelet of a more proportional world. "If someone doesn't suffer in the picture, it's not affirmative action," says Barbara Babcock, a Stanford University law professor. "That's what makes it so difficult. You're disappointing the established expectations of a white male. It's painful, but it has to be done." She, like other advocates, views the preference system as strictly temporary, bound to disappear after accomplishing its purpose of creating an integrated society.

Groups such as Jews and sometimes Asians that have been excluded from jobs, schools and club memberships but have been too successful economically to pick up the "disadvantaged" label may also suffer. Jews have traditionally been strong supporters of civil rights, but "racial preferences are just old-fashioned discrimination," says Nathan Perlmutter of the Anti-Defamation League of B'nai B'rith.

Jews (and also Arabs) have cases pending in the Supreme Court in which they seek to be defined as racial minorities so they can get damages for civil rights violations. The outcome of these cases is not expected to bear on the racial-preference question but should add to the turmoil over who should be defined as disadvantaged.

Paradoxically, blacks themselves can at times be victims of the new benign race-consciousness. A few years ago the 2nd U.S. Circuit Court of Appeals, based in New York, upheld a limit on black tenants in a public housing project on the theory that if their numbers reached a critical mass, whites would move out. "In the end, it leaves the alleged oppressors, the white males, open to further oppression by creating new categories for preferences," says the Civil Rights Commission's Pendleton. If counting by race and sex is as unpopular a policy as critics say it is, one might think there would be a move in Congress to clarify the federal laws. But most observers agree the support for such an action simply is not there, while the opposition from minority and women's organizations would likely be vocal and powerful.

Among Americans as a whole, polls show strong support for affirmative action in the abstract. Large majorities of blacks and whites favor such actions as aggressive recruitment of minority group members, special training programs and government educational assistance to minority groups.

But in a March 1986 article in Public Opinion magazine, John Bunzel, a former Civil Rights Commission member now at Stanford University's Hoover Institution, noted that blacks and whites differ sharply when asked their opinion of racial quotas. Blacks generally support them; whites do not. And neither blacks nor whites lent majority support to the proposition that schools should lower their standards to admit unqualified students. "It's all a matter of what questions you ask," says Bunzel.

One ground for hope for opponents of the new preference system might be the Supreme Court's own confusion about the issue, says the University of Illinois's Rotunda. Only three justices (Brennan, Thurgood Marshall and Harry A. Blackmun) vote consistently for preferences, while two others (Scalia and Chief Justice William H. Rehnquist) seem thoroughly opposed. O'Connor, Stevens and Byron R. White do not seem to have a consistent philosophy. "It may be years before the court comes to a majority opinion," he says. The Justice Department's Reynolds promises to keep testing the issue as long as possible.

Businesses and their lawyers take a more pragmatic view of the court's recent actions. Any company without an affirmative action program "is in jeopardy" of being sued by women or whoever else feels left out, says Sears attorney Morgan.

Concludes sociologist Nathan Glazer: "It's impossible to shut down something that has been this clearly established. The Supreme Court has made it clear that you can take race and sex into account in employment decisions, and there's nothing anyone can do about it."

Charlotte Low Allen

CHAPTER 10

*Practically unnoticed in the immigration
reform efforts of the late 1980s was a
congressional attempt to change the rules
on legal immigration. Two proposals, as
this September 5, 1988, article reported,
would have admitted more newcomers
based on skills and education while still
preserving current law, which has favored
those with relatives in the United States.
Supporters of the plan, which is used by
other countries, said skilled immigrants
would help boost the U.S. economy.*

GIVE ME YOUR SKILLED, YOUR ERUDITE

A Peruvian geochemist, fluent in English, spent two years and
several thousand dollars in attorneys' fees to gain legal immigrant status in the United States. He had no relatives here,
and although he finally gained admission, he emerged disillusioned.
Says his American wife, whom out of principle he married only after
getting his green card, "I don't think it's fair that we've got people
who are uneducated, illiterate, who don't speak English who can get
into this country and can bring in their families, when these people
can't."

Though it has received scant attention next to the landmark Immigration Reform and Control Act of 1986, which aimed to stop illegal
immigration, an effort is under way in Congress to change the rules
on legal immigration. Two new proposals would move the apparatus
slightly toward admitting more people on the basis of the skills and
education they bring with them, as opposed to kinship with people
in the United States.

The current system, established in 1965, is grounded on the principle of family reunification, giving heavy preference to those who
have relatives already in the United States. Some experts contend
the system unintentionally favors the low-skilled and uneducated

over the highly skilled, highly educated immigrant. In 1986 less than 4 percent of the 601,708 legal immigrants to the United States were granted entry on the basis of their ability to contribute to the economy, the so-called occupational-preference categories.

Of those 23,162 immigrants, 11,763 came as "professional or highly skilled" workers; the other 11,399 came as "needed skilled or unskilled" workers. They brought with them 30,463 spouses and children. These people are widely recognized as an important source of scientists, engineers, doctors, nurses, academics and other professionals. Many initially reach the United States attending graduate schools.

Aside from 104,383 refugees, the remaining 443,700 legal immigrants were admitted on the basis of their kinship to either a U.S. citizen or a permanent resident alien. Barry Chiswick, head of the economics department of the University of Illinois at Chicago and an expert on immigration, says this kinship system is a kind of "official nepotism" that "creates real inequities among potential visa applicants and undermines the potential value of immigration for bolstering U.S. productivity."

While no one calls for abandoning the principle of family reunification, many agree that U.S. policy should move toward something more akin to the "point systems" used by the three other major immigrant-receiving countries, Canada, Australia and New Zealand. The United States, which accepts by far the largest share of the world's immigrants, is the only one that bases admission primarily on family ties. By contrast, the point systems used by these other nations favor those who possess such attributes as education and work skills and an ability to speak English, giving less consideration to an applicant's having a relative in the country. About half of Australia's immigrants last year, for example, were admitted on economic grounds, only 30 percent as relatives of citizens.

A bill passed in March in the Senate, sponsored by Massachusetts Democrat Edward M. Kennedy and Wyoming Republican Alan K. Simpson, would establish a similar point system for 50,000 new slots to be added to the quotas for legal immigration. These slots would bypass the cumbersome process of individual certification by the Department of Labor, which requires an employer to prove that no American can fill the job going to an immigrant. Another 5,000 slots would be available to people willing to invest at least $1 million in the country and create 10 new jobs. The change does not, however, constitute a major increase in admissions and leaves intact the cornerstone policy of family reunification. Another bill, sponsored in the

House by New Jersey Democrat Peter W. Rodino Jr., contains a similar provision, but it more strongly reaffirms family preferences.

The current system was established by the 1965 Immigration and Nationality Act, which over the past two decades has shaped a surge in U.S. immigration that rivals the waves of the turn of the century. The act abolished national-origin quotas that had favored migrants from Europe, and it made family ties the primary basis for admission. While heralded as being fairer toward non-European immigrants, it was nonetheless widely believed at the time that the law would continue to favor Europeans. The idea was that through family reunification, U.S. citizens would bring in their primarily European relatives.

The effect was precisely the opposite: European immigration withered, while that of Latin Americans and Asians swelled. By 1965, U.S. blood relations with Europe had grown faint, leaving few immediate family ties on which to base entry to the country. Economic growth in Europe also had eroded the desire to leave such countries as Italy and Ireland. (African immigration remained minuscule; the national origin quotas had long blocked Africans, and few came under the 1965 act, because not since the days of slavery had there been the close kinship ties needed to gain admission.) In contrast, the 1965 act helped set off chain migrations from Latin America and Asia, as newly admitted immigrants began bringing in their relatives.

Making family reunification the basis of admission while ignoring a person's skills has established an unintended bias toward less educated migrants, says Chiswick, because the average skill level in many of the immigrants' countries is low.

"I don't think it was a conscious policy to favor unskilled workers and therefore make it difficult for skilled workers to come in," he says. "But I think the consequence of the policy has been to make it as easy or as difficult for low-skilled as for high-skilled workers to immigrate. By being neutral with respect to skill, what we get is primarily, from particular countries, low-skilled immigrants, and overall the skill level of the immigrants is lower than it would be if we had a policy that placed much more emphasis on the characteristics of the individual and what that individual could contribute to the American economy."

In a study for the National Bureau of Economic Research in Cambridge, Mass., immigration economist George Borjas says: "The 1965 amendments de-emphasized skills and occupational characteristics as a determinant of visa allocation . . . and made family reunification the main goal of immigration policy. . . . There is strong evidence that the major shift in the law in 1965 had some unforeseen consequences: post-1965 immigrants do not perform as well in the labor market as the earlier waves did."

The 1980 census, for example, showed that two-thirds of Mexican immigrants residing in Los Angeles County had less than ninth-grade educations. While the family reunification system does draw many skilled, educated workers, the bias of the policy is in the other direction.

Completely unforeseen in 1965 was the explosive growth of immigration from Asia. In preliminary discussion, Attorney General Robert F. Kennedy predicted that the act would draw 5,000 immigrants from Asia in the first year but said, "We do not expect that there would be any great influx after that." U.S. policy had for decades excluded Asian immigrants by various devices, from the Chinese Exclusion Act of 1882 to the 1924 national origins quotas. Consequently very few Asians had close relatives in the United States. But precisely because Asians could not gain admission through family reunification, the new immigrants applied under the 1965 act through the limited occupational-preference categories.

This planted a seed migration of highly talented immigrants; once established, they brought in family members through the reunification provisions. These family members tended to be highly educated as well. Today, Asians constitute roughly 40 percent of all those migrating to the United States. "One of the great ironies of the 1965 act is that this produced the most highly skilled set of immigrants in our nation's history," even though many assumed it would exclude Asians, says Kevin McCarthy, an immigration expert with the Rand Corp.

As the family provisions have begun to account for a greater share of Asian immigration, however, skill levels have begun to sink back toward the average of the population. "With the passage of time, the kinship relationship to the initial migrant gets more and more distant," says Chiswick. "So now we can have the siblings of the spouse of a sibling of somebody who was originally an occupational-preference recipient. If the seed migration idea seems to work, as demonstrated by the Asian experience, then I think it would work even better if that were the primary avenue for migration."

Prakash Sethi, associate director of the Center for Management at Baruch College of the City University of New York, recently surveyed high-skilled Indian migrants who settled in the United States in the past 15 to 20 years. He found that they outearn the average American household by 5-to-1, and 85 percent hold medical, academic, scientific or managerial positions. Increasing numbers of newer Indian immigrants are, however, "poor, generally unskilled, drawn to America mostly by what they may have heard from or about their distant successful relatives," according to Sethi.

Rand's McCarthy believes an admissions system that took into account labor market qualifications would "without question" have a positive effect. "Certainly in terms of the characteristics of the immigrants — that is, skill levels, education, language ability, certainly in terms of how well they've done in the country — I think you'd be hard-pressed" to say it would not have such an effect.

Chiswick argues that a point system also would be more fair than the current law. "Here's a government policy which tells people that how the government is going to treat you is not based on who you are, but who you happen to be related to, an accident of birth," he says. "Nowhere else in public policy do we have this kind of attitude. And as a matter of fact, much of what we like to think of as the progress America has made over the past number of decades is in viewing and evaluating people on the basis of who they are, not who they happen to be descended from."

Many ethnic and religious organizations, however, strongly prefer the reunification policy over a skill-based system. "That does not mean per se opposition to the seed immigration concept," says Dale Richard Swartz, president of the National Immigration, Refugee and Citizenship Forum, a coalition of 5,000 ethnic, religious and civil rights organizations. "The problem is when the new-seed concept eats into the family system," that is, diverts slots toward the skill-preference categories and away from the family categories. He maintains that family preference immigrants do bring skills. "It's not as if they're coming in with no skills," he says. "They're not blank faces."

Many studies have shown that an influx of even low-skilled workers has generally been beneficial to the economy. The Urban Institute and the Rand Corp. found positive effects overall from Mexican immigration to Los Angeles County, where legal and illegal immigration is heavily concentrated. The newcomers do not take jobs away from natives, as is often believed, but instead create them. Thomas Espenshade, a senior fellow at the Urban Institute, says, however, shifting to a point system "would tend to accentuate the positive economic effects of immigration."

Chiswick argues that such a policy need not abandon family reunification. "Nobody is talking about separating husband from wife, and nobody's talking about separating parents from minor children," he says. "Anybody who brings up those issues is bringing up a red herring." Immediate family members of those with skills could be automatically admitted; points could be awarded for other family ties. And, Chiswick argues, family members in the United States could provide help for education or job training, for instance, that would help a relative meet a skill test. He says a point system could be "really a very compassionate, pro-family policy."

He also argues that immigrants often voluntarily break up the family by immigrating. "There's quite a bit of gall involved in pleading the need for family reunification on the part of a person who voluntarily is responsible" for separating his family.

And unlike in decades past, Chiswick contends, immigration no longer necessarily entails permanent, gut-wrenching separations from one's family; jet travel and the telephone have made communication and visits comparatively cheap and fast, undermining the urgency of a family preference policy.

Patrick Burns, assistant director of the Federation for American Immigration Reform, a group that seeks to limit immigration, thinks ethnic groups favor family reunification as a means to admit more of their own numbers. "We have the Mexican American Legal Defense and Educational Fund pressing for special dispensation for Mexico," he says. "We see the Congressional Black Caucus pressing for special dispensation for Haitian immigrants. We see the Cubans pushing for special dispensation for Cuban immigrants. We see Senator Kennedy pushing for special dispensation for the Irish. We have seen a classic example, Congressman Peter Rodino, extremely concerned about Italian migration. We've seen [Senator] Barbara Mikulski from Maryland introduce legislation designed to give special amnesty to Polish illegal aliens. Often when I see congressmen interested in immigration legislation, it's to benefit an ethnic group of which they happen to be a part."

Some observers point out that while the current system scrutinizes the labor market impact of the less than 4 percent of immigrants who enter the country under the occupational preferences, using a cumbersome government certification process, it assumes no labor market impact from the vast majority of immigrants who enter under the family preferences. One observer calls it a convenient fiction that helps avoid larger questions about the economic and social role immigration should play, "the sort of basic questions about who we really want to come into the country."

The urgency of such questions promises only to rise with time. David Lewin, professor of business at Columbia University, believes the United States has already entered an extended period of serious labor shortages caused by a combination of strong demand from business and declining numbers of workers born after the baby boom. In such a climate, he says, immigration "is extremely important. We know that immigration is by no means merely low-skilled workers who take jobs in fields and light manufacturing. It includes a substantial proportion of people who go into scientific fields such as engineering, computer science, chemistry and physics, mathematics, business administration. The data on graduates of these programs in the United States show that very clearly."

Strikingly, he says, more than half of the people who received bachelor's degrees in engineering in the past four years from American colleges and universities were not U.S. citizens.

Carolyn Lochhead

PART 4

IMAGES OF
RICH AND POOR

HOMETOWNS COME IN ALL SHAPES AND SIZES

BRIG CABE

Main Street in America has many personalities, from the cavernous Louisiana Avenue in Houston (preceding page), to the commercial strips of suburban Atlanta (above), and the barber shops (right) and local churches (opposite) of Bristol, Pennsylvania.

JON A. REMBOLD

122

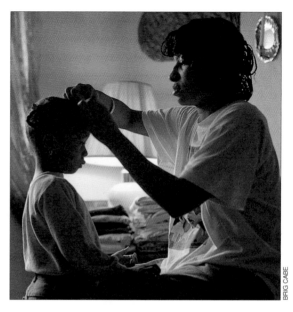

BRIG CABE

DOWN AND OUT AND
DOWN ON THE FARM

BRIG CABE

BRIG CABE

*The varied texture of American society,
urban and rural, included the single
mother on welfare caring for a child (top,
opposite), the farmer hard pressed but
determined to stay close to the land
(bottom, opposite) and the homeless, who
lived a life of poverty amid plenty (above).*

JON A. REMBOLD

The 20th century may be remembered as the era of regulation, despite conservative efforts to set businesses free. Congress, presidents, the courts and statehouses were embroiled in controversy over affirmative action (left), immigration reform (below) and handicapped rights (opposite).

GOOD AND BAD RULES, ALWAYS MORE RULES

RICHARD KOZAK

DENNIS BUDD GRAY

WEALTH AND POVERTY WITH AN ASIAN FACE

The work ethic was alive and well in much of Asia. The Hong Kong Stock Exchange (right) buzzed with activity, and prosperity enriched family life (above) in Japan. But industrialized Asia also began to pay a price for its good fortune, with workers (opposite) running ever faster to make a yen.

MILTON C. TOBY

128

BRIG CABE

Most of Southeast Asia has failed to keep pace with the continent. War still raged in Cambodia, producing a steady stream of refugees (left and below). Many Thai villagers were still dependent on the drug trade. The opium produced in their poppy fields (top, opposite) was often shipped through Hong Kong's port (bottom, opposite).

BRIG CABE

BRIG CABE

BRIG CABE

A demoralized, socialized Britain fell under Margaret Thatcher's spell and again became a dynamic nation (right). Her critics, however, never let up, from union members raising a strike fund at a Glasgow shipyard (below) to the IRA artists in Belfast (opposite).

THE FALL AND RISE OF MAGGIE'S ISLANDS

CATHALEEN CURTISS

BARE NECESSITIES IN THE LAND OF THE BEAR

CATHALEEN CURTISS

In the land where Lenin made communism a religion, a crisis of faith set in. The Soviet Union began a struggle to revitalize its economic life, but Moscow's famous onion domes (above) overlooked a nation in shambles, where the ordinary citizen played a perpetual waiting game to find scarce goods (right) as bureaucrats and soldiers (opposite) adapted to changed roles.

BRIG CABE

THE LITTLE GERMANY THAT COULDN'T

As the Soviet system staggered, its client system in East Germany fell. While slogans on buildings (right) long trumpeted the "other" Germany as a free state, the reality was soldiers (above) and Stasi, the secret police, until the Berlin Wall (opposite) crumbled under the weight of East German aspirations.

BRIG CABE

Chancellor Helmut Kohl's (left) West Germany maintained a strong defense (top, opposite) and an industrial-agricultural machine (below and bottom, opposite) that could absorb its impoverished East German countrymen.

BRIG CABE

THE BIG GERMANY
THAT COULD AND DID

BRIG CABE

BRIG CABE

BRIG CABE

RUTH FREMSON

OUT FROM UNDER
THE SOVIET HEEL

BRIG CABE

BRIG CABE

CATHALEEN CURTISS

As the Soviets packed to leave, Eastern Europe pondered its past, present and future. In Prague (top, opposite) there were honors for those who suffered under communist rule. In Hungary (bottom, opposite) people went back to work. And in Poland farmers tilled depleted land (above) to provide food (below) for a country in desperate straits.

CATHALEEN CURTISS

A STRUGGLE TO SURVIVE AS APARTHEID CRUMBLES

As black South Africans fought for an end to apartheid, they also struggled to eke out a living. They worked in mines and orchards (opposite), often with multiracial managements, and they ran small businesses such as general stores in the black townships (above).

RICHARD KOZAK

South African scenes included nannies with their white charges in city parks (above) and black shoppers at the windows of stores where they long were forbidden to shop (below). The South African regime, meanwhile, supported the UNITA rebel movement of nearby Angola's Jonas Savimbi (opposite).

RICHARD KOZAK

RICHARD KOZAK

DEVELOPMENTAL MUSIC
WITH A LATIN BEAT

Conditions in the Latin nations were as varied as their cultures, leaders and systems. Seed money to establish small businesses (opposite and above) gave new hope to Bolivia's peasantry, while Nicaraguans searched trash (right) for food following the Sandinista economic debacle.

RICHARD KOZAK

RICHARD KOZAK

Brazil was the largest and potentially richest of Latin America's countries, and one of the top 10 industrial nations of the world. Its vast natural resources provided the basis for a mining industry (opposite) and the wealth to create the urban skyline of Sao Paulo (left). It also witnessed an upsurge in the practice of Protestantism (below) on a largely Catholic continent.

BRIG CABE

PART 5

OLD FRIENDS

CHAPTER 11

*The dream of a united Europe is an
ancient one, surviving through centuries
punctuated by war and tempered by the
persistence of national differences. And
though the dream outlasted two World
Wars and a Cold War in the 20th century,
so too did the old prejudices, as described
in this article of June 20, 1988.*

A STATE OF ONENESS FOR WESTERN EUROPE

The 12 countries that constitute the European Community have been to war twice in this century and went to war like clockwork in centuries past. Nations as close to each other as New York and New Jersey harbor age-old resentments and nurture stereotypes — snobbish Brits, arrogant Frenchmen, boorish Germans — that belie their postwar sophistication.

Come Dec. 31, 1992, though — if all goes according to plan of European Commission President Jacques Delors — all barriers to trade, migration and capital among the members of the European Community will be abolished. In each phase of life — education, marriage, work, retirement — Europeans will face new opportunities and embrace new options. Political, military and cultural cooperation will soon follow, and never again will Europe see the ravages of the past. Amen.

The original idea behind the European Coal and Steel Community, the predecessor to today's European Community, was the creation of a Europe without national rivalries. The community was to turn on an axis of Franco-German cooperation, an idea so unprecedented in recent history that Jean Monnet, the father of the EC, hesitated in taking the giant step of creating the community for several years. Only in 1967 did the executive of the Coal and Steel Community merge with the European Economic Community and the European Atomic Energy Community to create one commission, what is now the EC.

Monnet's unwillingness to jump right into full cooperation while Europe was at the pinnacle of war-weariness is looked at askance today, but the continued amazement Europeans show at Franco-German military cooperation — only a recent development — highlights just how slowly national rivalries fade. Supranational forces such as today's European Parliament (the community's legislative body), the Council of Ministers (the decision making body) and European Court of Justice (the judicial branch) may well have been too much for a continent still recovering from the German Reich. Only as that specter faded could Europeans relinquish authority to a strong central power.

But, in an ironic twist, now that the countries of the community are realizing Monnet's postwar vision for a united Western Europe, the realities are changing, and Soviet leader Mikhail Gorbachev's policies of *glasnost* and *perestroika* are the wild cards. As the new openness seeps from the Soviet Union, the other Europe — the Eastern bloc — looms as a potential magnet to its Western neighbors. A comparatively underdeveloped but more open East could be a tempting market for Western European countries still suffering from a technological inferiority complex vis-a-vis Japan and the United States. These are the forces that counter the postwar imperative for a single European Community and may tempt its members to splinter.

The centripetal force that remains, however, is the threat of decline, a feeling that united they stand and divided they fall, to be crushed under the great political feet of the United States and the Soviet Union, under the economic feet of Japan. The minuet danced between the United States and the Soviet Union over intermediate-range nuclear weapons has brought even more urgency to Europe's quest for greater self-sufficiency. Etienne Reuter, aide to Lord Cockfield, European commissioner for the internal market, echoes the resolutely hopeful tone heard in the halls of the Berlayment, the headquarters of the community in Brussels: "I think it's going to work, and I think it's absolutely indispensable. If not, we will fragment and have no say in the world."

Businessmen don't need to be told twice. "Europe at the business level is consolidating itself for sheer pragmatic reasons," says Diana Pinto, a Paris-based cultural historian. "If you want to fight Japan, you've got to have a solid base here." The process of creating that solid base has meant a growing Euromanagement class for which movement throughout the community is becoming second nature.

But prejudices die hard, and governments are as loath as their citizens to relinquish old ideas just because some bureaucrat in Brussels thinks they ought to. And though Europeans' thinking has changed over the years, especially regarding political cooperation, some things will never change. A joke told 31 years ago, at the founding of the community, is still popular: Who is the perfect Eurocrat? Someone with the modesty of a Frenchman, the discipline of an Italian, the charm of a German, the imagination of a Belgian, the generosity of a Dutchman and the culture of a Luxembourger. Add six countries and the joke still gets a laugh. Sic transit gloria Europae.

Many Europeans cherish pejorative nicknames for their neighbors: Luxembourgers still call Germans Prussians, says Luxembourger Reuter. The British like "bubble and squeak" (oily leftovers) — cockney rhyming slang for the Greeks. The French like to tell "dumb Belgian" jokes, the Belgians like to tell "conceited Frenchman" jokes and the British are butts for their alleged insularity. After all, it was The Times of London that supposedly ran the headline "Fog Over Channel; Continent Isolated." And it was Prime Minister Margaret Thatcher of Britain who in an angry moment retorted to then-Prime Minister Jacques Chirac of France that "only a Frenchman could say that."

Even within the Berlayment there remains more than a trace of skepticism about the man in the street's enthusiasm for one Europe. "Coming closer to 1992 there are certainly reactions that could be labeled as archaic, nationalistic," says Carlo Ripa di Meana, the European Community's commissioner for culture. Almost all Europeans accept the rationale behind the single market and the abolition of internal frontiers, but the ramifications — free movement of labor, shared social programs, new and strange tax systems, shared professional standards — are far less understood, and consequently less popular.

The man who prefers to buy "pure British milk," as the signs in England's supermarkets say, is not the man who will easily accept a French or Greek lawyer, should one establish himself in London. Neither is the French farmer who went and burned Spanish trucks carrying early strawberries — over which the south of France had enjoyed a monopoly before the Spanish accession in 1986 — likely to be an enthusiastic one-Europer. For mid- and lower-level workers and small companies, the European single market of 320 million people is also a threat. According to Pinto, these are the people who feel they may be swallowed up, the foot-draggers in the march on 1992 for whom jingoism, as opposed to patriotism, is a refuge from integration.

When Europeans are asked what the community has brought them, they usually cite, with muted enthusiasm, a wider choice of products on the supermarket shelf or the availability of Italian cappuccino in London. And those good, cheap strawberries from Spain, which are a widespread symbol of an open market to many Europeans. Leon Hurwitz, author of a forthcoming book on the community, notes that those strawberries are a poignant image for many people: "Were the EC to disappear tomorrow," he writes, "and a competition held to select the epitaph, . . . a sure winner would be 'cheap strawberries.'"

Still, many emphasize that 31 years in European history is a very short time to understand an entirely new animal and to forget hundreds of years of cultural and political nationalism. Says Jacques Medecin, the mayor Nice, France: "In December of 1492 Europe discovered America, and 500 years later Europe must still discover itself."

A WEB OF SELF-INTEREST

The vision of a united Europe has inspired conquerors and reformers — Napoleons and Metternichs — for well over 1,000 years. In the post-World War II era their crusade has been taken over by economists like Jean Monnet, the father of the European Economic Community, and, more recently, Jacques Delors, president of the European Commission, whose maneuverings started the clock ticking down to one market in 1992.

With hardly a murmur of dissent, the governments of Western Europe have bought into a vision that requires them to drop their national economic defenses and subject their voters to direct competition with 320 million other Europeans in a single, continentwide marketplace. Where the legions of Napoleon and Hitler's tanks failed, the economists have triumphed, rallying the soon-to be-vanquished to a willing surrender under the banner of economic self-interest.

Among the inhabitants of the urban centers of Europe, unification is as sure as tomorrow's sunrise. "It's already happening," says a Portuguese cabdriver working the streets of Brussels.

The sentiment is echoed by thousands of like-minded souls in Paris, London, Frankfurt, Madrid and a dozen other cities where, for purposes of culture, trade and finance, Europe is already one. The European Community's citizens share a passport and a separate line at the Continent's airports. Many can save at banks in each others' countries and attend each others' universities.

Eurocrats, as the cadres of the growing international bureaucracy are called, radiate a faith that Europatriotism will prevail over deep and lingering cultural and national antipathies. To them, these ancient loyalties are the cobwebs of the past, to be swept aside by the ineluctable march of history. Why? Because there is no satisfactory alternative to European unity, says Carlo Ripa di Meana, the community's commissioner for information, cultural affairs and tourism. "We have to feel that we are all in the same boat, whether British, French or German," he continues. "Otherwise, we will always be pawns in the hands of the Soviets or in the friendly hands of Americans. We understand that if we do not have a European dimension, we can only become a museum of ourselves."

But only a minority of Europeans live in the cosmopolitan business centers where such sentiments are routinely and unquestioningly affirmed. What about the millions who still live in villages and provincial towns, who make their living far from immediate contact with the bustle of the world economy, where the ancient identities have not been eroded by global commerce? Observers already see a growing divide between those who are "Europeanized," who are already living the 1992 dream, and those who feel no part of One Europe. "We risk an increasing polarization in European societies," says Loukas Tsoukalis, a professor of European studies at Oxford University. "There is a large part of society that remains in its little village, insular."

Tsoukalis cities the example of Belgium, "probably the country that is the most European of the lot, with an elite that takes Europe for granted." Last year the Belgians — who are divided into French and Flemish-speaking populations — watched their government fall over a language dispute in a small town, a clue to the depth of feeling that still animates voters when questions of cultural identity are at stake. Indeed, side by side with the emerging consensus on unification since World War II has been the rise of numerous separatist movements, representing a bloody reaction against the forces of cultural homogenization.

A milder version of these sentiments has surfaced in the mainstream politics of the nation that, more than the others, has trumpeted the cause of European cooperation. In the recent French elections, Jean-Marie Le Pen and his National Front won 14 percent of the vote nationwide with the slogan "France for the French." In some regions he won upwards of 30 percent.

The Le Pen movement has opened a Pandora's box of ambivalent emotions, echoes of which are being heard all around Europe. In Marseilles, where Le Pen won 30 percent, his success was attributed to resentment against the huge number of newly arrived North African residents. But what about Alsace, which has no such "problem"? "People asked how Alsace could have gone with Le Pen," says Diana Pinto, a Paris-based cultural historian. "One of the answers was that it is on the border [with West Germany], and the people were terrified by the specter of 1992 and an open market. They went with someone who talked about national identity."

The disturbing lesson from Le Pen's strong showing, as far as 1992 is concerned, is the success of a platform based on xenophobia. Many believe that such antagonisms may become epidemic as certain regions or groups feel their traditional livelihoods threatened. This could invite a new political movement based on rejection of the European ideal. "The risk is, as Europe becomes more integrated, there may be groups of people in different countries who will see nationalism as a defense of the status quo," says Tsoukalis.

One of the thorniest questions facing the community is that of Turkish membership. With European Community headquarters in Brussels hovering on the brink (next year) of a decision to allow Turkey's application to proceed, all of the bugaboos of cultural hostility and economic insecurity are surfacing. Since its rapid expansion in the 1960s and 1970s, the Common Market has relied on a large influx of low-paid Turkish laborers to man the brooms and factory machines. But when Turkey applied for full membership last year, the request was met with hysteria in many quarters, especially Britain. Lord Bethell, a British member of the European Parliament, called the free movement decision "sheer madness" and described full Turkish membership as a "great peril to Western Europe's political and economic hopes."

Part of the objection is purely financial; members do not want populous and impoverished Turkey to soak up a big share of the community's social welfare budget. But many Europeans fear a new influx of Turks for reasons that have as much to do with religion and culture as jobs and housing. Like the North African countries that provide fodder for Le Pen, Turkey is a Muslim nation. Furthermore, like the North Africans, the Turks have a high birthrate, something that frightens the none-too-procreative Europeans who have witnessed the Levantinization of many of their towns and neighborhoods, says Ripa di Meana.

The experience has many convinced that the African invaders have no interest in being assimilated. Indeed, it often seems that way;

there are Muslim ghettos around many of Europe's capitals.

Many Europeans argue that the Turks, like the North Africans, are a special case because of their distinctly alien heritage and appearance. But Alfred Grosser, a professor at Paris's Institute of Political Studies, believes that they are just the latest victims of the resentment that Europeans have traditionally harbored toward foreign job seekers. At the start of the century the Italians of the chronically poor southern half of Italy were accorded sometimes violent receptions when they arrived in France and Belgium. The *Gastarbeiter,* or guest workers, who flooded the industrial regions of Northern Europe from Italy, Spain and Portugal in the 1960s brought forth a wave of resentment, even though they were welcomed by many employers. "At the end of the 19th century there were real pogroms against the Italians in southern France," says Grosser. "Now people say it is because [the new immigrants] are Muslims, and not Catholic, that they are not accepted. That is entirely untrue, as there have been mass xenophobic movements in France in the last and this century."

Others believe that fear of economic competition from foreigners is not limited to just laborers. One diplomat describes the fears expressed by professionals all along Europe's Mediterranean coast: "They think that British or German professionals will come down, enjoy the warm weather and steal all the tourists away from French doctors and lawyers." According to John Morley, head of the EC's employment policy division, these fears are justified, since foreign travelers frequently express a preference for being attended to by professionals of their own nationality.

Such concerns are another reason that the open labor market of 1992 may prove less than porous in practice. Professionals, the class of workers whose education and urbanity should make them the most likely to move around in an open Europe, have shown a marked preference for staying put. A 1985 survey suggested that there was surprisingly little movement of salaried workers among the various countries of the community. More than half of the foreigners holding salaried jobs were found to be from outside of the Common Market entirely. Given the difficulty that all other foreigners have in obtaining work permits in Europe, this is a feeble testament to labor integration.

In a study done on the migration of physicians within the European Community, Dr. Leon Hurwitz, author of a forthcoming book on the subject, describes a basic cultural intolerance. He surveyed a group of Belgian and French doctors. "All the Belgians are anti-

French," said one of the latter, in a comment Hurwitz found typical. Conversely, the Belgian doctors uttered sentiments like "all the French are anti-Belgian," "the French don't like foreigners" and "we Anglo-Saxons simply don't fit in with these Europeans." These findings suggest that trepidation about this selfsame intolerance is what keeps many people from moving at all.

The other side of the coin is an attachment to place, kith and kin that makes many professionals reluctant to try their luck elsewhere. Paul Taylor, a senior lecturer in international relations at the London School of Economics, says that the ideal of an efficient labor market will have to contend with a predilection for familiar scenes. Only when the economic gains greatly outweigh the separation anxiety will people be likely to uproot themselves.

Perhaps for these reasons programs to facilitate employment exchange have been mostly a flop. SEDOC, a communitywide service created to circulate information about job availability, lapsed into a near coma soon after its birth in 1968. Morley, responsible at the EC for its operations, does not remember what its initials stand for. "It's largely a bit of bureaucracy used by countries who really want to hire third-country labor but have to go through this formality to offer a job outside," he says. Lately, however, there has been renewed interest in SEDOC (which stands for System of Exchange and Documentation), as part of a long overdue effort to prove that there is something in integration for the man in the street.

Without such an effort, says Claude Cheysson, an EC commissioner and former French foreign minister, "there will be no 1992. The whole process will be blocked if there is no progress in the fields other than the single market" for corporate providers of goods and services. A recent stab in that direction was a 1984 committee on the "People's Europe." It was aimed at finding unifying cultural symbols to convince Europeans that there was more to integration than just big business. But its efforts on this front — among others, promoting a European flag, anthem and passport — have done little to win hearts and minds. And with cultural affairs getting less than 1 percent of the EC budget, little will change.

Ripa di Meana, whose job is to help stir up pan-European patriotism, has taken the trickle-down approach. He believes the proper note to pluck is the "humanistic common background" of Europeans. Predictably, such projects as the creation of a European Youth Orchestra and university exchange programs have changed the lives of few Europeans.

"Personally, I do not feel European at all," says Jean Tardito,

Communist mayor of the town of Aubagne, 8 miles east of Marseilles. "Sometimes I don't even feel French. This is where I am from — Provence." And he is far from alone, especially in the feeling that "the European Community is a community of capitals, of the interests of capital cities. The people who live in the member nations do not profit from this community."

Even defenders of the community ideal admit they have done a poor job of selling the broader public on integration. Etienne Reuter, an aide to Lord Cockfield, the commissioner for the internal market, says the strategy has not been to teach Europeans to crave each other's company but simply to convince them that a single market will put more money in their pockets. "I don't think the member states see Jacques Delors in the role of preacher, bringing understanding between the people," he says.

Despite the relative sophistication of the average European, stereotyping still enjoys a great popularity. Many Europeans judge each other by the figure they cut as tourists, which is seldom very flattering. "The British en masse on holiday — they drink too much and ask for fish and chips," says Britisher Morley. "And the Germans on the ski slopes — pushy and aggressive." Even Grosser, a believer in the success of cultural integration, shares in the common wisdom that "the British and German tourists, they are awful." Attitudes like these are hardly likely to be softened when Europeans find themselves competing side by side for jobs and professional advancement. Tardito predicts "bread will be taken from our mouths."

Ironically, one of the mainstays of EC activity is funding for regional development programs that encourage the unemployed to stick around rather than seek the jobs and opportunities that a wider Europe has to offer. "The February agreement to double the size of [the community's] social and regional funds is mostly to the benefit of the southern countries," says Taylor. "This is a policy exactly counter to people running around Europe in search of jobs." The regional grants do, however, serve as useful bribes to ward off what might otherwise be a nationalist backlash. The goal is to give backward areas a boost so they can attract labor and capital after 1992.

Even so, the kind of programs being developed can heighten the fears they are meant to soothe. Cheysson believes that many of Europe's decaying industrial regions should look to the growth of service industries for prosperity. But "less jobs in production, many more jobs in services" is not always what these people want, he says.

"Take our region," says Tardito. "It's power is as an open door to the sea, maritime commerce and ship construction. In Brussels they decided to close down the shipbuilding plants and no longer use the coal from our mines here. And what are they giving us instead? Europe up there is going to transform us — because they looked at the map and decided our region is very pretty — into a tourist paradise." Tardito, along with many other mayors of similar small towns across Europe, is furious. "And our workers," he asks, "what will they become? Luggage porters in hotels?"

A perennial dilemma for the One Europe advocates is that such people vote in national elections. Knowing which side their bread is buttered on, national governments look to the interest of their citizens before they look to the interests of Europe. "National political systems naturally reward a very different type of person" than the ideal Euroleader, says Tsoukalis. "The leader must be in the country all the time, and his international vision is not rewarded. On the contrary."

Politicians in different countries straddle this fence differently. Britain's Margaret Thatcher has assured her compatriots that "being good Europeans does not prevent us from standing up for British interests." Such strains are music to the ears of millions Britons who still cherish their country's separateness from the intrigues of the Continent. But for many others they are a disturbing reminder of the rebuke they received from France's Charles de Gaulle when they changed their minds and belatedly tried to climb aboard the Common Market in 1961.

Thatcher must balance the fear of not keeping up with the Joneses on the Continent with the desire to keep the Joneses and their continental ways out of Britain. A very different dilemma plagues the West Germans. "After the war, the generation in power could not be proud of Germany," says Wolfgang Stock, a West German journalist. "It was an obvious choice to be very pro-European." Yet the West Germans have also been bashful about asserting the leadership that is naturally theirs as the economic superpower of Europe. Also, many West Germans believe, once they lead Europe they lose any chance at reunification with East Germany.

West Germany's ambivalence has deep roots. "The ghost of Hitler is still around, so Germany refuses to take a leadership role," says Stock. That has opened the door for regional politicians in West Germany to become a powerful lobbying force in Brussels. By nature, their interests are narrow. Because of West German diffidence and British ambivalence, France, with its strong central government, is the kingpin of the community. (De Gaulle once said the unification of Europe would be performed by France and Germany, " France being the coachman and Germany the horse.") Not surprisingly, then, it is an enthusiast for integration, knowing that the pace and direction can largely be managed to benefit La Belle France. For most of the Continent's bureaucrats, an assignment to Brussels is considered a death knell. For the French, it is a choice posting. Even so, as the Le Pen phenomenon suggests, the French have their share of foot-draggers.

Then there is the host of smaller countries, all of which blow hot and cold from one day to the next, depending on the political temperature of the electorate. The Danish government, which has seen crisis after crisis of late (it has had up to 12 parties represented in its legislature), is "a dangerous little group right now, because they're very confused and not quite keen on being European," says historian Pinto. Italians, it is said, love the EC because their own government is so frequently in disarray. All this makes for confusing politics for Brussels. "There are real pressures on governments to work closely together," says Taylor, "and often you find them making what appear to be concessions. But when you look closely, those concessions too often disappear."

A classic example of a policy that vanishes when looked at too closely is that of equal treatment of workers. The only restrictions that countries are allowed to impose are, reasonably enough, on civil servants. But wait. What constitutes a civil service job? "In a number of European countries being a teacher is a civil service job," says Taylor. "In some countries a senior hospital position is part of the civil service, and nonnationals are excluded."

Another way in which national pride interferes in the labor market is in the suppression of unfavorable statistics. Governments are, for example, loath to admit that their citizens might find the grass is greener on the other side of the border. Several governments put a stop to the publishing of emigration figures a few years ago for just this reason, says one EC official. On the other hand, the bureaucrats in Brussels perform a genuine service for the member governments by serving as scapegoats.

Says Etienne Davignon, a former EC commissioner and director of the Societe Generale de Belgique SA, one of Belgium's largest enterprises: "Governments are very shrewd in relation to European questions. When there's a popular idea they say, 'With great difficulty I was able to make the stupid people in Brussels do this.' When an idea is unpopular, they go to the public and say, 'Of course, we thought this was a bad idea, but we couldn't stop it from happening.' "

An example is the egregious Common Agricultural Policy, which sucks up more than two-thirds of the EC budget and in which millions of consumers and taxpayers subsidize a relative handful of farmers. When faced with complaints from home, not to speak of infamous mountains of butter and rivers of wine that have been overproduced, the governments blame greedy foreign farmers.

Sometimes these attitudes threaten to turn the European ideal into little more than a giant catfight, as governments vie for a bigger slice of the European pie. Delors once observed that national governments treat the community as a supermarket from which they can take what suits them, giving nothing in return. The thing that impresses many is that even after 31 years, the market shelves still get replenished. The EC may not be loved, but it has staying power.

INTEGRATION'S DARK SIDE

"The big companies have decided that this Europe thing is really going to happen, and they are pushing governments to complete the internal market," says John Morley, head of the European Community's employment policy division. "They're the ones who are saying: 'Why do we have to wait until 1992? Why can't we do it next week?'"

This "Europe thing" is a single market of 12 nations and some 320 million people, where the only trade barriers will be the ones separating West Europeans from the outside world, and where unfettered competition will reign supreme. A report by analyst Paolo Cecchini recently released by the European Commission, the community's executive body, forecast bigger, more efficient and more specialized companies as a result of the single market. The same study predicted that integration will boost the community's gross domestic product by 5 percent, create more than 2 million jobs and cut prices by 6 percent on average.

This is indeed a rosy picture, but only the best and the brightest — and many fear the biggest — companies will survive. That has prompted an unparalleled period of introspection among Europe's smaller firms. Many of them are family-owned, some are hundreds of years old, and they are wondering if this brave new world is their death sentence.

Likewise, despite the halcyon predictions of prosperity for all, the first stage of integration is more likely to bring pink slips than paychecks to many European workers, a fact that is only now being widely advertised. Weighed down by the fears of those near the middle and the bottom of the labor force, as well as by reluctance to cede political control to the Eurocrats in Brussels, headquarters of the European Community, the national governments are dragging their feet all the way to 1992.

Anxiety and anticipation are evident throughout the European Community. Business pages of every major newspaper harangue their readers with questionnaires, polls and analyses: "Will France be ready for 1992?"; "Can Italy cope?"; "Are we big enough?" Many industries, accustomed to eking out a happy existence behind protective regulatory barriers, are asking themselves whether they are destined to sink or swim in a free, competitive marketplace.

Large companies, such as the West German and French telecommunications giants Siemens AD and Alcatel SA, are confident about the future. So are Bayer AG and Montedison SpA, two of Europe's most efficient chemical companies, which have long been hobbled by the protectionism that is rife in their field. Where these companies were limited by their national borders, and consequently restricted in size because of antitrust regulation, they will be free to operate throughout the European Community and regard its 12 countries as their home market. For them, 1992 is a dream soon to come true. With an enthusiasm fed by the flood of American investment bankers who have descended on Europe with deal-making skills, companies have been sizing one another up as suitable targets for merger or acquisition.

The Europe of 1992, as envisioned by European Commission President Jacques Delors in 1985, should be one big happy economic family. People will move from France to Greece, from Greece to Denmark as freely as Americans move from New York to New Mexico. Goods and services will enjoy the same facility of movement. Banks in Athens will lend to clients in Rome, and insurance companies in Paris will cover homes and lives from Lisbon to Copenhagen. A Jaguar sold in Belgium will no longer cost three-quarters as much as one sold in Denmark. National standards, still used as nontariff barriers to foreign goods, will be brought into line. Or so say the powers that be in Brussels.

But resistance to change is high. Take for example the not-so-vital coordination of lawn mower noise standards, an issue only recently resolved after 13 years of intra-European grappling. The noise levels were not the only bone of contention; questions of how to measure the noise, what actually constitutes a lawn mower and other imponderables kept governments, corporations and gardeners at daggers drawn. Imagine, then, the troubles in store for Lord Cockfield, commissioner in charge of the internal market and vice president of the European Commission, when harmonization of more contentious issues such as auto emission standards becomes necessary.

In 1985 a white paper compiled by Lord Cockfield's office on the single market listed some 300 directives necessary to achieve a barrier-free Economic Community. Thus far, just over one-quarter of them have been agreed upon by the community's member nations. But the kind of resistance that countries are showing is prompting skepticism from many corners. "My attitude is one of having to be persuaded that 1992 is actually going to happen in 1992," says Michael Stallibrass, London-based head of mergers and acquisitions for Shearson Lehman Hutton International. "I have no doubt that it will happen at some stage, because everything is moving in that direction, but I'm not at all convinced that it will happen in 1992."

Many observers believe that national governments are less enthused than big business in gearing up for 1992. "If you leave the process at the government level, they will clog up the works," says Morley. "By the nature of the game they have something to defend." So, ironically, while larger companies are working against the traditional antagonisms that have existed between European nations — one will not find hesitation about buying a foreign product or using a foreign financial service if it is cheaper and better — governments move more lethargically to remove barriers to economic liberalization and throw their internal markets into the competitive fray.

Certain countries are more accessible than others and, not surprisingly, it is the countries with the most to protect that are the most protective. For instance, monopolies commissions and government ownership are used to block cross-border acquisitions in West Germany, Europe's biggest single market. Conversely, Spain or Italy put up no such barriers, according to one London banker, but "there's nothing of interest there," he says.

This stonewalling — and that is the distinct impression in Europe's corporate world — often elicits from frustrated businessmen expressions of prejudices that a united European Community would theoretically obliterate: "The German position is consistent with the German personality," complains the London banker. "They want to have everything their own way."

Owners and top-of-the-ladder executives have been Europeanized for many years. But at the lower and middle levels, managers are still quite provincial in their attitudes. These attitudes, more than anything else, threaten progress toward integration, economically and politically. To combat the problem, companies are starting to go out of their way to cultivate a new generation of mid-level Euromanagers, says Andrea Wine, director of the London office of TASA International, a head-hunting firm. "There's movement to mix up management among more mature European corporations: send a Spaniard to Germany, a German to Italy, etc., to speed up integration," she says.

Ironically, it is the Americans who have embraced the movement toward Euromanagement most enthusiastically. Many European companies, despite years of experience in an increasingly common market, have been much slower to climb aboard. Wine says this is because Americans, unlike their European counterparts, have fewer preconceived notions about national characteristics.

During the initial stages of continental expansion, in the mid-1960s, there was a distinct predilection on the part of the corporate leaders to make sure that their foreign subsidiaries were run by people of the same nationality as the mother company. The first big move away from this was local management, a sort of halfway house that was popular in the 1970s. A West German conglomerate, for example, would go out of its way to hire an Italian to run its operations in Italy. But the final leap has proved more difficult. The resistance has come from both above and below. Italian workers in a West German-owned office might accept a German boss, would welcome an Italian one, but are hardly ready to submit to a Spanish one. "A lot of the reason we don't see a lot of this mixing, aside from questions of implementation, is trust," says Wine. Trust between those of different nationalities "is still absent to such an extent that it winds up determining a lot of decisions."

And the bottom line? While the occupants of the executive suite in many of Europe's biggest companies talk like starry-eyed idealists about the glories of One Europe, quite different noises are being made by mid-level management and below. These people are "always the most difficult to move," acknowledges Etienne Davignon, a director of the Belgian holding company Societe Generale de Belgique SA. "In a certain sense these people have moved up as high as they ever will, and any change is a menace. This is where the level of resistance is always the strongest." These are the people whose jobs are at risk in the "rationalization" of European business.

The negative repercussions of a streamlined Europe have been largely ignored, except in the case of international hostile takeovers. In their candid moments, however, even the most ardent supports of a unified Europe admit that the road to integration is likely to be anything but smooth as far as Jean Q. Publique is concerned.

The promise of future growth, after all, is founded on a premise of immediate restructuring — the merging of companies, the elimination of redundant jobs and the lifting of barriers that protect uncompetitive industries. The force of change will be felt most heavily at the bottom of the pyramid, especially in companies that, because they existed in protected backwaters, were slower to reduce labor costs and increase investment in mechanization than companies that have been competing internationally for years.

"Companies try to take Europe at the level of capital, at the level of the management, not at the level of the labor force," says Claude Cheysson, community commissioner for Mediterranean policy and a former French foreign minister. "A Europe that would become too much a Europe of the traders and the bankers will give birth to very deep social and cultural reactions."

This feeling — that the single market is not enough, that the eradication of trade barriers alone will not unify Europe — is not rare. Indeed, there is every reason to fear a retreat into cultural nationalism, even xenophobia, on the part of the many individuals who, as the Cecchini report states, will face more unemployment as companies streamline for competition.

But the proponents of integration shrink from addressing the role of national governments, the obvious channel for every parochial, defensive and xenophobic impulse. Leaders are unwilling to relinquish sovereignty over their monetary policy, as in the case of Great Britain, or their foreign policy, as in the case of Greece, which refuses to sign off on any policy benefiting Turkey. Despite the brave talk of the Eurovisionaries, these governments will remain disruptive forces far into the future.

A homogenized Europe, all will agree, is not in the cards, not economically, not politically and not culturally. But that has not stopped almost all European companies from rushing headlong toward 1992, come what may. It's a feeling in the air, says Loukas Tsoukalis, professor of European studies at Oxford University. "There isn't a conference or a meeting without 1992 pegged on to the title."

Danielle Pletka

CHAPTER 12

From its birth in 1957, the European Community was an economic body. But it also harbored the potential of becoming a political institution. With progress toward economic unity in the late 1980s, power inevitably trickled from national capitals to Brussels, the community's headquarters. Out of power at home, socialists saw this as an opportunity to achieve social welfare goals through the European bureaucracy. Conservatives deplored the loss of sovereignty. This article was published June 19, 1989.

JUGGLING THE SCEPTER IN A UNIFIED EUROPE

Is a United States of Europe, with a central government and a single leader, about to become a reality? Few in the European Community's 12 member countries would argue that it is, but there are signs that, as the EC proceeds with its ambitious plan to dismantle all internal barriers to trade by the end of 1992, more and more decisions — from trade to environmental protection to foreign policy — are being made in the community's institutions in Brussels rather than in national capitals. The bureaucratic decision-making process has been speeded up and streamlined, and new proposals to broaden the EC's scope of action surface almost daily. All across Europe, national politicians are starting to feel the political ground shift under their feet — and are looking to Brussels as the new center of power.

The notion that economic integration would lead, sooner or later, to some kind of political integration has been around since the Treaty of Rome, the community's founding charter, was signed in 1957. But only in the past few years, as the group extricated itself from sticky disputes over the budget and agricultural policy and finally settled on a step-by-step plan for economic integration, has unification shifted into high gear. The expected benefits of the 1992 plan, which some economists predict will boost growth by 5 percent, have quickened pulse rates from Ireland to Greece, and the traditional apathy that most Europeans have felt for the community and its faceless bureaucracy is being shouldered aside by a wave of Euroenthusiasm. "The transfer of powers from the member states to Brussels is already quite far advanced," says Peter Ludlow, director of the Center for European Policy Studies in Brussels. "We're not talking about issues remote in the 1990s — we're already in it."

Signs that Brussels is becoming the Washington of Europe are multiplying. The EC bureaucracy's headquarters has become a favored site for political demonstrations, and visitors can barely turn around without bumping into one of the city's 20,000 lobbyists. Community institutions have taken on a new allure and are no longer considered a dumping ground for political has-beens — in fact, they have started to attract a new breed of power seekers who see Brussels as the up-and-coming center of political action. The spreading fame of Jacques Delors, France's finance minister before becoming president of the European Commission in 1985, has inspired others to forgo the national political stage in favor of the European one: Martin Bangemann, who gave up leadership of West Germany's Free Democratic Party to become a commissioner earlier this year, is only the latest example.

Moreover, say observers, the politicians arriving in Brussels are becoming genuinely European, committed to the creation of a politically unified Europe, "There's no hope for a commissioner in Brussels who is chauvinistically nationalist — you're just not going to be effective," says Helen Wallace, director of West European studies at London's Royal Institute of International Affairs. "To be effective, you've got to be European."

Nevertheless, Europe still lacks a genuine government; decisions are made through a cumbersome process that might be described as bureaucracy tempered by diplomacy, and national governments are holding firmly to the reins of their own sovereignty. Moreover, community decision making is notoriously nondemocratic: The executive branch, comprising 17 appointed officials and collectively known as the commission, proposes legislation, which is decided on by Cabinet-level officials from the national governments who meet regularly in the Council of Ministers.

But a package of laws known as the Single European Act, passed in 1987, has injected a hefty dose of flexibility (and a less hefty dose of democracy) into the process, and its repercussions are starting to be felt. In the past, the council has had to reach unanimous decisions on key issues, setting off complex negotiations that could last for years. Under the act, most decisions now require only a majority vote — the equivalent of upgrading the community's motor from steam power to gasoline. Moreover, the act recognized foreign policy and environmental protection as issues that should be dealt with at the European rather than the national level and gave new powers to the European Parliament, the only directly elected EC body.

The new signs of life in Brussels have not, however, been greeted with universal joy. As the political implications of economic integration become clear — how should monetary and tax policy be set? for example, or how much of a welfare state is desirable? — a strident debate is breaking out between national parties of the left and right over the shape of post-1992 Europe.

It was the socialist parties that first recognized how extensive the changes wrought by the 1992 program were going to be and saw in them the chance to revitalize a left-leaning social agenda that had been stalled for years in most of Northern Europe. With centrist and center-right governments setting liberal, free market policies in place from Britain to West Germany, the left had found itself reduced to sideline status and even, in the case of Britain's Labor Party, contemplating decades of political impotence.

But new hopes have arisen in the socialists' camp that what they failed to achieve in their home countries, they could win at the European level. Their aggressiveness, and the warm reception they have received from a sympathetic community bureaucracy, has started to jolt the right into action. Two warring factions have emerged, one favoring a federalized Europe with a strong central authority, the other arguing that national governments should give up as little independence as possible, allowing a hands-off, free market Europe to emerge.

With the prospect of an increasingly powerful Brussels bureaucracy taking over more of the responsibilities of national government, feelings in both factions are running high, and higher still as recognition spreads that it is no longer a question of whether Europe integrates, but how. Commission President Delors has been the standard-bearer of those favoring a tightly unified Europe; in a widely publicized speech last summer, he predicted that 80 percent of the member countries' economic and possibly social legislation would be made in Brussels rather than in national capitals by the end of the century. Insisting that Europe must develop a "social dimension" to its economic integration, he has since been calling for a "platform of

guaranteed social rights" for workers. Delors's quasi-socialist view
of an integrated Europe was warmly received in many capitals but
has raised hackles in Margaret Thatcher's Conservative government.

Rising to what she saw as an attack against both British sovereignty and her own Tory, free market values, she struck back immediately. "We have not successfully rolled back the frontiers of the state
in Britain only to see them reimposed at a European level, with a
European superstate exercising new dominance from Brussels," she
said in a speech last fall at the College of Europe in Bruges, Belgium.

Decrying the emergence of what she describes as the "socialist
superstate" — a *dirigiste*, bureaucratic, protectionist and steadily
expanding technocracy in Brussels — she and her followers (known
informally as the Bruges group) have been arguing that market
forces should be allowed to determine Europe's future social policies. They insist that they are not trying to halt European integration, only to keep it from getting derailed by overambitious day-
dreaming. Building a powerful bureaucracy, they say, will only
backfire.

"There are still too many people in Europe with the spirit of
Napoleon in them who equate the social dimension with regulation."
Lord Young of Graffham, Thatcher's secretary of state for trade and
industry, said last month. "That is quite the wrong approach."

Thatcher's attack on Delors's "Marxist" vision of Europe has
taken on the flavor of a holy war, which many in her own party find
uncomfortable. But her antipathy and her determination to resist
appear solid. Last month, in launching the Conservative campaign
for the European elections, she warned the House of Commons that
it was in danger of losing sovereignty to the commission. To the
delight of the right wing in her party, she announced that she would
personally take control of Britain's response to all future community directives.

As the Thatcherites have sharpened their position, their ranks
have swelled with other conservative parties and interest groups.
"The socialist have a very bureaucratic conception of Europe, and
there are close ties between Delors and the French Socialist Party,"
says Michele Alliot-Marie, a former French education minister and
a member of the center-right Rally for the Republic party, who is
running for a seat in the European Parliament. "They want to see
the state become very powerful, with a strong administrative structure. This is something we are completely opposed to."

According to Alliot-Marie, the effort to share political control over the Brussels bureaucracy among the 12 governments is a key problem. Passing the presidency of the EC from country to country every six months, she says, means that the commission is running its own show for its own benefit. "During the Fourth Republic, we had in France governments which changed every three months. That meant that the only powerful people were the directors of the administration. And in the same way, the only ones in Brussels who have stability, and therefore power, are the commission's bureaucrats."

Other groups have joined the fray. The influential Brussels-based employers federation known as UNICE has been marshaling its forces against "social Europe," and Sir John Hoskyns, director of Britain's Institute of Directors, cautioned earlier this year that the spread of red tape from Brussels would undo any benefits from economic integration. "Sixties-style social engineering" and a "high-tax, corporatist Europe" would be the result, he warned.

The debate has generated much attention in Europe, due in large part to fears about the consequences of the 1992 program, and a spreading awareness that economic integration will create losers as well as winners. "The 1992 process is not value-neutral," says Helen Wallace. "Choices have to be made about how freely to open things up to market forces or whether to keep a gentle — or, some would say, not so gentle — hand on the tiller. That's why the social dimension is so important. It's not actually about worker participation and company law; it's about a much more important issue: Can you preserve a social contract through a difficult period of economic adjustment, what the costs are going to be, and how do you meet those costs?"

The EC has earmarked some $60 billion to cushion the blow on Europe's less-developed regions, but the debate goes deeper than money. The Delors vision is proving to be extremely popular, especially among those who see in it the creation of a Pan-European welfare state under the direction of a paternalistic bureaucracy in Brussels. Some, in fact, worry that Brussels will not extend its influence far enough. Says Jean-Marie Cambaceres, author of the French Socialist Party's election manifesto for the European Parliament. "People are afraid that social Europe will come at the lowest common denominator — and that France will be obliged to lower its level of social protection in order to stay competitive with countries like Spain, for example, where salaries are much lower."

Not surprisingly, labor and consumer groups have been quick to throw their support behind Delors. At huge rallies in Paris last month, leaders of France's powerful trade unions repeatedly vowed to fight for more Pan-European guarantees for workers' rights, while in Britain, the shopworkers union (one of the country's largest) abandoned its decades-old opposition to the European Economic Community and voted unanimously to push for a pro-labor Europe. "If completed on Thatcherite free market deregulated terms," said the group, "the European internal market could represent the biggest setback to the working people of Britain and the EEC this century."

Does all this mean that Europeanism is coming to equal interventionism? Despite the rhetoric, some observers doubt it. The philosophy of free market conservatism — conservatism with a small "c" — has dominated North European politics in the 1980s, but a shift to the left has already begun, and this, some say, is what the debate is about. "Social Europe is little more than a smoke screen," says Ludlow of the Center for European Policy Studies. "There isn't a consensus anymore in favor of interventionism or centralized bargaining. But we would appear to be moving within the next three to five years into a Europe in which the socialist parties are the dominant force."

But while Thatcher and Delors continue their standoff, the process of integration continues to gain momentum. The next big test comes in mid-June, when Europe's political parties will vie for seats in the increasingly powerful European Parliament. The winners, who will oversee the implementation of 1992 program, will have a strong say in the development of its social side. But the results will also give an indication of how strong popular enthusiasm is, not only for particular parties, but also for the very notion of government at the European level. If, as most observers expect, the parties on the left do well enough to capture a majority, Delors could find his vision of social Europe becoming a reality faster than even he expected.

Stephen Brookes

CHAPTER 13

The collapse of the Soviet Empire in Eastern Europe in 1989 quickly set the stage for the reunification of Germany. The early stages of unification, as this March 26, 1990, article reported, were fraught with uncertainty about how to proceed on economic and political integration. But Chancellor Helmut Kohl of West Germany never lost the momentum. And for a nation divided since World War II, no price tag for unification seemed too high.

GERMANY UBER ALLES, A 1990S JUGGERNAUT

Of all the countries making up the Soviet empire, East Germany was always considered the most important, the prize of World War II. It occupied a special place of awe in the hierarchy of totalitarian nastiness, having managed the transition from Nazism to communism almost without missing a goose step. Most people agreed that if communism were ever going to retrench, East Germany would be the last place the Soviets would let go.

Characteristically, Soviet leader Nikita Khrushchev was the one who put the Kremlin viewpoint on the chances of German unification most bluntly, taking certain liberties with the person of West Germany's octogenarian chancellor, Konrad Adenauer, in the process: "If you strip Adenauer naked and look at him from behind, you see very plainly that Germany is divided into two parts." And that, according to Khrushchev, who pushed the metaphor in a direction not fit for retelling here, was clearly the way things were meant to stay.

So when Chancellor Helmut Kohl on Nov. 28 stood up in the Bundestag and proclaimed his 10-Point Plan for a unified Germany, trying to give some direction to a political situation that was threatening to get out of hand, old man Khrushchev must surely have been rotating in his grave. Even some of Germany's friends abroad suggested that the chancellor was in a little too much of a hurry and were miffed that he had not consulted them beforehand. Kohl assured his listeners that the plan foresaw a gradual and measured movement toward unification and gave no specific time frame.

Today, even all this appears hopelessly outdated. Where the experts only months ago spoke of reunification within the next five to 10 years, they now speak of it within the next year — if not de jure then de facto. Unification has become inevitable, driven by the collapse of the East German economy and power structure. Because of the quick deterioration, the date for free elections in East Germany, first set for May 6, had to be moved up to March 18. Stated a jubilant Kohl at a political rally, "Never before since the division of our land have we been so close to our goal — the peace and unity of all Germans in freedom — as we are today."

After the fall of the regime of Erich Honecker in November and the resignation of his hapless successor Egon Krenz, the interim government of communist Hans Modrow, though forced to include the opposition and thereby putting the communists in a minority in the cabinet, has been a lame-duck government, unable to reach consensus on key issues. The new East German Parliament is expected to vote on reunification soon after the election, and the vote is expected to be massively in favor, since all parties have come out for it.

The crisis has been precipitated by the steady stream of people leaving: East Germany has been hemorrhaging to death, presenting the eerie prospect of a state peopled only by communists and old age pensioners. The ones who have crossed the border into West Germany are the young and educated, leaving whole sectors of industry and hospitals undermanned. In many areas, mail is no longer delivered. Some early scenes had an almost surrealistic touch to them. In one small city, a whole municipal bus company decided to cross over en masse and in uniform — as if in some special East German version of 12 drummers drumming, 11 pipers piping, 10 lords a-leaping. . . . To make up for the manpower shortages in industry, the government has had to resort to using army conscripts to do essential work.

Of a population of 17 million, last year 343,854 Easterners defected to West Germany, 130,000 of them legally, the rest through third countries such as Hungary and Czechoslovakia at first, then through the open Berlin Wall. Despite appeals from both Kohl and Modrow to stay home, the figure for January was 73,729 and continues at a daily clip of 2,000 to 3,000. At this rate, according to one precocious demographer, by 2006 nobody would be left, except perhaps a scraggly partridge in a polluted pear tree. At the same time, the call for reunification is becoming ever more urgent. According to one opinion poll, some 79 percent of East Germans favor it, up some 25 percentage points since November.

The communists themselves have been partly to blame for the rapidity of the collapse. They have been very slow in undertaking reform and have resisted the opening of the economy. It also did not help when it was discovered that the promised disbanding of the feared secret police, the Stasi, had been proceeding very slowly. And when somebody in the party got the bright idea of suggesting the creation of a new security service to protect the country from alleged neo-Nazi activity, many feared a communist attempt to grab power again; the exodus became measurably faster. The other factor has been sheer impatience. The East Germans feel that they have been paying the price for losing World War II for more than 40 years. Fancy foreign concepts like delayed gratification are not very popular.

Pressure for action is also coming from West Germany, where the continuing exodus has given birth to different concerns. The Bonn government all along has wanted very strongly to avoid a "reunification on West German soil," as the current phrase has it. That would only worsen the country's housing shortage and stretch its social welfare system beyond the limit. East Germans, who are granted automatic citizenship and are eligible for the same social benefits as West Germans, are now living in empty army barracks, in campgrounds and school gymnasiums, some even in the sleazy hotels of Hamburg's famous Reeperbahn red-light district, where business is slow because of AIDS. In one resettlement center in Bremen, 87 men reportedly have to share a single, hopefully very sturdy, toilet. West Germans are complaining that the newcomers have been receiving special privileges and preferential treatment. The head of the Saarland regional government, Oskar Lafontaine, a possible Social Democratic candidate for chancellor, has suggested closing the transit camps to deter more East Germans from entering.

Drastic action to slow the exodus is clearly on the minds of many Germans. What may be needed is nothing less than a new *Wirtschaftswunder*, the term used for West Germany's rise from the ashes of World War II — a new economic miracle, this time for East Germany. Engaging in a bit of rhetorical overkill, some have argued that the East is even worse off now than a divided Germany was just after the war, having been cut off from the world for four decades.

More aptly, perhaps, a British observer has compared it to Liverpool 20 years after the Beatles left, with a touch of North Korea thrown in for color. The country is massively polluted from all the brown coal being burned. As readers of spy thrillers know, a visitor returning from the East can always be recognized from the smell of his clothes. Experts estimate that it will take five to 10 years to bring the East up to West German standards.

To send a strong signal and to restore confidence, a new Cabinet committee on unity headed by Chancellor Kohl was set up Feb. 8. It will deal with such issues as the adoption of a single currency; the political, legal and economic aspects of unification; energy and the environment; ways to harmonize welfare and social systems; means of promoting quick economic reforms and building and reintegrating infrastructure. As a quick follow-up, Kohl and Modrow met Feb. 13-14 in Bonn, where they agreed to set up a joint committee on currency union.

The most immediate concern of the Kohl government is getting rid of the useless and inconvertible ostmark and the adoption by East Germany of West Germany's currency. This would turn over much of the East's economic sovereignty to West Germany and its Central Bank. In the old days, before travel restrictions were lifted, one ostmark officially equaled one West German deutsche mark. Now, the exchange rate is 3-to-1, while the ratio on the black market is 10-to-1. All in all, there are some 180 billion ostmarks that have to be replaced. The day the transition will take place from communist funny money to mighty marks remains secret and is referred to as Day X by the East Germans.

West German officials have attempted to calm fears and prevent panic among East Germans about the value of their savings (estimated to be about 10,000 ostmarks per person). Fearing that their nest eggs would soon be worth even less, East German savers had started to withdraw their money from banks and spend it on anything buyable, from clunky refrigerators made in Czechoslovakia to Meissner porcelain figures. West German Economics Minister Helmut Haussman assured them that their savings would be safeguarded after the switch, though without being specific about what these guarantees would entail. Kohl has also tried to assure them about pensions and social benefits.

Several possibilities have been discussed. First there was talk of a 5-to-1 currency exchange rate, then 2-to-1 and lately a 1-to-1 basis for the savings. That would be one of the greatest acts of charity of all time: It has been estimated that it would cost the West Germans about $100 billion out of pocket and perhaps undermine the deutsche mark and fuel inflation. One way of softening the effect would be to allow every person to change a fixed amount at first and then spread out the rest over some years. Such a law might also be made retroactive to Jan. 1, perhaps even to before the opening of the wall, since people have been spreading their savings over many family members in anticipation of such a move. For money in circulation, the first 1,000 marks could be 1-to-1, the rest 5-to-1, say. But the West German Central Bank is sticking to its announcement that no decision will be made until after the East German election.

At the same time, while seeking to provide hope and direction for the future, the Kohl government has carefully refused to give any substantial aid before the election, so as not to prop up the communists. He has insisted that all serious discussion will wait for the new government. When Modrow came, hat in hand, at the beginning of last month to ask for $9 billion in financial aid (which he described as "a contribution of solidarity"), the request was denied. Finance Minister Theo Weigel said it made no sense to fund a system "that has still not decided to make fundamental changes and has not shown it is capable of doing so." West Germany did, however, approve $3.6 billion in carefully earmarked aid for so-called immediate measures, such as road repair and the installation of a new telephone system to replace one that can perhaps best be described as hostile — but no money that would be at the communists' disposal.

Then, of course, there are all the constitutional questions involved: How does one merge what for more than 40 years have been two separate states? There are several possibilities. The simplest way, which would speed up the process of monetary union and economic reform and is favored by conservatives like Lothar Spath, the governor of Baden-Wurttemberg, is for the East to adopt the entire corpus of West German law. Under Article 23 of the constitution, parts of Germany outside the Federal Republic can accede to the basic law without further ado.

The other, more complicated, way — which could involve years of legalistic wrangling — is to write a whole new charter. Article 146 states that the present constitution ceases to be in force when the Germans adopt a new one by "free decision." This approach was initially favored by the East German and the West German Social Democrats, who argued that Bonn cannot just annex East Germany and even accused Kohl of having exaggerated the crisis in East Germany to hurry up the process. In view of the seriousness of the situation, they may change their position.

Josef Joffe, foreign editor of the daily Suddeutsche Zeitung in Munich, warns against throwing away a constitution that has proved its worth over 41 years, especially in Germany, which has thrown away so many constitutions in the past. But below all the government-to-government negotiations and constitutional deliberations, all kinds of practical links are already being forged, at the level of parties, cities, businesses, trade unions, even on what the newspapers refer to as the level of the flesh. West German youngsters go cruising into East Berlin in their shiny Mercedes-Benzes or BMWs and pick up the prettiest girls for a spin, leaving the poor young menfolk of East Germany with their little lawn mower-engine Trabants growling about show-offs in big, vulgar cars: "Speed fiends," mutter, mutter. "Motor fascists," mutter, mutter.

On the party level, West Germans have been scrambling to link up with their East German counterparts, who will be of great importance politically down the road. Indeed, East German left-wing intellectuals complain that the West Germans are in fact running the show. In West Berlin, the Social Democratic mayor, Walter Momper, is holding regular meetings with his eastern counterpart to improve traffic and communications links between the two parts of the city. They are also trying to find ways to merge transportation systems, phone service and garbage removal, all of which are close to breaking down in East Berlin. Momper is also urging the creation of a joint commission for administration, which most see as the first step toward a unified city government. Meanwhile, West German students facing a chronic housing shortage are already attempting to rent cheap vacated flats on the eastern side. It is Student Chic to live there now.

According to opinion polls, more than 70 percent of West Germans favor Berlin as the capital of a united Germany. Already, preparations are under way to make it so. City planners are speculating about what buildings could serve as ministries, while foreign powers are starting to think about new embassies. The old Reichstag building near the Brandenburg Gate, which has been unoccupied and ghostlike since its restoration after the war, waiting for the parliament of a united Germany to take its place there and in the meantime serving as a museum, would probably house the new parliament. Extra phone lines are already being installed, and the building is getting a general spruce-up.

Some interesting legal problems are expected to arise from all this. Some West Berlin landlords are now showing up in East Berlin to inspect what they consider family property, citing land claims before the war. One such putative landlord sent around questionnaires to residents of an East Berlin apartment complex asking whether the tenants had been members of the Communist Party. A West Berlin lawyer has laid claim to the land on which the East German Foreign Ministry is built. ("Get out of my ministry, you odious little man" sounds even more impressive when uttered in German.) It is estimated that around a half-million people have claims to buildings or land in East Germany that were confiscated without compensation by the communists after the war.

Just as significantly, in Bonn, the quiet university town on the Rhine that became the provisional capital of West Germany 41 years ago and which spy writer John le Carre dubbed "a small town in Germany," pessimism is spreading. For some, its choice as capital of the *Bundesrepublik* was meant to underscore the impermanence and unacceptability of Germany's division, while others saw its very modesty as a symbol of the nation's postwar conversion to democracy. In any case, politicians have called a halt to further government construction projects in light of recent events. Property prices have tumbled as much as 40 percent. At most, some hope there can be a kind of sharing of government functions between the two cities, but this sounds like wishful thinking. Bonn may well go back to academic slumber.

At the business level, things are moving, too. Among the airlines, cooperation between Lufthansa and its East German counterpart, Interflug, started early. They are now running inter-German flights at cut-rate fares and have been pressing the wartime Allies, which hold the airspace rights over the two states, for more flights. They would especially like to break the highly lucrative Allied monopoly on flights to and from Berlin. On the ground, trains running between the two parts are scheduled to double in number by May, by which time the ancient East German locomotives will have been refitted to run on invigorating West German electricity.

The West German industrial giants — firms like Thyssen, Siemens and Volkswagen — are busily preparing for One Germany, Volkswagen started a production line of engines last year under a licensing agreement in Karl-Marx-Stadt (which after election night will return to its old name of Chemnitz). Many famous West German companies — such as Carl Zeiss, a maker of optical and precision instruments, and Siemens, an electronics firm, and Dresdner Bank, the second largest bank in West Germany — have historical roots in what became East Germany after the war. To this, one can add hundreds of medium and small firms, which are busy scouting out the possibilities. But real action will have to wait until after the election, when the East's economy is opened up and the legal guarantees have been established to give Western investors confidence.

To make certain that all this rampant new capitalism does not get out of hand, the Metal Workers Union, West Germany's biggest, has offered its assistance in seeing to it that East German workers are not exploited by their new bosses. It intends to open eight offices in major East German cities. But according to Heiner Flassbeck at the German Institute for Economic Research in Berlin, the East Germans will have to make a choice. At a high ostmark-to-deutsche mark conversion rate, wages will be high and so will unemployment, at least at the beginning. Accepting lower wages would mean more jobs. Overall, a careful balance must be struck: Wages in the East must remain low enough to attract industries to invest, yet not so low that people will continue to cross over in hopes of making more money in the West.

Estimates vary widely over what the total cost of rescuing East Germany will be. The East German deputy premier in charge of the economy, Christa Luft, claims that investments of up to 1 trillion deutsche marks, or some $600 billion, are needed, while Haussman, the West German economics minister, thinks half that sum would do the trick. The fact is that nobody knows.

There are also some immediate risks connected with a single currency, and Kohl is taking a political gamble. Karl Otto Pohl, the head of West Germany's Central Bank, in the beginning was muttering darkly about the inflationary potential of a quick move to monetary union, in that it would require printing more money than was advisable to satisfy the East German need for deutsche marks. He was hushed up. This is clearly a case of political concerns outweighing economic ones.

Moreover, currency reform in itself is not enough. Also necessary are goods to buy with the money, and there must be fundamental industrial reconstruction. Half of East Germany's factories are considered unprofitable, their machinery dating back to Attila the Hun, and this inevitably means closings and major layoffs. According to the West German unions, this would mean donations of more than 100 billion deutsche marks over the next few years to finance unemployment benefits and pensions in East Germany. The head of West Germany's savings bank association has warned that this would probably lead to tax increases and budget deficits. Pessimists see cutbacks on social programs, housing and the protection of the environment in West Germany.

More self-confident souls claim that a substantial portion of the financing would come from private West German firms that stand to make big profits later. The chancellor thus far is sticking to his promise of no higher taxes (though there may be other "revenue enhancement" possibilities open to him down the road). The Kohl philosophy is that the government can lead the horses to water — by providing the right economic framework and climate — but the horses themselves will have to drink. Kohl has stated that if only one-third of the 100 billion West German marks invested abroad last year went to East Germany, this would give a tremendous boost. Besides, West Germany has the highest rate of savings in Western Europe, giving it enough capital to reconstruct the East German economy.

It is when Germans address themselves to the long-range prospects that most of them perk up, even the worriers. With patience and with foresight, West German corporations stand to make huge profits as the market grows. A nation of 78 million Germans will be an even bigger economic powerhouse of Europe. In addition, they will gain access to the East German distribution network for Eastern Europe and the Soviet Union. One businessman was quoted as saying, "While everybody else is cautiously knocking at the door, we are already inside having tea."

It was this kind of optimism that was reflected in Kohl's recent remark that the 1990s could turn out to be "the decade of the Europeans, and not of the Japanese." The Germans, after all, are very good at what they do.

Henrik Bering-Jensen

CHAPTER 14

*Many people mistakenly counted
Margaret Thatcher out at various times
during her tenure as Britain's prime
minister. Indeed, she faced a daunting
task and formidable opposition. Britain in
1979 was a country in precipitous decline.
The policies she pursued played a crucial
role in the nation's revival, and by
hanging tough and winning elections, she
established herself as one of the West's
foremost politicians. This article on her
appeared December 14, 1987.*

THATCHER LEADS A TRANSFORMATION

uring the course of a children's party held in Parliament, so the story goes, Margaret Thatcher did her best to see to the comfort of her young guests. Nonetheless, a tearful 4-year-old objected to the quivering dessert on his plate: "Miss, Miss, they have given me blancmange and I don't like blancmange."

"That," the British prime minister firmly admonished him, "is what parties are all about: eating food you don't like."

If the episode has the ring of folklore, it is only fitting. For Margaret Thatcher has become something of a mythic figure. With a 101-seat majority in Parliament and a string of three election victories, she has touched a record set by Lord Liverpool in the early 19th century. Indeed, early next year, she will become the longest-reigning British prime minister of the 20th century.

In an era when the two-term U.S. presidency is the exception rather than the norm, when the current occupant of that office has seen his power wane precipitously and when other Western European leaders seem only to be muddling through, Thatcher has gone from victory to victory and has become the senior Western statesman. As she put it in June, after her most recent victory: "I think I have become a bit of an institution — you know, the sort of thing people expect to see around the place." In conversation, a civil servant recently referred to the prime minister as "her majesty," which somehow seems an understandable slip.

Like the hostess hectoring her young guests, the prime minister often has had occasion since assuming power in 1979 to ask the British to do things they decidedly didn't like. That they should nevertheless elect her for a third time, and this despite a poorly fought election campaign, is seen by political commentator Brian Walden as a sign of political maturity.

David Butler, a leading elections expert and coauthor of a series of books on the subject, notes that while Thatcher has benefited to some degree from being attuned to general disillusionment with the ability of a centralized state to solve all problems, she for the most part has been the author of her own success. Says Butler, "I think many people would argue that she has made more difference than any postwar prime minister by sheer effort of will."

Most observers in Britain agree that she has shown herself to be a different kind of leader. Her postwar predecessors, Tory and Labor alike, basically saw themselves as managers of Britain's unavoidable decline, whose worst effects were to be cushioned by the welfare state. This meant adapting to "the winds of change," as the late Harold Macmillan, a Conservative, used to put it.

Thatcher, in contrast, saw herself as someone who could turn this decline around. "She has changed the parameters of British politics," says Tony Baldry, Conservative member of Parliament for Banbury. He describes how, as a young election aide in 1974, he found himself alone in Macmillan's library on the former primer minister's 80th birthday. Reflecting on the way Prime Minister Edward Heath handled the 1974 miners strike, which forced the Conservatives to call an election they subsequently lost, Macmillan stated half-seriously, "There are three organizations the British government ought never to take on: the Vatican, the treasury and the National Union of Mineworkers."

Margaret Thatcher has shown herself unbound by such conventional wisdom. Says Baldry, "In the [1984-85] miners strike, the prime minister made it quite clear that there were no established groups that she was afraid to take on." Fortunately, he jokes, "I don't think there has ever been any cause to take on the Vatican."

Norman Tebbit, who recently stepped down as Conservative Party chairman, describes the changes wrought by the leader in even stronger terms. "There has been," he says, "a constitutional, gradualist revolution going on for the past eight years, social and econom-

ic change combined." The depth of these changes, according to Butler, is suggested by the fact that Thatcher is the first leader since 19th
century Prime Minister William Ewart Gladstone to give her name
to a doctrine. "Churchillian," for example, applied more to a style of
government than to its substance. "Thatcherism" has content: a
reassertion of individualism combined with toughness from the central government.

In a recently published interview, the prime minister defined the
key tenets of the creed: "You live within your means; you have honest money, so therefore you don't make reckless promises. You recognize human nature is such that it needs incentives to work harder, so you cut your tax. It is about being worthwhile and honorable.
And about the family. And about that something which is really
rather unique and enterprising in the British character—it's about
how we built an empire, and how we gave sound administration and
sound law to large areas of the world. All those things are still there
in the British people."

The appeal of Thatcherism is partly that it can be reduced to such
simple everyday ideas, that it makes an easy connection between economic values and moral values. Says Walden, "The fact that she is a
woman of course leads to household analogies of good housekeeping.
A lot of people think that is what Thatcherism is. That this woman
counts up the bills and the money, giving money to those members
of the family who deserve it and withholding money from those who
don't."

Of course there is much more to it than that. Describing the way
the prime minister has managed to change popular perception and
expectations, Walden draws a comparison to the United States during the New Deal. "If you had put it to the American people that voting for Roosevelt meant they had changed their views of capitalism,
they would not have understood it. They were just voting for
Franklin Roosevelt and the New Deal." Similarly with Britain today,
he believes. While the average Briton would not think his views have
changed, they have been modified considerably by eight years of
Thatcher government

Since World War II, Britain has had one of the highest degrees of
state ownership in Europe — outside the East Bloc — and one of
the most comprehensive welfare systems. Redistribution was
emphasized rather than production. It is in this area, in perceptions
of the state and the workability of British socialism, that there has
been the greatest change in popular attitudes.

Looking back over the last two decades B.T. (before Thatcher),

Norman Stone, professor of modern history at Oxford, recalls the broken promises of the 1960s, when Labor Prime Minister Harold Wilson's vision of a new "white-hot" technological revolution that would get the country moving again failed to materialize. The '70s, he says, were even more bleak: "It was terribly depressing to see how this country simply functioned less well than France and Germany." The nationalized industries went creaking on, while endless excuses were found on both sides for a cozy arrangement between monopoly unions and monopoly employers and the taxpayers footed the bill. "You had the dismal Iron Curtain spectacle of tiny salaries being hugely overtaxed," says Stone. Spiraling inflation reached a peak of 24.2 percent in 1975 under Wilson.

The nadir was reached in 1978-79 under Wilson's successor, James Callaghan, in the so-called winter of discontent, when strikes by public service workers, including even the gravediggers, paralyzed the country for months. Union leaders, who often were compared to medieval barons, saw themselves as the national power brokers, able to make or break governments.

Eight years into Margaret Thatcher's reign, Britain presents a rather different picture. The 80 percent of the British work force solidly employed has become 15 to 20 percent better-off in real terms since 1981-82. Official figures show the economy has been growing by some 3 percent yearly since the early '80s, outperforming such major partners in the European Community as France, West Germany and Italy. Overall labor productivity increased 14 percent from 1980 to 1985. The transformation from an economy based largely on state-owned heavy industries to a more modern, diversified service economy has not been painless. And in some regions, particularly the industrial north of England, Scotland and Wales, the pain is still acutely felt.

One of the Conservative government's first targets on taking power in 1979 was the inflation rate, which during the 1970s had been higher than those of most of Britain's EEC partners. When the Conservatives came into power, the rate was around 10 percent, but it soared during their first year to 21.9 percent in May 1980. The 1980-81 budget, however, proved to be a watershed. Imposing strict monetary policies, adhering to the principle of sound money, the government reduced the rate dramatically to 3.9 percent by May 1983.

This accomplishment came at a heavy price: 20 percent of Britain's manufacturers went out of business, and the number of unemployed persons leapt from 1.25 million, or 5 percent to 6 percent of the work force, when the Conservatives gained power in 1979, to around 3.25 million, or 13 percent, in 1985. But halfway through Thatcher's second term, things began to turn around. The government eased its monetary policies, the slimmed-down industrial sector became more competitive, and productivity began a steady rise. Moreover, the number of unemployed persons has fallen by about a half-million over the past year, to a present 2.7 million.

Before the world stock market plunge in October, a growth rate of 3 percent had been projected for next year. A forecast by the London Business School, based on pessimistic assumptions about the U.S. economy, now suggests a growth rate of 1.5 percent may be more realistic. Christopher Smallwood, business editor of The (London) Sunday Times, argues that Britain remains in a stronger position than its trading partners because the impressive gains in productivity will continue to be felt.

An important part of the explanation for Britain's comeback lies in improved industrial relations — demographic, social and political factors have all conspired to reduce the power of the trade unions. For one thing, the shift from unionized heavy industries to largely nonunionized service and high-tech industries has caused the trade union movement substantial losses in membership. Since 1979 union membership has fallen by 3 million, to about 9 million total, and the percentage of unionized workers in the labor force has dropped from 51 to 37. Moreover, the Thatcher government has mounted a concerted effort to shift power in industrial relations from the trade unions back to the employees.

Roger Why, the director of group employee relations at Land Rover Ltd. and a veteran negotiator who has 15 years in the motor vehicle industry at the sharp end of industrial relations, recalls the old days; "I can remember as a relatively junior industrial relations officer having to handle six different stoppages of work on one track in the course of one morning."

According to Why, British Leyland routinely lost about 10 percent of its volume through disputes. Employers became so used to the restrictions imposed on them by the trade unions that, like a man grown accustomed to walking with a limp, in the end they found the constraints felt natural.

The Thatcher government, with significant pieces of legislation in 1980, 1982 and 1984, managed to curb the national power of the trade unions to a great degree. The key change was legislation requiring the trade unions to ballot their members first before strike action. As Norman Tebbit, who reshaped trade union law as secretary of state for trade and industry form 1983 to 1985, said at the time, "I use the word 'neuter' when talking about what I am doing to the unions, because I've been told I must not use the vernacular." Or as Conservatives like to point out more politely, they are making the unions more democratic, taking them out of the hands of power-hungry bosses and giving them back to the members.

The results for the British economy have been encouraging. Says Why of Land Rover, "We have had three tiny stoppages in the factory this year." Productivity in manufacturing industries went up 27 percent from 1979 to 1985, compared with 6 percent from 1973 to 1979. Within the newspaper industry, for instance, the effect has been dramatic, allowing for the introduction of computerized typesetting and the launching of three national newspapers.

The curbing of union power is reflected in a statement by John Edmonds, general secretary of the General, Municipal, Boilermakers and Allied Trades Union. "The unions," he said, "must develop policies which do not depend clearly and solely on the return of a Labor government." Furthermore, some unions, such as the Amalgamated Engineering Union, are signing no-strike deals with employers. It is also noteworthy that during the last election, a great many trade union members voted Conservative. While 42 percent voted Labor, 30 percent went Conservative and 26 percent voted for the Alliance parties. As recently as 1974, 55 percent voted Labor.

Britain has become attractive to foreign investors again, partly because the economy is sound and partly because of the past years' good labor relations record. Says one Conservative, "If someone had suggested that was going to be a reason for investment in Britain 10 years ago, they would have clapped him away for being insane."

Equally important social changes have taken place during the Thatcher years, perhaps none of greater significance than the prime minister's decision to promote, in one of her favorite phrases, popular capitalism. One of the major social engineering projects of the Conservatives has been the sale of council houses (public housing units) to their occupants. Under eight years of her government, Britain has moved from a nation in which 54 percent of the population owned homes in 1977, to one in which 67 percent did in 1986. Says Walden, "Thatcher thinks that private ownership is a virtue and that people ought to accumulate property and wealth, that it is good for their families and for society."

According to Butler, extending home ownership is an idea that goes back to the 1870s and Disraeli, who realized that by giving people a tangible stake in the country and its government he was increasing the number of Conservatives over the long run. The specific idea of selling public housing first was raised in the late 1960s, but the Conservatives were rather slow to seize upon it, thinking it too much of a hot potato. Under Thatcher, they have found it to be hugely popular. In electoral terms, the result has been to produce more Tories.

"If I were to describe the typical Labor voter," says Tebbit, "I'd say that he worked for a local authority, or for the state in some way, perhaps for a nationalized corporation, a member of a big trade union, living in a council house." But, he continues, "if you look at a man who owns his own house, who is a member of a properly funded pension scheme, over which he has increasing control himself, and who is working in the private sector — you have a strong assumption that that man is going to vote Conservative or Alliance perhaps, not Labor. The first group of people is falling in numbers, the second group is growing."

Another component in the Conservative search for permanent change has been the policy of privatization of nationalized industries, the selling of shares in such companies as British Aerospace, British Gas Corp., British Telecom and British Airways. The basic idea behind this policy is summed up by the Renaissance philosopher Francis Bacon's dictum: "Money is like muck, not good unless it be spread." Since the inception in 1981 of the privatization program, Britain's number of shareholders has risen from 3 million to 9 million. In the selling of shares, preference has been given to employees and small shareholders, with the aim of making it more difficult for a future Labor government to renationalize what has been sold off.

This aspect of popular capitalism already may have experienced a setback, due to the effect of plunging stock markets on public confidence, particularly among first-time investors, the so-called foot soldiers of the Thatcher revolution. Many may have been scared off by the experience. Say Smallwood, "The privatization program will go on, but most of the shares will be sold to large institutions, which takes away a lot of the political point, which was wider public ownership."

How lasting will be these changes wrought under Margaret Thatcher? Could they survive the test of another Labor government? A measure of how much Britain has changed is the change that has been forced upon the prime minister's political opponents. The September Labor Party conference in Brighton illustrated the difficulty facing that party after three successive election defeats in adapting itself to the new political scene in Britain.

Party leader Neil Kinnock told the conference, to dutiful if unenthusiastic applause, that all Labor policies would be up for review. Quoting union leader Ron Todd, he said, "What do you say to a docker who earns 400 pounds a week, owns his house, a new car, microwave and video, as well as a small place near Marbella in Spain, 'Let me take you out of your misery, brother'?"

Labor's attempts to catch up were discussed with relish at the Tory conference the following week. Elaborating on the theme that the other parties would try to imitate the Tories, Tebbit exulted, "The prospect of Mr. Kinnock trying to put on your clothes, Prime Minister, is hilarious." There is still some doubt, however, whether Kinnock's heart is really in such a change of hat. And there remains much resistance both in Labor's parliamentary group and in its rank and file to such changes, which have been described mockingly by its opponents as designer socialism.

What these Labor traditionalists may not have reckoned with is the difficulty of defeating a "conservative" government that is firmly forward-looking and committed to change. Some see an ironic role reversal in the two parties. "Just as the condition of the Conservatives getting back to power in 1951 was that they should accept the welfare state," says elections expert Butler, "in the same way the condition of Labor getting back to power would be that they should not turn the clock back."

THE SELLING OF SELF-DESTINY

Around 3 o'clock in the morning following the June 11 election, Margaret Thatcher arrived at Conservative Party headquarters in London's Smith Square. On the doorstep, she was received by Norman Tebbit, then the party chairman, with a bouquet of 100 red roses, symbolic of the size of the Tory victory. Relief and exhaustion prevailed at the gathering within, but as the prime minister stopped halfway up the stairs inside, she reminded them that this was no time to relax. To general laughter and some groans she told them, "There's plenty for us to do now. There'll be no slacking!"

For those in the party who favor a period of consolidation and a slower pace of reform, the prime minister had only scorn at the Conservative Party conference in Blackpool in October. "Would 'consolidate' be the word that we stitched on our banners?" she inquired witheringly. "Whose blood would run faster at the prospect of five years of consolidation?"

Clearly not Margaret Thatcher's. The tasks set for themselves in the Conservatives' third therm include the extension of existing policies: Trade union legislation will be introduced that would protect union members who break strikes from retaliation. Studies on the possible privatization of electricity and water will continue.

This time, however, the government is going further. For the first two Parliaments, the Conservatives had the advantage of carrying out policies that could be seen to have an immediately beneficial effect for a large number of people, such as selling public housing at favorable prices. The third presents more difficult challenges.

According to Tony Baldry, Conservative member of Parliament for Banbury, "The third Parliament is going to call upon individuals to take greater responsibility for their own lives and for the communities in which they find themselves." It has therefore been dubbed "the social affairs Parliament." Two of the priorities will be inner cities and education, both of them areas where, in the nature of things, results have to be long-term and no immediate political benefit can be expected. Much of the new legislation in these areas will concentrate on doing away with the last bastions of the left, the municipal power centers in places such as London and Liverpool.

The precepts behind much of the new legislation proposed by the Conservatives are the increase of competition and the extension of individual choice in matters of local services, most significantly in education and housing.

Much of the discussion in the field of education centers on how to restore standards and quality in the schools. Some critics of the present system look back longingly to the grammar school system, which was determinedly meritocratic, separating by tests at age 11 those who eventually would go to college and those who would not. This system was abolished by law in 1976 by Labor. The grammar schools, it was said, were too geared to middle-class values. To fail the exam was to fail a class test. Mention of Shirley Williams, the controversial minister of education charged with implementing the law, still brings horror to some Tory faces.

In its place, Labor established the comprehensive school, which everybody attends after age 11. The result, critics claim, was to make state education equally poor for all students, the clever being bored, the thick still unable to cope and the wealthy going off to private schools instead. Though the Thatcher government has no intention of restoring the old system, and indeed does not even talk of it, its proposals are clearly premised on the notion that there is widespread dissatisfaction with things as they are. Instead, Conservatives propose to raise standards throughout the country by introducing a national core curriculum, emphasizing traditional subjects such as English, math and science, with frequent achievement testing along the way.

They propose to allow parents and school governors to take their schools out of the control of the local education authorities and instead receive funding directly from the central government. When the state system of education was set up in 1944, extensive powers were given to these local education authorities at the expense of parents and headmasters. By allowing parents the possibility of removing schools from the local authorities' oversight, the Conservatives would give parents considerably more say over their children's education. And by giving each school its own budget, parents and headmasters would have greater say over how money is being spent. In this way, the Conservatives hope to stop what they see as left-wing local authorities squandering resources on a political agenda, under the guise of teaching such topics as gay studies and peace studies.

Giving parents these options, the Conservatives believe, is not just a policy for "the leafy suburbs," as Secretary of State for Education and Science Kenneth Baker puts it. It is particularly important in inner cities, where educational standards have been most eroded. Says Baker, "At the moment, choice is available to those who can afford it, who can make the sacrifices for it. What we're doing is extending choice to everybody; choice shouldn't just be something for the rich."

Another top priority for the third term is inner-city reform. The decay of Britain's inner cities became dramatically evident during the riots in the early 1980s in places such as the Toxteth area of Liverpool, Notting Hill and Brixton in London and the St. Paul's district of Bristol. More riots broke out in 1985 in some of the same places. The present misery of the slums has been compared to the London rookeries of Dickens's day.

Margaret Thatcher in her speech to the party conference said of the inner cities: "They are people trapped inside public housing estates governed by local authorities who are hostile to enterprise, who intend to milk industry and commerce for every penny." She further blasted postwar town planning as "social vandalism," referring to the huge concrete housing projects built in the 1960s, many of them now with windows boarded up, rubbish and graffiti everywhere, ferocious dogs, and stairwells stinking of urine. Underscoring the prime minister's determination is the creation of a special Cabinet task force on inner cities chaired by her.

The Conservative approach to the inner city differs fundamentally from past approaches. Lord Young, secretary for trade and industry, says Labor governments — and indeed past Tory governments before Thatcher—were profoundly statist, believing the state had an obligation to do everything. "What we believe now very strongly is to go back to one part of the Tory values, the part that says God helps those who help themselves. What we are really doing is helping people to help themselves."

Under the Conservatives the emphasis has been shifted away from social projects toward capital investment and economic regeneration. Conservatives favor a larger role for private enterprise as a force for social improvement. The idea is not only to draw business from the outside, but also to get the long-term unemployed involved in creating their own.

The state's role in this is to provide facilities, training and advice. To further this end, a variety of urban development corporations, local enterprise agencies, city action teams and task forces have been created in places such as Liverpool, Glasgow, Manchester, Birmingham and inner London. It is their job to establish cooperation directly between business and central government, investing in infrastructure and providing incentives for private firms in deprived areas.

The question remains whether such public sector investment will succeed in attracting sufficient private business to effect any real regeneration of such areas. Opponents complain that as yet the Conservative program has not been backed up by sufficient cash. While the resources of the total urban program grew in real terms from 186.3 million pounds (about $324 million) in 1981-82 to 236.8 million pounds in 1984-85, they then dropped to 219.5 million pounds in 1985-86 and are expected to fall again this year.

Furthermore, as Conservative Parliament backbencher Michael Heseltine has noted in a thinly veiled criticism of Thatcher's ideals on social self-sufficiency, "We have to be very careful before we assume strengths and values in those deprived societies that are characteristic of a more vibrant and richer community elsewhere. Self-help has a limited meaning in an inner-city community where 40 percent of the kids may be without work and, if they are black, the figure may be 60 percent."

Counters Lord Young, "I do not believe the state can cure those problems. If it could, it would have cured them a long time ago. Areas of great dereliction such as Liverpool, for example, have had and enormous amount of state money spent on them. Indeed, Mr. Heseltine was responsible for spending a great deal of money on Liverpool in the early '80s, and it does not look any better today."

According to Lord Young, money is not the answer "One of the great faults of the critics is that they tend to value a government by its input, by how much money they spend and not on the quality of the output, of what they actually get for it." Rather, he believes, fundamental attitudes have to change. "What we have to do is be able to create a society living in the inner city who believe that working life is the normal way and not the aberration. We have a large number of people living close together in local authority housing who got used to a way of life that does not include work." In the United Kingdom, people can receive unemployment benefits forever; there is no time limit.

An important part of the Conservatives' inner-city initiative centers on housing. As with the other new plans, self-determination and competition are emphasized. In the case of public housing, tenants will be allowed to opt out of the local housing authority and choose their own landlords. The aim is to break up the huge municipal tenements, which are often run by Labor-controlled local authorities and which Conservatives claim have been allowed to run down due to a mixture of mismanagement and ideological bias.

The second aim of the Conservative housing policy is the abolition of rent controls, which have all but suffocated the private rental sector in Britain. This, together with yearlong waiting lists for public housing, has had the effect of freezing the labor market, preventing those unable to purchase property from moving to where the jobs are, particularly in the southeast. "There is a hidden surplus of accommodation," notes Tebbit, "which would come on the market if this was economically sensible for people." The plan is not, however, to remove rent controls at a stroke. Instead, future rents will be the object of decontrol.

Potentially the most controversial part of the Conservative battle against the power of municipal authorities is the proposal to replace local rates, or property taxes, with a community charge, as the Conservatives refer to it, or, as it opponents at once dubbed it, a poll tax. Whatever the designation, this involves imposing a flat rate tax on every adult over 18. Proponents claim that the community charge is a simpler system than the present property tax and is designed dramatically to reforge the link between the local authorities, who set the rates, and the electorate, which pays them. At present, a large number of people do not pay property tax at all and have no reason to be concerned about the level of local authority spending.

Opponents of the community charge argue that, like any flat rate tax, it will hit the poor hardest. The propaganda potential of such an issue is obvious: the industrial baron in his huge mansion, paying the same percentage in community charge as the little old lady huddled at her electric fire. The critics also argue that the community charge may be difficult to administer, people being somewhat harder to track down and tax than houses.

Conservatives point out that the central government will continue to meet almost half the total bill of local authority spending and, as for the injustice of the flat rate, poor people will be required to provide at most about 20 percent of the community charge, or about 80 pence a week (about $1.40).

The squandering of political capital on what many see as a potential vote loser has been compared by one commentator to the Charge of the Light Brigade. Conservative backbenchers in the Parliament, who are called upon to do the riding, have voiced some concern over this, though at the October party conference the protest was very muted.

Finally, one issue that has dogged Thatcher from the start will continue on the Conservative agenda: how to reduce public spending. Says political columnist Geoffrey Smith of the (London) Sunday Times, "If you measure Thatcher performance against Thatcher intentions, that's one place where there's a gap."

She has succeeded in reducing the growth of public spending but has not actually been able to cut it back. When the Conservatives came into power, public spending as a proportion of the gross domestic product was 43.25 percent; today it is 44.25 percent. (In the United States, the comparable percentage for federal outlays was 23.7 in 1985.) While personal taxes have gone down, sales taxes have gone up. Social security accounts for 26 percent of total public spending (compared with 17.1 percent in the United States last year). The second-largest portion, 15.1 percent, goes to health and so-called personal social services. In 1979 the figure was 13.9 percent.

The British cradle-to-grave welfare system, which was started by Labor after World War II, provides free medical care for everybody, and costs are soaring. Just before the party conference, Social Services Secretary John Moor had spoken publicly about the need to reassess the universality of the welfare state, reserving state help for those who really need it, a theme he repeated at the conference. At the moment, all Britons regardless of income are eligible for benefits such as child allowances, state pensions and hospital care.

What Moore called for to bring down the cost of the health service was a "mixed economy in care" with more emphasis on private health care. Currently, about 10 percent of the population uses private care, which enables people to choose their own doctors and to decide when they want to be treated. The speech was interpreted by many as a trial balloon.

There are limits to how far this trimming can be pursued. Though the Conservatives might succeed in making people contribute a little more themselves, says elections analyst David Butler, it is unlikely that Thatcher would or could actually abolish the National Health Service or even alter it substantially. Agreeing, columnist Smith says, "The middle classes and the professional classes like the idea of cutting public expenditure, until they feel it themselves."

Says one commentator, "Health care is very popular. Neil Kinnock rightly stuck to it as his strong point during the election. Health service was one of the things the Labor Party did for the country in the 1940s and by doing that they changed the psychology of the country. In that sense Mrs. Thatcher has not changed the psychology. That will stay the same."

Henrik Bering-Jensen

CHAPTER 15

Canada's Prime Minister Brian Mulroney, the prime mover behind a 1988 free trade agreement with the United States, risked his political future over Canadian fears that the trade pact would leave his country dominated by its giant neighbor. As reported in this story December 12 of that year, voters rejected strident nationalism. They gave the go-ahead to implement the historic agreement, which some cited as a potential model for future bilateral pacts.

A FREE TRADE GAMBIT CARRIES THE DAY

It was, without doubt, the most divisive and fiercely contested election in Canada's 121-year history. Progressive Conservative Prime Minister Brian Mulroney, running on a record of healthy economic growth and the negotiation of a historic free trade pact with the United States was forced to defend that pact, and himself, against charges that Canada was being sold down the river.

By signing an agreement to bring the two largest North American economies closer together, the opposition parties charged, Mulroney was reducing Canada to a mere handmaiden of the United States; the trade pact, they charged, would sap Canada's independence, dilute its culture into insignificance and slowly pare away its welfare system, creating in the end a Canada as American as apple pie.

Overblown campaign rhetoric? Certainly, but it was heady stuff, and it looked for weeks as if it would work. What had started as an arcane and immensely complicated economic issue quickly became the central focus of a pitched battle for Canada's soul, and the country was treated to five weeks of a virulent, and at times literally bloody, campaign. As the rhetoric intensified and the accusations flew, Mulroney and his main rival, the Liberal Party's John N. Turner, found themselves neck and neck in the polls through most of the campaign. But when the smoke cleared Nov. 21, Mulroney had pulled off a decisive triumph; ratification of the trade pack is now assured.

Mulroney's victory, many economists believe, has avoided not only an economic catastrophe for Canada but also a setback for future bilateral trading arrangements. The country's export-oriented economy is closely tied to the United States; with trade between the two running more than $150 billion a year, it is the world's largest trading relationship. Direct U.S. investment is huge — American auto companies alone have 35 plants in Canada — and growing. Fully 75 percent of Canadian exports go to the United States, and about 70 percent of its imports come from the United States.

But for all its size and importance, the U.S.-Canadian relationship has been no less susceptible to protectionist pressures and trade disputes than any other, and it was this fact that drove Ottawa to seek the accord. The idea of a trade pact had been raised before — from a limited agreement in 1854 known as the Reciprocity Treaty, to broader attempts in 1891 and 1911 that went nowhere.

Trade between the two countries is, in many ways, already quite free: Both belong to the General Agreement on Tariffs and Trade, the world trade body, and about one-third of U.S.-Canadian trade has been regulated since 1965 under an agreement. But key areas of contention remained, and for trade in services, a key growth area, no agreement existed.

It was not until the mid-1980s that the idea of a full-fledged free trade accord met with support from governments and business communities in both countries. Canada's Liberals, under Pierre Elliott Trudeau, had begun a far-reaching debate on the future of the country's policy in 1980, setting up a Royal Commission under Finance Minister Donald S. MacDonald to look into developing a free trade pact. And while the Progressive Conservative government that swept into power with Mulroney at its head in 1984 was initially opposed to the idea, it soon shifted its position. ("Only imbeciles never change their minds," Mulroney was to say later.) In September 1985, he stood before the House of Commons and announced that Canada would seek a new agreement with Washington.

That agreement was to involve, as MacDonald had put it, a "leap of faith" for Canadians. In its final form, signed by Mulroney and President Reagan in January and approved by Congress in August, the accord is a complicated document that reflects the complexity of the U.S.-Canadian relationship itself. In its main points, it phases out all remaining bilateral tariffs over the next decade, creates a panel to settle disputes, eases restrictions on cross-border business travel, increases Canada's access to U.S. energy markets, liberalizes agricultural trade, phases out discrimination against sales of U.S. wines and spirits, and reduces Canadian screening of American investment.

The increased economic activity and reduced costs to consumers that should result from the agreement are expected to give a hefty boost to the Canadian economy. The University of Toronto's Institute of Policy Analysis released a report the week before the election arguing that the growth in productivity and decline of import costs would result in "significant permanent gains in incomes" and predicting that by the time the pact comes fully into effect it will have raised real wages by 4.5 percent, reduced unemployment by 0.2 percent and lowered the consumer price index by 7.4 percent. The volume of trade will have risen by 52 percent, says the group, and by the turn of the century exports will be growing faster than imports. Mulroney claims that the pact will create some 250,000 jobs over the next decade.

But for Canadians, the "leap of faith" means taking a calculated risk: that the economic changes that free trade brings will not destroy their national character or way of life. That risk is not taken lightly. Having a population and economy only about one-tenth the size of the United States', Canada's fear of domination is real. American investment in Canada's economy is huge, and its cultural presence is pervasive, despite extensive subsidies from Ottawa for homegrown culture. Foreign films, most from the United States, make up more than 95 percent of the movies shown in Canada, and a good 75 percent of Canadian television programming originates south of the border.

Moreover, says Charles Doran, head of the Canadian studies department of the Johns Hopkins University School of Advanced International Studies, "With two separate founding peoples, each with its own linguistic group, the country is inherently fragile. It's not surprising that such a country would feel cautious in all its dealings with its giant neighbor."

Nonetheless, when the pact was signed it appeared to enjoy broad support across Canada and was passed without incident by the Progressive Conservative-dominated House of Commons. But when the agreement was sent to the Liberal-dominated Senate, the Liberals' Turner saw his chance; he instructed the body to "withhold assent," turning the issue into an immediate political crisis and prompting Mulroney, on Oct. 1, to call a new election.

Turner's strategy was to play on the Canadian sense of vulnerability by threatening that the pact would turn Canada variously into a "colony," the "51st state" or a "junior partner" of the United States. In two televised debates — one in English, one in French — he and the leader of the small New Democratic Party, Edward J. Broadbent, hammered away at Mulroney. "You will reduce us to a colony of the United States," he shouted at the prime minister, "because when the economic levers go, independence is sure to follow."

The pitch seemed effective. Overnight, Turner shot past Mulroney in the polls. Some 54 percent of the public suddenly announced its opposition to the free trade pact, prompting columnist Peter Cook to write in The Toronto Globe and Mail, "The don't-knows have discovered that they do know, and have been hit with the blinding knowledge that comes to all those who acquire instant knowledge on arcane subjects."

Turner was selling an image of Canada as a kinder, gentler nation than the United States. "We don't have the same icon of rugged individualism, while social democracy is a legitimate part of the political spectrum," says political commentator David Suzuki. "Canada is not superior to or better than the United States, but different. Tighter economic ties with such a huge and powerful nation will inevitably reduce those important differences."

The Liberals were concerned primarily that, since there was nothing in the agreement that specifically protected Canada's social programs, they would eventually have to be eliminated. Once the pact was in place, Turner warned, Canadian companies would move to parts of the United States where taxes were lower, thus shrinking Canada's revenues and forcing cutbacks in social services.

Most economists reject that argument. "The free trade agreement will make a beautiful omelet, but to think that you can make an omelet without breaking eggs is nonsense," says Richard Belous, an economist who heads the Washington-based National Planning Association's Canadian-American Committee. "It will have some restraining impact on social spending, but it's very difficult to finance a social agenda if you have low productivity growth. We've seen that in the United States."

The C.D. Howe Institute, a Canadian think tank, agrees. Access to the U.S. market "will help Canadian firms generate the wealth that maintains our high relative living standards, and that is available for redistribution through egalitarian social policies," it said in a recent report.

Mulroney's victory may have broad implications for the shape of the world trading system as well. Frustrated with the slow pace of progress in resolving trade disputes, more and more countries are turning to bilateral trade agreements or limited trade blocs. The 12-nation European Community is well on the way toward its goal of a completely unfettered trade bloc by 1992, creating a single internal market of 320 million people, and U.S. trade negotiators are looking closely at the possibility of bilateral agreements with Mexico and Japan.

If Turner's campaign to scrap the free trade agreement had been successful, analysts say, it would have derailed U.S. attempts to strike any further bilateral deals. But Mulroney's victory has pushed the broad movement toward bilateralism significantly forward; while it will still be hard to overcome nationalistic resistance to such deals, the momentum has been launched, and it is widely expected that the U.S.-Canadian deal will serve as the blueprint for negotiating similar agreements.

Stephen Brookes

CHAPTER 16

Zionist pioneers knew there could be "no Torah without bread," and they worked hard to establish a viable economy for their homeland. But this article, originally published March 24, 1986, made clear the staggering nature of Israel's economic woes, brought on as they are by massive public expenditures, long-standing socialist policies in agricultural and industrial organizations and a workers' federation that in effect sets national labor policies.

TURMOIL IN ISRAEL, THE TEMPLE OF LABOR

The West Bank is relatively peaceful, for now. The Arab refugee camps there are abandoned, the windows of the cinder block buildings boarded up and the surrounding ground shelled into mounds of rubble. Jericho is back to being a sleepy Arab town and tourist trap. In the fields and citrus groves of the Jordan valley, the kibbutzniks scatter industriously or rest under the isolated shade trees. At Taba, the resort town on Israel's southern tip on the shores of the Gulf of 'Aqaba, an uneasy truce reigns. Machine-gun-toting soldiers stroll warily past girls in bikinis as negotiations between Cairo and Jerusalem drag on over the remote strip of beach.

Occasional bursts of violence still come from the Gaza Strip between Egypt and Israel, and mayors are still assassinated in the West Bank towns. But the incidents are random, perpetrated almost listlessly. Even the latest incident in the "security zone" along the Lebanese border (the ambush and capture of two Israeli soldiers Feb. 19) seemed the exception that proved the rule and was followed quickly by public debate on whether the 10-kilometer-wide security zone should be abandoned.

For the first time in recent history, the peripheral areas of Israel have enjoyed two years of relative calm. Preoccupied by plunging oil prices and the escalating Iran-Iraq war, Israel's hostile neighboring states have had little energy to divert to harassing the Jewish nation. The collapse of the Palestine Liberation Organization negotiations with Jordan and the continued ranting of Libya's Col. Muammar Qaddafi only reinforce the impression that, if the "Mideast peace process" has stagnated, a lull in hostilities has, at least for the moment, settled in.

Rather than focusing on defense or security matters, the public debate — in the halls of the Knesset (the Israeli parliament) and in the cafes of Tel Aviv — shifted inward last year. And the subject that transfixed politicians and public alike was the economy. "I don't think you can describe to anyone who's not been through it," says Marsha Brown, an Israeli who immigrated from New Jersey seven years ago, "what it means to wake up in the morning and they've just raised the price of bread and milk."

Early last year, inflation in Israel had been quieted to less than 12 percent a month (285 percent annually) after having reached annual rates of more than 1,000 percent in the fall of 1984. The elaborate system of wage indexing and subsidies for consumers could no longer keep up with the rampant price increases, and "money dissolved in your hands," as a Jerusalem shopkeeper puts it. Foreign currency reserves had slipped below $2 billion, so low that Israel had less than three months before foreign exchange would run out altogether. The budget deficit had reached unsustainable levels, and the government's expenditure had reached 60 percent of the gross national product (compared to around 24 percent in the United States). The foreign debt was the highest per capita in the world. Economic growth, which had reached staggering levels of 10 percent annually in the early 1970s, had stopped.

The series of package deals between the government and the Histadrut, the mammoth labor federation, that were designed to head off a massive economic calamity had failed dismally. In short, after years of unrestrained spending, rising standards of living and rampant inflation, Prime Minister Shimon Peres and his Cabinet came to the belated conclusion that, as Daniel Doron of the Israel Center for Economic Progress says, "The party was over."

What ensued was an unprecedented series of drastic economic steps taken after a marathon Cabinet meeting July 2. The next day, the government announced a comprehensive stabilization program, including:

• Reductions in basic subsidies to consumers, which helped cut the federal deficit from 17 percent to 8 percent of the GNP.

• A devaluation of the shekel and a stabilized exchange rate vis-a-vis the U.S. dollar, followed in the autumn by the introduction of the "new shekel." (A dollar now equals about 1.48 new shekels, compared with more than 1,500 shekels per dollar in mid-1985.)

• A wage and price freeze and abolition of most of the indexation linking wages to cost-of-living increases (which lead all Israelis to calculate their salaries only in terms of steady dollars, not the fluctuating shekel). With the reduction in subsidies, these measures meant a drop of 20 percent in real wages.

The economic plan was largely successful in stopping inflation. A Histadrut general strike only days after the plan was announced led to further wage negotiations, but the government accomplished the feats of lowering monthly price increases to less than 1.5 percent; reducing the government's share of the work force by a hiring freeze; lowering the foreign debt by $42 million in six months; diminishing personal consumption by up to 3 percent; and turning the corner on the declining GNP.

In fact, for the first time since 1954 (thanks largely to declining oil prices), Israel's income exceeded its expenditures for the last few months of 1985, and a surplus in civilian current accounts of up to $600 million is expected in 1986. The availability of funds has prompted a sharp debate among Israeli leaders over the proper steps toward real economic growth in the coming months — a debate that threatens to devolve into a wrangle over who gets the most funds.

But the success of the stabilization program and the growing dissatisfaction with Israel's hidebound, government-dominated economic institutions have led many to see the coming year as a turning point for the nation as a whole. Israel has a chance, as many see it, to overhaul its economy and move toward a modern, Western-style, productive society. But it runs the risk of reverting to spending beyond its means, stifling entrepreneurship and depending on American largess.

"From a security and political viewpoint," says Akiva Offenbacher, a senior economist at the state-run Bank of Israel, "the country has arrived. You can't live your life based on the assumption that you're going to be thrown into the sea anymore. We have a country and a state and a government, and we have a society that can enforce the type of institutions that are needed for growth at Western standards. So let's do it."

"The whole [economic] system is crumbling from within," adds Doron. "How it will come down and what will replace it is anybody's guess." The system for which Doron has such gloomy forecasts has its roots in the earliest stirrings of Zionism, as well as the harsh realities that faced the fledgling Jewish state after it established itself in 1948.

From the start, the Zionist pioneers understood that there could be "no Torah without bread." In other words, the survival of the Jewish beachhead in Palestine depended on the establishment of a viable economy. For each succeeding aliyah, or wave of immigration, "the initial priority clearly was to find employment," Howard Sachar writes in "A History of Israel." As early as 1898, Nachman Syrkin's manifesto, "The Jewish Question and the Socialist Jewish State," proclaimed that "Zionism must of necessity fuse with socialism," and the development of the *yishuv* (the name by which the Jewish community was known under the British mandatory government from 1917 to 1947) in general hewed to that doctrine.

The earliest settlers of the *yishuv*, most of them fresh from the working-class neighborhoods of Eastern Europe, often arrived imbued with the ideal of Labor Zionism: winning back the Jewish homeland through physical, largely agricultural, labor and collective organization. The "religion of labor" was trumpeted loudest in the writings of Aaron David Gordon (1856-1922), a Soviet Jew and devotee of Nietzsche and Tolstoy who emigrated to Palestine in middle age and wrote his essays in the evenings after days spent working in the fields.

By the 1930s, as European anti-Semitism grew in virulence, more than 150,000 Jews had settled in Palestine. Private capital from the Diaspora helped build the first factories in Haifa and Tel Aviv. The construction boom, which would for years drive the domestic economy as waves of new immigrants arrived, had already begun.

But the largely socialist ideology of the Zionists still held sway among the Jews of Palestine. The kibbutz, the utopian agricultural community, remains the abiding embodiment of that ideology, but Labor Zionism extended its influence to the cities as well. The earliest workers' organizations, like Poalei Zion (Workers of Zion) and HaPoel HaZair (Young Worker), had coalesced into an overarching labor federation. December 1920 saw the founding of the Histadrut — the massive "union of unions" which today controls a quarter of the Israeli economy and dominates the life of the average Israeli from cradle to grave.

"Israel is one of the few countries in the world," says Doron, "where the state created the nation rather than the nation creating the state. By the state I mean the self-governing institutions that the populace had created for itself in Palestine. Those institutions have absorbed the bulk of the population, and it's only natural that they became predominant in economic activity." After the declaration of nationhood and the bitter war with the Arabs, the Labor Party (then largely represented by Mapai, one of three labor parties which merged) under Prime Minister David Ben-Gurion began the dominance of political life which would be routine for almost 30 years. Ben-Gurion and the Labor Party had created the state of Israel virtually ex nihilo, housing and feeding new immigrants, finding them employment and powering the industrial and agricultural enterprises that changed the face of Palestine.

"To a certain extent, socialism was necessary during the early years of the state," says Dan Gillerman, president of the Federation of Israeli Chambers of Commerce. "In 1948 there were 600,000 people here, and we brought in three times that many in the first few years. To bring all those people and feed them and provide housing, there was no other way than by socialist means."

What resulted was an extraordinary blend of democracy and quasi-socialism, a labor- and government-dominated economy side by side with a contentious, often unworkable version of European parliamentary democracy. Fully 35 percent of the work force in Israel is employed by central and municipal governments, compared with 15 percent (nonmilitary employment) in the United States. By 1984 the government's budget had surpassed the GNP, and more than 90 percent of public and private capital savings are government-controlled. Ninety-three percent of the land and virtually all water resources are government-owned, as are many large industrial corporations (the oil company Paz, the chemicals giant ICI, the electronics firm Zion Cables).

Alongside this highly developed federal bureaucracy exists the huge, quasi-governmental structure of the Histadrut. The Histadrut is unique in its multiple role as federation of unions, worker-owned industrial conglomerate and manager of health and pension funds. Depending on whom one asks, it is either a many-tentacled octopus strangling the natural drive of the Israeli worker and entrepreneur or a benevolent guardian of the worker's rights and the traditions of Labor Zionism. Almost all the unions in the country (representing 80 percent of the labor force) are part of the Histadrut, and each individual worker is a full member of the larger body as well as of his local union. In other words, as Histadrut Secretary-General Israel Kessar puts it, "When I sign a contract with the government, it's in the name of each worker."

The clout of the Histadrut, along with the welfare orientation of the government, has led to extraordinary benefits for Israelis, including generous pension and health care plans, near-total job security and the system of wage indexation. They have also led to staggering taxation rates, an economy unresponsive to market forces and a general passivity on the part of Israeli citizens — a "tendency to put in eight hours and come home and let the government take care of me," as Eliyahu Kanovsky, chairman of the economics department at Bar-Ilan University in Tel Aviv, puts it.

But despite those factors, the Israeli economy worked, by any standard, exceedingly well for two decades. In the early years, the Israeli government turned the innovation and industry that had allowed it to triumph in the 1950-51 Arab war to the building of roads, housing and water lines, with the result that a modern infrastructure was fashioned in the space of a few years. Remarkably, Israel has built a viable export economy almost from scratch: Exports increased 3,600 percent in the first three decades of the new state, and growth rates reached 12 percent annually in the early 1970s, the highest in the so-called developing world.

At the same time, the standard of living for Israeli citizens grew commensurately, but not without a social price. The traditional rift in Israeli society between the Ashkenazim — the European Jews who brought Zionism to Israel — and the Sephardim — the later immigrants from North Africa and various Arab states — was gradually exacerbated. The better-educated Ashkenazim filled the professional and civil service sectors, and the more backward Sephardim were most often relegated to menial labor. This basic inequity was most acute in the outlying areas of Galilee in the north and the Negev in the south, in newly created towns like Kiryat Shmona.

The ensuing social friction found its expression in the rise to political power of Menachem Begin and the Likud Party. Begin's hardline Herut faction formed the core of Likud, and Likud's combination of fierce nationalism, determination to annex the biblical territory of Israel eventually and willingness to find a place for the disadvantaged Sephardic immigrants gained them a swelling following in the 1970s.

At the same time, a series of external setbacks was beginning to undermine the miracle of Israel's economic progress. The Yom Kippur war of 1973 was extremely costly in terms of both expense and public confidence in government and military leaders. The oil crises of 1973-75 and 1978-1980 were severe shocks to the small country's industry. And with the Camp David accords of 1979, Begin took the fateful, if unavoidable, step of signing away the Sinai oil fields, controlled (and developed) by Israel since 1967.

In 1972, Kanovsky estimates, Israel imported less than $100 million worth of oil. In 1977 the figure was $700 million to $800 million, and by 1982 Israel was spending $2 billion a year on oil. The effect was devastating. Part of the difference was covered by U.S. aid — now in the form of direct grants rather than loans. In fiscal year 1985, the U.S. government provided $1.8 billion in military aid and $1.2 billion in economic aid, and a $1.5 billion emergency supplement in economic aid for distribution in 1985 and 1986. Other sources of money, primarily from the United Jewish Appeal and the sale of Israel Bonds, amount to about $500 million a year. Since 1948, U.S. aid has totaled approximately $32 billion, at first mainly in the form of loans. Israel paid some $1 billion in interest to the United States in 1985.

But the social benefits continued. Despite the rightist orientation of Likud's foreign policy, its domestic spending habits were every bit as questionable as Labor's. After Begin's accession to the premiership in 1977, a succession of Likud finance ministers opened even wider the coffers of government and encouraged a spending spree which boosted personal consumption 43 percent from 1978 to 1985, while the GNP has grown at only half that rate.

Such a binge of public expenditure was almost inevitable, given the party-dominated structure of Israeli politics. Likud had built its support over the years by becoming beholden to a melange of smaller parties and splinter groups, acting in the interest of the poorer Sephardic Jews who had received scant attention from the entrenched, Westernized Labor hierarchy. So when Likud came to power it was only natural that it would have to reward its backers with political favors and government handouts.

The invasion of Lebanon in 1982 — which cost Israel dearly both in finances and world opinion — further damaged the consensus and national determination of the Israeli citizenry. The ensuing self-doubt and economic turmoil finally shattered both Menachem Begin and the Likud government, and the country's indecisive mood continued to be reflected in the factious 1984 election and its inconclusive results. The resultant coalition government, formed after weeks of negotiations, calls for a rotating premiership. (Labor's Shimon Peres has served out most of his 20-month term, due to end in October, at which point Yitzhak Shamir of Likud is to take the reins of power.)

By the time of the election, U.S. patience with Israel's economic policies had run out. In granting $1.5 billion in emergency aid (to supplement the $2.6 billion military and economic assistance package), the Reagan administration made it clear that strong austerity measures had to be taken. A board of American economists appointed by Secretary of State George P. Shultz, in fact, had presented a 10-point program of economic steps to the Peres government during a visit in 1984. The 10 "benchmarks" formed the core of the austerity plan enacted by Israel the last part of that year.

The dour, intellectual Peres has received well-deserved credit for his willingness to take the necessary stabilizing steps; but now, many fear, political pressures may once again be gaining ascendancy over economic common sense. "They haven't mended their ways at all," intones Doron of the Center for Economic Progress, sounding characteristically exasperated with Israeli politicians. "They want to start economic growth, which only means they want to start handing out goodies again to their political cronies."

Specifically, Finance Minister Yitzhak Modai leveled that charge at Peres in a bitter Cabinet meeting Feb. 13. The cigar-chomping Modai is an imposing figure and a mercurial character. It is he, rather than Shamir, who seems to dominate the economic discussion within Likud. He loudly threatened to resign if Peres went ahead with plans to devote $500 million to a discretionary "prime minister's fund" earmarked for stimulating economic growth and was quoted as telling the Association of Chambers of Commerce in Tel Aviv that "if they start operating the printing presses, I'll go home."

Peres, for his part, apparently fears a major infusion of funds after he steps down in October — a monetary expansion which would certainly reflate the economy and ease the austerity felt by everyone in Israel over the past few months and might perhaps lead to real economic growth. The struggles over reflation have threatened to bring down the coalition government, a consequence that all agree would also topple the carefully constructed program of stabilization. "Peres is thinking of his place in history," says Avi Temkin, an economics reporter for the Jerusalem Post. "Right now he is the man who saved the economy. But if there is a rise in standards of living after rotation, he may be remembered as the austerity guy while Shamir was the one who brought prosperity."

What persists, then, is a strong sense of uncertainty about the future and a realization that, if the immediate crisis of runaway inflation has passed, the harder task of developing a sound economy remains. "The great danger now," says Gillerman, "is that those people who control the economy have so much fallen in love with this Pygmalion which they have created. Everything we have achieved so far has been under artificial conditions, in a hothouse or laboratory. The time has come to try it out in the real world and see if it works."

There is unanimous agreement, in both of the main political camps, that Israel's growth must come in exports rather than domestic consumption, and that for the Israeli export industry to flourish, firms must have much greater access to capital.

The Tel Aviv Stock Exchange was nicknamed "The Slow and The Dead" by Israel Economist, an English language monthly magazine, in a review of 1985. Investment in Israel has always been fueled by infusions of foreign capital, and as the government outstripped its budget year after year, it gradually turned to the public savings to fund its budget. Temkin observes that "today there is not really such a thing as private debenture" in Israel: The government controls close to 100 percent of all forms of financial assets, whether they're in mandatory employee-savings schemes, provident (or pension) funds or foreign-currency-linked accounts. In addition, the successful economic plan has driven interest rates to levels that evoke disbelief from Americans: Forty percent a year is average, and 60 percent not uncommon.

Minister of Economics and Planning Gad Yacobi has submitted a comprehensive economic plan to Peres that includes freeing up at least 7 percent to 10 percent of the capital market, in hopes of reviving the moribund stock market, and channeling close to $200 million directly to public companies. Combined with tax incentives and government loans to export-oriented and sophisticated industries, the additional source of funds could help revitalize the economy — some say almost immediately.

"Israelis are great savers," maintains Gillerman. "There's something like $4 billion in private savings, in life insurance, in savings programs. People would like to have some alternative rather than having that money lay around in savings schemes. If you gave them incentives and got 10 percent of that money back into the economy you'd have $400 million overnight."

Yacobi's plan, like many of the measures advocated by Labor and Likud leaders, goes on to promote some fairly standard steps toward a free economy. It would lower the stiflingly high income tax rates, raise the standards of proof to qualify for welfare benefits, continue the dismantling of the old price subsidy system and alter the tax rolls to give encouragement to promising producers of export goods over older, uneconomic industries.

However desirable those moves might seem to an American businessman, each is fraught with much more political and emotional intensity than in the United States. Critics have termed the Yacobi plan politically motivated (Yacobi, like Peres, is a Labor Party member), and infeasible. But Yacobi defends it on purely economic grounds. "In spite of the criticisms I've been hearing," says the minister, "these are not proposals directed at political gains. They are very cautious, very solid, and they include no direct subsidies and hardly any budget increases."

The government also has to find a way to deal with a monumental internal debt: Because of its monopolization of public savings, the government now owes Israeli citizens $37 billion, a figure expected to balloon to $75 billion by 1993. After the bank shares crisis of 1983 in which the artificially inflated shares of stock in the banks held by the public collapsed, the government guaranteed compensation to those left holding the shares in scheduled payments through 1988. So far the government has successfully rolled over the debt, convincing the shareholders to hold on to the paper for promises of higher returns in the future. Nevertheless, the internal debt has been called "a time bomb" by more than one observer, and reports have circulated that the government is searching for a way out of the bank shares agreement.

The government intends as well to begin unloading many of the bigger government-owned industries, though controversy exists about the speed of the denationalization process. Among the companies to be sold are the highly profitable telephone company Bezeq, the oil company Paz and the electronics firm Zion Cables, though the size of the three and the small size of Israel's capital markets may force the government to seek purchasers abroad.

Should such a privatization occur, the prospects for Israel are good. The skilled work force, the proved industriousness and innovation of Israeli firms, the availability of large amounts of capital both from abroad and at home, and free-trade treaties with both the European Economic Community and the United States (Israel is the only nation so favored by both) all point to a potentially strong export economy along the lines of Belgium's or the Netherlands'.

The idea that Israel's future lies in high technology has been pronounced so often that it is now a cliche waiting to be fulfilled. As Doron points out, Israel has more Massachusetts Institute of Technology graduates per capita than any country except the United States and produces a disproportionate share of state-of-the-art medical instruments and military hardware.

High-tech success stories already can be found in Israel. The Elscint Co., founded in 1969 in Haifa, now holds a large portion of the world market in computerized axial tomography scanners for medical use. Rafael, the research and development arm of the Israeli Defense Forces, has developed the most sophisticated thermal night-vision instrument in the world.

The tendency to jump on the high-tech bandwagon is widespread — Peres himself has called for more emphasis on funding and research and for technological firms. But high tech cannot save Israel from its economic woes. "Just to say that 'high tech' is the thing isn't saying very much," says Offenbacher. "You have to find a specific good for a specific market where you can sell at an advantage. It's a very risky field."

Herbert Stein of the American Enterprise Institute, one of the Americans appointed by Secretary of State Shultz to the economic advisory board for Israel, points out that the Technion, the college of engineering and sciences near Haifa, already graduates more technicians than the country can absorb. "High tech depends on these highly skilled people," adds Stein, "and these high-tech people can earn much more in [Silicon Valley capital] Palo Alto than in Tel Aviv. When they have the constant security threat and the constant high taxes in Israel, what's going to keep these mobile people there?"

Stein's comment points up a fundamental conflict that underlies any economic program in Israel and threatens to undermine efforts to improve the situation. Israel's tradition of near-full employment is anachronistic for a modern, fully functioning economy; a certain amount of unemployment ("frictional employment") may be necessary to soften the labor market, keep wages down and encourage job mobility. But unemployment is concentrated in the impoverished development towns (30 percent of the jobless are in development areas, which have only 9 percent of the total population). And Israel, a society of immigrants that has seen emigration rise inexorably in the past decade, may not be willing to pay that price.

"In the States when there's high unemployment, the people living on the East Coast travel to the West Coast or the South to look for work," comments Kanovsky. "The problem is, in Israel they do the same thing: They go to California or Florida or Texas."

Structural factors make it difficult for any government, Labor, Likud or coalition, to make headway in transforming Israel's welfare economy into a free market one. The Likud government of 1977 came into office trumpeting a "New Economic Policy," but as inflation skyrocketed and entrenched political forces blocked efforts to reduce their share of the pie, government intervention and distorted prices only increased.

Closing down unproductive, government-supported industries carries a high social price. Israel Kessar threatens that if Solel Boneh, the troubled Histadrut construction firm which employs close to 15,000, "is allowed to collapse, then this country will collapse."

"The economy itself can't be separated from social trends," says Yacobi. "We cannot close our eyes to the fact that agriculture is in very bad shape, and some areas are close to collapse. And we cannot close our eyes to the fact that 30 percent of the young people are unemployed two years after they're discharged from the army."

"Certainly we believe that the government has to reduce its involvement [in the economy]," says David Brodet, an adviser to Minister of Industry and Trade Ariel Sharon. "The question is how to do it without too much damage." The potential damage extends not only to Israel's standard of living and financial institutions. The proposed changes could gnaw at the whole ethos that has carried Israel through the first decades of military siege, economic hardship and constant dedication to the future. To shift from Israel's current economic setup to a truly capitalist society requires more than technical and institutional changes. It requires a fundamental move from egalitarian policies and ways of thinking to an American-style ferment of self-interest and competition. Despite all the talk of achieving a free market economy, there is little indication that Israelis or their leaders are prepared for such a radical alteration in the national vision.

"One of the tragedies of the Begin government," says community leader Marsha Brown of Kiryat Shmona, "with its concentration on material gain, what I call 'bread and circuses,' is that they lost sight of some of the things that made people come here in the first place. Originally people were willing to sacrifice the good life for a national ideal. And that's changed in the last 10 years. Once you lose sight of why you're here, and you can't get that extra TV or new kitchen cabinet, then how is Tel Aviv any different than New York? That's when people start to leave and go to Europe or America."

As Doron has pointed out in frequent columns in The Wall Street Journal, a thriving economy involves some amount of risk and, inevitably, some failures, of companies and at times whole industries. Those are calamities that Israel has not been willing to undergo. As growth occurs, there will also ensue some expansion at each end of the economic spectrum, with more people becoming very wealthy and more dropping into poverty. Free market economics, says Offenbacher, means "basically survival of the fittest" — a social Darwinism entirely out of keeping for a state founded on democratic socialist lines. Continues Offenbacher: "The only way to reach a Western [economic] level is if the economy gets freed up, and that would represent a change in the whole philosophy here. The whole philosophy of central planning, of promoting not profitability and growth but just subsistence, might have been appropriate for the formative years of the state, but not for a healthy modern economy."

That change in philosophy would have to bring with it some diminution in the role of the Histadrut. In the phrase of David Kochav, a former government economist, the Histadrut is "two-headed," encompassing both labor unions and industrial enterprises. Much of the strength of the American economy has come from a healthy give-and-take of labor and management, a market environment where the respective claims of each — to fair wages and working conditions on the one hand and increased profitability on the other — maintain a competitive balance. Israel, the land of Labor Zionism, enjoys no such balance.

"Certainly, one would not expect a rapidly growing economy to have a large part of its enterprise in the hands of an organization like the Histadrut," says Herbert Stein. "But I think the most realistic hope is that the economy will grow up around it, and the relative role of the Histadrut would be reduced. It would be folly to make an attack on that system as it now exists."

Besides the obvious stake that the United States has in Israel's fortunes, the small, beleaguered country exerts a fascination as a sort of economic microcosm. The major problems of Israel — huge deficits, an intractable budget and entrenched interests which resist cutting of government expenditures, defense needs which are only expected to rise and large numbers of workers losing jobs in obsolete industries — are those of the United States magnified in relative terms. For Israel to survive, much less prosper, the conflicts of a controlled, labor-based frontier society vs. the realities of international competition and a rapidly modernizing economy — of a hallowed and idealistic tradition vs. the disinterested forces of change — must be addressed. The siege state has learned that the most implacable enemy may lie within.

Richard Martin

PART 6

AN EMPIRE'S END

CHAPTER 17

For years, the Central Intelligence Agency had consistently estimated that the Soviet economy was about half the size of the U.S. economy and growing slowly but steadily. Then came glasnost, and all of a sudden Soviet economists themselves started saying that the CIA estimates were way too high. They said their economy was a tenth to at most a third the size of the United States' and shrinking. For some economists who had long been critical of the CIA estimates, as this May 21, 1990, article reported, it was a welcome vindication.

THE BEAR IS BEARISH ON ECONOMIC ANALYSIS

How dead is dead? When the patient is the Soviet economy, even the experts can't agree. That's why a group of them gathered near Washington on a recent weekend to butt heads.

The unprecedented meeting was held under the auspices of the American Enterprise Institute, a research-oriented Washington think tank of mildly conservative reputation. Among those attending were officials of Goskomstat, the Soviet statistical agency whose numerology has long been received with snickers at home and abroad. Also present were analysts from the Central Intelligence Agency, once seen as a more reliable source but now coming in for the same treatment.

In the West, the CIA has traditionally dominated the business of guesstimating Soviet economic strength by dint of its unmatched resources. By the agency's lights, the Soviet economy is just over half as big as the U.S. economy.

This claim has been under quiet assault for some time, led by a group of economists with the Rand Corp., a research firm in Santa

Monica, Calif. More recently it has also been assailed by certain Soviet academics, who quip that they wish they lived in a country as prosperous as the one pictured in the CIA's statistics. Viktor Belkin, a member of the Soviet Academy of Sciences and perhaps the gloomiest of the lot, reckons that Soviet output is only 14 percent of America's. Others put it at 20 to 35 percent.

"If you believe the CIA's estimate, the Soviet economy is bigger than Japan's. If you believe these other estimates, it's smaller than Italy's. That's quite a difference," says Igor Birman, an emigre economist who has spent the last decade trying to persuade the CIA to lower its figures.

The dispute is more than academic; it goes to the heart of what policymakers know about the Soviet Union. Take the question of how fast the Soviet economy has been growing. According to the intelligence agency, it expanded by 2.4 percent a year from 1971 to 1985. While not exactly breathtaking, this performance could hardly be considered disastrous. So it is little wonder that Western politicians were thrown for a loop when Mikhail Gorbachev suddenly appeared on the scene, wringing his hands over the "crisis" of the Soviet economy and prepared to throw his empire into an uproar to fix it. In the world according to the CIA, such a development is hard to explain.

On the other hand, if the agency's critics are right and the Soviet economy has been stagnant or shrinking for a decade, the Soviet leader's panic becomes comprehensible. According to Anders Aslund, a Swedish economist and charter member in the CIA-bashers fraternity, "The high CIA estimates have been an important reason for the failure of most Western analysts to predict and understand the earnest craving for economic reform among much of the current Soviet leadership."

William Safire, the New York Times columnist and former Nixon phrasemaker, has played the role of chief publicist for the "Team B" view of the Soviet economy. He points to another vital area where rosy estimates may have led experts astray: in estimating the share of Soviet resources going to the military.

In a CIA-size economy, the Soviets were thought to be pouring 15 percent of resources into defense, just over twice the share spent by the Pentagon. But if Moscow is really spending 25 to 35 percent, it suggests the Soviets are even more armaments-crazed than once thought, with manifold implications for Western policy. Writes Safire: "The Soviet economy is much smaller than we thought, which means that the Kremlin is under far greater pressure than we imagined to reduce its spending on defense and empire."

John F. Kennedy once observed that the developing world was watching to see which would prove better at delivering the goods, communism or capitalism. The world then still marveled at the seeming miracle of the Soviet Union's rapid industrialization, and even a U.S. president had difficulty mustering a ringing affirmation of the West's inevitable triumph.

In its estimates of the Soviet economy, the CIA may likewise have lacked the courage of its convictions, say critics. Its main methodological error, they add, was failing to take seriously enough what textbooks teach about central planning's infirmities.

As Belkin, the Soviet economist, told the conference: "The non-market model is an impediment to structural change and an obstacle to demand-supply balance. In the long run, it lowers the use value of GNP. This fact was underestimated" by the CIA. For instance, in making its estimates, the agency pays a lot of attention to inputs, or the materials and labor that go into the production of final goods. The agency has long been impressed with Soviet claims to be the world's largest producer of energy, pig iron, fertilizer, tractors, timber, cloth and other so-called intermediate goods.

But what the agency takes as strength, others see as weakness. Western economists have calculated that, for each unit of output, the Soviet Union puts in three times as much energy, labor and material as a Western industrialized economy. The word for this is waste. As a former agriculture chief, Gorbachev himself has admitted that 20 percent of Soviet farm production spoils before reaching market, and other experts put it much higher. Belkin estimates that half of the country's industrial output is squandered.

Ironically, in a land notorious for shortages, some waste includes overproduction. Belkin says his country cranks out five times as many tractors as the United States because Soviet designers have yet to hit on the idea of one that can hitch up to every type of trailing equipment.

Another flaw in the agency's methods, the critics say, is its faith in the raw numbers that Soviet officials give for their economy's material output. According to Aslund, because Soviet farms and factories do their own reporting, "there is no serious control over delivered statistics." And Vasily Seluinin, a Soviet journalist who attended the conference, claims that the official books exaggerate the number of goods-delivering trips by the state trucking organization by a factor of five.

Critics also point to what they say is another systematic error in

CIA estimates: the failure to fully factor in inflation. Under central planning, with bureaucrats setting the price of everything, inflation is not supposed to exist, but it does — in overt and covert forms. Failing to recognize rising prices can lead to exaggerated ideas about the growth of an economy. In fact, central planning is not very good at controlling prices. Factories can win approval to mark up the price of their products just by claiming to have made some nonexistent improvement. They also tend to shift their production toward higher-priced goods. The supply of lower-priced goods goes down, and the average price of those goods that are actually available rises inexorably.

A particularly insidious form of inflation is the declining quality of goods. Pravda has recounted how, as their quota deadline approaches, those who assemble Soviet TVs use hammers rather than screwdrivers to put in screws. Paying the same and getting less is another name for inflation.

Birman has specialized in criticizing the CIA from the consumption side of the ledger, particularly for what he regards as its failure to fully account for the inferior nature of Soviet goods. The CIA, he says, has sent agents on shopping trips in Soviet cities to bring back goods. These are paraded in front of experts from Sears, Roebuck and other companies, who tell the agency what it would cost to produce them in the United States. The difference in cost is taken as a guide to quality differences.

But, as Birman points out using a pet example, differences in cost do not necessarily equal differences in quality: "In any Western dustpan, you have a little gap to keep the dust from falling back out. In the Soviet dustpan, they don't have it. And it makes the dustpan terrible. But the difference in cost is very small." Nor, he adds, are allowances made for the absence of variety, friendly service, plentiful supply or the ability to return defective merchandise. That such intangibles are hard to quantify is no excuse, he says, because ignoring them is tantamount to assigning them a value of zero, which is no less arbitrary than any other value they might be assigned.

Though the CIA attendees showed more inclination to entertain criticism than in the past, they remained skeptical of the critique, according to conference chairman Nick Eberstadt, a Harvard researcher and fellow at the American Enterprise Institute. "In the past, Soviet economists said their economy could do no wrong. Now they are saying it can do nothing right. I think there is some discounting [by agency analysts] of extreme statements."

Belkin sympathizes with the CIA's resistance to a view that

demotes the Soviet Union to the upper rank of Third World economies. "It is difficult to admit that a superpower, being at military parity with the United States and investing enormous resources in exploration of space, is smaller in terms of GNP than countries with one-fifth of its population," he said.

Still, the agency's estimates are important fodder for the making of national security policy. If the critics are right, the green-eyeshade gang has steadily overlooked the accumulating economic disaster that underlies the greatest shift in Soviet policy since the revolution. That would be a goof-up of monumental proportion.

Says Birman, "The CIA people are not working for themselves or for the scientific community. They are supposed to form a basis for our foreign policy, for our understanding of what is going on in the Soviet Union. And they didn't do it."

Holman Jenkins Jr.

Chapter 18

The plight of the Soviet consumer only grew worse during the early stages of Mikhail Gorbachev's perestroika, and thanks to glasnost, the West got a window on a world about which it knew little. This article, which originally appeared April 3, 1989, told some of the horror stories of centrally planned agriculture.

Russians Bemoaning Their Piteous Produce

A Soviet sausage is a curious object to behold. Small and shriveled to begin with, the poor thing turns limp and grayish after a couple of days in the fridge. Soviet consumers finally seem to be losing patience with it. As a result of reader compliants, a debate has been raging in Literaturnaya Gazeta for more than a year as to what goes into its making. The weekly magazine's investigators found it contains bits of cowhide and bones with plenty of salt added to cover the nasty taste. In some instances, nails, sand and glass had been added for extra nourishment.

The magazine is now being sued for slander and for "denigrating the meat processors' honor and dignity" by Yuri M. Luzhkov, chairman of the Moscow City Agro-industrial Committee. In response to what is evidently a conspiracy among consumers, Soviet sausage makers have barred state inspectors from entering the processing plants.

Anxious to avoid any taint of political bias, the magazine in January suggested using cats as taste arbiters, since they can be considered neutral in the debate over restructuring the Soviet economy. Of 30 cats on Literaturnaya Gazeta's test panel, 24 refused to touch the sausages and five would touch only the more expensive kinds. One kitten ate everything, but she was only 2 months old and clearly had no idea what she was doing. "Cats have always loved sausage, ever since people invented it. So why, for God's sake, wouldn't they eat this sausage? And why in the world should we?" asked the magazine.

The sorry state of the Soviet sausage only begins the catalog of woes opened at the plenary meeting of the Soviet Central Committee March 15-16. The committee net to consider what is known as the "food question," the perennial headache of Soviet leaders. Answering that question is considered crucial to the success of Mikhail Gorbachev's economic reforms. Says Zhores Medvedev, author of "Soviet Agriculture": "The shortage of food products has become the most serious source of public discontent," partly because expectations soared on the strength of the Soviet leader's promises. Without improvements in the food supply — basic items like sugar, cheese and meat are rationed in many parts of the country — it will be hard, if not impossible, to persuade people to make the sacrifices necessitated by Gorbachev's program.

How bad it is down on the farm can be gauged by the preliminary figures for the 1988 grain harvest issued by the State Planning Committee in January. Stepan Sitaryan, first deputy chairman of the committee, announced a 195 million-ton harvest — 16 million tons less than the 1987 harvest and 40 million tons below the target, which translates into less meat and diary products on Soviet tables. As a result, by Western estimates, the Soviet Union may import more than 40 million metric tons of grain this year, the most in five years. The Soviets will have to spend an additional $3 billion of their scarce hard currency on imported food products, according to Jan Vanous, research director of PlanEcon Inc. in Washington, which specializes in assessing and forecasting economic development in the Soviet Union and Eastern Europe.

Soviet agriculture has never recovered from the dual blow of the Bolshevik Revolution and Joseph Stalin's war against the peasants, which saw the forced creation of giant state farms and collectives, and the murder, deportation or death from famine of millions of kulaks, the wealthier peasants. There have been sporadic attempts to revamp the system, notably by Nikita Khrushchev, but mostly the solution has been to throw money at the problem.

According to Gorbachev, who himself was agricultural czar from 1978 to 1984, the state has invested some 680 billion rubles (roughly $1 trillion) over the past 17 years but reaped only an overall 25 percent increase in output. Grain and cotton output rose by considerably less, while the supply of potatoes actually decreased by 9 percent. Perhaps the greatest indictment of the system lies in the fact that the 1.6 percent of arable land that is not state-owned produces 30 percent of the food.

For two decades under Leonid Brezhnev, money was poured into gigantic irrigation projects that managed to shrink the Aral Sea into a salt desert. Similarly, fertilizer was misused on a gross scale, poisoning rivers with tons of chemicals and showing up in all kinds of undesirable places, such as in mothers' milk. Gorbachev has spoken on this period as a "rape of nature."

The waste of the Soviet system remains colossal. According to economist Murray Feshbach, about one-third of the crops never reaches the consumer because of poor storage, poor transportation, poor roads and poor refrigeration but pests aplenty. Apples from Central Asia, for instance, look less than appetizing after a 2,000-mile trip by train, traveling at an average speed of 15 mph. According to Komsomolskaya Pravda, the Communist Youth League daily newspaper, three out of four harvested potatoes go to waste.

Owing to the poorness of the feed, according to Vladimir Tikhonov, a Soviet agronomist, a Soviet cow yields only slightly more milk than an American goat. There are also examples where peasants, for want of proper feed, give bread to their pigs. Bread is heavily subsidized in the Soviet Union and consequently very cheap. "For society, this is a very expensive way to feed a pig. These subsidies have all kinds of side effects that the originators did not think about or imagine," says Semyon Reznik, a Russian emigre author. Prime Minister Nikolai Ryzhkov freely admitted to the Council of Ministers in October that "there is perhaps no country in the world that adopts as thriftless an attitude to its harvests as we do."

One decision for the Central Committee meeting was to abolish the ill-fated Gosagroprom, the superministry for agriculture created by Gorbachev in 1985 as part of his effort to streamline Soviet bureaucracy. Instead of overcoming the kind of glitches that the five ministries it replaced had specialized in — one supplying fertilizer, another forgetting to supply the spreading machines — the superministry only compounded them. Shortly before the meeting, a Pravda article by Vladimir Somov, the paper's agriculture expert, announce: "We did not destroy bureaucracy, but to the contrary strengthened it." According to Somov, experts have traced orders from the chairman of Gosagroprom passing through 32 levels of authority before they reach the collective farms. Naturally, the papers are signed and duplicated at each way station. "The best idea is unlikely to come through this bureaucratic density without losing its force," he noted. A new government body will replace Gosagroprom, though its powers have not yet been specified.

The other theme of the Central Committee meeting was the leasing of state land. Calling for the abandonment of "ideological stereotypes and dogmas" and for the use of "all effective forms of farming," Gorbachev asked on a recent tour of the Ukraine: "Do we really have to regard as the summit of socialist organization those chronic money-losers where sponging dominates and where wages bear no relation to the work put in? To maintain these enterprises further through credits from the state budget, money that they will never pay back, is impossible and makes no sense."

Indeed, a key theme of his speeches is that in the collective system, people have become "separated from the soil," reduced to the status of "day laborers." "The most important thing today is to make people full-fledged masters of the land," he stated in a televised speech in October. It was last summer, at a Central Committee meeting, that he introduced the idea of leasing land. Now the committee has proposed that families or groups of peasants be allowed to lease land for 50 years or more, with the possibility in some cases of passing it on to their children. This time around, Gorbachev even used the words "individual property," which sounds naughtily close to a capitalist concept.

Not everybody thinks this is a hot idea. Though expressing "full unity" on all basic questions at the meeting, Yegor Ligachev, long seen as the chief rival of Gorbachev, had noted sourly only a few weeks before at a televised rally at Omsk in Siberia that "it was not for this that we established Soviet power" — which has become the refrain of the antireform groups. Ligachev lost his position as chief party ideologist (the Soviet No. 2) in Gorbachev's September minicoup, landing in the hot seat as head of the Communist Party's Commission on Agriculture. He remains a member of the Politburo.

Ligachev is committed to what he calls "socialist continuity" and has pledged himself to maintain loss-making collectives and state farms in the interests of "social justice." He stresses the need for more resources to be spent on reversing the flow of migrants from the countryside and on revamping the food processing industry, neither of which would threaten the collective farm structure.

Ligachev is not without support on this issue. According to Soviet newspaper reports, innovative farmers have lately become the object of good old-fashioned Stalinist envy, denounced as latter-day kulaks or "Rockefellers" and subjected to chicanery by local officials who will suddenly become superfluous should Gorbachev's newfangled ideas go too far. Pig sheds have been burned down, farmers have been attached and manure has been thrown into milk cans, because less productive older laborers fear they may be thrown out of work.

The success of Gorbachev's plan all depends on the firmness of the legal guarantees accompanying it. It is not yet clear what would happen if the government should suddenly change its mind. "What we need is legal protection, not instructions," one chairman of a collective farm has been quoted as saying. What is more, according to Harvard University economist Marshall I. Goldman, peasants must still buy materials from the collectives and state farms, which often assert first priority for the materials. And as long as the state also still has priority for the crops it buys at fixed prices, progress is going to be less than impressive.

This pessimism was reflected in the latest, rather bleak prediction of leading Soviet economist Leonid Abalkin, a close adviser to the government. "The important thing to know is when people, sitting around their kitchen tables, finally will be able to say, 'Oh, life is so much better than it was.' I think that will happen only by 1995, and then we will be reaping the first palpable changes by then." Until then, all talk of improvement remains phantom food.

Henrik Bering-Jensen

CHAPTER 19

When Mikhail Gorbachev began singing the praises of Western investment in the Soviet Union, businessmen and bankers flocked to Moscow in a modern replay of the gold rushes of the 19th century. Their optimistic pronouncements on the Soviet market, however, were a mixture of high hopes and hype, with the emphasis on the latter. The problem, as this article of December 26, 1988, spelled out: Producing little of value for export, the Soviet economy generated precious little hard currency to spend on the products and services that Westerners had to offer.

TRULY TALKING SHOP AT THE KREMLIN

Call it the new kremlinology — the latest way of thinking about what makes Soviet leaders tick. No longer, as many Western businessmen and diplomats see it, are the Soviets willing to sacrifice their people's comfort and health for the sake of military might. According to the new school, a more wholesome priority has lurched to the top of the Kremlin's agenda: bringing the good life home to the long-neglected consumer.

But priorities are one thing and achievements something else. Last summer, when Mikhail Gorbachev dropped in on a group of Siberian housewives to ask how he was doing, the response was such bitter grousing about the deteriorating quality of Soviet life — shoddy merchandise, endless lines and barren shelves — that even the Kremlin leader seemed to blanch. The emptiness of *perestroika*, Gorbachev's celebrated slogan of economic rebirth, was brutally displayed to the world by Soviet television.

"The party builds its relationship with the society on its ability to successfully manage the economy," says the Brookings Institution's

Ed Hewett. "Gorbachev is worried, the whole leadership is worried, that the party is losing its foundations of its support." Says a Swiss businessman: "Gorbachev knows that if he is going to survive, he must do something for the average person. And soon."

He has upped the ante in recent weeks, painting the crisis of the Soviet economy in bleak colors. Central Intelligence Agency estimates have been sunny by comparison, leading the spooks to claim that Gorbachev is exaggerating for dramatic effect. The CIA's critics, who have long said things were far worse, point to egg on agency faces.

In November, the existence of a Soviet budget deficit, given as 36 billion rubles, was admitted for the first time, helping to account for an unsocialist epidemic of inflation. Next came the repeal of Gorbachev's sobriety campaign. Besides winning back some of the regime's flagging popularity, reopening the vodka spigot was a desperate maneuver to boost revenues and reduce the sea of rubles sloshing around a stagflating economy.

Three years of fruitless reform have backed the Soviet leader into a corner. But there may be an escape route: massive borrowing and buying from the capitalist world. The Soviets have already sweetened the pot for foreign investors, thanks to a revised joint venture law that permits them a controlling share in partnerships with Soviet agencies. Soviet economists are flogging the idea of importing Western merchandise as a way of rally workers to *perestroika*'s banner. Gorbachev has been at pains to be encouraging. In a recent speech, he came closer than ever to singing the praises of a mixed economy, hinting that the Soviet Union might become a nuclear-tipped Sweden.

For businessmen, this looks like the marketing opportunity of a lifetime, more mouth-watering even than the opening of the People's Republic of China, that perennial lust object of Yankee traders. "You are talking about a billion Chinese with an average income of only $300 a year, compared to 270 million Russians who earn that much in a month," says Gianni Montezemolo. "That's a lot of people with a good income." Montezemolo is in charge of finding new markets for Johnson Wax, Raid insecticide and other goodies from S. C. Johnson & Son Inc.

But there is one problem: No country can buy for long without also selling, and the Soviet Union, a dismal failure as an exporter of finished goods, has little to entice the outside world. Even its fertilizer sells at a sharp discount because of poor quality. Seven decades after taking over, the Bolsheviks still get the vast bulk of their foreign cash from auctioning off the exhaustible riches — oil, gas, gold, diamonds — that came with the real estate.

Last year, they raked in a mere $30 billion. After shelling out for vital imports, interest payments and the upkeep of a wastrel empire, little is left for discretionary spending, and none for imported fripperies like British candy bars and Japanese VCRs. "There's no point in getting worked up about the Russian market," says Fred Halliday of the London School of Economics. "There's just not that much market there."

The cash squeeze is the biggest obstacle to business, and Gorbachev and his foreign suitors are at odds over how to bridge it. The Soviet leader wants investors who will supply at their own expense the technology to make Soviet industry competitive. This approach will not only conserve his own cash, it could also help him develop the manufactured exports to supplement his dwindling oil income.

Businessmen, however, may prefer to fry other fish. "Over the years, the companies that did the best were the ones that sold the Soviets a piece of equipment and left it at that," says Harvard University's Marshall Goldman. Not only do they avoid the hassle of setting up shop inside the Soviet Union, but they can quickly cut their losses if the Soviets turn xenophobic, as they have in the past. While companies are eager to do business, they want Gorbachev to pay cash, even if he has to borrow from the West to do it.

Luckily for the salesmen, banks are just as eager to provide the necessary credit. The Kremlin is regarded as a top-notch customer by international moneymen. Says a Swiss investment banker: "They are excellent payers — never a day late."

During the 1970s, in an age of reckless lending and borrowing, the Soviets were notably restrained on the receiving line. To the bankers, Soviet balance sheets now look like a model of financial rectitude. Installments on their $40 billion in foreign debt consume 20 percent of annual export revenues. The way the bankers reckon, the Soviets could double their borrowing before this ratio would reach the danger zone. "Anybody who deals with the Soviets knows they are almost paranoid about hard currency," says George Clark of Citibank N.A. "The danger today is that they won't borrow enough for good investment purposes."

Western bankers seem determined to prevent the Soviets from making that mistake. Cheered on by their respective governments, European banks trotted out a total of $6 billion in new credit lines this past fall, some with taxpayer guarantees. The fanfare was unprecedented. Unlike U.S. banks, which have legal and political complications to worry about, the Europeans always had cash to spare for the Soviets, so there was little reason for trumpeting the latest bundle — except as a token of support for Gorbachev. "There's always a certain amount of hype in international financing," says a New York banker. "But this sort of thing is really somewhat unseemly from anyone's point of view except the Russians'."

"Nobody in Europe considers it unpatriotic to lend to the Soviet Union," sniffs the Swiss financier. Never mind about the thousands of Warsaw Pact tanks arrayed across the border in Eastern Europe; they are mere vestiges of a past misunderstanding, and anyway the Soviets will be taking some of them out. "Because of Gorbachev, there is a feeling that the Soviets are no longer on an aggressive path."

That feeling has become contagious, as has the desire to sanctify it with commerce. Politicians as well as businessmen have descended on Moscow in droves to glad-hand Gorbachev and assure him of their desire to sell.

Prime Minister Ciriaco de Mita of Italy was so dazzled by the "unimaginable commercial advantages" that he proposed a new Marshall Plan to rebuild Soviet industry. Chancellor Helmut Kohl of West Germany, who once compared Gorbachev to Nazi propagandist Joseph Goebbels, stopped by to introduce the Soviet leader to 60 of his closest friends from banking and industry. Even that entourage was puny beside the mob — 500 corporate bigwigs in their own jumbo jet — that tagged along with Commerce Secretary C. William Verity Jr. in April.

Only the Japanese government, still smarting over the Toshiba Corp. scandal and the lingering issue of the Soviet-occupied Kuril Islands, was absent from the parade, though that has not stood in the way of business. When one Western businessman recently complained about the difficulty of telephoning a Soviet customer, he was told that Japanese salesmen with automatic dialers were tying up Moscow's overworked lines.

The sales calls have paid off — an auto factory deal for Italy's Fiat, a nuclear plant for the West Germans, several petrochemical projects for U.S. and Japanese companies — but some of those eager for more business worry about whether these noisy deals are the tip or the entire iceberg.

Western salesmen would take heart if the Kremlin began drawing heavily on its new credit lines, signaling a large role for imports in Moscow's game plan. There are plenty of reasons for them to hope it might. The Soviet Union's own machine-building factories, confused by conflicting orders to improve both quality and quantity, have done neither, taking much of the wind out of Gorbachev's plan to increase output of consumer goods.

But a wholesale binge of foreign borrowing would be a defeat for his original *perestroika* blueprint, one that called for bootstrap reform: shifting resources from guns to butter, getting bureaucrats off the backs of managers, rewarding good ideas and hard work — exactly the script that Soviet economists have long peddled as a means of escaping dependence on the West.

"This is still a country where the unanimous view is that you import only what you cannot produce, and you try to produce everything you can," says the Brookings Institution's Hewett.

For many of the reformers, the relevant lesson is the failed tenure of Leonid Brezhnev, who latched onto Western technology and credit as a means to keep things going without provoking the bureaucracy. As it turned out, the unreformed system wrecked any hope of imported machinery being efficiently employed. Poland and Hungary, two communist debtors that have been recent beneficiaries of strings-attached bailout packages from the West, are the ultimate cautionary tales for Gorbachev.

Gorbachev has tried to resist the Brezhnev model. That does not mean he has given up on getting foreign capital and technology to put some oomph into his reforms. It just means he is not willing to pay cash for it.

Enter the new joint venture law, making Gorbachev the first Soviet leader since the sainted Lenin to allow foreign capitalists to invest directly in Soviet homeland. Westerners who visit Moscow are impressed with the fervor Gorbachev has instilled in his managerial class. "They sound like broken records," says one lawyer. "Somebody told them to talk about joint ventures and now that's all they want to talk about." Fealty to the party line is not the only reason. By attaching themselves to a capitalist partner, Soviet managers enjoy much greater freedom to run their businesses, and even become eligible to travel abroad.

The advertised goal, spelled out in the law itself, is to accelerate the arrival of happy days for the Soviet people. Businessmen who peruse the small print quickly learn better. Every venture is required to satisfy its own hard currency needs. That means that if the Western partner expects to take profits home, he will be looking abroad and not to the Soviet people for customers.

No surprise, then, that investors have been flocking to the country's few export sectors, such as petrochemicals. Companies like Chevron Corp. and Combustion Engineering Inc. are bringing in the know-how to goose production from Soviet oil and gas wells. Their profits will come from the resulting exports.

Some also see opportunities in such areas as food and technology, where imports eat up much of the Kremlin's precious foreign reserves. Companies that can help the Soviets become self-sufficient are claiming a slice of the hard currency that would otherwise go for imports. Siberia, for instance, will soon host the world's largest soybean refinery, courtesy of Archer-Daniels-Midland Co. If all goes according to plan, the resultant gunk will bulk out Soviet meat and milk supplies, allaying the need for food imports.

By the latest Soviet count, more than 1,000 protocols of intent have been signed with would-be joint venturers. But only a handful will find room to hitch a ride on the Soviet Union's meager foreign trade, and few others are likely to get beyond the drawing board. Many companies frankly admit they are only humoring a large customer by making upbeat noises about investing, hoping the payoff will come in the form of straightforward sales. "When the Soviets want to talk about something, you talk about it," says Robert Scallon of Britain's Barclays Bank PLC. "If nothing else, it keeps the door open."

For a lot of companies, the Soviet market is still more trouble than it is worth. Businessmen face a thousand headaches, from the scarcity of office space to the need to bring along their own paper clips and typewriter ribbons. Hiring and firing in the Soviet system is still a tricky proposition, and so is dealing with local authorities, who are in the habit of dragooning workers from nearby factories for leaf raking and other public projects.

On top of everything else is *perestroika* itself. One of its central tenets is giving individual managers their heads and letting the marketplace punish wrong guesses. That may win plaudits from academic economists, but Western businessmen are not necessarily free marketers. "It's a bit hypocritical, really," says John Howell, head of Soviet operations for the accounting firm Ernst & Whinney. "But what makes the market attractive is guaranteed prices and sales."

Archer-Daniels-Midland, a firm with long experience in the Soviet Union, finds itself puzzling for the first time over whether the Soviets can really deliver customers for soy sausages and soy milk. "Before *perestroika*, if the appropriate person at the appropriate ministry issued an edict that something should be done, it would be done," says Vice President John Reed. "Now we aren't sure that even if an edict was issued, it would be carried out."

Perhaps the boldest roll of the dice is being taken by Johnson &

Johnson, the purveyor of Band-Aids and dozens of other health products. The company sees huge potential in the Soviet Union, a medical purgatory where thousands of rural hospitals lack running water and where bandages are routinely washed and reused. According to people close to the firm, it is willing to sacrifice any foreseeable payback to get an early foothold. "They're saying, 'We want market share, and we are happy to sit on the ruble until it becomes convertible, even if we're all dead by then.' "

That is a leap of faith few firms so far are willing to take. In economic terms, nothing would symbolize the end of Stalinist isolationism like a convertible ruble — one that floats on world currency markets, allowing money and goods to cross Soviet borders as freely as they do in the West. Economists reckon the ruble should be devalued by 80 percent. Though that would be a powerful tonic for Soviet industry, it will not happen soon. Lifting the lid on domestic prices, a necessary prelude to floating the currency, could trigger Gorbachev's worst nightmare: a full-scale revolt by his volatile provincials.

Seventy years of a fixed pricing system have taken a heavy toll on the Soviet economy. The favorite example of Western economists is the collective farmer's habit of feeding his cattle on subsidized bread and saving his grain to sell to the state bakeries. Any collision between the free market and an economy built of such distortions could be explosive. Toss a floating ruble and a flood of imports into the mix, and it might be chaos — a possibility that has certainly occurred to more than a few people in the Kremlin.

Holman Jenkins Jr.

Chapter 20

*Poland was first in the breakup of the
Soviet empire. It was a breathtaking
transformation: all those Solidarity
leaders who had spent the martial law
years down and out or in jail now heading
for their offices in major government
ministries. Once unshackled, as this
November 13, 1989, article reported,
Poland faced the problem of how to keep
itself together while undoing the economic
damage that communism had wrought.*

THE BLOCBUSTERS
OF POLAND ON A ROLL

The Polish city of Gdansk is best known as the birthplace of Solidarity, the East Bloc's first independent trade union, full of idealism and high-mindedness. But it is also a Baltic seaport, full of both sailors and tourists.

In the new era of *glasnost* and *perestroika* in Eastern Europe, tourism is doing a brisk business in Poland, up 10 percent this year. Germans in particular come here to have a good time. Some arrive in traditional dress, complete with feathered hats to hunt wild boar; many are elderly and are returning to visit the haunts of their youth, when the place was known as Danzig, A. Hitler was in charge of Germany, and the Germans derived strength through joy and joy through strength. Today, they derive joy through money, though the service is not always up to expectations.

At a restaurant one German asks for mustard with his pork chop, only to get an indifferent "We don't have it" from the waiter; another complains that his smoked eel appetizer is half-frozen, eel sorbet rather. Bon appetit!

In the evening, Gdansk turns into a garish honky-tonk. One whole hotel is dedicated to the nocturnal needs of tourists. Unlike Warsaw, which is said to have the best-educated hookers in the world, subtlety is not the style here. Some of the girls look as if they are built in the local shipyard. But one attracts special attention. She sails in wearing a skirt so short and tight that all good men are appalled while everybody else breaks into noisy applause. Hers is clearly a huge talent. "One million zlotys," shouts one enthusiastic German, hauling out a massive wad of bills. "You need a suitcase to carry all this money around," he roars with Bavarian abandon.

Down south, in Krakow, ancient seat of the Polish kings, Sin has also made inroads. A new hard-currency casino, the first of its kind in the East Bloc, has opened on Florianska Street under a discreet sign offering everything from blackjack and roulette to one-armed bandits. "The response has amazed us," says its British manager, Kevin McLean, a veteran of the business who has set up gambling casinos all over the Third World, from Egypt to Kenya to Thailand. The overseers are Turkish; the dealers are local students from Jagiellonian University, as well as a professor who decided to give up his teaching post. "They are as good as any in Vegas," boasts McLean.

Twenty percent of the hard currency comes from tourists, the rest from Poles. "There is a lot of the stuff around," says one dealer. Some of it has been stashed away for a long time. Among the prized trophies are a 1907 U.S. $5 bill and a well-worn 1921 silver dollar. No photographers are allowed inside when the casino is open, to guarantee the anonymity of the customers. The country's second casino has just opened in Warsaw, and a third is scheduled to open in Poznan in December.

This is the Poland experienced by tourists and visitors, a land of black-market operators and Pewex shops where Western goods and comforts can be had for hard currency. It is not the Poland known to most who live here. Their world is one of misery and chaos, with signs of breakdown and dysfunction everywhere: Elderly ladies wait for hours in queues, only to find they cannot afford the scraps of meat for sale; soup kitchens run by the Red Cross have opened in many cities, serving what the newspapers call *bryja*, which according to one Pole is best translated as "thick, gooey gruel which triggers the vomit reflex"; it takes 30 years to get a public sector flat, 20 years to get a telephone. There is anger and frustration among people, an atmosphere both volatile and dangerous.

Sometimes the two worlds meet, as happened recently to two fat and happy Canadian professors on the train to Krakow. They were subjected to the so-called artificial crowd treatment: A group of toughs suddenly surrounded them, pushing and shoving, relieving them of their cash and valuables. In extreme cases, these gangs have used acid to blind their victims. Tourists are advised to avoid the

Krakow train and get there by plane or car instead.

Such is the situation that faces the new Solidarity-led government of Tadeusz Mazowiecki, who was confirmed Aug. 24 as the first non-communist prime minister in Eastern Europe since 1948. If Mazowiecki looks like a man who carries the world on his shoulders, it is with good reason. One legacy the new government inherited from the communists is a $39 billion foreign debt. Inflation is running at close to 200 percent and if unchecked could reach 900 to 1,000 percent by the end of the year, according to government ministers.

The budget deficit is running at $2.3 billion and could reach $4.4 billion by year's end if drastic action is not taken. Industrial output is down, and the industrial base is outdated. A third of the country has been classified as an environmental disaster zone. Life in Poland sometimes seems like life in a giant ashtray. Smoke comes from all sides: from the factories, from the cars, from the fields where peasants burn stubble, from the Poles themselves, puffing away on their cigarettes.

Poland's government thus confronts a task of historic proportions, nothing less than overcoming 40 years of economic malfeasance and converting the country's Stalinist system into a modern capitalist one. "Our most important task is to catch up with the rest of Europe before it leaves us behind for good," says Lech Walesa, the burly and mustachioed electrician who has led Solidarity since 1980 and who this summer decided that it was a worthy gamble for the movement to accept government responsibility. Adds Solidarity's parliamentary leader, Bronislaw Geremek, "We have to try to move from a planned economy to a market economy. Nobody has ever achieved that."

More immediately, according to Mazowiecki, the government must avert "economic catastrophe" — a complete collapse. The situation has been compared to the devastation of war or natural catastrophe. Polish papers carry dire predictions of an icy winter with World War II-type hardships: coal shortages, power blackouts and bread riots.

To complicate matters further, this economic transformation must be accomplished without upsetting relations with Poland's Warsaw Pact partner and big neighbor to the east, the Soviet Union. Following hints dropped by Solidarity activists that Poland would quit the Warsaw Pact when the chance arose, Mazowiecki has worked hard to reassure Moscow that the government has no plans to leave the pact. "The new government will respect Poland's alliances, and this is not just a tactical move but stems from our *raison d'etat*," the

prime minister stated in his inaugural speech in September. But his
government will seek reforms that make it impossible for one Warsaw Pact country to interfere in the affairs of another.

In October, Finance Minister Leszek Balcerowicz outlined an austerity program aimed at qualifying the country for Western aid. A
first phase of emergency measures is designed to stop further deterioration of the economy over the next three months. It is to be reinforced by a program of far-reaching changes: restructuring the tax
system; ending indexation of wages; liberalizing foreign trade rules;
unifying the exchange rate; creating a convertible zloty and a Warsaw stock exchange; shutting down money-losing industries and privatizing whatever can be run profitably; and abolishing most price
controls. There has also been talk of cutting defense and police budgets by 15 percent.

The plan offers shock treatment for the Polish economy. It is based
on the premise that only a quick conversion to a market economy
can bring an end to the crisis. According to Balcerowicz, traditional
solutions, such as price controls, rationing and centralized distribution, would only drag out the pain and delay the cure. The plan was
first unveiled privately at a meeting of the International Monetary
Fund in Washington, at which Poland asked for $2.7 billion in aid. It
met with a combination of admiration and concern about the break-
neck speed of the proposed changes.

The government plans to slash subsidies, which account for about
40 percent of the budget, on everything from milk to public transportation. At the same time, it has proposed a cutback on a system
that ties wage increases to inflation. Originally demanded by Solidarity as a means of protecting workers from inflation, indexation
has instead contributed to hyperinflation. Wages will now be indexed
at 80 percent rather than 100 percent of the inflation rate, with a
view toward ending indexation after Jan. 1. Balcerowicz has freely
admitted that his policies will cause bankruptcies and industrial closings, and that unemployment may affect 10 to 20 percent of Poland's
work force of 17 million.

Underlying the program has been an intense debate in recent
months within Solidarity. Throughout the fall, Western economists
like Harvard's Jeffrey Sachs, an expert on indebted Third World
economies, have been making the pilgrimage to Warsaw to offer their
advice. Conservatives have called for a harsh cure, something like
the one Ludwig Erhard successfully administered to postwar West
Germany. The now-or-never advocates argue that austerity measures can only be taken during the new government's honeymoon

and that the shock may be the only way to convince Western creditors that Poland is serious about reform.

More cautious reformers have warned that Poland is no West Germany, with a massive Marshall Plan behind it, nor is it a banana
republic with a pliant peasant population. They worry that doing too
much too quickly will shake the country and create civil unrest.
When the president of the Polish Senate, Andrzej Stelmachowski,
recently talked with a representative of the World Bank, he demanded to know how one evaluates the importance of social peace. "That
is not an economic problem," the bank official answered. "This is
your main fault," answered Stelmachowski, who argues that the
shortcoming of all economic estimates is their failure to take into
account the importance of social stability. Left-wing Solidarity officials are beating the drums as well; they say an austerity program
such as the one proposed by the government could push two-thirds
of Poland's 38 million people over the edge.

Even the cautious crowd acknowledges that in order for the situation to get better, it first has to get worse. And that it certainly has.
In one of its last acts, the communist government of Prime Minister
Mieczyslaw Rakowski on Aug. 1 took the lid off food prices. Since
then they have skyrocketed: Meat has gone up 1,200 percent, milk
950 percent and butter 500 percent. A pack of Popularne cigarettes,
without which life seems unimaginable for most Poles, now costs 70
percent more, and everybody is constantly asking everybody else for
matches to light them. At gas stations, prices went up 120 percent
over two weeks in September. These days, it is common to see as
many as 60 little Polski Fiats, with engines the size of a lawn mower's,
waiting in line. A typical monthly wage of 200,000 zlotys translated
into $28 on the black market in mid-October.

"I have learned to live without money. As long as I have something
interesting to read, I can get by," says Aleksander Nelicki, a young
psychology instructor at Jagiellonian University in Krakow, as he
waits in line for his monthly salary — a sum that varies unpre-
dictably according to the leaps and bounds of inflation. One thing he
cannot do, explains Nelicki, is get married. His apartment in the new
Nowa Huta district of Krakow is so diminutive, he says, that he has
to be something of a contortionist to live there; his kitchen measures
1 square meter. After some time, the ancient payroll clerk finally
shuffles in, clutching two huge stacks of bills. Zlotys are handed out
by the thousands — no need to worry about pay slips or direct
deposit.

But not everybody has Nelicki's enviable ability to get by on nothing. Particularly worrisome for the government has been an ongoing exodus, especially of the young and educated. The flow has increased since the June election, along with rising pessimism over the economy. Some 230,000 are expected to seek permanent residence in West Germany this year — a 60 percent increase over last year and more than four times the figure for 1987. West German papers now carry ads from women in Poland looking for eligible German bachelors.

Twenty percent of university graduates leave Poland each year, and doctors are leaving the country in greater numbers than the medical schools turn them out. With all of the newly won political freedoms, emigrants can no longer be classified as political refugees, only as economic refugees. In his inaugural speech before the Polish Parliament, Prime Minister Mazowiecki acknowledged the urgent need for "creating favorable conditions for enterprising young people."

To soften the effects of the austerity program, the government has promised to create unemployment insurance and other welfare benefits, including food stamps for the country's more than 4 million pensioners, entitling them to free milk, cottage cheese and bread. The government has also promised emergency action to improve housing and health services. The chronic housing shortage greatly reduces the mobility of workers and gives them little choice but to hunker down or seek their luck abroad.

Crucial for success, as Poles see it, is prompt support from the West. "Our friends must not wait until we suffocate in our difficulties," Mazowiecki said after his selection as prime minister. Now that communist domination of Eastern Europe has eased, something the West has hoped for for 40 years, it would be both illogical and immoral to be ungenerous, Poles argue; if the West is unforthcoming and the Polish experiment fails, the West will deserve most of the blame.

In his role as Poland's chief fund-raiser, Lech Walesa has repeatedly called for an infusion of $10 billion in capital and investment over the next few years. "Political transformations in our country have gone far already," he says. "Unfortunately, they have not been paralleled with economic progress. This imbalance threatens us with social disturbances and protests and even may result in upsetting the process of democratic reform and the loss of our political gains. This would be a momentous tragedy for Poland, which for the first time in 45 years has a realistic chance to get on its feet economically." Walesa plans to be in Washington to address Congress Nov. 15 as part of a week-long visit to North America. He is expected to deliver an impassioned plea for cash.

During President Bush's July visit, when it still looked as if the communists would be leading Poland for several more years, he offered the country $119 million in economic, technical and environmental assistance. Following the dramatic changes there and in Hungary, Bush, under congressional pressure, changed the proposed assistance for the two to $455.5 million over three years, the majority of which would go to Poland. He now finds himself outbid by Congress. On Oct. 19, the House passed a measure that will allow the two up to $837.5 million over the next three years. West Germany is expected to offer Poland credits worth more than $1 billion, and France is offering $642 million.

Part of the reason for the Bush administration's initial reluctance to step in is fear of the backlash that might result if the United States is seen to be meddling too openly in Eastern Europe. There is also concern about the staying power of Mikhail Gorbachev, who has one or two domestic problems of his own. Equally, while many Poles may feel that they have done their bit by throwing off the communist yoke, business decisions are rarely made on idealistic grounds.

Skeptics note that the country remains entangled in inefficient and unprofitable East Bloc trade obligations and that even shock treatment may not succeed in opening up the Polish economy, with its huge state-run monopolies. Though a book by British Thatcherite author Jeffrey Archer — "Not a Penny More, Not a Penny Less," which is full of good Conservative business values — is at the head of the Polish best-seller list, there is no skilled managerial class. Moreover, the infrastructure is worn down: The telephone network, which had always been in notoriously bad shape, was further damaged after martial law in 1981. For instance, a phone call from Gdansk to Warsaw can take more than an hour to make. "How can you do business with such a system?" says a Polish businessman in disgust.

That is what the Solidarity government is up against; a key test of success will be its ability to seize full control of the levers of power. A symbolic incident dates from one of Mazowiecki's first days in power. For fun, he pressed a button under his desk. From a hidden niche in the wall sprang an armed soldier claiming that he was there to defend the life of the prime minister. Nobody had cared to tell Mazowiecki about his jack-in-the-box bodyguard.

The government has to find a way to metamorphose the Polish bureaucracy from a party-controlled, parasitic *nomenklatura* into a nonpartisan executive apparatus of state. Thus obstreperous officials recently decided to exempt collective farms from an increase in diesel fuel prices, for example, sticking to the time-honored communist practice of bestowing preferential treatment on state enterprises. "If we don't manage to overcome the routine of the system and these old, constantly repeated ways of governing, then even the best programs may turn out to be impossible," said Geremek at a news conference.

At the local level, there is no doubt that some old scores are being settled. Who enjoyed what privileges and at whose expense is not soon forgotten. An example is furnished by the miners of the Kazimierz Juliusz coal mine in Sosnowiec. The old bosses now have the opportunity to work off their paunches some 400 feet below ground.

At the same time, the government has emphasized that it does not want a witch-hunt, a purge that could touch off civil war. As Geremek has warned, "We are not making the mistakes that the Afghan *mujahideen* made. They offered the communists nothing. The Kabul government were all going to lose their jobs, maybe their lives. So there was nothing for them but to fight on. We want to change the fundamentals of Polish society but without bloodshed." The new emphasis will be on performance.

Already, the government has taken some significant steps. An amendment to the constitution that will officially end the leading role of the communist party, the Polish United Worker's Party, is expected to be passed soon in Parliament. In addition, though the Ministry of the Interior has remained in the hands of the communists, the hated Zomo paramilitary units have been disbanded. The Zomos, with their dirty gray-blue fatigues and long white nightsticks, have long been considered by Poles to be no better than organized hooligans. They played a detested role in imposing martial law in 1981 and were used throughout the 1980s to disperse pro-Solidarity demonstrations. Communist Interior Minister Czeslaw Kiszczak has explained that a part of his pledge is to dismantle the oppressive apparatus of the state.

The Zomos will be replaced by a smaller force, Ogpo, and the number of professional paramilitary officers will be cut from 12,000 to 5,000. The new Ogpo units will be placed in only 22 of Poland's 49 provinces, and among their main duties will be soccer crowd control (as usual, the dreaded hordes of invading Brits are mentioned in this context) and other things decidedly nonpolitical. Their deployment will be under the control of the prime minister's office, not the provincial police chiefs.

More tricky is the problem of what to do about crimes committed during martial law. In September, the Parliament formed a commission to look into allegations of police brutality and criminal wrong-doing against members of the opposition. The problem again is to balance public pressure against the need to placate an army and a police force already upset over budget cuts.

Concentrating on the misdeeds of the 1950s has emerged as a safer course, at least for now. The government has announced an intention to take legal action against those responsible for the torture and murder of thousands during the Stalinist era. Labeling them crimes against humanity on the order of those committed by the Nazis during World War II, Justice Minister Aleksandr Bentkowski has stated that the crimes of this period are not covered by the statute of limitations and that families of victims are entitled to material and moral compensation.

Now that the media are Solidarity's business, censorship has seen a sharp decline. Gone are the days when censors with almost perverse arbitrariness banned subjects ranging from plant and cattle disease in Poland to the plans of Ugandan dictator Idi Amin to erect a statue of Hitler. Moreover, there will be an end to privileges for the communist press RSW Prasa, which in the past had got more than half of the country's chronically low paper supply.

Mazowiecki has appointed pro-Solidarity writer Andrzej Drawicz as head of the crucial Committee for Radio and Television Affairs, long the key propaganda tool of the communists. The new chairman's first act was to fire the three national news anchors, who were closely identified with the communists. Solidarity activists are calling for more personnel changes. Licenses for private radio and television stations are also in the works.

A diversification of the media is one means of decentralizing power in the country. Another is the emphasis Mazowiecki is placing on the creation of noncommunist centers of power at the level of local government, which is regarded as crucial for reform. He has appointed a minister for local government reform, Jerzy Regulski, who will supervise local elections and work for local autonomy in finance and other areas. Currently, all appropriations have to be decided by Warsaw; local officials need to raise and keep their own revenue. This is the only chance many towns will ever have for fixing their streets, repairing their houses. Patronage jobs must be taken away from the communists. Discussions are under way on whether local elections should be held in 1993 as scheduled or moved forward considerably.

Perhaps the greatest challenge of all lies with the dual nature of Solidarity itself. It is at once a trade union and a reform movement.

Many of its members are employed in the outdated heavy industries that are such a burden on the country. Most workers want a more prosperous economy, but they also want austerity eased by welfare, and they want their places of work protected. Wrote columnist Piotr Wierzbicki in Tygodnik Solidarnosc, "The trade union character of Solidarity naturally makes it difficult for it to support economic liberalism. Many of its members have become used to socialism, do not want to renounce 'socialists achievements' and are afraid of free competition."

Take the steel plant of Nowa Huta just outside Krakow. It looks like an evil furnace from a Tolkien novel and has been belching fire and smoke for four decades. Deliberately placed there, some say, by communists in the early 1950s as a punishment for the town and a counterbalance to its old aristocracy and its intellectuals, the plant has been poisoning Krakow ever since.

One-third of Krakow's population suffers from respiratory ailments. Its ancient, soot-covered buildings seem to be crumbling before the eyes of the visitor. But the plant produces 30 percent of Polish steel, and 3,000 factories are dependent on it; it employs 10,000 workers.

Leszek Maleszka of the local Solidarity factory bulletin, whose pages recently ran a series on the environmental problems brought on by Nowa Huta, fully acknowledges the dilemma. On one hand, he is defending workers; on the other, reforms. "I have great difficulty in balancing these two attitudes of mine," he says. "I am not saying it shouldn't be closed in the end. But it is a very hard decision. It means the closing of 10,000 jobs and nobody knows how many in the dependent industries."

The problem was also illustrated last fall, when the communist government threatened to close the Gdansk shipyard — the cradle of Solidarity but, in business terms, a highly dubious operation. The decision was an obvious provocation, and the communists later backtracked. But these are exactly the kinds of tough decisions that Poland faces if it is ever to emerge from economic ruin.

Much of the success of reform seems to ride on the persuasive powers of one man, Lech Walesa. He played the crucial role in creating the new political arrangement in Poland. For himself, however, he did not want to be saddled with government responsibility. Instead, he emerged as the kingmaker, with more room for maneuver — the person who can shape events and who could step in if things go wrong. Someone not directly involved in making unpopular decisions, Walesa is still able to serve as a symbol. He has lately taken to projecting himself less as a labor leader, more as the father figure of the country, a kind of independent moral authority.

In describing Walesa, journalist Mariusz Ziomecki uses the analogy of Marshal Jozef Pilsudski, the Polish nationalist leader between the world wars, whose only official title was comptroller general of the army and who lived quietly in Warsaw's outskirts, but without whose consent nothing could happen. Walesa now acts as a kind of shadow president to the real president, Gen. Wojciech Jaruzelski. He is said to have his eye on winning the presidency in six years, when Jaruzelski's term ends.

As someone above the political fray, Walesa cannot allow himself to be too closely identified with government policy. He has repeatedly blamed the government for failing to explain the recovery program in the detail required to win public acceptance, and thrice within a short period he warned that the economic crisis could explode into civil war unless a consensus is reached. Before the government released details of its economic plan, he said, "If someone fools around with prices, they do so at the expense of this government. I warn that if there are more price rises we will not be able to keep people working normally."

But the important function for Walesa now is to urge popular restraint. Unofficially, Solidarity has called for a six-month strike moratorium to give the government a chance to get its program going. Says Walesa, "Solidarity unionists are aware that Solidarity must weaken itself until the situation of the enterprises improves itself."

At the Royal Palace in Warsaw, an exhibition of jewelry collected in 1938 eerily recalls another period of turbulence for Poland. Mound upon mound of silver jewelry lies there, rings, armbands, silver purses, reminders of a fragile, glittering prewar Warsaw that can now be only distantly recaptured through the faint sounds of Django Rheinardt music emanating from ancient radio sets late at night. The silver was sent abroad to purchase arms, but it came too late. "Poles were willing to make sacrifices then," says Olena Skwiecinska, a young Solidarity journalist. "Perhaps they will be willing to do so today." Today, the Poles have no silver and gold to offer, only their continued endurance.

Henrik Bering-Jensen

CHAPTER 21

As communist leaders began facing up to the disastrous results of central planning, condemnation of capitalism gave way to disenchantment with socialism. The more radical reformers went beyond advocating market discipline for state-run enterprises to calling for private ownership. That raised the question of how to dismantle state ownership and create real capital markets. The answer, according to this report of August 7, 1989: with great difficulty.

HOW TO MAKE MARKETS WHERE NONE WERE

As somebody once said, there's only one thing worse than being exploited by capitalists, and that's not being exploited by them.

The pacesetters of the communist world are reluctantly coming to the same conclusion. A decade or two ago, when they first began throwing Marxist dogma overboard, one shibboleth they refused to jettison: Market forces might have to be used to whip socialist steel mills and shipyards into shape, but that was no excuse for tinkering with anything as fundamental as state ownership.

Countless disappointments later, the reformers have begun sidling up to a naughty idea: that state ownership may be as much to blame as central planning for socialism's ills. But how to ring down the curtain on an era in which the government holds title to everything? From Beijing to Budapest, the boldest voices are touting the creation of real capital markets as the crucial next step in the flight from communism.

To see why, look at Poland. In the early 1980s, it adopted the usual formula for reinvigorating a sluggish state sector: Enterprises were cut loose from central control and threatened with having their subsidies withdrawn. Managers, it was hoped, would respond by cutting costs, improving productivity and making their factories "self-financing."

The theory may have been fine, but the results were dismal. The regime balked at weeding out firms once they proved themselves hopelessly unprofitable. Bankruptcy, it turns out, is no more appealing to the party loyalists who occupy the executive suite than to the Solidarity-led workers who threaten rebellion from the shop floor. Today, the state continues to shovel out ever-larger subsidies to keep its factories afloat, financed by printing money and trying to raise food prices faster than Solidarity can demand offsetting wage increases. Poland, as a result, teeters on the brink of Argentina-style economic chaos.

Reforming communists everywhere face the same grief. To Stalin and his acolytes, smokestack industry was the essence of socialism, and bigger was always better. Their legacy is Poland's sprawling Lenin Shipyard, Hungary's massive Ozd steelworks and hundreds of other industrial brontosauruses. All over the communist world, from these rusting ramparts an unholy alliance of party hacks and workers fend off change. Chinese reformers call this coalition the "iron rice bowl."

In the West, smokestackers faced their Waterloo a decade ago, brought on by surging energy prices, competition from Japan and an explosion of synthetic materials. Smart communists could only admire the ruthless efficiency with which capitalists fired workers, closed money-losing plants and shifted investment to sunrise industries like computers and telecommunications.

Their own agricultural reforms provide further proof that private ownership works better. One-quarter of the Soviet Union's groceries come from the 3 percent of farmers who work their own land. Poland's farms were never nationalized, and their efficiency contrasts starkly with the bumbling of state-run industries.

But legalizing family farms is one thing, transferring entire industries to private hands is another. First, it means trashing the monolithic banking systems of the Stalinist era. In the old days, communist banks were little more than printing presses, to be cranked up whenever the party needed money for a new project. Now they must become competitive, Western-style institutions, capable of enticing the public's savings out of mattresses and guiding them toward profitable enterprises.

Hungary leads in this transition by a couple of light-years. In the early 1980s it launched the socialist world's first bond market and began to plumb an untapped pool of dormant savings. For want of better opportunities, Hungarians traditionally had invested their spare cash in gold jewelry or fancy homes. Now they could earn a hefty 11 percent on bonds guaranteed by the state.

By this year, more than 350 issues had been floated, some with enticing bonuses. For example, to raise funds to speed up the installation of telephones, the post office peddled bonds that entitled investors to jump ahead of a 10-year waiting list for phones. (Since the bonus applied only to the original purchaser, the bonds plummeted in secondary trading.)

Until two years ago, bonds often traded briskly at weekly sessions at the Budapest Bank. But an upsurge in inflation triggered a rush of sell orders in October 1987, just as Wall Street was suffering an unrelated crash of its own. Worried that big losses might sour investors on future issues, state-sponsored banks began buying up bonds to slow the market's collapse. Today, with investors having yet to shake off their jitters, dealers spend more time trading insults than bonds.

Yet the interbank bickering over the collapse of the bond market is testimony to an even more far-reaching reform. Two years ago Hungary began laying the groundwork for a truly competitive banking system. Five new banks were crated, and between them were divvied up the industrial clients once served by the National Bank of Hungary, now retreating to the loftier vantage of Western-style central banking.

The new banks are meant to be profitmongers. Though some of their funds still come from the state, they can raise extra capital by selling bonds, shares or certificates of deposit. And they are supposed to be careful about how they lend their funds. After a six-month standstill period, they were even allowed to start shucking off the deadbeats inherited from the state and begin vying for the patronage of Hungary's blue-chip enterprises.

Not surprisingly, the best portfolio was inherited by Hungarian Creditbank, whose chairman, Sandor Demjan, is a party bigwig and the hard-charging founder of Skala-Coop, an enormously successful department store chain.

Demjan was quick to test his powers. Declaring that "there is only one economic law," he clamped down on new loans to the Ozd steelworks and gave management a deadline for turning the factory around. Over the grumbling of party officials, 2,500 workers were fired right away, and Demjan called for shrinking by half the remaining work force of 10,000.

He made his unsocialist demands in the name of the plant's "stockholders." Until recently, that meant the employees themselves, who were the only ones entitled to own shares under an earlier reform that invited state enterprise to sell stock. But things are changing again. Rolled out in January was a new law that permits individuals to own 100 percent of a company that employs 500 people or fewer. (There are some Hungarian officials who have intimated that by organizing as a holding company, even this restriction can be gotten around.)

Yet action at the Budapest Stock Exchange remains listless. Because the legal formalities have yet to be worked out, the market still is not open to the public. But bankers have high expectations for the future. Plans for a modern building are being drawn up, and the London Stock Exchange is giving advice on computers and software. The tentative site for the new stock market: on the campus of Karl Marx University.

Behind the grand hopes is new legislation that allows foreigners to buy 100 percent of the shares of Hungarian companies. With an entire economy to privatize, the government is clearly counting on Western money for help. In February, Trade Minister Tamas Beck traveled to West Germany to flog more than 50 enterprises the state would like to unload. There was only one taker, a multinational group of investors that bought Tungsram, a light bulb manufacturer. True to form, the new owners quickly got about the dirty work the old socialist overseers had put off. The plant's top managers and 28 percent of the work force were sent packing.

Other foreigners look forward to joining the fun, including the New York investment bank Bear, Stearns & Co. Inc., which has cobbled together a $50 million investment fund. One of the contributors is George Soros, the Hungarian-born founder of Wall Street's Quantum Fund. "It's highly significant that the opposition [to economic reforms] is coming from people in heavy industry," he noted.

Soros displayed his mettle as an investor during a decade when Wall Street was engineering a sometimes brutal restructuring of the West's recalcitrant rust bowlers. Could a similar raider-led revolution be in the cards for Hungary?

The Tungsram deal already has some of the earmarks of a hostile takeover, and the prospect of more companies passing from state to private hands has sparked a hauntingly familiar debate about the rights of owners and the duties of managers. With the new stock market and the licensing of foreign ownership, the arena for all kinds of takeovers and leveraged buyouts is taking shape. Though Hungarian managers may resist putting themselves at risk by issuing shares, a liquidity squeeze engineered by the central bank leaves them few alternatives for financing modernization.

Among the other communist reformers, Poland has also talked about setting up a stock market and recruiting foreign buyers for state enterprises. Part of the Lenin Shipyard, Solidarity's birthplace, has already been sold to a union-busting Anglo-Polish group. But despite a paucity of domestic savings, Poles have little hope of getting foreign investors to finance the renovation of those salvageable industries or to hire workers left jobless by the closing down of the hopeless money losers.

As Miklos Nemeth, Hungary's prime minister and an alumnus of the Harvard Business School, told his colleagues in Parliament recently, "Nobody would invest in a place where they had to fear civil war breaking out the next day . . . or that 'those communists' will change their minds and nationalize it in five years."

He might have been describing Poland. The 10-year struggle between Solidarity and the Jaruzelski regime has produced a dizzying number of U-turns on economic policy. As a result, most Polish entrepreneurs keep their gaze firmly fixed on the short term, earning a reputation as the East Bloc's nimblest traders in black market goods but avoiding anything that smacks of taking a longer view. As for foreign investors, they turn a noticeably colder shoulder to Poland than Hungary.

With the crackdown on protesters in China, the odds makers have started taking a less sanguine view about the propensity of communists to change their stripe. As one bemused Western businessman complained, "Everybody thought they had become capitalists."

After Hungary, China had traveled farthest down the road of privatization. Three years ago, the city of Shenyang, launched what is called a "stock market," the first since the revolution. Similar exchanges have popped up in Shanghai, Beijing and other cities. In fact, most of the instruments they sell are more like bonds, paying a fixed return but not entailing ownership rights.

Still, the goal was capitalist. Like the Hungarians, the Chinese hoped not only to mobilize hidden savings but also to begin introducing market discipline to the allocation of investment capital. Though foreigners are not yet allowed to play the markets, the prohibition does not extend to the Chinese citizens of Hong Kong, Macao or Taiwan, and at least one enterprise has asked permission to issue securities denominated in U.S. dollars.

Building up the embryonic securities trade was a top priority of Zhao Ziyang, the zealous reformer recently knocked from his perch as party chief. His sponsorship assured wide publicity for the views of Li Yining, an economic gadfly who argued that ending state ownership was more urgent than getting rid of price controls. As recently as February, the influential Guangming Daily editorialized: "Any form of ownership should be considered reasonable as long as it fosters economic development."

Long before the Tiananmen Square massacre, Prime Minister Li Peng and a group of hard-liners were intent on pushing Zhao to the sidelines and turning back the clock. Yet in one area of reform, even the prime minister calls for full steam ahead. In April, he gave a hearty blessing to Zhao's plans for a national exchange.

With good reason. China has been remarkably unsuccessful at getting industry's snout out of the national treasury. Despite a bankruptcy law on the books in some cities since 1986, not a single enterprise is known to have been shut down. And unlike its fellow travelers in the East Bloc, China has the extra handicap of being a sprawling and populous place. The usual tribulations of reforming communists are magnified by an outbreak of so-called economic warlordism — regional authorities running amok with instruments of central planning that Beijing has let slip from its control.

At the heart of the problem is China's unreconstructed, printing-press banking system. With the reforms of the last decade, regional branches have begun ignoring directives from Beijing and paying more attention to the demands of local officials. Credit is pumped out willy-nilly to finance their pet investment schemes and sweetheart loans, whether or not the deals make economic sense.

As a result, China has lost control of its money supply. Last year, cash in circulation was supposed to expand by 17 percent. It grew by 58 percent instead, spurring inflation and forcing Beijing to scale back its capital spending plans drastically.

Before Tiananmen, China was a hotbed of schemes for privatizing state enterprises (and homes and land, too). Proponents hoped to do more than just break the inflationary embrace of politicians and industry. They aimed at healing a politically explosive rift between rich and poor provinces that threatened to destroy the reform campaign.

Along the coastal regions, capitalist money from Hong Kong has been calling the investment tune for years, and people have prospered mightily. In the rest of China, where party bosses still hold sway, stagnation remains the rule.

Unlike their coastal cousins, the inner provinces are cut off from the financial and trading opportunities offered by the outside world.

Their only hope for growth is through more efficient development of local resources and markets. That means the kinds of real reforms — floating prices and full property rights — that communists still shrink from. Now that foreign money is having second thoughts about China, the old-style Stalinists may hope to close the gap by restoring the coastal areas to bureaucratically engineered poverty. But such policies are becoming harder to sell at party meetings.

Like their counterparts in Eastern Europe, Chinese communists are learning to enjoy reform. When markets are half-free, half-communist, they provide excellent opportunities for bureaucrats to become plutocrats. State-subsidized resources can be funneled to private firms in return for a bribe or a share of the profits, and managers at state factories can pocket a nice bonus by selling goods on the black market. In Poland, a large chunk of the private sector consists of firms set up by party bureaucrats to milk their connections with state industry. Even the son of Chinese leader Deng Xiaoping has been accused of using family influence to make a bundle from importing consumer electronics.

Top communist officials sometimes decry the tendency of those lower down to engage in "swindling, profiteering and preying on the market's imperfection," as Poland's Gen. Wojciech Jaruzelski recently put it. Hungary's justice minister, Kalman Kulcsar, even felt compelled recently to declare that privatization is not a plot "to safeguard either managers or others in positions of ownership."

But a better gauge of official sentiment may be the fate of Hu Yaobang, the popular Chinese party chief who was deposed two years ago. His sins included noticing too loudly how well the sons and daughters of the party elite seemed to be doing off reform.

As far as the party faithful are concerned, *perestroika*'s selling point may be the opportunity for graft. Otherwise, all they have to gain is an end to their privileges. Hardened cynics long ago were resigned to the idea that capitalism would be entrenched only when a quorum of the politburo have their bit.

Holman Jenkins Jr.

PART 7

ENIGMAS
OF THE EAST

CHAPTER 22

In the course of a few decades, Japan transformed its economy from war-ravaged disaster to the second largest in the world. The Japanese themselves took pride in their achievements. For many, however, pride was not enough. They began to ask why the nation's fabulous riches had not been translated into more dramatic improvements in the quality of everyday life. The cost of living in Tokyo became fabulously high. Tiny apartments were selling for hundreds of thousands of dollars, and the Japanese dream of home ownership looked to be receding rapidly. By 1990, as this September 3 article reported, even key government ministries were starting to fret. They pledged to make consumer issues a higher priority.

RICH JAPAN, POOR JAPANESE

Masuo-san gensho, the Japanese call it, in their penchant for catchphrases. Translated, it means "the phenomenon of Mr. Masuo." Mr. Masuo is a cartoon character in one of Japan's most popular and (after 20 years) longest-running prime-time TV programs, an animated version of Ozzie and Harriet. Recently, however, he has come to symbolize the increasing number of Japanese shut out of the real estate market. Poor Mr. Masuo has never been able to afford a house of his own and suffers the indignity of living with his mother-in-law. The six-room Tokyo dwelling the family of newspaper comic strip characters began in back in 1946 would cost about 1 billion yen in today's market. At 150 yen to the dollar, that is nearly $6.7 million. A lot of money for a cartoon character.

But no laughing matter. The Japanese have created an economic juggernaut. The nation has become a world leader in technology. Its investments span the globe. Its huge reserves of capital prime the international financial markets and, some say, keep the United States from sinking in its own deficits. But just as Japan's tireless efforts have come to fruition, the Japanese find themselves stalled at home, confronted by diminishing personal expectations. Though they have attained the highest per capita income in the world, they are less able than at any time in the postwar era to buy a home of their own, and owning a home is the dream of every Japanese.

The hyperinflation of the real estate market has had both direct and indirect effects on the quality of life in Japan. In numerous polls, more than half of the highest-paid people in the world say they do not feel affluent, a sense shared even by Japan's truly wealthy. Those with incomes double the national average complain that they are frustrated with their standard of living — the tiny, ravenously expensive apartments; the long, crushing commutes to work; the tedious days at the gray office. A refrain from a Japanese folk tune repeats: "Getsu, Getsu, Ka, Sui, Moku, Kin, Kin." It is a recitation of the workweek: "Monday, Monday, Tuesday, Wednesday, Thursday, Friday, Friday."

MITI, the Ministry of International Trade and Industry, the bureaucratic engine propelling Japan's economic miracle, calls it the "paradox of prosperity": rich Japan, poor Japanese. The government worries that without the incentive of home ownership, Japanese workers will lose their will to do the hard work that keeps the economy booming. And so for the past year, Prime Minister Toshiki Kaifu has been holding regular meetings on "The Society We Should Aim for in the 21st Century."

Such talk has been heard in Tokyo before, however. Shuichi Kato, a noted commentator on Japanese society, doubts that change will come easily or soon. "The extraordinary growth of Japan over the last decades and the lagging quality of life are two sides of the same coin. To a large extent, we grow at the expense of our living standards." Tinkering with such trade-offs, he fears, "might result in economic catastrophe." But he also acknowledges that there may be little choice. "In the years immediately after World War II, it was all right to live in this state of emergency. But after 40 years? And with all this prosperity? These conditions are not acceptable."

Just how bad are things? Tokyo is to Japan what Manhattan, Washington, Chicago and Los Angeles together are to the United States. The city serves as a compass of national priorities, the heart of cultural, financial, industrial and political life. This metropolitan center, with nearly 12 million residents, has taken the brunt of Japan's headlong rush from a war-ravaged economy into the 21st century. And the people of Tokyo say the pressures are becoming intolerable.

Yumiko Miyakawa lives with her husband, an art teacher at a design school, in a middle-class section of western Tokyo called Shibasaki. She looks much younger than her 38 years. She works at home three days a week doing word processing for a company that promotes sales of Philip Morris Inc. cigarettes in Japan. Together, the Miyakawas, both of whom have college degrees, earn approximately 4 million yen a year, about $27,000, close to the national average. "Japan became rich," she says, "but most of the people are not rich."

Her apartment, which is favorably situated just a short walk from the local train station, is about a 75-minute commute to central Tokyo. The apartment building the Miyakawas live in is about 15 years old and, from the outside, resembles the sort of small complex that might be found on the outskirts of many American cities.

The obvious difference between this apartment and its U.S. counterpart is size. The Miyakawas' place consists of a dinette kitchen, a bedroom, study and bath. The bedroom and study are both about 8 feet wide, just a little wider than the outstretched arms of a man. It is about twice as long. The kitchenette serves as an entryway to the apartment and is cramped by a small dining table. Altogether, the space measures about 450 square feet, half the size of a typical Manhattan apartment. *Usagi goya*, the Japanese mockingly call their places: rabbit hutches.

For this, the Miyakawas pay 90,000 yen a month in rent, $600. They pay an additional $100 a month to park their six-year-old car in front of their building. (Filling its tank costs $33.) And they pay all utilities — water, gas, electric — which tacks on an average $113 per month. To secure the place, the Miyakawas paid four months' rent in advance, of which they will get back only two when they move out, a common scenario in the Tokyo real estate market.

Usually, apartments like this offer no Western-style amenities. They do not offer such fundamental appliances as a water heater, customary even in the poorest U.S. dwellings but rare in Japan. The Miyakawas had to buy their own. What is more, the apartment came without washer or dryer. No dishwasher. No refrigerator. No stove. No microwave. Few Japanese homes have ovens. The Miyakawas cook on a double hot plate, which they had to buy for themselves.

There was no air-conditioning. No central heat. Again, a standard arrangement. Kerosene is delivered to their door in winter and they warm themselves with space heaters. Without a trace of irony, such apartments are offered by real estate agents under the designation "mansion." This is a standard mansion.

Yumiko says hers is a little better than average. She is accepting of her situation. The phrase she uses is echoed through Japan's big cities, *Shonagai*: It cannot be helped. This apartment is not a halfway house to a brighter future, either. She does not expect to be able to buy a home. "Not in Tokyo," she says. "Too expensive." And like many Japanese, she must live in Tokyo, because it is bad form for Japanese to change jobs in search of greater opportunity. It brands them as unreliable. Most Japanese spend their lives with one firm.

The western suburbs of the city where Shibasaki is located are generally considered well-to-do. Like the rest of Tokyo, it is a warren of winding streets little more than one car wide. There are no sidewalks, except in the center of town, and only a broad white road stripe marks the way for pedestrians between the two-way traffic cramming past.

Many of the homes here are detached single-family dwellings. This is where Kayo Yoshikawa and her husband, Giichi, live, with their two sons, age 23 and 19. Giichi heads a branch office of the globe-trotting Mitsubishi Trust & Banking Corp. He earns a yearly income of more than 10 million yen, or $67,000, double the national average.

His wife, who has completed two years of college, works part-time, 20 days a month, as a hotel domestic. She considers herself "middle-middle class." Her pleasant two-story home has five rooms and one bath. Out front is a small, immaculate garden, a reminder that nature has not entirely been lost to the city's concrete. Downstairs, in what would correspond with the dining room in the United States, is a traditional tatami room, named for the floor mats of woven rice straw. Only stockinged feet are permitted on tatami. It is a ceremonial room, a formal receiving and dining room that often doubles, as it does for the Yoshikawas, as a bedroom. They sleep on traditional futons, large folding cushions, hidden during the day behind wooden panels at one end of the room. Upstairs the two bedrooms are reserved for the sons.

The Yoshikawas bought their home 20 years ago and now place its value between $600,000 and $1 million, possibly more. The rule of thumb for home ownership is that the cost of a property should not exceed five times the family's gross annual income. Today, despite the

Yoshikawas' substantial earnings, they could not afford to buy the home they live in — which is why Kayo Yoshikawa can say in all candor, "We don't feel that we are rich."

Home ownership is down from 62 percent of all households in 1983 to 61.1 percent in 1988. Although the percentage of ownership is high, the trend is troubling. As a November 1989 "White Paper on the Life of the Nation" produced by the Economic Planning Agency said, "The main reason for the decrease is the rising cost of housing in recent years. . . . For those who rent their dwellings, the situation is bleak."

The deliriously high cost of Tokyo housing becomes plain from a quick perusal of listings at the city's real estate offices. Cubbyholed in racks outside the entryways of each office are sheets of red, green and yellow floor plans describing each apartment's offerings and monthly charges. The average price for a home in Tokyo is $432,000. Its size is 675 square feet. Nationwide, in 1986 (the last year for which figures are available), it was $192,700 for 788 square feet. But land prices skyrocketed after 1986, and that figure is now grossly low. By comparison, last year the average price in the United States for a new home was $148,000, with about 2,000 square feet of floor space, according to the Department of Housing and Urban Development.

In Tokyo's Ikebukuro section, a lower-middle-class residential area close to the center of town, there are offerings for a 512-square-foot apartment at $552,000 and a 133-square-foot apartment at $185,300. In the more tony Shinjuku section, which will soon be home to the city's towering new government buildings, a 420-square-foot apartment is offered at $1,033,000. In the less desirable east end of Tokyo, in the old Edogawa section, a newly built 660-square-foot condominium is on the market for $466,000, plus $100 per month for maintenance.

Last year, 60 of Japan's top 100 taxpayers made their money in real estate. Since 1955, the price of land in Japan has risen an average of 54 times. Prices in Tokyo and five other major cities have ballooned 128 times, according to a May report by Japan's National Land Agency.

Perhaps the most dramatic example of the high cost of land in Japan was produced by Masaru Yoshitomi, the director general of the Economic Research Institute of the Economic Planning Agency, a government think tank. In a 1988 speech, he noted that the land under Tokyo's Imperial Palace was more valuable than all the land in Canada. Today, he would add the state of California into the bargain.

Yoshitomi's office is located in Tokyo's Kasumigaseki, the nation's seat of bureaucratic power, inside the same four-block power quadrangle that holds the mighty Ministry of International Trade and Industry and its economic counterpart, the Ministry of Finance. Two "mansions" could easily be fit in the area occupied by Yoshitomi's large desk and the conference table opposite. A noted economist, he was one of the first Japanese to hold a directorship in the 24-nation Organization of Economic Cooperation and Development, the powerful international market council.

Yoshitomi begins explaining the stifling price of housing by talking about Japan's limited land resources. What he says is heard everywhere in Japan, at many levels of government, and has grown into something of a catechism. Although the figures sometimes vary, the essential proposition is the same: Japan is about the size of California. Seventy percent of the land is mountainous. Only about 17 percent of the available land is suitable for housing and farming. Nearly 124 million people call this home. Hence, the high price of land.

But the explanation is not entirely sufficient, as Yoshitomi explains. "Land value comes from economic activity," he says. The measure of economic activity he employs is gross national product per acre, the amount of money earned on an acre of land. For example, the gross national product per acre in Germany is seven times that in the United States, and land values are about seven times U.S. land values. In Japan, however, the gross national product per acre is 40 times that in the United States, but land is 90 times more valuable.

The huge gap between actual land prices and GNP per acre is partly explained by the combination of low interest rates and high expected growth rate, Yoshitomi says. The economic rule of thumb is that when interest rates are low, asset prices are high. Interest rates in Japan are considerably lower than anywhere in the West. And economic forecasts call for continued high growth rates for the Japanese economy, as much as 5 percent a year, promising ever higher value added per acre. Put another way, there is good reason for speculators to bid up the value of land.

"So if you have low interest rates and high growth rates, you might explain this gap," he says. "But to what extent is very difficult to say. The remaining difference could be a bubble, speculation. But bubbles burst, and the Japanese bubble hasn't, so perhaps it is not a bubble."

One result of these prices is that people are moving farther and farther from the center of Tokyo. This makes commuting, which has always been a problem, an issue of public policy, and it raises questions more easily dodged than dealt with. "Commuting time in Tokyo is not so far from New York," Yoshitomi says. "There, it is one hour, 10 minutes. Here, it is one hour, 20 minutes" each way. There are important differences, however. Nearly everyone in Tokyo uses mass transportation to commute to work. But more to the point: The rigors of commuting make it life's single worst indignity.

Fifty-five percent of Tokyo's workers travel more than two hours to and from work; of those, one worker in five travels more than four hours each day. And commuter trains, though running at three-minute intervals with added cars during rush hours, fill to 250 percent of the capacity for which they were designed. At times, riders have the sense that their feet do not touch the ground or that the forces of acceleration or deceleration on the packed car will crush them. Subway attendants help jam people into trains so the doors can shut. Riders complain that they are physically and psychologically molested by the daily experience, and they arrive at work exhausted.

Between commutes, they endure one of the longest workdays in the developed world. Usually, Japanese office workers — known in Japan as "salary men," who are roughly the U.S. equivalents of white-collar workers but who harbor an ethic of total company commitment — arrive at 8:30 in the morning and stay long past their 5:30 quitting time. Almost always, they are at their desks until 8 in the evening, with many working even later.

Schmoozing after-hours is a virtual institution for salary men, in many cases a requirement. (In Japan, corporate expenditures for entertainment are greater than the government's expenditures for defense, according to the Economic Planning Agency.) With the long commute, it is not uncommon for them to arrive back home at midnight.

A health elixir popular among Tokyo's working stiffs is called Regain. TV ads for the energy drink pose a high-powered salary man asking, "Can you fight 24 hours a day?" Regain, of course, will make this possible. Its ingredients include caffeine, nicotine and vitamin C.

Drinks like Regain are popular in Japan because work hours have actually increased as the country has grown in prosperity, up from 2,064 in 1975 to 2,111 in 1988. Last year, a national record for overtime hours was set in Japan, with 190. U.S. workers average about 1,900 hours per year on the job, German workers, 1,600. The six-day week is still commonplace in Japan. Overall, only 30 percent of

Japanese workers had two days off a week. However, in those companies employing fewer than 100 persons — the vast majority of firms — only 5 percent offer a five-day week. Most often, companies work one weekend out of two or three.

Japan's giant Nippon Telegraph & Telephone Corp., for example (a company larger than American Telephone & Telegraph Co. and International Business Machines Corp. combined), still keeps office hours every other Saturday. This, four years after the government promised a campaign to reduce hours below 2,000 a year by 1990 and 1,800 a year by 1992.

The possibility of working even longer hours than at present is taken so seriously that there has been resistance to moving the nation onto daylight saving time, or "summer time," as the Japanese call it. Starting in May in the Land of the Rising Sun, the sun will rise at 4 a.m. The economics of switching are obvious to this energy-starved nation, which is fueled almost entirely by oil imports. But the Japanese fear that whatever gain summer time may bring in terms of conservation, it will ultimately lead to more hours at the office.

Makoto Takei, who works for the giant telephone company, says he is resigned to his arduous schedule. Until he was promoted to special assistant to the senior vice president for international affairs, he rarely left the office before 10, often not until midnight. Now things are better. He says he is usually home by 9 p.m. and has time for himself and his family after dinner, usually about 10 p.m. "The situation is not so bad," he says, although he spends little time relaxing. "I seldom watch TV." He is back at his desk the next day at 7:30 to catch up on reading or to prepare for assignments.

In return for his conscientiousness, Takei earns a good bit more than 10 million yen a year and can look forward to Japan's system of lifetime employment, at least until age 55. Then, in the typical pattern, he will retire to a less prestigious position, with considerably lower pay, in a subsidiary of his firm. Contrary to conventional wisdom, only one worker in five enjoys such guaranteed lifetime employment in Japan.

Technically, Takei gets 22 paid vacation days each year. But he rarely takes more than a week or two off. Few Japanese make full use of their vacations. In fact, the free time taken has decreased 10 percent since 1980. Nowhere do employees allow themselves more than 50 percent of the time they are due, according to the November 1989 Economic Planning Agency white paper.

Largely, this is a result of peer pressure. No one likes to be seen as shirking work, and only hard workers who put in long hours are rewarded with promotions. But there are also pressing financial considerations driving the Japanese. The 1989 report found that 55 percent of employees age 30 to 39 keep their brutal schedules because they need the extra wages, which they earn in addition to their vacation pay.

When Takei does take time to himself, he rarely travels. "Everywhere you go is crowded," he explains. Because Japanese usually take their vacations at the same time of year, resort areas are frequently overcrowded. So are the already jammed roads. A weekend jaunt from Tokyo to the seashore some 60 miles away can take up to six hours. And highway tolls are exorbitant, gouging riders for $41 between Tokyo and Nagoya, a distance equal to a trip from New York to Washington. From Tokyo to Osaka, a distance equal to a trip from Chicago to Cleveland, costs a staggering $67 one way. Just to ride the narrow two-lane expressway cutting over Tokyo's maze of winding streets costs $4.

Unlike most Japanese, Takei says the majority of his income goes to pay for his home loan, instead of into savings. He lives in a modern, well-appointed house, located in the wealthy suburb of Kamikitazawa in western Tokyo. His home resembles a small two-floor subdivision town house in the United States. It is built on land owned by his father. "Otherwise, I could not afford it," says Takei, whose income is nearly three times the national average. "I would still be living in company housing."

Company and public housing are Tokyo's answer to the high price of real estate. A 1987 survey of 742 Japanese firms found that 96.2 percent of them offered some form of housing. In the past, such places, with their low, low rents, were a way for people to salt away cash for home purchases. Such places are often undersized, even by Tokyo standards, but they are usually well-located, just a short commute from the office. Such subsidized housing bears no social stigma. Even small and medium manufacturing firms, which form the backbone of Japanese industry, offer their workers housing.

Near the Edo River, which forms the city's eastern boundary, is an industrial-residential area crammed with such small factories. These firms do not have names, only owners, like Shinsaku Seto. His business, which chrome-plates metal tool parts — rollers for extruding plastics, for example — was founded 35 years ago by his father-in-law. The company remains closely held and last year had revenues of about 400 million yen, $2.7 million, about average. He has 40 employees.

The front office of the factory could pass for any small manufac-

turing company anywhere in the world. The industrial-grade decor
— gray furniture, metal cabinets — gives the place a gritty air. There
is no computer, only a copy machine and a facsimile machine. An
abacus sits at the ready on one desktop. Only Seto's office, which is
up a flight of steel spiral stairs, is air-conditioned against the humid-
ity of the summer rainy season. It is a small, immaculate room.

"Once we employed 100, but automation has replaced workers,"
he says. Just as well, perhaps, as labor shortages are now a serious
issue in Japan. Compounding the problem is a shrinking birthrate,
which reached an all-time low for the postwar period last year. Young
people claim that cramped housing makes it impossible for them to
have more than one child and still live close enough to their offices
to maintain some semblance of family life.

"When this business began, money was a problem," Seto says.
"Now the problem is finding young workers." The young shy away
from what they call 3-D jobs (or 3-K in Japanese): those that are
dirty, dangerous, difficult. Like many employers, Seto turned to foreign workers, but he found them unreliable, leaving work to take language classes in midday, he says.

Seto's workers earn 1,000 yen an hour, about $6.60. Overtime in
Japan earns time and a quarter. The first Saturday of each month is
an unpaid holiday at Seto's. Wages average about $20,000 a year.
There is an employee restaurant on the floor above the plant, where
the men take half an hour for lunch. Today the menu calls for salad,
rice, hamburgers, eggs and pickles. Food odors waft through the
room. An upright cabinet stands against one wall. It holds the workers' drinking cups and chopsticks. The various designs on the uten-
sils suggest the personalities of their owners.

Four of the workers in the factory make use of company housing.
There is a row of individual rooms down the hall from the lunch-
room. Each is the size of a storage locker, about 8 feet by 12 feet, and
costs 10,000 yen a month, $67. The walls are paneled in wood veneer.
They buckle in places and show their age. The carpeted floors are
stained. There is no air-conditioning, just one sliding window glazed
with corrugated translucent plastic.

Across the hall is a game room where the workers have pushed the
few pieces of furniture to one side. Here, they relax on the floor after
work, playing cards or mah-jongg. A red ashtray the size of a hub-
cap spills over with cigarette butts.

But for the incandescent light, this could be a sweatshop scene
from the 19th century. The floor where the men sit and smoke is
located above the factory's plating vats, where rainbows of chemi-

cals are puddled on the factory floor. The atmosphere is part Dickens and part gold rush. The $800 a year Seto's workers pay in rent, the free board, leaves much of their yearly $20,000 in earnings for savings.

If the living conditions Seto reveals are questionable, they are nonetheless typical. Some of the men have lived here for years and may never move. Though they have money to spend, there is little room for storage or furniture — some stereo equipment, televisions, an auto. "They do this to buy a house," Seto says, "but that is getting difficult." In a survey done by the Bank of Japan, 32 percent of Japanese in 1978 said they were saving to buy a home. In 1988 that figure had plummeted to 19 percent, a symptom of the despair Japanese feel over real estate values.

Savings rates are also down from 1979 levels of 18.5 percent to 15.1 percent in 1988, although the overall value of savings has grown. Last year, the average Japanese family had a 13.1 million-yen nest egg, $87,300, according to a March survey by the government's Management and Coordination Agency. Significantly, however, over the same period, debt for the average worker showed the greatest increase in 10 years, up 20.9 percent in 1988, to $25,000.

Indications are the Japanese are on something of a spending bender. Says social critic Shuichi Kato, "People cannot afford to buy homes, so they buy other things." Prestigious cars are becoming a substitute for home ownership. "More and more, you see Benzes parked in front of shabby houses in Tokyo." The Japanese do not say Mercedes-Benz, Kato points out. "They say 'Benz,' as if the word had power."

Here, too, the paradox of Japan's prosperity emerges. "The cars are largely a psychological satisfaction," Kato observes, "because there are no roads." In all of Japan, there are only 7,100 miles of expressway, a number the government has promised to triple this decade.

Although there are 46 million passenger cars in Japan, few are used for commuting. In Tokyo, traffic is nearly impacted, and parking is virtually impossible. Those who do commute by car leave their homes at 5 a.m. and can be seen parked on the street, snoozing or eating a brown bag breakfast before restaurants and offices open.

The freewheeling spending evident in luxury car sales is visible elsewhere, in other ways, particularly among young working people. Japanese marry late, so their early 20s are years blessed by disposable income. Tokyo's shopping districts — such as the Ginza, Shinjuku and most especially Rippongi — are promenades, teeming with handsome, well-dressed young people. This is Japan's answer to the trendy fashion parade along Paris's Boulevard St. Germain.

Most of these young bons vivants, like Yuki Nakajima, 22, live with their parents. "Women like me lead a good life if we are not married," she says. She has recently returned from a weekend in Okinawa, a former battlefield that has metamorphosed into a tropical island resort.

Nakajima works for Japan Air Lines Co. Ltd. and is a graduate of Tokyo's prestigious Sophia University. She exemplifies the young women captured by the phrase *Hanako gensho*. Hanako is the name of Tokyo's most popular magazine for young women. It is a life-style magazine, but the weekly is more than a Japanese version of Mademoiselle, Glamour or even Elle. Hanako is to shopping what travel guides are to touring.

With an average take-home pay of 100,000 yen a month, nearly $700, and no rent to pay, young women like Nakajima are wellsprings of disposable income. A recent magazine survey found that young women dished out an average of $554 a month on clothing, food and drink. Nearly 10 percent of the record 9 million Japanese who traveled abroad last year were women age 20 to 24.

Seated in the cushy environs of the Rainbow Lounge in Tokyo's pricey Imperial Hotel, Nakajima is in her milieu. She glances through her crowded appointment book to recall what she did on her last night out. Her date book is organized with colored stick-on symbols. It is almost a childlike touch. There are green circles to indicate holidays and gold stars to mark office events, such as meetings and conferences. The red heart posted over Saturday night needs no explanation. Last Wednesday, she notes, pointing to a gold star on the calendar, she attended a casual after-hour party thrown by her company.

High-priced real estate is something Nakajima says that she worries about. A friend recently related a story to her regarding a young woman in her early 30s who was unmarried. Although she was conducting a far-reaching search for the right man, she was fussy. She wanted to find a fellow who was born and raised in Tokyo. The reason for this particular qualification was immediately apparent to Nakajima. The woman wanted a Tokyo native because it was more likely that his parents would own a home in town. *Masuo-san gensho*. Inheriting a place is the only hope most young people harbor for owning a home of their own in the city.

Such an attempt at accommodation is one way the Japanese are dealing with their diminishing expectations. Still, the lack of public outcry about the real estate crisis is surprising to many observers. The past two parliamentary campaigns bubbled with talk of consumer unrest, but such sentiments never boiled over into vote-casting issues.

Masao Kunihiro, an opposition member of the Diet, Japan's parliament, blames this seeming indifference among voters on national character. "The Japanese are like sheep," he says. "They call themselves *shachachiko*" — a portmanteau expression, he explains, that means corporate livestock. "The word is pronounced very wryly, very sardonically," says the former television personality, whose flare for the dramatic has become a political asset. He thinks the Japanese have armored themselves against adversity with large doses of cynicism.

The ability to endure harsh circumstances is basic to the social compact and has its roots in the culture. There is even a word for it: *gaman*, a mix of fighting spirit and true grit. It explains as much about the quiet resignation of the Japanese in the face of this paradox of prosperity as does *shachachiko*.

Not to be overlooked, however, is the more practical circumstance. For despite the hardships, Japan has made huge strides in living standards since the war. Stores overflow with food. Everyone has shelter, excellent medical care. The Japanese electronics and auto industries are the envy of the world. The country has become a direct challenger to U.S. technological leadership and ranges ahead in many areas. The nation has real economic muscle. Japanese businesses own Rockefeller Center, Tiffany's, 50 percent of the prime real estate in Los Angeles, 30 percent of Houston, Washington.

The people count such accomplishments as their own. Their sacrifices are realized — and assuaged — by the nation's achievements. And they may be proud that their nation works. The trains run on time, as do the ultrasafe subways; the mail gets delivered; streets are clean; crime is virtually nonexistent; drugs are no problem. One may more safely drink the tap water in Tokyo than in Paris.

Philosopher Kato points to still another factor in the lack of reaction by the Japanese electorate: "The relationship between the government and the people is different in Japan from the West." He cites taxes as an example. "People hate taxes but they never question them. [The exception was a fire storm last year over a 3 percent consumption tax.] We just had a royal wedding in Tokyo. No one talked about the budget."

Grass roots movements in Japan are practically unheard-of, particularly in recent years. For the most part, people are too consumed by their long hours to become involved. Instead, when change is in the winds, it flows down from the lofty and powerful ministries. That is why a recent "vision paper" issued by the Ministry of International Trade and Industry drew so much comment. While the paper ranged over such issues as Eastern Europe and Japan as an emerging global power, it took the unusual step of calling attention to consumer issues.

Such "visions" have been issued each decade since the 1960s. They have set the agenda for Japan's ascendancy in computer hardware, autos and consumer electronics. MITI's reputation for realizing its visions remains virtually unchallenged.

And now, says the ministry, the target is consumers. "To date, in Japan, we have adopted policies in response to the times," says Kunio Morikiyo, director of the policy planning office at MITI, who introduced this latest vision. "In the 1990s, that calls for programs that benefit the people. We call our industrial policies of the 1990s 'human-oriented.'"

The summary report delivered by Morikiyo, which was uncharacteristically issued in English as well as in Japanese, came right to the point: "If we simply look at numbers, there is no question Japan has left a trail of superior economic performances. However, there is increasing doubt among the Japanese people that their standard of living has risen accordingly. The problem is too serious to simply say that it is a 'matter of personal viewpoints' or 'an extravagance of a newly wealthy Japan.'"

MITI says it is concerned about public reaction. The fear, however, is not that the paradox of prosperity will result in civil unrest, or even that it might send Japan's ruling Liberal-Democratic Party to its first outright defeat since 1955. Instead, the ministry worries that the mixing of Japan's deep cultural strength, *gaman*, with its dark opposite, cynicism, will result in nihilism. "If changes are not made to realize this goal, and there are increasing gaps in wealth and among regions, a feeling of frustration may permeate society. This in turn could undermine motivation and creativity in individuals," the paper warned.

MITI delivered its vision for the 1990s just as the yearlong Strategic Impediments Initiative talks ended across the street at the Ministry of Foreign Affairs. Its timing raised brows among the skeptics. Much of the trade talks focused on Japanese promises to pump up its skinny infrastructure and to make progress on land prices. Such impediments have so much impact on the Japanese economy that the United States believes remedying them will improve the one-sided trade imbalance between the nations. (The prohibitive cost of real estate, for example, excludes midsize U.S. companies from opening their doors in the Japanese market.)

Unofficially within MITI, it was acknowledged that the vision was issued for external consumption, to form a coda to the Strategic Impediments talks. Doubts about the true significance of the vision even percolated up from those who contributed to the document: 200 independent consultants from giant corporations such as Mitsubishi Heavy Industries Ltd., Nomura Securities Co. Ltd., Dentsu Advertising; foreign firms like Citibank NA; powerful associations like the Keidanren (the Japan Federation of Economic Organizations) and Nikkeiren, its nominal counterpart in labor.

Hidehiko Sekizawa, a consultant on the vision and executive director of Hakuhodo Institute of Life & Living Inc., a subsidiary of Japan's No. 2 advertising firm, remains cautious. "We must keep our eyes fixed on what MITI will do, not what they say."

To gain perspective on Japan's living standards for the vision, Sekizawa says he interviewed 30 Westerners who had been working in Japan for more than three years. He wanted to know how the quality of life in their home countries differed from Japan's. The study found that the Japanese lack three things. As Sekizawa summarizes, "We lack space, because we live in rabbit hutches. We lack time, because of long hours, long commutes and no leisure. And we lack private lives, because most of our time is spent with colleagues or clients."

In search of a catchphrase to vivify the findings, Sekizawa arrived at the Japanese word *manuke*. "The meaning of *manuke* is that 'we lack three things,' " he says: "time, space and family interaction." The purpose of the catchphrase was to attract press attention. The hope was to galvanize public opinion, because the Japanese instantly recognize that the catchphrase is a stinger. It has a double meaning. "*Manuke* is also the Japanese word for 'stupid,' " he says. "We are stupid to live without these three things."

But Sekizawa is not entirely discouraged by the situation. He takes MITI's invitation to him and to other top marketing people as a signal that the ministry is aware of the issues. "I have little knowledge of industry," he points out. "I study consumers." Asking him to join the study "may show that MITI is serious about understanding consumer needs." Still, he adds, the question remains: "Can MITI change anything?"

One potential target of reform for the ministry is Tokyo's urban farmer. In people-packed Tokyo, farmers control 15 percent of the land. Only 1 percent of the city's people live on these preserves. The National Land Agency survey found that within one hour's commuting time from central Tokyo, 17,400 hectares of land, nearly 43,000 acres, were suitable for housing. If only 15 percent of that land were developed, there would be enough room to build 500,000 detached homes. At 3.19 persons per household, Tokyo's average, that is enough housing for almost 1.6 million residents, 13 percent of the capital's population.

The farmers who own these lands are at great advantage, borrowing against their huge land assets to make lucrative investments or subdividing the land and selling it for substantial profits. Then there are the tax breaks. Because land prices are so high, the effective tax rate has shrunk to almost nothing, about 0.1 percent, compared with 1.5 percent in the United States. "Farmers pay about one-fiftieth the rate paid in the rest of Japan," says the Economic Planning Agency's Yoshitomi. That means that a farm plot worth $10 million would pay yearly taxes equal to a dinner for four in Tokyo's Ginza, about $200.

The largest, most luxurious homes in most of Tokyo's neighborhoods are those owned by local farmers. In the little town of Takaido, for example, in the wealthy western suburbs, a family of farmers who have lived in the area for years keeps large parcels of land nominally under the till. A wag in the Ministry of Construction has said that if this one particular owner's land were sold in a single year, its buyer would become the largest taxpayer in Japan.

On one section of the land is a chestnut grove the size of two football fields. It is worth millions. In season, the chestnuts from the grove are sold by the side of the road in paper bags for 500 yen, 35 cents a bag. There is an honor cup to collect the 500-yen coppers. The small transaction that takes place atop that chair seat satisfies the definition of farming in the tax code. Nearby stands a sign that says, "This agricultural land is maintained as greenery for the benefit of Tokyo's children." The sign sits behind a 4-foot concrete wall, too tall for young children to get the message.

Says the Economic Planning Agency's Yoshitomi, "There are two separate questions: Do we deal with the price of land or the more effective use of land?" The government prefers the former, he says. But he thinks higher land prices are inevitable. "The purpose of our policy should be aimed at increasing the utility of the land for the people." In other words, more space, lower unit prices. "That obviously will end up raising land prices on the underlying property."

Tokyo is a low, flat city. Across its endless urban sprawl, few buildings rise up above the treetops, about 2½ stories. The city's seismic instability partly explains this low-slung phenomenon. But Yoshitomi says that buildings can be built to withstand earthquakes. "We are technology optimists," he says. "The problem we are trying to overcome now is glass." During an earthquake, glass shattering from skyscrapers could have terrible effects on those below. "So we are developing special windows." The future of Tokyo, he believes, will be upward.

"We are not talking about turning Tokyo into Manhattan," he says. Instead, he sees a city of 20- to 50-story buildings in Tokyo's 10-kilometer radius inner core. "In the next 10 kilometers there would be seven- or eight-story Paris-style apartments, with their own parking garages. Beyond 20 kilometers would be American-style suburbs."

What he describes is known as the Tokyo Doughnut. It is an idea so well institutionalized that it is taught in elementary schools. Most consider such plans for the city to be dreams, virtually impossible to implement. MITI's paper suggested a second solution, reducing the pressure on Tokyo by directing national resources to other cities. That scenario also seems unlikely.

A more realistic near-term solution, which is already being acted upon, is leveraging out living space through the tax code. The government's Tax Commission began hearings on the subject in May. A full report on real estate, farm and inheritance taxes is expected in October.

Yoshitomi says the effective tax rate for real estate will certainly be increased. Higher real estate taxes would be balanced by lower local taxes. The effect would be to maintain purchasing power but to reduce the incentive to hold on to housing. "We have to squeeze the people to make them sell their land." Already, he says, a consensus is forming in the government to support the change. "It will take five to 10 years to accomplish."

While these are not draconian measures, the message they contain is not a pleasant one. The dream of owning land, at least in Tokyo and possibly in the other large cities, is coming to an end. "Encouraging young people to buy land is mistaken," Yoshitomi says. To avoid the downward spiral that comes with diminished expectations, the loss of incentive, he suggests an alternative. "They should have more space in a less costly apartment. This would make them happy."

By trading expectations, land for living room, the government hopes to make a dent in the paradox of prosperity. It entails sacrifice. But this is the only possible future, Yoshitomi says. This generation of Japanese now in their early 30s will be the generation of *Masuo-san gensho*.

"Young people, sorry to say, must give up the idea of owning their own land in Tokyo," says Yoshitomi. "It is not economical. We will build more comfortable apartments with more reasonable rents. They won't have to pay the high price of land to own their own homes. We must put an end to that illusion."

Jeff Shear

CHAPTER 23

One of the reasons U.S.-Japanese trade relations started deteriorating during the 1980s was the Japanese penchant for explaining barriers against imports in terms of Japan's cultural uniqueness. As this article of July 18, 1988, reported, the explanations ranged from the long digestive tracts of the Japanese, invoked as a reason to exclude U.S. beef, to the wetness of Japanese snow, a reason for excluding foreign-made skis. This fortress Japan mercantilism meant high prices for consumers; but even the young, eager for a better standard of living, seemed unwilling to break with the status quo.

THE CLOSED SOCIETY OF A SUPERPOWER

O ver a traditional Japanese dinner one evening, Hiroshi Yamada, at 30 the youngest member ever elected to the Tokyo Metropolitan Assembly, attempts to explain why the world does not understand the hub of the trade issue with Japan, which he sees as not simply a matter of the country opening its markets. The Japanese, he says, just cannot consume more imported food than they already do.

Almost no rice, for example, can be imported. "Rice," he says, toying with a piece of sushi, "is the core of the Japanese civilization." Asked about the fact that the price of rice to the Japanese consumer would be cut drastically if Japan ended its policies of protection and subsidization of rice farmers, Yamada responds, "the Japanese want quality products, not low prices. Comparison shopping is not the Japanese way. This is our system, and we want to continue it. We want the safety of domestic production."

The view that Japan's trade policies are in large part cultural is

certainly not original to Yamada. In January, Tsutomu Hata, a former agriculture minister who now leads a farm trade lobby, told a
group of American legislators that the United States should not
expect Japan to import much more U.S. beef, because the Japanese
have trouble digesting it. Their intestinal tracts are longer than those
of Americans, he maintained.

The idea of Japanese uniqueness also has made it difficult for
many foreign companies trying to sell to Japan. American-made sup-
positories have been rejected by the government on the grounds that
Japanese physical differences make them unsuitable for the population. Foreign pharmaceutical makers are often turned away
because their tests are judged inadequate, having been conducted on
non-Japanese.

The government claims that Japanese construction work is different from any other; a regulation requires that foreign companies
must prove they can meet exacting Japanese standards before they
can be admitted to do business. Ski manufacturers are trying to get
the government to declare European-made skis — one of the few
European import successes — unsuitable for the market, because
Japanese snow is "wetter" than the European variety.

Whether these ideas are ingrained in the culture or are propaganda tools used by producers to avoid foreign competition is difficult to determine. "I happen to support beef imports, but this is a
matter of Japanese taste," says Kobo Inamura, a young bureaucrat
at the Ministry of Posts and Telecommunications. One recent letter
to the editor in a Tokyo daily ascribed U.S. trade frustrations to "bar-
barians who do not appreciate cultural relativism and subtlety."

But surely some of the attempts to discourage imported products
fall into the propaganda category. This spring, Japanese farmers
took to burning President Reagan in effigy and erecting signs charging that imports bring acquired immunodeficiency syndrome. A
film produced by Zenchu, the Central Union of Agricultural Cooperatives, which has 5.5 million members among farm households, is
being shown throughout rural areas. It depicts widespread health
problems — disfigured fetuses float in lab jars, hospitalized children
have mysterious skin diseases — purportedly from food imports
treated with toxic chemicals. The film concludes: "Once you sent us
this lovely gift of friendship, and now you send us poison. . . . If
Japanese consumers are being poisoned, is it good to have this open
trade with the United States?"

The ire of the farmers has been raised by the latest installment in
the battle over import policies, negotiations between the U.S. and

Japanese governments that have focused on lifting limits on imports of beef and citrus products. The next go-around will likely address the volatile issue of rice import prohibition.

Such negotiations have resulted in revisions in import quotas but no change in overall Japanese policy. For example, on the beef issue, Japan agreed to phase out import restrictions over a six-year period. But as the Japanese phase out the restrictions they will raise tariffs on beef from 25 percent to 70 percent, later reducing them to 50 percent, to keep prices in line with domestic levels. U.S. officials want a substantially lower tariff. Despite the high prices such import limits mean for the consumer — a steak costs about $35 in a Tokyo market — there is little consumer pressure for the government to make such concessions. (The country's total food bill accounts for fully one-quarter of all consumer spending, while the comparable U.S. figure is 17 percent.)

"The public is not in favor of perfect markets," says Takashi Kiuchi, the general manager of the economics group at the Long-term Credit Bank of Japan Ltd. "We would like to preserve the substance of our culture. If we move to free trade, we may lose Japanese virtue in the process."

Compounding this is the disproportionate clout rural Japan has long had in the Diet, the national legislature. Says Nobutaka Machimura, a member of the Diet's House of Representatives, "In my constituency there are dairy farmers and rice growers. They are rather anti-American in their sentiments. They don't want compromise."

In the United States, there seems to be a growing concern that the trade barriers are the result of Japanese insularity, traditional preoccupation with self-sufficiency and an "us against them" mentality — and thus may be nonnegotiable. In a recent speech, U.S. Commerce Secretary C. William Verity Jr. said, "They tell us they have to protect their markets because of their culture. They haven't joined the world yet."

A more precise way of putting it is perhaps that the Japanese have not yet let the world in. On the other hand, they now have a world market for their products far larger than ever envisioned in the Greater East Asia Co-Prosperity Sphere, a concept of a Japan-led economic bloc born in the last Japanese drive for rapid industrial expansion that spilled over into ultranationalism and war.

There is no sign that fundamental attitudes toward trade liberalization are changing in Japan. In fact, officials and industrialists have gone on the offensive of late, arguing that the reason for the U.S. trade

deficit "lies in the characteristics of the U.S. economic system," as the
Bank of Japan recently said in a report. In an article in a leading
business magazine in the spring, a prominent economist, Ryotaro
Komiya, wrote, "The reason for the imbalance in U.S.-Japanese
trade lies on the U.S. side. If the imbalance is to be corrected, it is first
necessary to find a means to decrease its national debt." He also criticized Japan's diplomacy as a failure for giving in to "one-sided
American demands."

Businessmen, especially those in export-dependent industries,
have shed their previous quiet diplomacy and taken a more con-
frontational stance. Eishiro Saito, chairman of the Nippon Steel
Corp., regularly chides the Japanese government for its "passive"
listening to U.S. trade complaints. Some have also warned of the dangers of American protectionist measures, while denouncing any U.S.
criticism of Japan protectionism as "Japan bashing."

Another theme that the Japanese have long propagated — that
their success is culturally determined — is making a comeback,
especially with regard to competitive threats from neighbors such as
South Korea and Taiwan. The soaring yen, for example, should make
the South Korean Hyundai a big seller in Japan; the car has enjoyed
such success in the United States. But there are few Hyundais for
sale in Japan because dealers who carry Toyota or Nissan cars fear
losing their dealerships should they sell them.

"At a time when the nations of Asia are having problems in their
economic relations with Japan, the argument, 'What's wrong with
Japan making goods of high quality?' is given considerable credence.
What this means is that the other peoples of Asia don't work hard
enough," says Loke Pooi-choon, a Chinese Malaysian who reports
from Tokyo for a major Singaporean Chinese-language daily, Lian
He Zao Bao.

Examples of the dynamics of the Japanese trade thrust are by now
the stuff of legend among foreign competitors. The Ministry of
Finance backs industries in which it perceives high demand by
directing the allocation of development funds to private companies
through the banks it controls. Support originally went to textiles,
then switched to automobiles, steel, electronics, semiconductors and
now to financial services. To do this, the Japan Development Bank
draws on Post Office savings accounts, which, thanks to an exemption from taxes and generous interest rates, have grown to a sum
greater than the assets of the 10 largest American money center
banks combined. (Japanese law forbids any private bank to pay a
higher rate on savings than the Post Office.)

In addition, in the early stages of the push in exports, the Ministry of Finance allowed companies an exemption from tax on up to 80 percent of profits earned from exports. This was later changed to give companies depreciation allowances in direct relation to their export performance. The Ministry of International Trade and Industry targets the countries and markets to be penetrated. It also can bring together large producers into one company to achieve economies of scale — a practice U.S. antitrust law would prohibit — and effectively shut down industries that are judged unable to compete.

Extraordinary measures undertaken to maintain an internationally competitive posture are common. Many exporters are willing to go to extreme lengths to keep overseas markets, subsidizing vulnerable items in foreign markets by raising domestic prices and shielding home markets.

While tariff rates are roughly equal to those of other industrial nations, they are spiked with special tariffs in industries that are considered vulnerable to foreign competition. In addition, Japanese markets are protected by a maze of nontariff barriers. Foreign cigarettes, besides bearing a tariff of 20 percent, are allowed on sale at less than one-tenth of the country's 250,000 tobacconists, and their importers are forbidden to advertise except in English-language publications.

Clyde V. Prestowitz Jr., a former trade negotiator in the Reagan administration with responsibility for Japan, says that the Japanese simply do not understand the term "open" the way it is understood in the West. "Culturally, it's an alien concept for them," he says. But now there are signs of discontent in Tokyo about the price paid by the consumer to maintain this mercantilist fortress. Many Japanese are coming to realize that the country's economic strength, even as Japan's per capita gross national product exceeds that of the United States, has yet to be translated into much improvement in everyday life.

In a recent speech, Prime Minister Noboru Takeshita acknowledged as much, saying, "The focus of manufacturing, efficiency and exports has been harmful to the spirit of the Japanese culture. The Japanese economy is structurally slanted toward excess supply and insufficient at-home demand." He committed himself to a "pleasure-doubling plan," stressing an increase in domestic consumption, shorter working hours and a more relaxed society.

The younger generation is particularly concerned about the disparity between Japan's industrial might and everyday quality of life.

"We have to wait 10 or 20 years to reach the top now. When there were higher rates of growth, it didn't take so long," says Kiuchi of the Long-Term Credit Bank of Japan. "It used to be that if you graduated from the University of Tokyo and you worked for this bank it was almost a given that you would rise to the top. Now, it is not so clear."

The younger Japanese also complain that Japan has not yet reduced the work year to 2,000 hours and workers are not encouraged to take the holiday time they are allotted. Surveys show that leisure time with friends ranks high on the list of things young people want. A 1986 study of 1,000 single people age 20 to 39 conducted by Infoplan, a market research concern, showed that 38 percent gave priority to work over family.

Even so, says Kiuchi, "A good job at a good company is still what the average young man aspires to." That is unlikely to change soon, especially given the alarm bells set off with the older generation by any talk of loosening up. Says Machimura, the Diet member, "My daughter, in her 20s, is very lazy. The whole young generation is that way. But we won't let that affect Japanese production,. You know, hard work is the Japanese tradition."

These new pressures are unlikely to produce any great trend toward liberalizing the economy. More than anything else, the attitude of Japan's youth toward work signifies confidence that in economic terms, at least, Japan has made it. This has so far bred not a propensity to change but a more conservative impulse — to protect the status quo that old and young see as responsible for their country's success.

David Brock

CHAPTER 24

*Under pressure from its Western allies,
Japan began increasing its foreign aid,
surpassing the United States in 1988 as
the world's top donor. What began as a
regional effort designed mainly to create
new markets for Japanese companies and
goods metamorphosed into a program
that, while still self-interested, bore a
greater resemblance to the aid programs
of other countries. But as this article of
March 27, 1989, pointed out, when Japan
began asking for clout commensurate
with its contribution to organizations like
the World Bank, Washington started
having second thoughts about the
ambitions it had encouraged.*

JAPAN GIVES MORE — AND ASKS FOR MORE

The hard figures will not be in for a few months, but observers in both Tokyo and Washington believe that sometime last year Japan leapfrogged over the United States to become the world's largest donor of aid to the developing world. The aid is running at more than $10 billion a year, a good part of the expansion having come from the rise in the value of the yen, which has pushed up dollar-denominated aid grants without causing much of a dent in the Japanese budget.

But the rise also has been fueled by an aggressive push on the part of Japan's prime minister, Noboru Takeshita, to defuse claims by the United States and other developed countries that Japan has been getting a free ride on the global economy and not picking up enough of its responsibilities for the world's financial health. In addition to opening up its own market to more imports, Japan last year began implementing a five-year $50 billion aid program that could give it an unassailable leadership role in the world's development into the

next century. That is something that the United States and other aid
donors have been encouraging for years. As its partners in the Organization for Economic Cooperation and Development cope with
budget deficits and growing resistance on the part of voters to
increased aid spending, Japan may be the only country well-posi-
tioned to spend heavily on the Third World.

It contributes aid to some 134 countries, and the total of its financial flows (including all forms of official development aid, loans and
private investments) amounted to $20.5 billion in 1987. And with a
trade surplus approaching $100 billion a year, the largest such sur-
plus in the history of the world, Japan is aggressively investing. Its
assets abroad are worth almost $300 billion.

There is room to do more. The nation spends about 0.31 percent
of its gross national product on aid, less than the 0.35 percent average of the donor countries in the Organization for Economic Cooperation and Development's Development Assistance Committee. It
ranked 13th out of the 18 committee members in 1987, ahead of the
United States (0.2 percent) but well behind countries like Norway
(1.09 percent) and the Netherlands (0.98 percent).

But as Japan spends more in such organizations as the World
Bank and the International Monetary Fund, it is starting to demand
more political clout in those organizations. And U.S. critics of
Japan's aid programs say that the distinctly nonaltruistic, even
opportunistic, way that the nation spends money in the developing
world is aimed at laying the groundwork for an expansion of private
Japanese investment, often at the expense of American business.

What worries U.S. policymakers is the way the aid is granted and
the way it is linked with private investment by Japanese companies.
Some analysts say Japan has its own interests at heart, rather than
those of the developing world, and that it has been channeling funding into development projects aimed at extracting key resources like
timber, natural gas and coal, on which it depends for its own economic growth.

Many in Japan admit that Tokyo's aid policies in the past have
been characterized, as one leading economist put it recently, "by
pragmatism and opportunism." Until the mid-1970s, Japanese aid
was designed to promote exports and economic interdependence,
and almost all the aid was "tied" — that is, recipient countries had
to spend it on Japanese products and services. Moreover, the lion's
share of the aid, both grants and loans, went to Asian countries,
where the nation hoped to reap the most political and economic benefits. In an effort to reverse this, Japan has been increasing its aid to

non-Asian countries, particularly those in Sub-Saharan Africa, and putting a more altruistic face on its donations. It is trying to shift to a greater emphasis on grants rather than loans, to make the loans less expensive and to give the beneficiary countries more leeway in how the money is spent.

Officially, only about one-third of the aid is described as tied. But analysts say that what Japan calls untied aid is often only partly untied: Governments can use it to buy goods either from Japan or from their own producers, but not from anywhere else. "Japan's definition of untied is a little more lenient than some other countries'," says Gretchen Green, analyst at the Japan Economic Institute in Washington.

The extensive tying of aid has led to complaints in Washington that Japan is using its aid to compete unfairly for Third World markets. "It's true that the Japanese program, much like nearly all the European aid programs, is frequently tied to contracts for their own exporters," says Richard Bissell, an administrator at the U.S. Agency for International Development. "The United States is uniquely focused on development needs, rather than the needs of our own exporting sector. That's an issue which concerns us, as the Japanese aid program has grown."

Japan uses other, subtler means to ensure that its aid pays off. With a minuscule field staff, the Overseas Economic Cooperation Fund, which administers official loans, does not want to get involved in recipient countries' development policies, preferring to grant loans in response to requests for specific projects. This "request-only" policy has led savvy Japanese businessmen abroad to suggest projects to host governments and to draw up design plans. Since the projects are designed by Japanese, for Japanese machinery and know-how, the contracts tend to go to Japanese suppliers. "Even with untied aid, an awful lot of it ends up going into the pockets of Japanese businessmen," says Edward J. Lincoln, a senior fellow at the Brookings Institution in Washington.

Private Japanese investors abroad also benefit by coordinating their investments with officially funded development projects. Close to 40 percent of Japanese aid goes for major capital projects like power plants, dams and transportation infrastructure, which open up possibilities for Japanese industrialists. Analysts say there are close ties between the public and private sectors. "Official aid and private capital investment are blended very neatly and effectively, more so than we have been able to do it. If that continued to be their principal style, it could hinder our efforts to expand our investments and development assistance," says a Japan specialist at the Center for Strategic and International Studies in Washington. Lincoln agrees: "You end up getting a preference for Japanese direct investment because a lot of foreign aid comes along with it."

Some observers say the picture is changing. "Increasingly, Third World contractors are doing better on aid contracts generated by the Japanese," says Susan J. Pharr, a professor at Harvard University's Reischauer Institute. Last year, Japan began to gradually unite the engineering parts of its official loans and to allow foreign contractors to participate in grant-financed development surveys. But despite the progress, only 40 percent of grants are untied, according to the OECD.

The Japanese argue that, even if Tokyo's official aid does benefit the nation's businessmen, the economic growth that results from it is good for the whole world, including the United States. One analyst points to the Japan-funded road that links Thailand's main airport to downtown Bangkok, a road that has played a crucial role in Thai development, allowing it to approach middle-income status. "Development produces higher productivity and more purchasing power, which benefits everybody," says Saburo Okita, a former Japanese foreign affairs minister and now head of Tokyo's Institute for Domestic and International Policy Studies. "It's not a zero-sum game."

Other leading Japanese economists, such as Terutomo Ozawa, believe that a completely altruistic program is less effective than commercial motivations in guiding developing countries toward sustained economic growth. He says the development of business relations and industrial ties, as well as access to new technologies and exposure to managerial techniques, promote long-term growth.

Under pressure from the United States and other major aid donors, Japan is increasing the number of grants, but lending is still strongly preferred over donations of money. "Japan gave so many loans because they wanted to promote economic self-sufficiency and avoid welfare-type aid," says Green of the Japan Economic Institute. "They gave loans in order to give countries the incentive to get their economies functioning and pay the loans back." The Ministry of International Trade and Industry, in particular, has strongly favored continuing loans with harder terms.

Loans are disbursed through the Overseas Economic Cooperation Fund, which is starting to offer more concessional terms on its loans (most of which charge 3 percent interest for 30-year loans, with a 10-year grace period). The rate was lowered to 1 percent last year on loans to the poorest and least developed countries. The Development Assistance Committee has called for further softening of terms.

Aid analysts say the Japanese are likely at least to make an effort to do that. They are aware that as the yen has risen the loans have become more difficult to pay off. But Japan may be limited in how far it can shift from loans to grants. Unlike the U.S. aid program, which is entirely appropriated by Congress, much of the funding made available for Japanese aid is borrowed in the nation's capital market. So as the country struggles with its own budget deficit, expected to be about $55 billion for fiscal 1989, most observers expect loans to remain the primary means of aid.

The nation is also starting to recycle some of its trade surplus into loans through the Export-Import Bank of Japan. Japan has pledged to recycle some $30 billion over three years; how it will be spent has not been fully decided, but about one-third will go through the World Bank and the International Monetary Fund; much of the rest will be lent in tandem with private-sector projects. That kind of spending, says Ozawa, points to a "hybrid form of economic cooperation, a combination of official aid alongside private-sector transfers of productive capacities — for the most part in the form of direct foreign investment."

While Japan has been increasing its loans, grants and recycled surpluses, it is fast coming up against the limits of its small and bureaucratically tangled aid institutions. While the Overseas Economic Cooperation Fund disburses loans and the Export-Import Bank handles recycling, grants are given by the Japan International Cooperation Agency, which also administers the Japan Overseas Cooperation Volunteers program, Japan's version of the Peace Corps. Authority over the different agencies is split among multiple sections of the government, including the Finance Ministry, the Foreign Ministry and the Ministry of International Trade and Industry, which have different approaches to aid and do not work well with each other.

The bureaucratic confusion reflects the fact that there is no overriding philosophy guiding the expansion of foreign aid. When the aid budget was doubled last year, officials said only that they wanted to contribute to global security and stability. That suggests to most analysts that the decision was really taken in response to pressure from other countries. "Japan has been donating more because other countries feel they should, not because they have any agenda about what they want to see happen in developing countries," says Lincoln.

That search for approval from its partners in the Organization for

Economic Cooperation and Development has also led Japan to funnel more of its aid through multilateral development agencies such as the World Bank, the International Monetary Fund, the Asian Development Bank and the United Nations. While they are still keen on garnering the kind of economic and political benefits that come from direct bilateral aid, Japanese planners are said to welcome the access to information and experienced personnel that the multilateral channels bring. More important, Japan's larger role in the multilateral agencies gives its aid a more cooperative and altruistic look and helps to cement its newly found leadership role in the world economy. "If Japan is going to take on more global responsibilities, it is going to want to get credit for it," says one analyst. "The World Bank and the IMF are good places to get that credit."

But Tokyo wants more than credit—it wants clout. And that worries some in Washington, who fear that Japan's gain in influence will be the United States' loss. Voting share in the multilateral aid organizations is determined by the size of a country's contributions, so as Japan ups its aid, other countries — in particular the United States — would lose influence.

That is something that U.S. policymakers are fiercely resisting. When Japan proposed an increased contribution to the World Bank last year, Washington vetoed it. "We want the Japanese to spend more money, but we don't want them making the decisions," says Lincoln. Echoing suspicions about Japanese ambitions, the U.S. development agency's Bissell says: "In the multilateral organizations, there is always the question of what strings come with the increased Japanese financial role. That's simply a reality of life, and we have to consider whether we are willing to pay that price.

Given its influence over how fast and how far Japan goes, Washington is facing some important decisions about the signals it will send to Tokyo in the months ahead. "We're at a critical juncture," says Susan Pharr of Harvard. "For the Japanese to go forward in a major way, they need, in effect, a nod of approval from Washington. And if the U.S. is starting to say that this is detrimental to American interests, then they'll back off. But if policymakers in Washington think more deeply about this, they'll see that it's in their long-term interest for Japan to increase its aid."

Stephen Brookes

Chapter 25

*Beginning in 1980, U.S. presidents each
year granted China most-favored-nation
status — a designation meaning that
goods made there escaped the ruinously
high tariffs applied to imports from the
handful of countries not so favored. This
article of June 4, 1990, described the
pressure that was put on George Bush to
reverse course, as a way of protesting
Beijing's brutal 1989 crackdown on the
pro-democracy movement. Though many
felt that this would punish the wrong
people — pro-Western Chinese
businessmen and poor U.S. consumers —
few spoke out for renewing the status.
Bush did it anyway.*

CHINA AS LEAST- AND MOST-FAVORED NATION

"Most-favored-nation" is not a term for countries that the United States is especially fond of. It means only that a nation's exports are eligible for the minimum tariffs levied by the United States, a privilege offered reciprocally to most of the world's countries. Among the most-favored and least pleasant are Iraq, Syria and Burma, which under the alias Myanmar has recently murdered thousands of anticommunist demonstrators.

President Bush must decide by June 3 whether China should remain in this unselect company (only 16 nations fail to make the cut). If most-favored-nation treatment is withdrawn, duties on Chinese goods would triple or quadruple or worse, pricing most of them out of the U.S. market and signaling Washington's dissatisfaction over the bloody course of recent events in the world's most populous country.

By the consensus of China experts, this could be the most portentous decision faced by U.S. policymakers since President Nixon in the 1970s ended 23 years of Chinese isolation and began to establish ties.

"Business is a major symbol to the Chinese of the relationship," says China analyst Paul Kreisberg of the Carnegie Endowment for International Peace. "When relations were normalized, it was with the clear understanding that the process included most-favored-nation." Adds Myles Neinstadt of the Brookings Institution: "The Chinese would take cancellation of MFN as a severe slap, and it would have a major impact on relations at least until there is a leadership change in Beijing."

The current deadline arises because of the Jackson-Vanik amendment, a 1973 law that prohibits most-favored-nation treatment for communist countries unless they allow free emigration. The president can waive the law in individual cases, as presidents have done for China every year since 1980. In the past, these waivers have been almost controversy-free, but that was before the bloodshed in Tiananmen Square last spring and the subsequent imprisonment of thousands of protodemocrats by the government. Now the most-favored-nation issue threatens to provoke a full-blown confrontation with Congress over the White House's go-gentle approach.

Bush, who fancies himself something of a China expert because of his role as first U.S. ambassador to the communist regime, almost certainly favors renewing favored status despite the crackdown, though he has been acting Hamlet over the issue. Many legislators and much of the business community similarly favor renewal, though most have been equally reticent.

Still, they have solid arguments on their side. For one thing, most of China's exporting is done by private enterprises or foreign joint ventures, the sector of the society most sympathetic to Western ideas and values. Taking away most-favored-nation status would roll up a good chunk of the economy of southern China, where most of these enterprises are based.

"Impoverishment of southern China would not damage [Premier] Li Peng and his colleagues," says Roger Sullivan, president of the U.S.-China Business Council. It would only "help them in their campaign to bury what they call the putrefying corpse of bourgeois liberalism."

Or, at least, the bourgeois liberals would face duties on their goods that would shoot up to levels established under Smoot-Hawley in the 1930s. For example, Mattel Inc. would pay 70 percent on its made-in-China Barbie dolls, compared to 12.6 percent now. Levies on garments would balloon to 70 percent from 6 percent. And since Chinese manufacturers take advantage of cheap labor to aim their goods at the low end of the U.S. market, the change would hit the poorest Americans the hardest.

Then there is the near certainty of Chinese retaliation, which could affect not just the $6 billion a year in exports from the United States but also $4 billion in U.S. investment there. A likely victim would be McDonnell Douglas Corp., joint owner of an aircraft assembly operation in Shanghai. At risk would be a deal for 150 medium-haul jets for China's internal routes. If awarded to McDonnell Douglas as expected, the job could be worth $8 billion. Another target could be U.S. wheat sales, which brought home $1 billion last year.

Another major clobberee would be the British colony of Hong Kong, which was a stopping-off point last year for 70 percent of China's $16 billion in exports to the United States. John Kamm, president of the American Chamber of Commerce in Hong Kong, says that most-favored-nation status is a "life-or-death issue" for the hyperventilating colony. Its loss, he says, could fatally weaken Hong Kong's already sagging confidence level and engender "anti-Americanism in one of the world's most pro-American cities."

But perhaps the strongest argument is that business ties have been stunningly successful at worming Americans into the nether regions of Chinese society, promoting two-way traffic in people, ideas and information. Says a lobbyist for a major U.S. company: "That's what this is all about: Do we shut the door and risk driving them in another direction, or do we keep the door open so there is always communication between our countries?"

On the other side, opponents worry about how a renewal will play in Beijing, particularly among the factions that are already believed to be gathering their forces for a succession struggle. Wouldn't it enable the hard-liners to claim that their iron grip on dissent is a cost-free exercise?

Good question, but most who are raising it actually favor renewal — with conditions. Holly Burkhalter, Washington director of Human Rights Watch, argues for tying renewal to political prisoner release. She points to the recent freeing of 211 jailed dissidents, which according to a memo leaked by a defecting Chinese diplomat in Washington was aimed at influencing the debate. Though "pretty paltry," she says, the gesture suggests that "if the administration and Congress ask for more, they just might get it."

Winston Lord, the former U.S. ambassador to China who coined the memorable phrase "fawning emissaries" for the secret missions dispatched to Beijing last year by Bush, is less sanguine about behavior modification. His recommendation: renew most-favored-nation status but couple it with a host of other economic and political sanctions so Beijing cannot claim that Washington has endorsed its crackdown.

In the end, though, the arguments are likely to take a backseat to partisan politics. In response to a recent Supreme Court decision, the House and Senate are fine-tuning Jackson-Vanik to bring it into line with the Constitution. If the Senate has its way, under the new version Congress will have 105 days, rather than the present 60, to thumbs-up or thumbs-down a presidential waiver request. That would bring the issue to a head — with the possibility of a presidential veto and an override fight — just before the midterm congressional elections in November.

George J. Mitchell, the Senate majority leader, has made a career lately of trying to embarrass the president on foreign policy. When the Berlin Wall was opened up, it was Mitchell who criticized Bush for not rushing to the scene to welcome the East Germans to freedom. On a Sunday morning news show in April, the Maine Democrat became the first major figure to take a negative stand on most-favored-nation status.

"I'm a Democrat, but I really think on the part of the Democrats there is a political element to all this," says Kreisberg. "It's a chance to give the president a whack, and if they can do it even closer to the election, it may be even more attractive."

With that in mind, some wonder whether the White House really has the stomach for another fight of the kind that attended the visa extension for Chinese students. William Abnett, president of the Washington State China Relations Council, suspects that some Bushies may have preemptive surrender in mind. "There are only three or four advisers close to Bush in the White House who favor MFN for China."

As far as public and media opinion are concerned, the president's China policy has been one of his few serious missteps. In April, the White House was clearly sending signals to the business community to step up and take some of the heat for renewal. "The sad result so far is that a lot of businesses haven't responded to the call," says Abnett, who represents a state that accounts for one-seventh of U.S. exports to China. "There are a million and one reasons why MFN makes a lot of sense, but it's very hard to make those arguments over the din of emotions."

Secretary of State James A. Baker III, who is often credited with whispering political wisdom in the president's ear, has taken pains in the past to distance himself from Bush's China diplomacy. Some now suggest that if he had warned Bush off his earlier gestures the president would now have more room to maneuver on MFN. "Ironically, in this case, the president's policy might have benefited from Baker's involvement," says Brookings's Neinstadt.

Ultimately, though, the fate of most-favored-nation status may lie with a boat bobbing in the South China Sea, the Goddess of Democracy, which plans to beam pro-democracy radio messages to the mainland. If Beijing tries to torpedo the broadcasts, it could cost precious votes in Washington. And even if China passes that test, it may face another in September when foreign television cameras — and potentially more student demonstrators — gather in Beijing for the Asian Games. Says Neinstadt: "If we wake up with a different set of headlines next morning, the picture can change quite dramatically."

Holman Jenkins Jr.

CHAPTER 26

Many stock markets enjoyed a banner year in 1989, but none could match the performance of those in Asia's developing countries. This article of February 12, 1990, examined the growing pains of four young financial markets: in Indonesia, Thailand, Malaysia and India. All had enjoyed monumental rates of growth and all were faced with the problems, both technological and political, of how to gracefully join the financial big leagues. Most needed were modernization of the exchanges and the political will to make them level playing fields for investors.

PEP, PROFIT AND PAIN IN NEW ASIAN MARKETS

The hottest financial markets in the world last year were in Southeast Asia: Thailand's stock exchange more than doubled in value, as did Indonesia's. And these were not the only developing markets to turn in a grand performance. But having proved that they can meet investors' wildest expectations and more, Asia's emerging markets now must wrestle with the consequences of their explosive growth. Most of them, small and large alike, are not equipped to deal with success: Brokers, underwriters, clearinghouses are overwhelmed with new issues and new money. If the region is to continue growing, its financial markets are going to have to make a leap into 20th century technology and provide the logistic support that high turnover demands.

Inefficient markets are of course appealing to some: Earnings can be higher than on a mature exchange, a paucity of information means handsome payoffs for investors in the know, and slow reactions can cushion the shock waves when larger exchanges crash. But such appeal is necessarily limited over the long haul to insiders, speculators and the naive. Rapidly growing exchanges must bolster confidence that when the market booms, their success is linked to solid economic fundamentals, not simply the financial hocus-pocus that an antiquated exchange permits. The keys to this transition are a favorable legal environment and modern technology.

A MAD DASH IN DJAKARTA

Though it is more than a decade old, Indonesia's central stock exchange was nothing until 1988, the year the government decided to turn the capital into a financial center. The goal was to move from 24 listed companies on the Djakarta Stock Exchange to 400 within four years. "Everyone thought that was a bit of a joke," says Peter Everington, investment director at Thornton Management in Hong Kong (which runs the Jakarta Fund, a closed-end mutual fund specializing in Indonesian securities).

Few people are laughing now. After languishing at about 100 points for years, the market leapt to 500 last year, and 115 companies listed or announced their intention to list. Investors lined up to shift money from bank accounts to the market after the government evened up taxes on bank deposits and capital gains.

The market's biggest boost came last August, with a further liberalization of the foreign investment laws. Before then, foreigners were cut out of much of the trading on the Djakarta Stock Exchange because of limits on foreign ownership. That law was changed to accommodate trading in companies that were already majority foreign-owned — firms such as Goodyear Indonesia and Pfizer Indonesia — which until recently dominated the Djakarta exchange. Foreign investors flooded in, and trading volume quadrupled nearly overnight.

Foreigners are still restricted to owning 49 percent of a company's traded shares and as a result are paying handsomely for their stocks. This scramble for paper has driven a wedge between local brokers and the state's investment trust, Danareksa. The trust holds one-third of all new issues and has been accused of making sweetheart deals with foreign groups for a share of the profits.

The market's success has also been too much of a good thing for overworked brokerages and the Capital Market Executive Agency, which oversees the stock market. Share registration is backed up weeks and months, and the 13 underwriters (the government has delayed licensing any others) who cover the capital are sitting on piles of cash as they fill orders. New issues of stock are oversubscribed by as much as a hundredfold, and investors have been frustrated with tiny allotments. Where these issues were once sold in lots of no fewer than 100 shares, the minimum has now dropped to one share.

The mad dash at the Djakarta exchange has put the government in a difficult position. Under pressure to go ahead with a privatization program that would sate some of the demand for new issues, the government, some analysts worry, will be tempted to dump the least promising state-owned companies onto the exchange or reduce exchange standards to allow other losers, albeit private, to list shares. The listing of cement maker P. T. Indocement confirmed their worst fears. Owned by a friend of President Suharto, Indocement was listed on the the exchange with the aid of a special dispensation from the Ministry of Finance, required because the company had not registered a profit in the prior two years, as the exchange's listing regulations demand.

But the hunger for shares is such that Indocement was snapped up and did not precipitate the collapse some had predicted. In fact, since the issue, the share price has risen 10 percent. Nor is the government likely to fiddle with the market much in the future. "There is room for political scandal," says Richard Chenevix-Trench, director of Baring International Asset Administration in Hong Kong. "But on the whole, face is a very important thing around here, and I don't think governments want to float companies that are going to let everyone down."

YEN IS KING IN THAILAND

Thailand's stock exchange rose 120 percent last year, buoyed by a tide of Japanese money. With the boom came a wild West atmosphere, replete with bad guys. One brokerage was recently suspended for price-fixing on a magnificent scale: On some days it reportedly accounted for more than 30 percent of market turnover. Another house was nailed for trying to manipulate the market with rumors of Prime Minister Chatichai Choonhavan's resignation.

Congestion and overloaded phone systems take their toll on the market as well. Getting across Bangkok through epic traffic jams can take hours; calling across the country is nigh impossible, and regulations that are little short of ridiculous exacerbate every other aspect of daily life at the exchange. Share issues require two company board members to sign each certificate. Trading has yet to be computerized (though there are hopes for it to happen this year). London's Financial Times recently reported that on the exchange floor, traders in active stocks need to have the physique of a bouncer to reach the board.

Despite the hassles, foreigners are fighting to get into the market. Indeed, Japanese investors dominate to the extent that political woes in Tokyo can hurt the market as much as domestic trouble. The market slid sharply for several days running on news of the dissolution of the lower house of the Japanese Parliament in late January.

Banner headlines around the world trumpeting super profits have raised expectations. But, say Thai officials, they should be lowered. "Foreigners cannot expect us to be like New York or London," says Udom Vichayabhai, managing director of the Thai Mutual Fund Co. "And they have to accept that when they want to take money out it takes a long time." Long indeed. Repatriating profits can take months.

The government may yet give foreigners an even better reason to steer clear of the Securities Exchange of Thailand. In its efforts to cool off the economy, there is serious talk of raising interest rates or taxes or both. Cutting inflation means cutting liquidity, though, "and if it all dries up, a lot of people will be left holding very expensive stocks," says David Scott, a senior analyst with W. I. Carr, a British investment firm in Bangkok.

Others are more dubious about the government's willingness to act. "The finance minister has big investments in the stock market himself," says Paul Ensor of Baring Securities in Bangkok. But if the government does not soak up the excess cash in the economy one way, it must find another. Long-awaited privatizations — new issues would immediately release upward pressure on the market and provide the government with the money it needs to fix up Thailand's lousy infrastructure — do not appear likely this year.

The prime candidates for sell-off are Thai Airways International, the nation's flagship airline, and the Electricity Generating Authority of Thailand. But political infighting is delaying a sale. The airline is proving particularly difficult to unload. A job there is like the proverbial gold watch to retiring Royal Thai Air Force officers: Everybody gets one.

MALAYSIA ON THE FAST TRACK

The Kuala Lumpur Stock Exchange went up only 57 percent last year, a sorry performance by regional standards. Still, Malaysia is on track to become the region's next newly industrialized country, and its exchange is one of the biggest in the region. Market capitalization is equivalent to 98 percent of gross national product (compared with 1.2 percent for Indonesia and 28 percent for Thailand), and the infrastructure is up to the standard of the industrialized countries — a legacy from Mother England and colonial days. Phones work; roads go somewhere, almost everywhere.

The Kuala Lumpur Stock Exchange works too. Transactions are cleared in five days, and a new computerized trading system will handle 250 million shares a day, a far cry from the chaotic clearing and settlement in other regional exchanges.

This year's biggest question was supposed to be the emergence of the KLSE from Singapore's shadow. Once twin exchanges, the two split and delisted each other's shares at the start of the year. Far from collapsing, however, Malaysia's market shot up. More troubling are bad signs for the country's huge plantation sector. Though the long-term outlook is good, thanks to agrotechnology and the fact that the nation is the world's largest producer of rubber, Patrick Lim, president of the Malaysia Investors Association, predicts at least a 10 percent decline in the market because of falling world commodity prices.

Unlike Thailand, Malaysia's market is not driven by foreign cash, despite being relatively open to foreign investment. But even without foreigners the market has been able to sustain a bull run of more than two months, leaving brokers falling over themselves to keep up. The source is a huge pool of domestic savings looking for somewhere to go. "The Malaysians are very liquid. Savings is at around 36 percent" of gross domestic product, says Lim, "and Oriental people are very speculative."

Furthermore, foreign investment has recently begun to pick up. New funds specializing in Malaysia are on the drawing board in Britain and Japan, and three are already operating. Several upcoming privatizations have stirred interest. The national airline went private in 1985, followed by Malaysian International Shipping Corp. Soon to follow are the railways, the container ports and possibly the airports.

INDIAN INVESTORS WAITING

Investors all over the world hyperventilate at the thought of the Bombay Stock Exchange opening up, but the latest signs are discouraging. The defeat of Rajiv Gandhi and election of V. P. Singh are expected to slow the liberalization aimed at opening up India's economy to market forces.

Singh, who as finance minister under Gandhi designed many of the economic reforms of the 1980s, owes his election to rural constituents and not to businessmen. The government's new budget is expected in late February or early March, and the Bombay Stock Exchange has been tumbling in anticipation. The government has made it clear that it intends to devote its money to the peasant and not the pinstriper. "If they're going to spend a large amount of their resources in agriculture, they're going to have to get their money somewhere," says a manager at DSP Financial Consultants, one of India's leading private merchant banks. "So taxes, here we come."

Things are looking down for would-be foreign investors too. An ominous sign is the treatment of Pepsico, whose welcome last year was seen as a bellwether of openness to foreigners and Western consumerism. Pepsi's majority-Indian-owned (by law) affiliate announced in late January that the government was trying to shut it down. A socialist minister alleges that the project was an "illegitimate" deal done by the former government.

The Pepsi episode bodes ill for moneymen dying to get a piece of Bombay's frenetic action of the last few years. An 800 percent rise during the 1980s and a spate of megaissues have highlighted the presence of a large and wealthy middle class that will fuel the country's already high economic growth rate. But it looks as if outsiders will have to wait for the first issue of convertibles that will pave the way to an open market.

"It will come," says an official of Unit Trust of India, a state-run merchant bank. "But it will take some time. One has to wait and watch; it cannot happen that fast."

Danielle Pletka

PART 8

LATIN
LABYRINTHS

CHAPTER 27

The economic damage to Panama that resulted from the U.S. effort to oust Gen. Manuel Noriega came in two waves. The first was the result of stiff economic sanctions. The second, in the wake of the U.S. invasion, was the looting of Panamanian businesses. But the long-term prospects for the country, thanks to its strong middle class, looked good, as reported in this January 29, 1990, article.

PANAMA AT LIBERTY TO SORT OUT ITS MESS

If they gave an award for the most billboards per mile, Colon would probably win. This port city at the Panama Canal's Caribbean entrance is plastered with them. Sony, Panasonic, Seiko, Reebok, Spaulding. The signs scream a who's who of the world's premier makers of consumer goods.

In normal times, this city is a mecca for Latin America's moneyed classes. Merchandise pours in by the shipload from the Far East, Europe and North America, filling 341 acres of warehouses and showrooms. A buyer from Brazil or Peru can select goods, pay in dollars and ship them out by airfreight. There is no waiting, no tax and almost no paperwork, making Colon a refuge for Latin America's inflation-harried, tax-dodging businessmen. "There is no place outside of Hong Kong where you can see such a variety and quantity of goods at competitive prices," says Larry Berger, whose company sells sporting goods, perfumes and musical instruments out of Colon. "If a guy comes looking for a certain brand of tennis racket and I don't have it, someone else always does. It's instant gratification."

Unlike the rest of the country, which is mired in depression, this little piece of Panama was booming until last month's invasion. Last year, the Colon Free Zone did $4.8 billion worth of business, its best year ever. And with Latin America beginning to step off the stagflation treadmill, the happy days seemed set to last. Imports shot up twice as fast as exports, a sure sign that companies were boosting inventories.

Washington's economic sanctions, imposed in early 1988, proved only a momentary nuisance. Without the steady flow of canal and pipeline fees, corporate taxes and other payments, Panama soon ran desperately short of the U.S. dollars that serve as its national currency. Banks, needing to ease their cash shortage, called in loans to local businesses and froze savings deposits. For industry and agriculture, the effects were devastating. They have invested nothing in the last two years. For the Free Zone, however, the disruption lasted only as long as it took to arrange for fresh credit lines outside the country, often with the help of Japanese and South Korean suppliers.

Not even the Mafia-like rule of the Panama Defense Forces seemed to faze the dozens of foreign trading companies based in the free trade zone. Cheerfully, they paid a 1 percent levy on outgoing shipments to Transit SA, a protection racket run by Noriega's hand-picked presidential candidate, Carlos Duque. An official of the American Chamber of Commerce even suggests that the scheme be continued for the benefit of the new government.

But the Colon Free Zone was not able to duck the latest calamity, a plague of looters that came in the wake of the U.S. invasion. Troops have sealed off the main docks at Cristobal and are sifting through the wreckage of 1,500 looted containers. According to Naomasaki Murakoshi, economic counselor at the Japanese Embassy, only the virtually indestructible container cranes were spared. "They stole everything, even the light bulbs," he says.

Coco Solo, the second-biggest port in the Free Zone, fared little better. It was the scene of a fierce shoot-out between Panama's Naval Marine Company and four platoons of the U.S. 7th Infantry. Three weeks later, the roads are still festooned with barbed wire and every intersection is covered by a machine gun. On one of the docks, a motorized ketch is taking on a few dozen cases of Balboa beer for the isolated inhabitants of the San Blas Islands. Otherwise, the port is out of business.

Across the bay is downtown Colon, a "pirate town from way back," as one U.S. Army officer puts it. Here, amid the vast warren of shops and warehouses that are the heart of the Free Zone, the damage was less severe. A group of Lebanese businessmen held the mob at bay for two days with weapons prized from an illegal shipment that happened to be passing through when the whirlwind hit. Only a handful of shops were sacked, and those mostly by looters coming in after the Lebanese had been disarmed and relieved by U.S. troops.

To some of the locals, the Free Zoners, many of whom are foreigners or recent immigrants, are like the ships that fly the country's flag of convenience. Their comeuppance was long overdue. If anything, though, the storm hit with even greater violence in Panama City. For two days, the streets were under the control of the digbats, or Dignity Battalions. "They did the breaking and entering, and whole neighborhoods rushed in behind them to do the looting," says Berger. Perhaps 80 percent of the capital's shops were wiped out.

The generalized plunder no doubt contributed to the jubilation with which the poor greeted the liberating gringos. Only later will it become clear at what price. "What was pillaged and destroyed was our working capital, some of it accumulated over generations," says Berger.

Ezra Cohen, a Colon businessman, already bugged out once. In 1988, he shipped his family and nine containers of stereo equipment to Miami after local bankers, caught in the liquidity squeeze engineered by Washington, yanked his credit. Miami proved expensive, so when a handful of European and Chinese banks began offering credit to Panamanian importers, he moved back to Coco Solo—just in time to lose $3.5 million in stock to postinvasion looting.

His father, the owner of two Sony dealerships in Panama City, was no luckier. Though some of his best customers were high-ranking Noriega cronies, that did not stop the digbats from cleaning him out. They stole the toilet and even a photo of him shaking hands with Sony's chairman.

Like everybody else, the Cohens have been stiffed by their insurance company, which says wartime looting is not covered. In fact, insurers here have long enjoyed a closed market and some of the highest premiums in the world, a favor they returned by buying the government's IOUs, now essentially worthless. So even if they wanted to, the companies cannot pay the mountain of looting claims. "For our family, this has been a very big disaster," says the younger Cohen. "But I also have 70 employees and my father has 64. If we don't receive some kind of compensation, those people will be on the street yelling at the government."

Flory Saltzman, a grandmotherly dealer in native handicrafts who lost $70,000 in stock and another $1,000 in uncashed checks and MasterCard slips, takes an even dimmer view of liberation. "They are all thieves, just different thieves," she says of Panama's political classes. "At least when Noriega was in the chair, I had business."

Vice President Guillermo Ford is the new government's economic point man. He knew he faced a severely depressed economy and
a public sector riddled with ghost employees and career criminals.
He knew the government had not paid a dime on its $3.9 billion debt,
the largest in the world per capita, in two years. What he had not
counted on was Noriega's scorched earth farewell. "Christ, this
country is a mess," he says, sighing.

How much of a mess? A canvass of its members by the local Chamber of Commerce came up with $2.2 billion in looting damage. A gov-
ernment survey says $660 million. Even that may be too high, say
several businessmen. One reason is the tendency to overestimate
damages whenever there is a prospect of compensation. Another is
the problem of double counting: What one firm calls an inventory
loss, another calls an uncollectible IOU.

So far, aside from the release of $140 million in frozen funds, Uncle
Sam's main contribution to the cleanup has come in the form of bulldozers operated by the Corps of Engineers. But everybody here
assumes that serious money is coming. At this end of the dialogue,
the phrase that keeps coming up is moral obligation.

Noriega was Washington's man, goes the argument, so Washington
should clean up his mess. In particular, they blame the United States
for following the Clausewitz principle of concentrating on the
enemy's main forces and not scattering troops in vulnerable knots
to police the looters. When a visitor balks at a $14 bottle of suntan
oil, a shopkeeper jokes, "Somehow we've got to make you Americans
pay for what you did to our economy." Ricardo Arias Calderon, the
other new vice president, figures $1.5 billion should cover it.

If the new government of President Guillermo Endara could be
seen delivering such a bankroll, it would be a sure popularity boost-
er. The price may be too high for Uncle Sam. Says a State Department official: "Have you looked at the federal budget lately? We're
giving only $200 million apiece to Poland and the Philippines, and
those countries are important to us."

So, of course, is Panama, with its strategic geography and famous
ditch. But these days, the Japanese use the place more than Americans do. Half the Toyotas destined for the U.S. market pass through
the canal. Japan accounts for the lion's share of the merchandise that
moves through the Free Zone and the majority of the tonnage on
Panama's worry-free ship registry. Both Panama City and Washington are hoping for a big donation from Tokyo. Meanwhile, the hole
is making a reasonable effort to fill itself. Companies send out teams
to roam the neighborhoods and summarily repossess heisted mer-

chandise. Others are ransoming back, for a few cents on the dollar, goods that looters stole in the heat of the moment but have little use for: truck tires, machine parts, golf club shafts.

More than money, the problem here is confidence. Until the government or insurance companies step forward to take up the liabilities, a great number of companies are technically insolvent. Banks refuse to lend, and companies fear doing business with each other. "The fact is, if somebody came tomorrow and looked at our books, we'd be finished," says one executive.

Another drag on the recovery is the caginess factor, as businessmen jockey for position in the relief queue they expect to be opened soon. One well-known retailer swears a blue streak that he was cleaned out, but a friend in the neighborhood where he lives just laughs. "He has a spare apartment piled to the ceiling with merchandise," the neighbor says. "He could open for business tomorrow if he wanted to."

Such maneuvering may already have hindered the postlooting paper chase. Typical is the problem of an importer of household goods who is trying to reconstruct his accounts receivable from a computer tape he took home in September. "I do a lot of business with the local supermarket chain," he says. "We both know they owe me money, but neither of us knows how much." Adds a former chief of the Panama Chamber of Commerce: "If you owe somebody money, you can be pretty sure he'll let you know. But if he owes you money, why should he tell you about it?"

Since the question of liability is rapidly becoming a political football rather than a legal one, dissembling is likely to become pandemic. Ford makes it clear that the government will be picking and choosing when it comes time to dole out relief money. "We're not going to indemnify people who want to take a check and go live in Miami."

Carlos Valencia, president of a local industry group, agrees. Help should go first to strategic industries, meaning those that spur domestic production. "Large supermarkets are important because they buy food produced locally. A jewelry store is not important." An industrialist, Valencia is a different kind of businessman from the traders who dominate the Free Zone, many of whom abhor politics, humored Noriega and have little proprietary feeling for the canal, the most potent symbol in local politics. Valencia is a nationalist as well as a capitalist. He has been jailed for his role in the National Civic Crusade, the largely middle-class movement against Noriega's thugocracy. "The most important thing for Panama now is to prepare to take control of the canal and see off the last American soldier," he says.

With Panama under new management, much of it sharing Valencia's viewpoint, Colon may find its style a little cramped, at least for a while. Certain activities—gunrunning, drug smuggling and end-running the U.S. boycott of Cuba—are likely to find less tolerance in official quarters. But these pursuits counted for only a small portion of the Free Zone's business. A bigger part was illicitly catering to domestic consumers.

Before the invasion, Colon was known also for its brazen flouting of Panama's import taxes, which are 50 to 80 percent for most goods. Goods were not so much smuggled as dumped into the local retail market, making life nearly impossible for law-abiding importers. "That place was a goddamned supermarket," says Ford. "We've shut down all those retail shops." That may be, but in the long run the high tariffs for the domestic market are likely to give way.

In any case, as long as Brazilians like to spend and Japanese to sell, the Free Zone's future seems secure. As the smoke clears from last month's battlefields, it is the prospects for Panama's other world-class industry, its banks, that will be worrisome. Once again, Uncle Sam is the villain. "If the U.S. government succeeds, no more bank center in Panama. That's the simple story," says one diplomat.

More than 100 international banks, from Chase Manhattan to the Bank of China, have subsidiaries here, attracted by laws that ensure anonymity for depositors and by the fact that Panama uses the free-flowing dollar as its de facto currency. Not all of this money comes from drugs. For example, much of the business done by Citibank and Chase Manhattan reportedly concerns the payment of canal tolls. American Express Bank serves the U.S. military. Many others are engaged in trade finance for customers in the Colon Free Zone. Still, the biggest part of the business consists of taking deposits from wealthy South American citizens whose only crime may or may not be a desire to stay wealthy. For years Washington has lobbied for the right of foreign governments to peek at these accounts. Now some bankers fear it has finally found, or rather installed, a regime that will go along. Ford's answer: "Bankers are not policemen, though we do expect them to be honest bankers."

What that means is still being negotiated. But at a meeting with Panama's Jewish business community, Endara warned that airtight secrecy is a thing of the past, according to one who was present. In one area at least, Uncle Sam is giving good advice: Dismantle the bureaucratic controls that have made manufacturing and agriculture poor relations of the international service sector. Together, these account for less than 20 percent of the economy, compared with 51 percent for banking, insurance and the Free Zone.

The state sector is the legacy of Omar Torrijos Herrera, the charismatic, hard-drinking dictator who negotiated the treaty that will transfer the Panama Canal to local control in 1999. Though his base was in the military, his ideas were vaguely Marxist and his swash-buckling persona appealed to many poorer Panamanians. Torrijos was killed in a plane crash in 1981, but crowds at political rallies still sometimes break into chants of "Feel it, feel it. Omar is present."

Omar is present today in the shape of the state's sugar mills, cement factories, banks and other enterprises. Omar is present in the price controls on rice, meat, potatoes and other items deemed to make up the bill of fare for the poorest residents. And he is there in a labor code that makes it difficult and expensive to fire workers. This last item is the one most urgently in need of reform. Says Valencia, "Panamanians are used to it, but companies from abroad, mainly from the Orient, find it very cumbersome." Not all Panamanians are used to it. Some older businessmen privately say the looting has given them an opportunity to get out of business cheaply.

What Panama needs is more jobs, not fewer. Many three-paycheck homes have become single-check ones. Perhaps 25 percent of the population lives on a family income of less than $150 a month. The solution for these people is to make farming and industry as welcoming to foreign investment as trade and financial services.

Will investors come? Almost certainly. Panama's middle classes have proved their worth, providing the ballast that carried the nation through stormy seas. There was none of the carnage of El Salvador, no attempt to abandon the dollar and print bales of money, as in Peru and Argentina. "Even under a thug like Noriega, our basic economic institutions were respected," says Valencia. "This country can continue to be a haven where people can park their money and feel secure, a place to invest and do business."

Holman Jenkins Jr.

CHAPTER 28

*In Nicaragua, the Sandinistas took power
in 1979 backed by the rising expectations
of the middle class. And they were voted
out in 1990 in large measure because of
public disenchantment with a decade of
economic collapse. This article, originally
published October 31, 1988, described the
mess made in Managua.*

THE BITTER FRUIT
OF SANDINISTANOMICS

A visit to one of the many impoverished barrios that ring the Nicaraguan capital of Managua is no longer necessary to measure the extent of economic decline in the country. Now, mothers send children from their tin and mud shacks each morning to search for food in the leafy section of the city that houses government buildings and foreign embassies. One recent morning found three barely clothed young boys, their stomachs distended, crawling through the brimming trash bins outside the apparently well-stocked Libyan People's Bureau, or embassy. From a large photograph in a glass case hanging nearby, Libya's Col. Muammar Qaddafi looked on with a wry smile.

The economic crisis is so explosive an issue in Nicaragua that most analysts say it is the greatest threat to the Marxist-Leninist Sandinistas' ability to rule the country, far more serious than the civil war against the democratic resistance forces. "Hunger is the No. 1 issue in the country," says Ramiro Gurdian, acting president of the Nicaraguan Democratic Coordinating Board, an umbrella group for the civic opposition. "It is bringing people into the streets to demonstrate against the government."

Certainly, scores of Nicaraguans who had long been sympathetic to the Sandinista revolution are now turning against the government chiefly over economic conditions. The Nicaraguan Socialist Party, founded in 1939 as the first Nicaraguan party tied to the Soviet Union and part of the ruling Sandinista coalition for four years, went into all-out opposition to the government last month, saying: "Nicaragua is living through one of the worst, most profound crises in its history. . . . Workers and peasants are being made to pay the price of the revolution."

The economy is in its fifth year of steep decline. The most pressing problem is hyperinflation. The government's own figures show that inflation ran at 1,800 percent last year, and private estimates are that it may top 10,000 percent by the end of 1988. Real incomes have fallen more than 90 percent since 1980 due to a combination of inflation and government wage controls.

Nicaragua's economic plight is perhaps best summarized by two words: declining production. For 1987 the Ministry of External Commerce has reported total exports worth $251 million. This represents a 41 percent decline since 1983 and a 61 percent drop from levels in 1977, two years before the Sandinista revolution.

The country has always been dependent on its agricultural exports. Under the regime of Anastasio Somoza Debayle, who was ousted by the Sandinistas, agriculture had grown rapidly, becoming ever more industrialized in the Fifties, Sixties and early Seventies. By the late Seventies, Nicaragua produced enough cotton to meet its domestic needs and to export as its No. 1 crop. The new cottonseed industry, which makes cooking oil, was a sign of healthy diversification in the economy.

Today, there is a shortage of cotton in Nicaragua's hospitals and not even enough cooking oil to ration. Last year, cotton exports were one-fourth of the 1978 level. Much the same is true for other big export crops such as coffee, down by 50 percent last year from the level of a decade ago. At the same time, the country experienced an 80 percent decline in industrial exports from 1977 to 1986.

The number of industrial companies operating in Nicaragua has been halved since the revolution, and the state has confiscated or imposed direct control over more than one-third of the remaining enterprises.

Although imports have declined from nearly $900 million in 1985 to about $750 million last year, there is nonetheless a trade deficit that is double the annual export earnings. This deficit is financed in large part by the nearly $500 million in Soviet economic aid Nicaragua will receive this year, as well as the essentially free Soviet supplies of petroleum and basic foods that are rationed through state stores. Nicaragua has a foreign debt of more than $6 billion and is paying no service on its debt. So the Sandinistas now are surviving on charity in the form of development grants, foodstuffs and trade credits from Western democracies such as Sweden, the Netherlands, Norway, Canada, France, Italy and Spain, and additional aid from Libya and such East Bloc countries as Yugoslavia.

The Sandinista regime has contended that the seven-year war with the U.S.-backed Contra rebels is to blame for the state of the economy. But nongovernment economists maintain that the economy was in deep trouble owing to government mismanagement and corruption even before the civil war got under way. In addition, much of the cost of fighting the Contras has been assumed not by the Sandinistas but by the Soviets, who provide all of the Sandinistas' weaponry free. The government says it spends about 60 percent of its annual budget in defense and security matters, a figure that has grown consistently every year since the revolution, regardless of the status of the civil war. Only about half of this military apparatus is engaged in the war.

In any event, the Nicaraguan public no longer seems to accept the Sandinista explanation for the declining economic fortunes, according to a July poll by the Central America University's Managua campus. Asked what they considered to be the principal reason for the country's economic woes, only 19 percent of the respondents named the civil war or the U.S. trade embargo. Eighty-one percent referred generally to "bad government." Enrique Bolanos Geyes, chairman of the Supreme Council of Private Enterprise, Nicaragua's largest business federation, says excessive state control, lack of respect for private property and "contempt for the law of supply and demand" are responsible for the economic collapse.

The Sandinistas took power on the crest of a revolution of rising expectations among the middle class. After a 1972 earthquake that virtually flattened the capital, economic growth and modernization began to level off; economic output started to fall slowly, as did real wages. The economy's failure to grow at previous levels, combined with Somoza's caudillo style of government, led to the leader's downfall. But the Sandinista junta proved either profoundly ignorant of, or indifferent to, matters economic. Only Jaime Wheelock Roman, the minister of agriculture, was schooled in the fundamentals of Marxist economics. The second tier of economic officials and advisers included Soviet bloc central planners, especially Bulgarians; North Americans who advocated maintenance of the status quo; Latin American dependency theorists; and Guevarista moralists out to develop a "new" Nicaraguan.

Thus, from the outset, Sandinista economics took one leaf from the Cuban model, which emphasizes the moral over the material;

and, in a curious twist, one leaf from Latin fascism, which holds that the state does not have to own the means of production so long as it directs all of the decision making in the economy.

Studies conducted by the Supreme Council of Private Enterprise show that about half of the economy is directly in the hands of the state, evidence cited by the government to show that Nicaragua has a "mixed economy." But whether one is a manager of a state farm or a private owner, the government determines consumer and producer prices, the distribution of raw materials, salaries, product mixes and production rates. Products must be sold to the state at prices set by the state.

Both public and private producers also are hampered by the government's failure to maintain the country's infrastructure. A serious shortage of electricity, for example, has been a prime factor in the plunge of industrial production. No new electric plants have been brought on-line in recent years, and the government is not even maintaining the old ones. The industrial sector has also been badly hurt by the emigration of skilled workers and professionals, while the agricultural sector lost workers in the mobilization of young peasant men for the armed forces.

There is little incentive for businessmen, who lack confidence in the economy and fear having their companies expropriated, to innovate, invest or even maintain production. The Sandinistas recently have stepped up their confiscation of privately owned land and businesses, including the property of all of the officers of the private enterprise council.

In July, as part of a major crackdown on political dissent, the government confiscated the country's largest private business, the San Antonio sugar plantation, which had been a symbol of private enterprise for nearly a century. "The Sandinistas have said that this plantation was evidence of their commitment to a mixed economy," says Gurdian, who owned and operated the country's largest banana farm until the government seized it a few years ago. "They have now sent the message that no private property is safe from government seizure."

Spread over 7,200 acres in the western province of Chinandega, the San Antonio plantation had been owned and managed by the Pellas family since 1890. The mill refines half the sugar consumed in Nicaragua and provides sugar for 90 percent of the country's liquor production. In announcing the seizure, Wheelock expressed concern over what he called low productivity levels. While conceding that the level of production had fallen, the Pellas family maintained that this was due to the Sandinistas' failure to provide the foreign exchange needed to buy machinery, parts and fertilizer to maintain the farm and refinery. They also said that existing state-owned plantations were in even worse shape than the San Antonio.

Wheelock also denounced "outbreaks of worker indiscipline" at the mill, a reference to what likely was the real sticking point with the government, which was rebuffed in its efforts to organize workers into a Sandinista union. Prior to the expropriation most had chosen to affiliate with the opposition Confederation of Labor Unity. Now, those who have not been fired all work for the government.

The San Antonio expropriation was but one instance of the Sandinistas' long-standing propensity to play politics with their economic policy. The regime realized early on that scarcity had its uses in population management. The system of rationing could hardly be effective without chronic shortages. The average Nicaraguan now spends hours in line seeking basic foods and household goods each week.

The government had provided its supporters — government workers, Sandinista union members, the armed forces and their families — rationed amounts of basic goods at low prices through so-called neighborhood "defense" committees. The system, however, has all but collapsed, since producers are refusing to sell at prices offered by the state. Higher-level Sandinistas are allowed to purchase dollars at preferred exchange rates to buy imported goods at dollar stores. Dollars also enter the economy from Nicaraguans who have fled the country since the revolution and send hard currency to relatives left behind, and the government has recently opened the dollar stores to anyone who can manage to acquire greenbacks.

There is a thriving black market. Thousands of people survive by selling state property, or goods that should be delivered to the state, to black marketers, who offer a better price than the state while still selling at a profit. Their problem is finding customers who can afford the goods.

Faced with this desperate situation, the government undertook a series of radical moves in February that ended up exacerbating the situation. The Nicaraguan cordoba was sharply devalued against the dollar, boosting the cost of imports and spreading price increases through the economy. The government also quintupled wages, increased the prices of 46 basic goods and froze them there, raised sales taxes and eliminated gas and transportation subsidies. The price of a gallon of gasoline went from the equivalent of 15 cents to $1.50. President Daniel Ortega Saavedra ordered all state ministries to slash their budgets by 10 percent and combined several agencies into one Ministry of the Economy under Luis Carrion Cruz, one of the nine members of the ruling junta.

Many saw the new policies as a politically motivated "attack on private business," as the private enterprise council's Bolanos puts it. The government cut producer prices in half. The revaluation of the cordoba hurt the country's private companies, who had owed their existence for years to a government subsidy that provided them with dollars at a giveaway rate of exchange. Managua eliminated the subsidy, and for the businesses a dollar was suddenly 143 times more expensive. In addition, under rules set by the government, no individual could exchange more than 10 million old cordobas for the new revalued ones. Many unlicensed market vendors and other merchants, many of them women in the Eastern Market, the largest in Managua, had stockpiled much more than that amount.

In June prices were freed from government control, and the cost of basic goods in state stores — once heavily subsidized but now notoriously short on supply — are nearly the same as on the black market, where goods are more plentiful.

The Managua-based Central American Historical Institute, a pro-Sandinista think tank, said of the government's February and June moves in the latest issue of its monthly publication, Salvo: "In the view of the popular classes, the central weakness of the measures was that the government did not know what it was doing. This conviction tends to grow with each new package, because the standard of living continues to deteriorate." The average worker's salary is now $2 a week. In a recent interview with the Sandinista daily Barricada, Ortega acknowledged that "a large part of the population" is dissatisfied but insisted that "the discontent . . . does not reflect the political position of the population toward the revolution."

What Ortega may — or may not — realize is that the revolution itself is responsible for the country's economic woes. Bolanos and others say that the only move drastic enough to make a real difference — demobilization of the Sandinista military — is unlikely to come soon, if ever. With the civil war winding down on terms favorable to the Sandinistas, the argument that the war was responsible for the military buildup will be put to the test.

David Brock

CHAPTER 29

*The 1970s and '80s saw an explosion of
evangelical Protestantism in once-
monolithically Catholic Latin America.
The biggest advances came among the
very poor in Brazil, Chile and Central
America. With conversion, in many cases,
came new habits of behavior: no more
booze, a new dedication to family, a
devotion to work. This July 16, 1990,
article described some of the potential
economic consequences.*

THE PROTESTANT ETHIC IN LATIN AMERICA

On walking into his church one evening 10 years ago, the Rev. Joaquin Atenas, a Pentecostal pastor in Santiago, Chile, discovered a bloodshot and bedraggled down-and-out drunk sagging forward on a bench. "The voice of the Holy Spirit told me to lay hands on this man and suppress his spirit of drunkenness," he recalls.

Atenas called the drunk to the altar, took his head in his hands and said, "Spirit of drunkenness, be gone from this body."

"Pastor, I want to talk to you," said the drunk.

"Sit down and listen to the word of God," Atenas commanded. At the end of the service two hours later, "the man was completely sane and sober," Atenas insists.

Still, the man could not find work. A butcher by trade, nobody would hire him. "He would work 10 days and drink for 15," the pastor explains. Some months later, the congregation held a retreat. Once again the Holy Spirit moved in the pastor. At the direction of the Spirit, he asked the sober but jobless butcher, "Do you have faith?"

"Yes," he answered.

"Then the Lord will give you a butcher shop." Within a year, says the pastor, the Lord had provided the butcher shop.

Still, there was no meat-grinding machinery. One day, a salesman offered the butcher the requisite machinery for a down payment of 30,000 pesos. The butcher borrowed 15,000 pesos from his son and then turned once more to the pastor for advice on how to raise the rest. "I will lend you 15,000 pesos," the pastor told him. Thanks to the Holy Spirit and some timely intercession by the pastor, the butcher made the down payment and paid off the balance in 28 monthly installments. He now owns a second butcher shop as well.

The butcher has now come into the church and taken a seat beside the pastor. At the conclusion of the story, the two exchange a glance. With evident pride, the butcher reaches into the inside pocket of his suit jacket and pulls out a checkbook — proof that he has got his head above water.

Latin Pentecostals tell stories like the one about the butcher over and over. The academic evidence remains patchy in a localized, case study way, but the anecdotal evidence is abundant: In Latin America, there is a correlation between Pentecostal conversion and material improvement, albeit modest and incremental. Clean living, reordered patterns of consumption and a helping hand from the pastor now and then add up to a ramp into the stable lower middle class. The linkage must be "couched in terms of frequent concurrence and mutual reinforcements," according to sociologist David Martin, author of "Tongues of Fire: The Explosion of Protestantism in Latin America." "Evangelical religion and economic advancement do often go together, and when they do so appear mutually to support and reinforce one another."

In parts of rural Chile these days "the first question asked of a prospective employee is, 'What religion are you?' " says Guillermo Prado, a Chilean journalist. "If you answer evangelical or Pentecostal, you have the job."

Carmen Galilea, a serious, methodical sociologist at the Bellarmino Center for Sociocultural Research in Santiago, frankly admits that she has little hard data establishing a connection between membership in a Pentecostal church and economic advancement. But she knows what she knows and fearlessly generalizes about the typical Pentecostal: "He is well-regarded. He is responsible. He doesn't drink and is better motivated and better paid. As a result, he rises economically."

Sociologists and cultural historians have debated the link between Protestantism and economic mobility ever since Max Weber first posited one in the classic "The Protestant Ethic and the Spirit of Capitalism" in 1920. Weber traced the spirit of capitalism (the unique and surprising combination of worldly acquisitiveness and worldly asceticism preached in the "Autobiography of Benjamin Franklin") to the Calvinist doctrine of predestination.

Calvinist orthodoxy left believers without any way of knowing whether they were predestined to eternal salvation or eternal damnation. To relieve the anxiety and suffering this uncertainty caused among the faithful, practical pastoral advice departed from orthodoxy, recommending intense and sustained worldly activity as the best means of attaining proof of election. "In practice, this means that God helps those who help themselves," wrote Weber. "Thus, the Calvinist ... creates his own salvation, or, as would be more correct, the conviction of it." He created this conviction through "a system-atic self-control which at every moment stands before the inexorable alternative, chosen or damned."

That is one way of attaining the conviction of election, but there is another way. Weber contrasts the two: "The religious believer can make himself sure of his state of grace either in that he feels himself to be the vessel of the Holy Spirit or the tool of the divine will. In the former case his religious life tends toward mysticism and emotional-ism, in the latter to ascetic action."

To all appearances, Pentecostals in Latin America embrace both means and exhibit both sets of characteristics. The Pentecostals, observes Martin, are characterized by "effervescence in the chapel on Sunday and, beginning Monday, disciplined endeavor during the workweek."

"Pentecostal preaching puts great emphasis on the demand to develop yourself," says Bishop Francisco Anabalon of the Apostolic Pentecostal Church in Chile. "You have to get ahead. You are a son of God, and you are supposed to be the best. You are constantly exposed to this kind of preaching. To paraphrase a famous Bible verse, you are called to be the head, not the tail." God's blessings, Pentecostals are told, are material as well as spiritual. Still, this is a far cry from the practice of "positive confession," or "name it and claim it," developed by American Pentecostals.

Prayer dedicated to a specific material outcome ("If you pray for a camper, tell God what color," the Rev. Jim Bakker once told his viewers), or "name it and claim it," is unrealistic in the Latin Amer-ican context. The preaching in the slums of Latin America is closer to "inch by inch, everything is a cinch," says Anabalon with a laugh.

The reasons for the apparent link between Pentecostalism and modest upward mobility are varied. They include withdrawal from the Roman Catholic fiesta system; rejection of the Latin male ideal of hard-drinking, promiscuous, violent machismo; the mutual material support available within the Pentecostal faith community (the churches provide a network that often functions as a job or housing referral agency); and the acquisition through lay participation in church activity of skills (speaking and organizing) and attitudes (self-confidence, initiative) that assist professional advancement outside the church.

Martin cites a study by Mary O'Connor during the mid-1970s contrasting the material advancement of Mayo Indians in Mexico who became Pentecostal with the stagnation of Mayos who retained a traditional folk Catholicism. Those who became Pentecostal "initiated a major change of life, notably by gaining freedom from the fiesta system and the obligation of *fiesteros* to give away huge quantities of food," writes Martin. "Rejection of the obligations of the fiesta helped them get together more money for consumer goods and the education of their children. They also saved money by their rejection of all entertainment, especially drinking. Yet the rejection of waste and drinking was not a rejection of wealth. Pastors encouraged their congregations to work hard, educate their children and improve their material conditions."

Martin remembers a Pentecostal pastor telling him that "the traditional male ideal in Latin America is the man who shoots three men and sleeps with three women; the Pentecostal male ideal is the man who can successfully cope with one woman for one lifetime." He cites the work of anthropologist Elizabeth Brusco among Protestants — both Lutheran and Pentecostal — in El Cocuy, Colombia, as an illustration of how evangelical religion assists economic and social advancement through the taming of machismo. Martin summarizes Brusco's findings: "Machismo is a major drawback, because the more women a man 'conquers,' the less he can provide. In her view, the effect of Protestantism is to reduce drinking and fighting and to increase concern for the home and family. Whereas Catholics aimed to acquire a radio, the first priority of Protestants was a domestic table. Their concern, she says, was with wholesomeness, with learning and with being productive. Evangelical households ate better and exemplified new priorities in consumption."

"By far the largest conduit for evangelical Christianity," writes Martin, "is provided by the massive movement of people from countryside or hacienda to the megacity. The new society now emerging in Latin America has to do with movement and evangelicals constitute a movement."

The move to the city dissolves all the traditional ties of family, community and religion in which the migrant was bound up from birth. When he arrives in the big city, the new arrival is independent; he is no longer "tied down." But he is also alone: He is not yet "tied in."

The Pentecostal churches offer what Martin calls a "protective social capsule." It is a surrogate family of brothers and sisters providing emotional support. It is a ready-made social network that helps people find work or housing. And it is volunteer work that occupies almost all of a person's free time in church-related activity. The work utilizes people's talents and creates opportunities to develop new skills that may give them a sense of usefulness and fulfillment for the first time in their lives. "In the Pentecostal Church, every member has a role," says journalist Prado. "The man who has been a construction worker all his life suddenly finds himself speaking to his brothers from the altar. He feels like he is doing something important, relevant. Everyone has a role. They may not all preach, but, for example, one will play in the band, another may direct the choir. People feel they fit in." And in the Catholic Church? "They don't have a role."

Pentecostals assume a range of responsibilities "from little domestic ones like maintenance of the church building all the way to being a missionary and preaching in the streets, which is a carefully planned endeavor," says sociologist Galilea. "They have bulletin boards in all the churches where they all read the preaching plan for the week. And they all participate in this."

The skills, the attitudes and the contacts developed within the network give people an edge in the workaday world outside the church. The network "offers opportunity for developing skills of expression, organization, propagation and leadership," writes Martin. "Such skills cannot, in the long run, be irrelevant to survival and modest advancement in the conditions of contemporary Latin America, especially for the pastorate. By molding individuals with some sense of their own self-hood and capacity to choose, it may well be building up a constituency well-disposed to a capitalistic form of development."

Daniel Wattenberg

CHAPTER 30

*International development agencies
traditionally had nothing to offer
directly to the poorest of the poor. They
gave resources to governments and
hoped for the best, usually without
much luck. This May 28, 1990, article
described a different approach, a
program aimed at giving poor people
small loans to improve their business.
The results in La Paz, Bolivia, were
impressive. People quickly started
making more money and repaying the
loans with interest.*

NO SMALL CHANGE FOR BOLIVIA'S POOR

The workday at the Rodriguez market in downtown La Paz begins in the dark hours before dawn. By 4 a.m. the patrol of stray dogs and the few military police in green woolen capes and helmets clear the rough cobblestoned streets for trucks coming in from the verdant valleys below. The run-down, open-air, diesel belchers rumble up the hilly streets, swaying side to side, laden with crates and sacks of produce upon which 30 or more passengers are precariously perched. Within minutes the dimly lighted streets are seething with the complexly ordered activity of an ant farm as men and women rush to set up the market.

Don Panchito (everyone uses the old Spanish form of address of Don or Dona; the letters stand for "of noble origin"), 70, is ready for business. His tiny bar-styled cafe, in a row of several others on the edge of the street, is warmly lighted and inviting with the aroma of strong coffee.

"I work every day of the week," he says, pouring three spoons of sugar into a steaming mug. "If one doesn't work, there's nothing. I don't rest. The stomach doesn't rest."

The market doesn't rest either. Every day of the week the routine is the same for the more than 30,000 that make their living here. The Rodriguez market is but one of more than 20 markets that dot the city of about 1 million. The majority of the city's inhabitants are former peasants who have come from the countryside in a steady stream since the 1950s in search of a better life. Their expectations have been largely frustrated by excessive government regulation of economic activity, forcing them to find work where they can.

Virtually every commercial vendor is an Aymara Indian woman, wearing her trademark bowler hat, fringed shawl, layered skirts and a multicolored blanket called an *ahuayo*, which is slung across the back and serves to carry a baby or a load of produce. Most of these women are trapped in a never-ending cycle of trying to make enough money for their families to survive. A good number are beholden to the truckers who haul the produce from the countryside, who act as wholesalers as well.

Most of the women do not have the cash to pay the truckers up front. For their part, the truckers are willing to sell on credit — but at usurious interest rates, as high as 10 percent a day. Desperate to eke out what they can, the women have no choice but to accept the truckers' conditions. Many of the women just hope to break even, taking some of the produce home to eat instead of leaving with some extra change. Others buy what goods they can, which they hope to sell just so they will have some money with which they can buy more the next day.

In the past couple of years, word has got around the Rodriguez market about a private, nonprofit organization in La Paz that gives credit at commercial interest rates to vendors and small-time manufacturers and artisans. Known by its Spanish acronym as Prodem, which partially stands for the Foundation for the Promotion and Development of Microenterprise, the institution is an affiliate of Accion International. Based in Cambridge, Mass., Accion is a privately funded organization that has developed a system for making credit available to the self-employed, underfinanced workers of the Americas — those who labor outside the mainstream economy in what is loosely termed the "informal sector."

Traditionally considered economically unproductive and high credit risks, the poor who compose the informal sector — more than 50 percent of La Paz's economically active population and growing three times faster than the formal sector — had little possibility of advancement until Prodem came along. Yet it is estimated that these nonregistered workers contribute more than 25 percent to Bolivia's $4 billion gross national product. Their ranks swelled even further when the government launched its austerity program in 1985 to try to rein in the 24,000 percent annual inflation, forcing many in the formal economy out of work.

In its 2½ years of disbursing loans, Prodem has found that with an initial loan worth as little as $50, incomes increase from 50 to 100 percent and the repayment rate is more than 99 percent — paid back with 3 percent interest. The very poor, it turns out, are very bankable indeed.

Jacinta Avila de Acosta, in her 50s, has heard about Prodem from a friend and is interested in getting credit. She hopes to meet with one of the 17 credit counselors from the program as soon as she sells off her produce. Huddled in a black woolen shawl, her bowler hat cocked to the side, Dona Jacinta waits at her vending stall in the so-called enclosed market — a structure of vertical 2-by-4s supporting a patched roof of corrugated tin and plastic — for men to unload her produce from the truck. Dona Jacinta started out at 1:30 a.m. from the farming community of Palomar, one of the nearest to La Paz, with her daughter, son-in-law, baby grandson and 30 others. They balanced themselves on top of their produce for more than three hours as the old truck negotiated rocky dirt roads to the city.

A tiny, aging man delivers some of Dona Jacinta's produce. Wearing a colorful, knitted Aymara woolen cap with ear flaps and a cape of thin cotton material on his back to protect his clothing from the cargo, he and his similarly dressed colleagues look like Andean Supermen. Doubled over with the weight of the produce, they jog from the street to the corresponding stall, whistling for people to move out of the way. Some chew coca leaves in the same way that tobacco is chewed. Mastication of the leaf has long been used to combat hunger and fatigue. Dona Jacinta pays the men 50 centavos (about 17 cents) for each crate of tomatoes and one bolivano (33 cents) for each large burlap bag.

Surrounded now by bags containing romaine, parsley, radishes and peppers that have been packed with grass for protection, she waits for the shoppers. "We're here only to sell today," says Dona Jacinta. "Around 6 o'clock we should start. Then we'll head back home in the afternoon. When there's produce we come back into town every day, otherwise two or three times a week."

Dona Jacinta is vastly better-off than most women. She has her own plot of land and sells her produce wholesale. An early shopper arrives and inspects the parsley. Soon they start haggling over the price, hissing in Aymara, an ancient Indian tongue that predates the Incas. Dona Jacinta soon concedes to the lower price and tosses 10 bunches into the woman's *ahuayo*, which is spread on the dirt floor. "Soon as I'm finished here, I'm going to Prodem," she says, stashing the money into a pouch inside her shirt. "What's the address?"

Prodem does not advertise and there is no sign identifying the office. People learn about it by word of mouth. The inconspicuous, small building near the top of the steep, cobbled street of Almirante Grau is more readily identified by the groups of Indian women gathered on the sidewalk than by the three digits, 625, above the iron gate entrance.

The offices open at 8:15 in the morning, but on Tuesdays there are always a few groups of *cholitas*, as the women are called, who have gathered by 7:30. This is the day that loans are disbursed for commercial vendors. For Maria Manani and Andrea Luna Viuda de Quispe, it is a red-letter day: They will be receiving their first loan.

One of the requirements of the program is that those seeking credit form "solidarity groups" of four or more trusted friends, each of whom guarantees the loan. For first-time loan recipients, the entire group has to present itself to sign the promissory note. Sitting on a doorstep across the street, the two women are anxious because the two other group members have not arrived. Dona Andrea, rubbing her callused hands to keep warm in the cold mountain air, explains that the four women in the group, which they have named Chama after a village, sell either vegetables or meat and work near each other in the market.

"I used to work for a lady and then she let me go, but she would sell me some of her meat on credit," says Dona Maria. "I've always been short on money and had nowhere else to go. I was dependent on her and whatever meat she wanted to sell me. Now with the loan I can buy where I please, buy more and buy better quality."

When the check is presented, says Dona Andrea, "we have to go to the bank." She laughs: "We've never gone to get money before. We've only gone to pay taxes."

"Most of our clients and the vast majority of the nonformal sector pay a proportionately higher-level tax than do those in the formal sector," says Francisco Otero, director of Prodem. Otero is uncomfortable with the term "informal" because of the connotations of illegality and uses "nonformal" instead. The tax levied on the informal sector is a government estimate based on sales. In addition, each woman in the market pays 50 centavos a day for her vending spot.

Fernando Mendoza, the World Bank's representative in La Paz, explains that these 50 centavos daily are "a fee. It is paid to the municipality and is called 'the right to be sitting' on the street. Taxes as such are given only to the central government. But the fee is like a parking fee, and they have to pay that to the municipality."

The door next to the gate of Prodem is opened, and many *cholitas* pass through a garage and climb the steps on the left to the second floor. The office consists of three large areas, each on a separate floor, that have been subdivided into smaller rooms. Above the doorway on the first floor is Prodem's logo, prefaced by a symbolic braid — the *cholitas* traditionally wear braids tucked into their shawls. They enter what resembles a classroom and sit on orange metal chairs that all but disappear underneath their layers of skirts. Mothers take the time to nurse their crying babies while chatting with their friends.

An older woman, who identifies herself only as Dona Ilda, is also a first-time loan recipient. She speaks quietly and softly, as most Aymara do. "It's so difficult. Because selling in the market is our custom, we can't just leave it. And now that I'm getting on in age, I can't really switch to something else. For this reason I'm continuing. I've been selling fruit now for 28 years and I haven't advanced, having to pay off the credit I buy the fruit with all the time. God willing, with this loan I'll get to move forward. I want to travel to buy my fruit because by traveling you can get cheaper prices," Dona Ilda says.

"We're new to the program and we're still not understanding that well all that they've been teaching us, but I know the loan will help us progress with our work and move ahead," she says, repeating what she has learned in the many information and training sessions Prodem holds for loan recipients.

Prodem's challenges are many. Most clients have never had to deal with financial transactions that involve accounts, checks and deposit slips. Many are also illiterate.

"We hold many sessions throughout the loan cycle," explains Mario Usnayo, director of the credit counselors. "There's an information talk, which we hold every day, where we explain what Prodem is and what the requirements are. Then groups that think they've met the requirements fill out an application form. Once these facts have been verified and an economic evaluation of their needs has been assessed by a counselor, they have to attend two sessions before they receive their loans. In the first session we discuss the importance of group solidarity, and in the second we discuss the loan amount and payments and how to deal with the bank. Once they receive their first loan, there are various training sessions with each new loan where we discuss problems, money management, marketing, public relations within the group and with customers."

It's standing room only now, as credit counselors organize and ready loan checks. Jiovanna Meneses, another credit counselor, meanwhile gives an information talk on the first floor to a mixed group of both men and women. While 98 percent of commercial vendors are women, some 90 percent of artisans are men. Prodem's loan portfolio is equally divided between the two, though 70 percent of the 9,500 clients are commercial vendors who receive smaller loans. Their average loan amount is the equivalent of about $315, while the loan for an artisan averages $372.

Meneses explains the program's requirements, which include at least one year's experience in the line of work, being owner of the vending place or shop, selling only domestic products and having a responsible solidarity group. The concept of the group (which cannot be composed of family members) is stressed at every turn.

"If Dona Maria decided to spend her money and go dancing all night and the next day forgot to make her installment on Monday when it was due, was she acting responsibly?" Meneses asks rhetorically. The group softly titters. "No, she was not. Ladies and gentlemen, we must be responsible, we must be punctual with our payments. This is our obligation. The money is part of a rotating fund. The money we repay goes to another group for their loan. If we don't repay on time, we hurt the program."

After the session, participants receive a piece of paper with a stamp to prove they have attended. This piece of paper must be presented if they want to continue with the next step and apply for credit with their group. On average, 10 new groups join the program weekly, but there is a waiting list and the wait is approximately one month. One woman folds the piece of paper in half and puts it carefully inside the lining of her hat.

"There is a tremendous demand for our services, and we're nowhere near satisfying this demand," says Otero, who also oversees Prodem's branch in El Alto, a town just outside La Paz, and is starting up a new operation in the city of Santa Cruz. "We really work only five or six markets, and there are more than 20 in La Paz. We're very limited because of the limited amount of resources for the revolving fund," which is about $3 million lent and donated by international development agencies, foreign governments, the Bolivian government and private individuals. "I believe some 140 markets have been identified in La Paz and in El Alto, and we're not even supporting one-tenth of them," he says. "In La Paz alone, if we had $12 million, we would still be short of satisfying demand."

"This group is receiving its third loan and also has a little star, which means they have made all their payments on time," says Marta Duran, a credit counselor. "This is a good group. They're hard workers and responsible." They get a round of applause. Duran beckons two of the representatives of the group to come up and sign the promissory note. (After the first loan, only the coordinator of the group and another member need to show up to receive the check.) "Will you sign?" asks Duran. A heavyset woman pushes her hat back and bends over the desk, carefully writing her name. The second woman presses her thumb on the ink pad and has Duran place it next to her name.

Juan Ancasi, another credit counselor, reviews with the gathering of about 70 groups how to stand in line at the bank, how to cash their checks and how to deposit their weekly installments.

"We want two to go to the bank," Ancasi tells the group. "Two people can't be robbed. We don't want that excuse. Once the teller gives you the cash, go to the side and count it right away. If it doesn't add up go back to the teller. Don't lose your money."

Duran continues with the disbursement, calling out groups by name: "Super Amigas," "Jewels of the Aymara," "Hearts of Gold," "White Stones." "This group received a black stripe because they have been delayed in making their payments," Duran says. "This group is on the verge of disappearing. What do we say to them?" The crowd jeers and whistles. The women approach the desk and sign for their check. Heads bowed, they quickly shuffle out.

"The principle of the solidarity group also serves as group pressure for the clients to pay their installments on time. The only agreement that exists between a group is a word contract, which in this country is still very strong," says Ronald Reque, the resident credit counselor for the commercial vendors. "It's up to the group to also work out any problems they may have. We let them sort things out; that's not the counselor's domain. We don't want to foster paternalism. We treat them professionally like clients, and they respond in kind."

Otero says that this approach fosters a sense of self-worth among the clients. "Because we're not paternalistic . . . and because we expect the money back and consequently treat them as clients, there's an important aspect in terms of their self-esteem. . . . The lack of self-esteem is the greatest obstacle to development. If people feel they can't better themselves, or society is telling them this and we develop a welfare state mentality, then we really have set the basis for sustained underdevelopment. The issues of trust and the accessing of resources on the basis of your own self-worth has a tremendous

impact on self-esteem." Otero, a warm and energetic man, passion-
ately believes in providing the wherewithal for the poor to improve
their standard of living.

"If you belong to the poorest sector of the country, not only are
you hungry and you don't have shelter and things like this, but more
important than anything, you are destitute emotionally," Otero says.
"So to give them more things simply makes them more destitute.
They say, 'Well, we're basket cases, we have to be given things.'
Whereas, if you came up with a scheme where you would give them
something that would increase their self-esteem and their dignity,
they would all of a sudden improve their lives."

The Rodriguez market is a roiling sea of people in the afternoon.
The mountain air is cool, but the sun is hot. From the top of any
steeply inclining street, Illimani, one of the most imposing snow-
capped mountains in the Andean range, is visible. It looms just outside the city, standing like a sentinel. Farther up on a busy corner of
Rodriguez Street is Margarita Castillos de Estrada's vending stall.
She is too busy to admire the beauty of Illimani.

"It's been ages since we had this place on the corner here. My
mother left it to me as an inheritance. I've been working here for
more than 30 years now," says Dona Margarita, a weathered woman
in her late 40s. "Before the loan I couldn't buy so many products,"
she says, stirring three large vats of floating olives. Neatly lined up
on wooden crates of different heights stand jars of honey, bottles of
vinegar, coffee, corn seeds, some produce. "It's been a tremendous
help for me because I have three sons who are studying in a private
school. I am their mother and father at the same time. I alone provide for the home," she says proudly. And her husband?

"Unfortunately I don't have one. He's an alcoholic, so I told him
to get out and end his life as he pleased," she says. "Before, when my
husband worked and was a normal man, he collaborated. But then
he became a drunk, and I didn't have any sort of collaboration so I
decided to rid myself from him. That's the way it is. And now I'm the
sole provider, and with the loan I have the money to buy the products I need."

Dona Margarita is on her ninth loan and is now receiving the
equivalent of roughly $340, which has to be paid off in weekly install-
ments of $17 in five months. "In a week my profits are about 20 boli-
vanos [about $6.50 after the loan payment], 10 bolivanos or 5. Just
as in a day I can earn the same amount. This is true during the holidays. But days like these it's slow," she says. "We wait for holidays
like Holy Week or the 16th of July," the anniversary of the founding

of La Paz. "Before the loan, I sometimes would earn as little as 4 bolivanos a week."

The focus on women who sell in the market is one of the features that distinguish Prodem from the few other credit-giving organizations.

"We first work with the poorest of the poor that are economically active. We usually go for the market people," Otero explains. "Many programs say, 'Why support these unproductive women out in the street?' In this sense we're unique. There is a bias against the street vendors in many programs, whereas we realize their importance. Their argument is, 'If it doesn't have paid value, we shouldn't fund it.' From there they take the leap and say, 'In the countryside one papaya costs 10 centavos, in La Paz 50 centavos. Since they haven't done anything to the product, they haven't transformed raw materials into anything, they're not a productive unit,' which of course is not true. If you think they have not added any value to the product, then go and buy your papaya in the countryside."

Near the market on Rodriguez, in what is a minimall of parallel tiny shops separated by a narrow dirt walkway, Johnny Ticona makes bowler hats. Back in the late 1800s, when the British (along with many other foreigners) came to the mining town of Potosi, the English bowler piqued the fancy of Aymara women. They adopted the hat and added it as an accessory to their layered skirts and fringed shawls, which they copied from the Spanish wives of the conquistadors.

Johnny, 17, is fashioning a bowler by pressing a hot iron on a woolen hat that is placed on top of a wooden mold. This is his father's shop, a small booth. Johnny has been making hats now for three years. "Before the loan my dad just fixed old hats because he didn't have any capital to buy material to make new ones. But now we've been able to buy these new wooden hat molds and material from Argentina and Brazil. The material from Brazil is finer than the Argentine and those hats are more expensive, running for 70 bolivanos."

The greatest advantage of the loan, Johnny says, is that they can now buy their material in bulk. "We now pay about 30 to 35 bolivanos [$9 to $11] for each hat when we buy the material in bulk vs. 45." Turning down a large radio playing rock sung in Spanish, Johnny says, "I like the work a lot. I'm going to develop new models." What variations can be introduced to a basic bowler? "The height has varied," he explains. "Before the hats were higher. Only a few ladies ask for this type of hat now. Fashion has changed and the majority ask for this model [which is lower]. We have to change the models periodically to keep up with the fashion. You see, they also like to wear the hats now tilted to the side."

He says his father is on his fourth loan. The amount he received for three months is the equivalent of $483. "My dad hopes to get a bigger store," Johnny says. "We're running out of room here with all of these hats. They keep taking up more space."

With Prodem, people aspire. The program also enforces a savings plan for its clients, deducting 5 percent of the clients' loan and putting it into an account. They can claim it when they leave the program. "Progress is not just a question of resources, it's also a question of attitude," says Otero. "So all of a sudden they start thinking about the future."

Nancy Lecona de Toledo and her husband, Benjamin, are dreaming of the day they will export their leather jackets to the United States with the label "Made in Bolivia" instead of the one they sew on now, which says "Made in Argentina." They work out of their bedroom in a tiny house in a dusty, southeastern neighborhood of La Paz.

"We stitch on 'Made in Argentina' labels so we can sell," explains Don Benjamin. "People prefer things from Argentina. If we put 'Made in Bolivia' no one would buy the jackets. They would say, 'Oh, it's not good.' We have a very narrow mentality here."

With the loan, they have been able to hire two workers. "Before, we only had one worker, along with my husband," says Dona Nancy. "Then with the loan we bought one machine and then another, and we could hire workers with the increase in work." Depending on the design of the jacket, each worker is paid 3 to 5 bolivanos for the two jackets they make daily.

"We make more during the winter," she says. "We have clients from Chile, two women who come directly here and buy the jackets to sell in Chile. We sell according to the models, some we sell for 120 bolivanos and others for 90. The women come every week during the winter and other times once every two weeks or monthly. The Chileans are our only clients for export right now, but we periodically go to Peru to sell. Maybe someday we'll ship to the United States," she says, laughing.

The profit margin for each jacket is the equivalent of $2.50, and they sell about 25 each week. Their next hurdle is to try to get people to accept jackets with the "Made in Bolivia" label. "We're going to get people used to the idea bit by bit," says Don Benjamin. "But we can't do it right away. There are legal questions and paperwork that we have to put through first, and there are some additional taxes we have to pay." In order to put his own label on the jackets, Don Benjamin has to register a patent trademark — in other words, register and formalize his shop.

"The government is full of technocrats who, to start with, don't know the sector and the way in which the artisans work," says Jorge Aranda Mercado, a credit counselor for artisans. "The paperwork and procedures are incredibly slow. They demand a lot of investment in money and time."

It is the endless, complex bureaucratic maze that keeps many in the informal sector. Otero does not believe many people "make the leap" to register and become formalized. "I don't think anybody's really doing it because it's such a ridiculously long process. It's like falling into a corrupt trap," he says. "They will never get their permit, and they will pay hundreds of bolivanos and will probably end up frustrated. All they will do is create problems for themselves because they're not going to improve their life or their business."

In Palomar, one of the farming communities south of La Paz, Damian Quispe Apaza inspects some of his tomatoes. His plot of land, about 2½ acres, is one of many in the community of 120 families. Palomar, like the other three farming villages in the area, is in a lush, green valley wedged between two mountain ranges. The region is idyllic: Sheep and cattle graze, a river provides for natural irrigation, and the valley supports crops year-round.

"The bulk of the tomatoes were already harvested last week," says Don Damian. "We'll start to seed potatoes around May 20. They will be ready for harvesting in August and September. Until then we have lettuce and parsley to harvest and prepare the land for potatoes."

The agricultural sector remains completely informal. There is no government regulation. With Bolivia's social revolution of 1952 and the accompanying agrarian reform, the land automatically went to anybody who had worked it. About 60 percent of Bolivia's population is rural, though only about 1 percent has any irrigation. Prodem has six groups that are composed of farmers. While it would like to expand, it cannot for lack of funds.

"We're dying to do a rural program," says Otero, "but for this we need extraordinary sums of money. I would not go into the countryside unless there was at least $2 [million] to $3 million available to begin with. Otherwise you get these hordes of people at the door asking for loans, and you can't satisfy them and you start getting a bad name."

Don Damian is a member of the first farming group to receive a

loan from Prodem, two years ago. Erasma Calle de Aluse, another
member of the group, is visiting. She has taken her shoes off and sits
down to nurse her baby. "I heard about the program while I was
working in the market," she says. "So we formed a group — we've
known each other since we were babies — and were the first farmers to get a loan. At first our loan was small, only 100 bolivanos each.
But with that we were able to buy seeds. We were told that each loan
would increase." Now on their fifth loan, the group is receiving 2,000
bolivanos each, or $645.

"Two thousand is still not enough," says Don Damian. "Our costs
run more or less up to 4,000 bolivanos. Each time the soil has to be
prepared, we need to rent a tractor to till it. That's about 80 bolivanos an hour and we need it for at least four hours each time. We
need to buy fertilizing chemicals and chemicals against insects. We
also have to pay 10 bolivanos a day for each worker. We have between
five and 10 workers depending on what needs to be done. With meals
we pay them 5 bolivanos. Then we have to serve them breakfast,
lunch and dinner."

"But before the loan we couldn't afford 10 workers when we needed them, so we would work with four or five, depending on what the
land needed," says Dona Erasma.

Delfim Reyes Ortiz, another member of the group, has wandered
over to chat. His farm is in the most remote farming village of Tahua-
palca, which gets fresh water from the melting snows of Illimani.
Because soil conditions are better, Don Delfim is also able to grow
fruit.

"We're earning 40 to 50 percent more with the loan," he says. His
wife stays in La Paz and sells their produce in the market, as does
Don Damian's wife. Dona Erasma just sells wholesale. Each goes in
to town at least twice a week. "It costs 5 bolivanos to ride to La Paz.
People are packed in with the produce and ride like monkeys for
more than three hours," Don Delfim says. "It's very uncomfortable
to travel. The roads are bad and it's very dangerous. Some trucks
fall over the cliffs, their steering fails, brakes fail. You can see them
in the ditches. But there's no use complaining. We've got to go into
the city."

"Before we knew about Prodem, we approached one of the agricultural banks and one of these guys, one of the engineers, asked for
200 bolivanos and nothing was done," says Dona Erasma. "We were
ripped off," says Don Damian, shaking his head. "And many others
were ripped off too."

"Besides, the loans are for one year or two years, and the capital along with the interest has to be paid back in one lump sum," Dona Erasma explains. "Once this money is spent, it's not possible for us to return it all at once. For us it's better to pay once a month or even every three months along with the production cycle."

Most banks simply are not structured to meet the needs of farmers and others in the informal sector. Says Otero: "Commercial banking in Bolivia is for a modern, Western economy. We don't have a financial system for the genuine, authentic, criollo economy of Bolivia, which is what we are. So the banks suffer from many difficulties that don't allow them to satisfy the credit demands of these people. . . . They're not interested in these tiny amounts of loans."

In an effort to better aid the informal sector and reach more farmers in the future, Prodem is forming its own bank, which it hopes will be ready to disburse its first loan in 18 months.

"Prodem is a star project. We've got the people, we've got the market, we've got the resources, we've got the sympathy, but it's not a solution," says Prodem Chairman Fernando Romero. "We've got to go one step further. We have got to set up an institution that is there to last and is self-sustaining. It's got to be a bank. It's got to be a business. . . . The moment you make it self-sustaining — the moment it can live its own life and doesn't depend on charity or donations — then you got something going."

Dona Erasma would agree. Placing her baby inside her *ahuayo* and over her back, she says: "Without money, one can't move, one can't do anything. Without money, there's no work."

Susanne Sternthal

PART 9

AFRICAN QUAGMIRES

CHAPTER 31

*Economic pressure proved the undoing of
South Africa's racist apartheid edifice.
But it was less pressure from the outside,
in the form of sanctions, than the
economic aspirations of the South African
people that made the Afrikaner's
hodgepodge of racial regulations
untenable. This July 31, 1989, article
described those pressures as manifested in
the "informal" sector of South Africa's
economy — made up of black
entrepreneurs, hawkers and taxi-drivers
who were unwitting agents of change.*

THE COLOR OF MONEY
IS WHAT COUNTS

Just over 20 years ago, Raymond Ackerman introduced the American-style supermarket to the southern tip of Africa, building dozens of stores surrounded by oceans of parking. His insight into the suburban yearnings of affluent whites paid off, and his Pick 'n Pay chain soon vaulted over its downtown rivals to dominate the business.

Like everybody in South Africa, Ackerman is worried about the future. A few years ago he tried taking out what he calls an "insurance policy," setting up a chain in Australia, until the government there forced him to sell. Today he preaches a "caring capitalism" that he hopes will survive the passing of white minority rule, which he considers only a matter of time. "I've put too much into this country — and gotten too much out of it — to leave unless I'm chased out with the barrel of a gun," he says from his headquarters in a leafy suburb of Cape Town.

Not far away, among the black squatter camps of the Cape Flats, is another successful retailer. Like most of his neighbors, Victor Mbauli came to the Western Cape from the Transkei region in search of work in the 1970s. After a stint as a well digger, he tried his hand at selling groceries from a jerry-built shack in Khayelitsha township.

Today he is the owner not only of a thriving *spaza* shop — the Zulu word means camouflage, echoing a time when any sign of black enterprise drew the wrath of the white authorities — but also an enormously profitable, if not quite legal, Coca-Cola distributorship, which he operates from a shed built of corrugated iron. Even at today's sanctions-battered exchange rate, his monthly sales are worth the equivalent of nearly $100,000.

Whites are learning that there are thousands of Mbaulis in their midst. Ackerman now reckons that such *spaza* shops are his biggest competitors, with combined sales equaling those of his national chain. If measured in terms of the volume of goods and not the distorted exchange rate, the total is about $4 billion, he says.

And blacks are doing more than just selling groceries. Their *shebeens*, or unlicensed saloons, account for about 80 percent of the beer sold by South African breweries. Operating outside formal premises and without formal licenses, black men and women repair cars, build homes, perform surgery, make clothing. By some estimates, their efforts, if properly counted, would increase the economy pictured in official statistics by 30 to 40 percent.

This evidence of the failure of apartheid, a system of legal discrimination that for a long time aimed at keeping economic opportunities out of black hands, is being gratefully received by many whites. They take it as a sign that whites and blacks — trapped in an economy that the official numbers claim has been steadily shrinking in relation to population — may not be doomed to beat each other's brains out after all.

"This is a second chance for South Africa, maybe the last chance," says Theo Rudman, as he navigates his Mercedes-Benz along the mud boulevards of a sprawling squatter camp near Cape Town. Rudman, a former businessman, is the founder of the Self-Employment Institute, which offers training for informal businessmen. Tellingly, his office is located in the shell of an old British Leyland factory, a casualty of international disinvestment.

Khayelitsha is one of his favorite haunts. He ricochets energetically from shack to shack, peeling back curtains to reveal a world of individual enterprise: a beauty parlor, a traditional herb shop, a place to get flat tires fixed. Wherever he goes, Rudman hands out his business card, offers advice or exchanges shoptalk with the proprietors, many of whom he has visited before. "In terms of physical comfort, this is the bottom end of life," he says. "Yet there is an incredible vitality here."

A lucky thing, too. The country's schools turn out 350,000 students a year, which is just about that many more than the formal economy can absorb. Rudman believes that the informal sector is the only thing keeping the lid on South Africa's social caldron. True, some blacks have turned to crime and others to revolution, he says. "But the third alternative, fortunately, is to create self-employment, and that's what many of these people have done — with very little capital, very little education, very little help all around in a hostile economic environment. The squatter camps are the only places in South Africa where there is true free enterprise."

The last statement might be regarded as subversive, except that the government is now saying the same thing. A recent full-page ad by the Ministry of Information in a black business magazine began with the words, "Let's face it, we do not have a Free Enterprise economy in this country."

Louise Tager, dean of Witwatersrand University's law school, has been delving into apartheid's legal morass as director of the pro-deregulation Law Review Project. "The laws designed to prohibit the development of black business are so harsh that even South Africans who might have believed in the apartheid system are shocked that they could have existed," she declares.

Besides being excluded from white areas, blacks were forbidden to own land in their own communities, form corporations, or work at home. Any kind of manufacturing was also outlawed completely, and scarce retail sites were at the disposal of imperious white bureaucrats, against whose decisions there was no appeal. These seldom saw their jobs as encouraging competition for white stores, even though the nearest might be miles away.

Such a vacuum does not go unfilled for long. A furtive economy of shebeens, *spaza* shops and other illicit businesses has existed for decades to serve the needs of the crowded townships. Yet so great is the gulf of ignorance that most whites were oblivious to it until recently. That changed when the black economy began bursting out of the townships and into the white cities.

Each day, township commuters line up for dingy blue buses, which groan along expressways at half the speed of surrounding traffic. For years the white-owned monopoly bus company, Putco, had the market to itself, but no longer. More and more of its customers are choosing the more convenient service offered by black entrepreneurs driving sleek, Japanese-built minibuses.

Most are members of the Southern African Black Taxi Association, which has become the textbook case of black economic power.

From a small beginning, the group now claims 50,000 members. Toss in the estimated 50,000 unlicensed operators and all the people who make their living from the taxi sector, and the industry accounts for about 350,000 jobs, almost as many as the entire gold mining industry. Taxi drivers are the biggest private consumers of gasoline, tires and auto parts, not to mention vehicles (their favorite is the Toyota Hi-Ace, nicknamed the Zola Budd for the South African-born runner).

Their significance assured that they would have powerful allies when a governmental commission, upset over rising bus and rail subsidies, recommended stamping them out in 1980. The attack was deftly turned back, and now the group has expanded into service stations, auto dealerships and muffler shops. Last year, it even mounted a nearly successful takeover bid for Putco. This year it has opened a chapter in neighboring Mozambique.

When they are not dodging the black taxis, urbanites can be found browsing among the wares offered by the black hawkers who have flooded the cities. Alistair Sparks, a white journalist who just returned from a two-year stint at Harvard, recently wrote of his amazement at the sudden "blackening" of Johannesburg.

Like the taxi drivers, the hawkers have had an uphill fight against officialdom. From time to time, policemen still confiscate or destroy their goods or slap them with fines. But the battle is being won. Central business districts have been opened to all races in dozens of white cities, and municipal authorities are relaxing their hawking laws, a move that has more than a few shopkeepers objecting. Tager shrugs. "In South Africa today, you don't have much choice. Either you're going to have a man outside your door selling onions, or you're going to have him there with a knife trying to rob your customers."

But hawking is more than a safety net; it is also a launching pad. Mark Headbrush, who owns a successful trucking service and employs 23 persons, was selling cosmetics from a suitcase until he spotted his chance — in 1985, when white companies stopped sending their delivery vans into Soweto during the riots. The life histories of a remarkable number of black entrepreneurs include stints as hawkers.

The legalization of the taxi and hawking industries "did not happen because the government felt like Father Christmas," says John Kane-Berman of the South African Institute of Race Relations. "The government simply surrendered. There were not enough policemen to enforce all the regulations."

That has been the story of apartheid in the economic sphere. After having made an average of 760 arrests a day for 40 years, Pretoria dumped its notorious pass laws in 1986. Despite the panic among some whites, nothing much changed. The flood of black migrants into cities the laws were supposed to prevent was already a done deal.

In the same way, blacks have won the right to unionize, to compete for white jobs and to live in certain white areas. Next on the agenda is a bill that would sweep away most of the licensing requirements that keep many black businesses on the wrong side of the law. After that, more refinements in the Group Areas Act, which carves the country up into white, black, colored and Indian areas. Though final repeal of the law is not just around the corner, black and white businessmen are already bickering over the phasing of the assaults on each other's turf.

In fact, among the most *verligte*, or enlightened, bureaucrats in the economic ministries, there is warm applause for getting rid of laws that hobble black money-making. Says one official, "You would not find a single person in the Treasury who would restore hard-line apartheid."

The reason is simple. Without property rights or legal businesses, the townships are fiscal black holes; they generate little in the way of tax receipts but consume huge subsidies for a host of services — transport, housing, utilities, medical care. Even more money goes to support the quasi-independent homelands, a patchwork of territories where blacks can enjoy the illusion of self-determination at their leisure because there are no jobs. For whites, who make up a mere 15 percent of the population, apartheid has meant a tax burden that has quietly grown to crushing proportions.

One result is the popularity of the opposition Conservative Party, which promises to send blacks packing from white South Africa. Another is the steady loss of white talent. Two years ago, a survey of emigrants sailing to Australia found that almost all were leaving in search of a better life-style and not to escape ethnic strife.

But the most important consequence is the growing unviability of a key tactic for hushing black opposition to white rule. "The government is trying to buy out blacks with multibillion-dollar programs to upgrade black areas," says economist Leon Louw. "But it's destroying the economy, and a point may come when whites say, 'Look, this is worse even than handing over power.'"

Such thoughts are echoed by many white businessmen, who are the biggest cheerleaders for the licensing of black competition. But often their conviction weakens when it comes to opening up their own industries. Even Ackerman gripes about having hawkers in front of his stores who can beat his prices because they pay no taxes or rents. Yet he is willing to put up with them, he says. "Our attitude is, let's be as competitive as we can, let's create a real Hong Kong approach."

This is more than bigheartedness. Wholesaling to hawkers already accounts for 5 percent of his turnover, and the firm is trying to reach more of them through new wholesale outlets. The same attitude is filtering down to small shopkeepers, once the sworn enemies of hawkers. Many are realizing that the hawkers represent not just a potential new market, but that having them nearby draws pedestrian traffic and reduces crime. In Johannesburg many shops now give hawkers discounts.

Thanks to the Small Business Development Corp., which is jointly owned by the government and a group of private companies, informal operators are even eligible for subsidized credit. The many losses on loans to small-timers are made up from profits on lending to bigger firms. Of course, most informal operators get their financing the old-fashioned way: from their personal savings, loan sharks or informal mutual funds known as *stockvels*.

Still, the group's director, Ben Vosloo, epitomizes the casual attitude toward legalities that is essential when doing business in the informal sector. He laughingly describes a client who deals drugs out of his SBDC-financed muffler shop. "From time to time, this guy falls in arrears and then he'll suddenly come along with a bankroll of money. That means he's been out peddling his marijuana."

Though not precisely in this form, such alliances between formal and informal businesses are being touted as a cure for what ails the South African economy: the shortage of capital caused by the drying up of foreign investment and the depressed gold price. Partly because of apartheid labor policies, South African industry is among the most capital-intensive in the world. In the metals industry, it takes about $1,000 to create a single job. But the informal sector can create a job — as a hawker, a tailor or a fender mender — for as little as $75.

But there is more to it than jobs, according to Rudman and other experts. With the sanctions gun to its head, South Africa's is a true export-or-die economy, and exploiting the efficiency of its informal sector could help it compete with the export powerhouses of the Pacific Rim. Rudman points to the example of big Japanese companies, many of which farm out much of their actual production to smaller operators with low overhead, low wages and no lifetime employment policies to uphold.

Though South African companies are taking halting steps in this direction, apartheid has left enormous obstacles. One is the periodic waves of anarchy that sweep the black townships, disrupting business and often victimizing those who are seen as collaborators with the white regime.

Another is entrenched attitudes among white businessmen. Despite the fact that his *spaza* shop does a hefty turnover, Victor Mbauli cannot get most white distributors to deliver goods. "They don't like to come here," he says. "The ceiling leaks when it rains and the floors are dirt." And though Mbauli is a pillar of the Khayelitsha business community, when he goes to a white distributor, he is often shunted off on the junior executive who deals with hawkers.

The exception is Coca-Cola, which has sent its trucks into the shantytown to keep him stocked. Even so, according to Rudman, the local bottler is missing a chance to penetrate a burgeoning market more deeply, an opportunity that would not escape notice in another setting. "They are taking Victor for a bit of a ride," he says. "But if they gave him more profit, they'd sell a lot more Coke."

That so many black entrepreneurs have grown up in the deep shadows of the white economy poses another set of problems. Few have the planning, marketing and accounting skills that white businessmen expect. The scarcity of telephones in black areas is also a handicap. Take the case of a shop owner who wants to stock a new item. "He might walk five miles and spend a whole day doing something that takes you or me half an hour," says Rudman. "And blacks are always pitching up without an appointment, which drives whites crazy."

Nor does black capitalism sit well with all members of the black community, as demonstrated at a recent meeting between the National Council of Trade Unions, a black labor group, and the African Council of Hawkers and Informal Businessmen. James Mndaweni, the union leader, warned the hawkers against becoming "an appendage of the business captains and the ruling class." Successful blacks are "often singled out for attack as sellouts and stooges and race traitors," says Louw, whose Free Market Foundation is leading the effort to gauge the size and shape of the informal sector.

For that, the government can take the blame. Over the years, the closing of every avenue of black enterprise was accompanied by a shrill insistence on attachment to Western values. "The selling of South Africa as a free market system was counterproductive because it simply wasn't," says a Finance Ministry official. "People in the black community have a right to say, 'The free market means they become rich and we become poor.'"

Now that the government is burbling about free enterprise for blacks, many old campaigners are suspicious, accusing white politicians of trying to buy black acquiescence in minority rule. Ironically, according to a recent survey by the South Africa Foundation, a liberal business group, most black businessmen think so too. Despite their genuine gains, there is "a deep and pervasive skepticism over the reality of black advancement," the foundation reported. "They remained unconvinced that unfettered free enterprise alone could correct the social injustices accumulated by centuries of discrimination."

In that, at least, they are the soul mates of their Afrikaner rulers, who over the decades used political power to gain economic power. Except in the case of the blacks, the process runs the other way.

Last year, in the village of Boksburg, Conservative Party politicians restored segregation in public places. Now the economy is a shambles, the victim of boycott by black consumers. Though the government has quietly enjoyed the embarrassment of its Conservative rivals, the ruling National Party knows that it is potentially whistling past its own graveyard too. Blacks account for half of all consumer spending nationally, and much more within many of the major municipalities.

"If blacks succeed in changing policy in Boksburg, they're not going to spend the rest of their lives watching television," says Kane-Berman. "The government knows a weapon forged successfully in Boksburg is going to be used someday in Pretoria."

A MARKET OPPRESSED

South Africans expect their leaders to be honest, churchgoing men. So their next president may have felt a little nervous standing before the television cameras in May and absolving Pretoria of any blame for the country's decade-long economic crisis. It was all the fault of foreigners.

A bolt of lightning did not descend on the broadcast studio to immolate Frederik W. de Klerk, the new boss of the ruling National Party. If there was divine retribution at all, it was only the guffaws of the liberal opposition and the business press. Most of his listeners, de Klerk could comfortably assume, found the party line only too plausible.

After all, signs of foreign perfidy are all around. Companies that protested for decades their commitment to South Africa disappear overnight. Familiar brand names are replaced with dubious substitutes like Phipp's Milk of Magnesia and Anadin. The rand, once a Gibraltar of currencies, is shunned by overseas investors. "South Africa is the polecat of the world," complains a government official. "Our planes aren't even allowed to land in New York."

As far as the average South African can make out, the treachery of foreigners is the reason that Toyota and VCR prices are climbing out of sight. Just a few weeks before de Klerk's speech, Pretoria clamped down on consumer spending and aborted the healthiest growth spurt in a decade. The reason: An import boom was soaking up foreign exchange needed to repay overseas loans — loans that foreign banks should have been only too happy to extend, given the country's peerless record.

More egregious debtors, like Mexico or Hungary, can wangle all kinds of slack, but none of that for South Africa. Miss a payment, and sanctioners would have all the excuse they need to impound Pretoria's ships, cargoes and bank accounts, chasing a once-great trading nation out of the world payments system. South Africa would be reduced to bartering for a living like North Korea or Albania.

"We are driving along the edge of an economic abyss," says Tony Norton, president of the Johannesburg Stock Exchange. "One gaffe, one chap really blowing it, can tip us into a situation where we can't be part of the world anymore."

More or less steadily for a century, South Africa was a place that money came to. A constant wash of foreign cash left a glittering residue of skyscrapers, modern mines and factories, not to mention a white life-style that lured thousands of Western immigrants to the Dark Continent. But now the foreign money cannot get away fast enough, draining out at a rate of $2 billion to $3 billion a year.

As chief of the South African Reserve Bank, it has been Gerhard P. C. de Kock's unenviable job to steer the country through this dramatic reversal of fortunes. "It's OK for Switzerland to be a capital exporter," he growls. "But for little South Africa to pretend to be Switzerland, that goes against all common sense. Yet we have been doing it for four years."

For one thing, Switzerland has savings to spare, but South Africa is a capital-hungry land. Much of its natural wealth lies untouched, and a large part of its more than 35 million inhabitants live in Third World poverty and clamors for something better. For another, Switzerland's warring minorities made their peace five centuries ago. South Africa's have yet to do so.

Church groups and student protesters marching in front of corporate headquarters happily claim credit for steering the tides of international finance. But, despite de Klerk's disclaimer, they got plenty of help. The Wall Street Journal recently named South Africa as potentially one of the world's richest countries. Policies made in Pretoria have kept this promise unfulfilled.

Ever since 1948, the hand on the tiller has belonged to the National Party, which rose unexpectedly to power on the economic hates of poor Afrikaners, the descendants of the earliest Dutch settlers. In a hint of things to come, foreign money read the election returns and rushed for the exits. Another exodus occurred in the early 1960s, triggered by the Sharpeville massacre of black demonstrators and Pretoria's exit from the British Commonwealth.

Capitalists had reason to worry. The success of the Nationalists owed as much to resentment of English mine owners as fear of the *swart gevaar*, or black danger. On taking office, the party toyed with the idea of nationalizing the mines, the country's dominant industry, as part of its grand apartheid strategy for building an Afrikaner place in the sun. Though rejected at first as too expensive, the idea resurfaced when Pretoria shook off the Commonwealth's costly compensation rules.

But the party finally settled for merely harnessing big business to Afrikaner aspirations. Apartheid labor laws turned the mines into welfare agencies for white workers, obliging owners to reserve most jobs for "civilized labor" despite an abundance of cheaper black workers. Half the profits from gold mining were skimmed off to build an edifice of Afrikaner socialism. Subsidies were rained down on rural folk to keep them on the land, and the state bureaucracies swelled to provide jobs and upward mobility for thousands more who had been flocking to the city steadily since the Great Depression.

From 1950 to 1965, the public payroll doubled to nearly 200,000, and more than 300 state corporations were formed. By the 1980s, the public sector had long surpassed private business in terms of total investment and was routinely consuming 38 percent of the national income. Not incidentally, the policy of *baantjies vir boeties* — jobs for the boys — helped cement the National Party's support at the ballot box. At last count, 60 percent of the Afrikaner electorate was on the state payroll, and thousands more rely on it for their livelihood. Armscor, the state weapons giant, is the meal ticket for 63,000 workers in the private sector.

Ironically, only in South Africa was the dream of a generation of African socialist leaders realized. An entire tribe was lifted out of rural poverty and into urban plenty. With the state as the lever, the cost was deftly shifted to the backs of foreign capitalists and black workers. And it was done with a minimum of outright graft and gross inefficiency.

Afrikaner businessmen profited too. Under the wing of the Nationalist patronage machine, firms grew until they rivaled the English ones. Of the five giants that control companies that make up 24 percent of the Johannesburg Stock Exchange, three are Afrikaner-owned. (A whopping 56 percent, though, is still controlled by the distinctly un-Afrikaner Anglo American Corporation of South Africa Ltd.)

Behind this triumph was the guiding hand of the Broederbond, a secret organization devoted to the advancement of all things Afrikaner. It made sure government funds were withdrawn from Barclays Bank and Standard Chartered and deposited in Afrikaner institutions like Volkskas. When tempted by milder English cigarettes, members reminded one another to "smoke and cough for *Volk* and *Vaderland*." Their cozy relationship with Pretoria gave many Afrikaner capitalists a less jaundiced view of the visible hand than their English counterparts had. Because their interests (and passports) were more exclusively South African, they were also more apt to thumb their noses at overseas pressures.

The glory decade for Afrikaner business began with the shootings at Sharpeville. As dozens of foreign investors packed their bags, exchange controls forced them to sell out to the locals at bargain prices. Pretoria obliged the new owners by slapping heavy surcharges on competing imports. Fanned by the regime's self-reliance kick, manufacturing led the economy to growth of 6 percent a year in the 1960s.

Aside from leaving, foreign investors contributed little to the party. Yet investment took off. Domestic savings financed a host of new state industries like Armscor and homeland development banks. Free from foreign meddling, apartheid shifted into high gear as Pretoria poured millions into homeland industry, hoping to reverse the flow of blacks to the white cities. "Afrikaners emerged from the Sharpeville crisis owning a larger share of the economy and with a greatly expanded state apparatus," writes economist Merle Lipton.

The hothouse economy of the 1960s even lured back foreign investors. Those were the go-go years for U.S. capital, which rained freely on the just and unjust alike. By decade's end, more than 200 U.S. companies had sunk roots in South African soil. But the investment boom was short-lived. By 1974, two years before the Soweto uprising, money was already steering well clear of South Africa again.

Foreigners had seen what Pretoria still refused to admit: that apartheid was an economic disaster. Forbidden to own property, and cut off from upward mobility, blacks, the nation's majority, had been transformed from a potential asset into a huge liability. Their productivity was abysmal. Their townships and homelands, bereft of viable industry and economic opportunity, became massive drains on white taxpayers. If exchange control made it too expensive to withdraw, foreign companies could at least stop funneling new investment to their South African subsidiaries.

Not that it was missed at first, thanks to a meteoric rise in gold prices in the mid-1970s. Further disguising the absence of foreign investors in the early 1980s was an overseas borrowing binge by Escom, the state electricity corporation. By 1985, even this fig leaf was no longer available. Fed up with being sworn at by clergymen or afraid of being the last out, foreign bankers called in $14 billion in old loans and yanked Pretoria's unused credit lines.

Suddenly, being the polecat wasn't fun. By starving the economy of skilled labor, apartheid had made industry addicted to imported machinery. Now the nation could no longer afford a growing economy; the money to pay for new machinery had to be husbanded for loan repayments instead. The financial crisis sparked a clamor for a return to the go-it-alone approach, led by Fred du Plessis, who until his recent death was chairman of the giant Sanlam insurance empire, originally founded on the savings of farmers and fattened on capital flight. He called for bringing in even more bureaucrats to man the economic battle stations — rationing imports and credit, setting prices and wages. This time, though, the aim was not a free hand to pursue apartheid. It was an economic hot wire to relieve the "revolutionary situation," as he called it, of 5 million jobless blacks.

That his advice was ultimately rejected is evidence of something new in Afrikanerdom. De Kock, the central banker, led the counterattack, warning that direct controls would only invite stagnation and corruption. "Proponents claim their approach can be reconciled with free enterprise and a market economy," he said. "They are sailing under false colors. What they are proposing is a system of central planning."

The backlash against Afrikaner socialism had simmered at least since business executive Andreas Wassenaar provoked fury with his 1977 book "The Assault on Private Enterprise." But the credit for

Pretoria's late conversion to capitalism may actually belong to Margaret Thatcher, who is admired almost as much for the turnaround she engineered in Britain's fortunes as for her steadfast opposition to sanctions.

Even before the loan freeze, market thinking made a strong comeback under State President P. W. Botha. Despite his reputation as a Nationalist hack without an inkling of economics, he lent an ear to de Kock and Finance Minister Barend J. du Plessis, who made the liquidation of Afrikaner socialism the centerpiece of their program for battening down the South African economy against the turmoil ahead. "South Africa is bound to come out of this process leaner and fitter and better-equipped for growth based on its own resources," says the finance minister.

One of the most promising steps, still only half-taken, is the opening of the economy to blacks. Last year, the last job reservation vanished from the books when blacks were allowed to become mine blasters, a hotly debated move because of the presence of explosives. Blacks are also winning greater freedom to operate businesses and own property.

Privatization is another matter. However appealing in principle, Pretoria is not keen on retrenching its own voters. Thousands of civil servants have already rushed to the banner of the opposition Conservative Party, which promises to restore the Afrikaner-first policies of yesteryear. Under the circumstances, the regime figured it was no time to break its unbroken record of election-year pay raises for bureaucrats. The checks started going out in May.

The privatizers' most noteworthy trophy is growing somewhat musty. It has been a decade since 70 percent of Sasol, the state gas-from-coal operation, was peddled to private investors. Among other big properties, phosphates, steel, electricity and parts of the sprawling South African Transport Services empire have also been tapped for the auctioneer. But brokers are not holding their breath.

What to do with the proceeds of privatization is another debate. The free market men want the money for tax cuts that they hope will spur growth in the private sector. The politicians, hoping to buy off black discontent, want it for the flagging effort to equalize black and white education and such. Now that former Treasury boss Chris Stals has got the nod to replace the retiring de Kock, it may signal the ascendancy of the welfare spenders.

Theirs may be an impossibly tall job. The state spends seven times as much on educating white children, and blacks outnumber whites by 5-to-1. There is plenty more inequality where that came from.

"We will bankrupt this country if we try to close that gap," moans a white executive.

Another problem for the privatizers is the hostility of black leaders whose presence might be needed at a future negotiating table. Many of them regard privatization as a scam for locking in white control of the economy before letting blacks into government. The African National Congress, whose exiled and imprisoned leaders rate highest with blacks, wants to nationalize even more industry as part of a "rapid and irreversible redistribution of wealth."

Says Sampie Terreblanche, an adviser to the Democratic Party and an advocate of immediate negotiations with the ANC: "It's completely the wrong time to talk about privatizing things. Why should we sell off property that in theory also belongs to the 75 percent who are black?"

Well, one reason might be that down that road lies the answer to South Africa's racial conflicts. Without a rich, powerful and intrusive state up for grabs, blacks and whites would have less to fear from each other, less reason to fight over control of the political levers. "The going mood here is about privatization, about growth, about freeing up the economy," says Riaan de Villiers, political editor of Leadership magazine. "The unspoken concomitant is that it will also lead to political freedom."

If so, that day is still a long way off. Economically, the 1980s have been a bad decade for blacks. Even taking the underground economy into account, black unemployment is 40 percent and destined to climb even higher, since half the black population is still of school age. Warns economist Ronald Bethlehem, "There is no need for sanctions to ensure a disaster a decade hence." Yet because of the debt crisis, the government must stomp the economic brakes whenever growth creeps above 3 percent. Anything more, it says, and a scramble among debtors and importers for foreign exchange could trigger hyperinflation. But even if it manages a steady 3 percent, the economy will still come up 8 million jobs short by 1999.

How long will South Africa have to wear this straitjacket? Until foreign bankers are no longer embarrassed to be seen in its company, according to de Kock. And the only way to win them back is through "adequate political and constitutional reform," he warned in a blunt speech to a Cape Town audience in May.

Abroad, antiapartheid activists trumpeted the statement as proof that sanctions were working. South Africans glumly interpreted it as a warning to expect no help from the economy as they grope for an exit from their national nightmare. "It's when you have more rats chasing less cheese that the conflict potential rises," says Ben Vosloo, head of the Small Business Development Corp.

Within a few blocks of Vosloo's office, in the rich suburbs north of Johannesburg, the evidence is everywhere. One by one, the homes are disappearing behind high walls, iron bars and guard dogs. Though the traditionally liberal residents applaud the opening of downtown to blacks, they are increasingly afraid of going there themselves, according to pollster Philip Frankel. A growing paranoia about security is sapping their reformist outlook, he warns. At the same time, many are convinced that violence no longer threatens the state, if it ever did. Not only did the regime handily quell the township riots of four years ago, but it drove the guerrillas of the African National Congress from their refuges in neighboring countries.

"We just went through the worst political violence in a century, and as far as I can tell, it was contained without using machine guns," says John Kane-Berman of the Institute of Race Relations. "The balance of military power is overwhelmingly on the side of the racist regime, as they call it."

Yet life goes on to a steady drumbeat of miscellaneous bloodshed. The papers carry regular updates of the body count in Natal, where thousands have died in battles between black radicals and Zulus. White supremacists and police vigilantes are suspects in a string of slayings of antiapartheid activists. A black cabdriver recalls being unable to eat for two days after receiving a summons to John Vorster Square, site of the Johannesburg police headquarters, where prisoners have been known to fall out of windows during interrogations.

In September, white voters will go to the polls and, if the pundits are right, give the National Party its shakiest mandate in 40 years. If a vote against the incumbents-for-life is a protest vote, then at least half the electorate is expected to join the ranks of the disgruntled. Among them are large numbers of white farmers, workers and petty bureaucrats, once the backbone of Nationalist support. Powered by disaffected voters' economic aches and racial fears, the Conservative Party, led by Andries Treurnicht, a former leader of the Broederbond, hopes to repeat the Nationalist upset of 1948. "Today, for the ordinary voter, the bread-and-butter issues have become very important again," says Casper Uys, a Conservative legislator and economic spokesman.

Yet the Conservatives offer little relief beyond cutting funds for black welfare and bashing big business. The party's platform of racial partitioning is hardly calculated to restore the flow of foreign capital. "We're not going to commit suicide to satisfy the outside world," concedes Uys, a farmer from near the Mozambique border. "So we'll simply have to sweat it out."

For those who would rather not, an option is the Democratic Party, created by the recent merger of three liberal groups. The union came at the prodding of big business, which is scared stiff of the pro-sanctions viewpoint prevailing in Europe after 1992. "Our economic problems can be solved by nothing short of getting a government acceptable in the eyes of the West," says Harry Schwarz, the party's economic spokesman.

That means sharing the ballot box with blacks, a recipe that most whites still find unappetizing, however much it may be sweetened with Western aid and the protections afforded by a bill of rights. But the party may still make a strong play for "New Nats," Afrikaner voters who have grown more liberal with affluence.

The only group without a simple prescription for the future is the ruling National Party. One of its new leader's first acts was to give the heave-ho to a rival who talked too explicitly about the future. De Klerk's own promise of a "totally changed South Africa" electrified voters not nearly as much as the invitations it brought from the White House and No. 10 Downing St. His election manifesto was equally strong on adjectives and weak on verbs. Yet de Klerk's ascension is being greeted enthusiastically by liberal businessmen, who are relieved to see the last of Botha and his "foulmouthed, bullyboy style," as one U.S. diplomat put it.

Though quick to distance themselves from the victim, businessmen were shaken by the treatment recently meted out to Christopher Ball, the outspoken chief of South Africa's biggest bank. After Botha badgered him publicly about the financing of an anti-apartheid ad, Ball quietly quit his job and slipped out of the country. "The episode had a dramatic effect on the business community," says de Villiers. "They saw what could happen if you stuck your neck out, so they scuttled back to base."

When Botha was ushered into retirement after a stroke in January, the relief was palpable. The Nationalists are the only game in town, and good relations pay off in contracts, tax breaks or getting a son excused from military duty in the townships. And whatever their political beliefs, most whites look to the National Party as the final guarantor of their personal safety.

For his part, de Klerk has already earned a reputation as a listener. His decision not to execute the Sharpeville Six, a group of black revolutionaries, earned the applause of businessmen. They worried that an execution would draw more sanctions at a moment when the balance of payments was hanging by a string.

Norton, the stock exchange president, looks forward to even more influence after the election, thanks to the expected strong showing of the Conservatives. "De Klerk is going to have a different political constituency in four months," he says. "He won't be able to go on out-righting the right."

When that day comes, industry bigwigs will be pushing an ambitious deal with the West. "If the world will reinvest in our country, we will get rid of apartheid and negotiate with real black leaders," says Raymond Ackerman, chairman of the nation's biggest supermarket chain. "Unless I'm being carried away, that seems to be the thinking of de Klerk."

Others are skeptical. Denis Worrall, a former ambassador to London and now a Democratic pooh-bah, charges that de Klerk put Botha up to his notorious 1985 Rubicon speech. A finger thrust in the eye of the world, the speech scuttled crucial negotiations over South Africa's debt. Others say de Klerk's new moderation is an attempt to outflank Finance Minister du Plessis, who ran second in the leadership balloting and is popular with the so-called *verligte* yuppies of the party's liberal wing.

But whatever the urgency of de Klerk's reformist impulses, he is no less bound by Botha's famous admonition to "adapt or die." That much, at least, has changed for good since Ben Vosloo, as a young economics graduate from Cornell University, visited another Nationalist leader, Prime Minister Hendrik Verwoerd, and got a lecture on the virtues of grand apartheid. "He was a professor of anthropology and sociology," Vosloo recalls, "and he thought the way to avoid conflict in Southern Africa was to unscramble the omelet. You took the black pins and put them on the black blocks, and the white pins on the white blocks."

That piece of social engineering lies in ruins. Only the redneck right still believes that millions of blacks living in and around the white cities are "temporary sojourners" from distant "homelands." Botha was the first to acknowledge that they were becoming the dominant consumers and workers in a single South African economy. Ten years ago, blacks unions won recognition from the government because factory owners could not think of an alternative to negotiating with them. By the middle of the next decade, says Kane-Berman, Johannesburg will find itself in the same boat.

"Nine out of every 10 rand spent in this city will come from black pockets," he says. "You've got a lily-white government that thinks it can run a great city while being accountable to a diminishing proportion of the people. You can't run a factory like that, and you won't be able to run Jo'burg like that." Once voter rolls are opened in the biggest city, he adds, the national rolls will not be far behind.

Not all whites consider that day worth waiting for. Half the country's 1.2 million English-speakers are said to carry British passports, and several thousand trickle out every year. More might leave if they could take their money with them, but exchange controls make that tricky. One U.S. cousin tells of receiving a parcel of uncut diamonds, and an epidemic of exchange fraud led to a recent shake-up at the central bank.

But many have roots too deep to pull out, and no place to go if they did. Thousands are refugees from Marxist takeovers in Mozambique, Angola and Zimbabwe. Antarctica is the next stop south. "I have no other fatherland than South Africa," says Casper Uys, the Conservative farmer. "If the worst happens, we'll simply have to fight it out."

Others believe the answer is to face the music soon, before a slow-motion economic disaster gradually robs whites of their bargaining power in the postapartheid world. One is Rudolf Gouws, the influential chief economist of Rand Merchant Bank Ltd. From his office near Sandton City, a luxurious development in suburban Johannesburg, he argues for a rapid march to democracy. He only hopes the period of socialist experimentation will be short.

"One has to bear in mind what blacks want," he says. "They see that whites have used the levers of power over the years to create a very comfortable situation for themselves. And in all of Africa, the way to riches has not been seen to be by business and individual effort but by jobs in government. This is the reality of South Africa as well."

Holman Jenkins Jr.

CHAPTER 32

*As with many African nations, the
economic fortunes of Ghana, the "Black
Star of Africa," sagged under the
weight of statism in the years following
its independence from Britain. But as
this September 12, 1988, case study
reported, Flight Lt. Jerry Rawlings was
willing to reverse course. That turned
his country once again into one of the
brighter lights of black Africa.*

GHANA ON THE ROAD TO A FREER ECONOMY

Perched among the dunes along the highway east of Accra, the capital of the West African nation of Ghana, is the target range for the nearby military academy. Here on a sunny morning in 1979, commuters left their cars along the road to watch the execution of three former heads of state and five other top military officers. It was a dramatic performance. After the first volley, only one of the victims remained standing: Gen. Akwasi Afrifa, the ruthless strongman who helped oust Ghana's first civilian government more than a decade earlier. "I'm not dead," the general reportedly roared. "More bullets!" The soldiers obliged, and the job was finished. Several miles away at the University of Ghana, where students had been watching on television, an exultant cheer arose. The celebration was echoed in many parts of the country.

Red hoods and execution posts were the calling card of Flight Lt. Jerry Rawlings, the charismatic 32-year-old pilot who had already been convicted once of plotting against the country's ruling generals. At his trial, Rawlings denounced his superiors for corrupting the military and destroying the nation's economy. Now, sprung from jail with the help of fellow mutineers, he seemed bent on throwing out the greedy old soldiers and replacing them with a gang of bloodthirsty younger ones.

Neighboring governments watched in horror. Two decades earlier, Ghana led colonial Africa on the path to independence. Kwame Nkrumah, the hallowed leader of the independence march, was featured on the cover of Life magazine, and Vice President Richard M. Nixon led a gaggle of dignitaries to celebrate the continent's coming of age. But Ghana's promise was quickly squandered by a parade of corrupt and incompetent leaders who pioneered the economic blunders that are a hallmark of modern Africa. Would the anarchy unleashed by Rawlings engulf its neighbors?

"The coup made people very nervous," recalls Deborah Pellow, an anthropologist from Syracuse University who was living in Accra. "What happens in Ghana often spreads to the rest of Africa. Here you had these teenage boys running around with submachine guns and a real sense of power. There was a feeling that the whole place was up for grabs."

Ghana today is anything but a pariah nation. Politicians, potentates and scholars come to marvel at its resurrected economy and praise its dictator. In a speech last year to representatives of the international banking community, Ronald Reagan singled out Ghana as one of the few bright lights in Africa. President Kenneth D. Kaunda of Zambia, in the self-appointed position of spokesman for the Third World, recently declared that "Ghana is our mecca."

Development agencies in the West tout Ghana as a showcase of cures for what ails the Third World. To prove their point, they have poured vast sums into the country over the past five years. "This experiment is sending a very important message," says Seung Choi, the World Bank's representative in Ghana. "It shows that the countries of Africa are coming to grips with reality."

Ghana's disastrous foray into central planning in the 1960s was copied by all but a handful of its African neighbors, and as a consequence the continent, possibly the richest in terms of agricultural and mineral resources, now lives on the international dole. In the last few years, as many as 25 countries have begun to mend their ways. Like Kaunda — at least before he abandoned his reforms to placate rioting copper miners — many attribute their change of heart to the dramatic turnaround in Ghana.

The unlikely hero is Rawlings, the self-professed revolutionary who is routinely photographed embracing the likes of Libya's Col. Muammar Qaddafi and Cuba's Fidel Castro. Six months after his first coup, he became a legend by stepping aside for a civilian government. Two years later, disgusted by his country's collapsing economy and the government's harassment of himself and his friends, he staged a fresh rebellion, this time promising to extend to the whole country the housecleaning he had administered to the military brass.

But the airman soon realized that his newly declared "holy war" would be going nowhere on an empty bank account. A close associate was dispatched to Libya and the Soviet bloc to fetch the blank check needed to rebuild the country's decaying infrastructure. The emissary came back empty-handed, and the economy continued to spiral downward. Swallowing his pride and ignoring the tantrums of the die-hard radicals in his entourage, Rawlings turned west for salvation. "It has been a wonderful transformation," says a Ghanaian businessman and ex-government official. "These people, when they came in, were really quite radical. Now that they've had to make things work, their ideas have changed. Of course, they don't like to admit this publicly."

"The options that confronted us were completely exhausted," says P. V. Obeng, the regime's top bureaucrat. "Most of the people involved in the revolution were relatively young, with some political idealism in their heads. The debate nearly broke the government." In the end, there was simply no choice but to negotiate with those bastions of imperialism, the International Monetary Fund and the World Bank.

With the surrender came swarms of Western economists, descending by the hundreds to offer advice on dismantling the state economic machinery, liberating the marketplace and attracting foreign investors. "The World Bank has been pushing a major overhaul of all kinds of institutions in Ghana," says Jon Kraus, a political scientist who has frequently visited and written about Ghana. "They really want to work it into a totally capitalist economy."

The government, enfeebled by the constant drain of talented people to better lives abroad, was overwhelmed. Few of the bank's recommendations have been rejected, and in many cases bank personnel have been responsible for drafting not only the proposals but the government's reponses to them as well. "The ministries have been denuded," says a Ghanaian management consultant. "So they have just swallowed everything, hook, line and sinker."

If the government's claim to authorship of the economic program rings hollow, it still earns full credit for gung-ho implementation. Thousands of bureaucrats are being woken up and shown the door, a gaping budget deficit is being narrowed, and the first cluster of state-owned enterprises are on their way to the auction block. Where the government once set prices for more than 6,000 commodities, it now controls only five. Where corrupt bureaucrats once controlled the price and availability of foreign currency, the marketplace now does the job. Thanks to such reforms, the local currency, the cedi, has undergone a nearly 7,500 percent devaluation against the dollar, a terrific blow to urban consumers but a godsend to farmers and other exporters.

"The government took some bold decisions, and really only a military regime could have done it," says James Phillips, head of the Ghana Employers' Association. "The civilian governments were never able to come to grips with the economic problem. They were too afraid of being overthrown." In return for its boldness, the regime was rewarded with an economic boom. Growth surged more than 6 percentage points in each of the past four years, inflation retreated from 125 percent to 30 percent a year, and exports nearly doubled.

For all the good news, the government is reluctant to advertise the capitalist thrust of its reforms. "Anti-Western rhetoric has sunk so deep into Africa," says George B. N. Ayittey, a Ghanaian economist who teaches at Bloomsburg University of Pennsylvania. "People are bombarded with it for years, so the intellectual climate is very hostile to the West." Over the past decade, the IMF emerged as a particular villain, thanks to the recipe of austerity it tried to serve up to many an African client.

In the early days, when the regime first began courting Western aid, the paranoia ran deep. Local representatives of the World Bank were instructed to fly secretly to neighboring Ivory Coast before telephoning the bank's Washington headquarters. When the deal was struck, it outraged the regime's more radical members, contributing to the smoldering resentments that have sparked several coup attempts. Altogether, at least nine plots have been foiled, thanks to the aptly named Maj. Courage Kwashigah, leader of the commando unit that looks after internal security. Many of the disgruntled leftists have been silenced or driven into exile.

Still, the regime bends over backward to avoid labeling itself. "Ours is not a capitalist or communist or socialist government," says Obeng, a mechanical engineer who was recruited by Rawlings from his job directing a private fishing company. "It is a government of people of varied experiences and persuasions."

Though "copybook socialism" has been discarded, he adds, the regime does not draw the lesson from the miserable record of the state-run industries. "It is true that at the time we took over, the state sector commanded the greatest proportion of assets and resources and that their contribution to production has been minimal," Obeng says. "But we don't jump to the conclusion that they are inefficient just because they are in the state sector." Instead, he attributes the superior performance of private companies to willingness to exploit the opportunities afforded by the black market.

Skeptics find plenty of other reasons to doubt the depth of the regime's conversion. Kwesi Botchwey, who as finance secretary is often credited with bringing the country to its senses, told one visitor that his program was modeled on Lenin's New Economic Policy, a scheme of forging temporary alliances with capitalists in order to build the foundation for socialism. And Ghana keeps cozy relations with communist governments from Nicaragua to Vietnam, and it takes special pleasure in thumbing its nose at the United States, even though this costs untold millions in lost foreign aid.

Observers worry that the regime's antics may rebound on the economic program. They are concerned about the country's image before foreign investors, who are desperately needed to give work and training to people left jobless by the shrinking state sector. "We worry whenever Rawlings puts down his script and ad-libs," says a businessman and strong supporter of the government. "He gets very emotional and it's a little disturbing. People get the impression that things are unstable."

Another worry is the government's failure to sell the program to the man in the street. Indeed, by continuing to mouth radical pieties and refusing to permit a free debate on the relative merits of capitalism and socialism, the regime may be inviting its own overthrow. Disgruntled intellectuals and entrenched civil servants are already muttering that Rawlings is really the two-faced puppet of international finance. That makes powerful ammunition for the countless coup plotters. "The scenario is not hard to imagine," says Ayittey, the economist. "Some leftist idiot overthrows Rawlings and says Ghana has been sold off to the imperialists. Everything the government is doing is thrown overboard, and that's it for Ghana."

That might be it for other would-be reformers too, say supporters of more Western lending. Sudan, Liberia, Zambia and Guinea have already backed off because of political resistance, and dozens of other regimes are waiting on the sidelines to see whether the new loans are worth the price of reforming their economies and endangering their own power.

BURNED OUT ON STATISM

Tetteh Quashie is the Thomas Edison of the Gold Coast. In 1879 he returned from the island of Fernando Poo, where he worked as a laborer, and with him came a pocketful of smuggled cacao seeds. He set up a nursery in Mampong and was soon traveling the hinterlands, distributing seedlings and advice to peasant farmers. Within a few decades, the British colony had become the world's largest exporter of cacao, from which cocoa comes.

"This amazing achievement," wrote an early historian, "was accomplished entirely by African farmers, with little help from the government beyond the provision of the necessary transportation system." Peasants pushed back the forest, planted seedlings and tended the young trees for the several years it took before they yielded their first crop. By 1938, the British government estimated, the trees were being grown on 300,000 farms of less than 5 acres.

On the other side of the Atlantic, African labor had been employed under duress to produce the exports that financed the development of a continent. In the Gold Coast, the same people were building a nation of their own through sweat and ingenuity. "Cocoa enabled the Gold Coast to pay for substantial imports of cement, machinery, flour, and so forth, commodities unknown to the country in the 1890s," write historians Peter Duignan and Louis H. Ganns. "Carriers and canoes gradually gave way to steam locomotives, trucks, and bicycles, and conditions of life underwent a massive transformation."

The same was true in other parts of Africa. Western-built roads and railways were opening up world markets to native farmers, producing rapid leaps in material welfare. Peanuts, palm oil and cocoa became staples of the West African economy as British railroads penetrated the hinterlands. Uganda, Kenya and other East African colonies became heavy exporters of coffee, tea, cotton and other crops when the railway link between Kampala and Mombasa, Kenya, was completed early this century.

West Africa's "golden bean" lived up to its name. When the Gold Coast was granted independence in 1957, it enjoyed a higher standard of living than Portugal. Ghana, as the new nation called itself, boasted the best roads, ports, schools and hospitals in Africa, a literate and skilled work force and a hefty $481 million in foreign reserves. No wonder it proudly proclaimed itself the Black Star of Africa. But by 1983 Ghana was hopelessly mired in debt, hunger was rampant and virtually the entire economy sat idle because of a shortage of imported parts and materials. Outside Accra, the capital, the roads were nearly impassable and the railways in disrepair. Bags of cacao rotted at regional depots, unable to reach the coast. Cacao exports, accounting for 60 percent of Ghana's crucial foreign exchange earnings, plummeted to less than one-third of their peak volumes in the mid-1960s.

Ghana's story replayed itself in many of the African nations founded on the remains of Europe's colonial empires. The enormous agricultural potential of a continent was squandered in pursuit of a pipe dream of instant modernity. Today, writes Robert H. Bates, author of a landmark study of agricultural policy in the new African states, "the collective optimism of the nationalist era has given way to a sullen and embittered recognition that the sacrifices of the many have created disproportionate opportunities for the few."

Kwame Nkrumah, the nationalist visionary who led Ghana's independence fight and the most admired African statesman of his time, did not live to see the fruition of his work. He died in 1972, having spent his retirement in Guinea, which had taken the unusual step of making him honorary cohead of state after he was overthrown in his own land. There he spent his last years still writing and preaching the ideas of a disastrous African socialism.

Twenty-five years before, after spending most of his adult life as a professional student in the United States and Great Britain, Nkrumah had returned to his native land to become the director of the United Gold Coast Convention. Founded by lawyers, businessmen, tribal bigwigs and leading cacao farmers, the group lobbied for a gradual transition to independence. Nkrumah had other ideas. Chanting the slogan "Self-government Now" and playing on the discontents of the so-called veranda boys, a growing corps of landless workers and students, he drummed up an angry mass movement. "If we get self-rule," he promised, "we'll transform the Gold Coast into a paradise in 10 years." Liking neither his rabble-rousing methods nor his radical ideas, the respectable burghers and farmers disowned Nkrumah, earning his undying distrust.

Nkrumah's big break came in 1951. Just before the elections for the new colonial Parliament, he was arrested by British authorities. The publicity won him the office of prime minister and release from jail. It was a token job, but he gladly took it, knowing that in the fullness of time a pleasant exterior would win him Britain's blessing to become the leader of an independent Gold Coast.

Similar men would come to power across the continent, often with the tacit support of the retreating colonials. Julius Nyerere, a dreamy-eyed schoolteacher with a degree from the University of Edinburgh, would take the helm in Tanzania and be called the "conscience of Africa" by Western admirers long after his socialist vision brought his country's economy to its knees. Guinea's Ahmed Sekou

Toure, a protege of the French Communist Party, would decline Charles de Gaulle's invitation to remain under France's wing, choosing instead a future of Albanian-style stagnation, which he would label "mental development." Only a few countries would be luckier. British-trained Jomo Kenyatta, who copied Nkrumah's leap from prison cell to prime ministership, would chart a capitalist path for Kenya. So would Felix Houphouet-Boigny of the Ivory Coast, eventually leaving next-door Ghana far behind in cacao output and per capita wealth.

"Seek ye the political kingdom," Nkrumah preached to this generation of leaders, "and all else will follow." It came to pass March 6, 1957, the day the Union Jack was hauled down and the red, yellow and green stripes of Ghana took its place. Nkrumah inherited more than a flagpole and some colonial architecture. Since the 1930s, the British had been abandoning their laissez-faire approach to the colony's internal life and trade. Eager to appease the growing clamor for progress and colonial self-rule, they raised taxes and began spending more on roads, schools and other trappings of modernity. With World War II came controls on prices, interest rates and rents, as well as the creation of the cocoa marketing board, which tapped into the savings of farmers to finance the purchase of war supplies. In the 1950s, as socialism triumphed at home, the British even set up an agency to nurture state-owned industries in the Gold Coast.

Peter T. Bauer, a free market economist and historian of British West Africa, regards the panoply of bureaucratic controls left behind by the colonials as imperialism's most damaging legacy. "Without these controls, and especially the state export monopolies, the prizes of political power would have been far less," he writes, "and there might have been less scope for large-scale organized oppression and brutality."

At the time, Bauer's was a minority view. Most of the big-name development experts gave their blessing to an expansive role for government. "Because of the many deficiencies in backward countries," said Gunnar Myrdal, the Swedish Nobel economics laureate, "the government will have to take over many of the functions which in the most advanced countries are left to private business."

Simply put, Myrdal and others believed that countries were poor because they were poor and that only a "big push" could lift them out of stagnation. Instead of "husbanding scarce resources of capital and entrepreneurship," argued economist Albert O. Hirschman, government planners should create "inducement mechanisms" to speed development. In practice, this meant borrowing huge sums to build industries overnight and then shielding them from competition with the use of high tariffs and subsidies.

The theory was highly congenial to Nkrumah and his colleagues throughout the developing world. It licensed borrowing and spending on a grand scale, and it practically demanded that leaders build huge projects to match their egos. Most of all, the big push gave the state enormous clout to reward its friends and punish its enemies.

The annual meetings of the Organization of African Unity, a group that Nkrumah helped found in 1963, became a favorite forum for their displays of extravagance. In 1963 the Ghanaian spent $17 million to build a conference center and host the first meeting. Since then, the tab has gone up. President Omar Bongo of Gabon spent $1 billion for the honor in 1977. Sierra Leone anted up $200 million in 1980.

Development was the soul of independence to Nkrumah, and he eagerly set about turning Ghana into an industrial giant. During the early years of independence, his approach was downright Rotarian, with most of the money going into roads, railways and ports, which greatly sped the growth of the country's exports. In the early 1960s, however, cocoa prices dipped and Nkrumah came to the end of his colonial cash inheritance, leaving him hard-pressed to find the dollars and sterling needed to finance his schemes.

The crisis only inspired him to greater ambitions. By borrowing heavily and taking strict control over the money generated by exports, he would not only maintain the development rate but step it up immeasurably, with the creation of state-run factories and farms. "The goal is the complete ownership of the economy by the state," he proclaimed. The pattern was dutifully copied by his acolytes. "Virtually all of the African nations continued to pursue Nkrumah-type statist policies of centralization, state enterprises and price controls," according to Ghanaian economist George B. N. Ayittey, who now teaches at Bloomsburg University of Pennsylvania. "The results have been economic ruin."

"It was a dismal history," recalls James Phillips, who was recruited to tame Nkrumah's menagerie of white elephants a few years later. "Many of the state enterprises were run as extensions of the social services. They were expected to absorb the unemployed and provide jobs for relatives of government officials. There wasn't much business sense."

Tony Killick, author of an exhaustive study of Nkrumah's development efforts, provides examples:

• The Bibiana gold mine kept on several hundred employees into the mid-1970s, even though the last ounce of gold-bearing ore had been scraped from the deposit in 1968. The cost was five times what it would have taken to pay every worker the minimum wage for staying at home.

• With the help of newfound friends in the Soviet bloc, Nkrumah built a state-of-the-art mango cannery. Only later was it realized that supply was limited to a few trees growing in the wild and that it would take five to seven years to bring newly planted ones to fruit. Even then, Ghanaians had very little appetite for mangos, and the plant's capacity would exceed the entire world trade in the fruit.

• Nkrumah created a host of state farms, which he believed would liberate the socialist state from dependence on a hostile peasantry. But even with hundreds of imported tractors and tons of fertilizer, they managed less than half the yield per acre of the peasant farmer.

Overall, Killick writes, the performance of the state enterprises was abysmal even by the standards of other socialist and mixed economies. In Nkrumah's last year, they operated at a feeble 29 percent of capacity, and only four out of 53 earned a profit, despite the virtual monopolies many of them enjoyed in their respective markets.

To keep these industrial cripples stumbling along, the government created a raft of price and import controls designed to keep wages and production costs low, block competing imports and make sure that the state got first dibs on available foreign exchange. In fact, the controls were managed so badly that many factories sat idle for months or years at a stretch waiting for parts or materials. Meanwhile, food prices skyrocketed as farmers abandoned fields or turned to the black market and smuggling to earn a decent income. In a pattern that was reproduced throughout Africa, Bates says, "the market became the setting for the struggle between the peasant and the state."

It was a battle that neither side won, especially in the case of cacao farmers, whose only access to their overseas customers was through the state-run Cocoa Board. Like most of his neighbors, Nkrumah did not hesitate to exploit this power. Three years before independence Nkrumah froze the price paid to growers and then ratcheted it steadily downward thereafter. By the time Nkrumah was given his walking papers, the government was shoveling 75 percent of the proceeds of the cacao crop into the ravenous maw of the state. Though farmers kept picking the beans for the pittance they earned, they no longer found it worthwhile to do the weeding and replanting. From the mid-1960s onward, the annual crop got smaller and smaller.

The pattern repeated itself wherever governments usurped the profits of farmers. During the late 1970s and early 1980s, Tanzanian producers retained less than half the world price for their coffee, cotton, cashews and tobacco, and output fell by 35 percent. Such practices explain why Africa, a continent peopled by 300 million farmers, must import 45 percent of its food. Only countries such as Kenya and the Ivory Coast, which permit farmers to enjoy the proceeds from their labor, remain exceptions to the trend of declining production and deepening poverty.

Nkrumah might be forgiven for not noticing the damage such policies were doing. He was busy mutating into a semidivine figure, adopting the title of *osagyefo*, meaning "victor in war." Giant posters of his face began to blot out the scenery, and his palace guard was turned into a private army, loyal only to him. Criticism seldom breached the circle of toadies that surrounded the self-proclaimed Lenin of Africa. "Toward the end of his rule there was little of the pragmatist left in him," Killick writes.

Along with the leftward march and the deepening cult of personality had come political repression. Within a year of winning independence, Nkrumah beefed up the preventive detention law inherited from the British and began filling the jails with dissidents. In 1960 his party won a rigged referendum that junked the country's mushy parliamentary system in favor of a strong executive concentrating power in Nkrumah's own hands. Four years later he outlawed the opposition altogether, turning Ghana into a one-party dictatorship. Most of these moves were aimed at silencing the opposition of businessmen and farmers who balked at his rabid spending and authoritarian rule.

Throughout Africa, economic catastrophe has proceeded hand-in-hand with tyranny. Since 1960, the continent's food production has declined by 20 to 25 percent, while its population grew steadily at 3 percent a year. The result: hunger, debt and retreating standards of health — and political upheaval. In the years since Ghana's independence, there have been more than 100 changes of government in Africa. Only five were accomplished though constitutional means. In 1966 Ghana's hated capitalists found allies among older, British-trained generals, who resented Nkrumah's plan to displace them with Soviet-bred subordinates. A coup, allegedly helped along by the CIA, was staged while Nkrumah was flying to Hanoi to bring peace to Vietnam. The people, fed up with food shortages, inflation and heavy taxes, said good riddance.

The military and civilian regimes that followed lacked the

courage, the good sense or the longevity to shuck the budgetary mill-stone of the state sector and restore incentives for cacao farmers and other private entrepreneurs. From the late 1960s until 1983, the economy shrank at a rate of 1 or 2 percent a year.

Nkrumah's other great legacy was the near-total corruption of everyday life. As his bureaucracy spread its tentacles over the econ-omy, monumental opportunities for graft were discovered, creating the model of the modern socialist kleptocracy. Government became a form of organized crime. People in positions of power bought state-produced goods or imports at controlled prices and then reaped for-tunes by reselling them on the black market. "You could become a millionaire overnight just by laying your hands on an import license," says Seung Choi, the World Bank's resident representative in Ghana.

"There was a rampage for easy wealth," recalls a native business executive. Local buyers for the state-run Cocoa Board issued worth-less chits to farmers and kept the cash for speculating in the black market. One of Nkrumah's top ministers charged a 10 percent com-mission for issuing import licenses, and the *osagyefo* himself was reported to have taken $30 million to comfort him in retirement. In the hands of Gen. Ignatius Acheampong, who ruled during much of the 1970s, graft became an art form. He contracted loans with shady offshore finance companies in the government's name, pocketed the proceeds and left the taxpayer to honor the IOU.

Illegal trading became the only lucrative activity. "People were chasing fewer and fewer goods, buying and selling," says economist Ayittey. "Nobody was producing anything." Of the producers who stuck it out, most either had to find domestic buyers on the black market or smuggle their goods across the border to make a living. In 1986 as much as 20,000 tons of Ghana's cacao was sold in the Ivory Coast while Togo managed an impressive $90 million in gold exports even though the nearest mine was across the border in Ghana.

Dozens of African nations came to similar grief. President Mobu-tu Sese Seko of Zaire, the kingpin of a government that is notorious for theft, enjoys a fortune estimated at $5 billion to $8 billion. In the 28 years of Mobutu's reign, the real income of the average Zairian has shrunk almost 90 percent, and his government owes $5.4 billion to foreign banks. When once-prosperous Uganda disintegrated under madman Idi Amin, people simply left their homes and jobs and wandered into the jungle to live on wild bananas. Across the con-tinent, avaricious states drove farmers to stop producing for money and settle for growing only what it takes to feed their families.

Because it rations scarce goods among those not well-connected enough to get them at fixed prices, the black market is a vital escape hatch from self-destroying official economies. "If it weren't for the underground entrepreneurs, there would be more hunger, unemployment and misery," Peruvian novelist Mario Vargas Llosa has observed of the role of black markets in the Third World. "Thanks to them, the poor can work, travel and have a roof over their heads."

It was left to the military regime of Flight Lt. Jerry Rawlings to prove the truth of this proposition in Ghana. Outraged by epidemic corruption and rocketing prices, he declared war on *kalabule*, local slang for illicit trading. Soldiers zealously enforced price controls with beatings and shootings, and bulldozers rolled over Accra's famous open-air Makola Market, fingered by the regime as a hotbed of economic crime.

The shortages became acute. Goods were buried, destroyed or smuggled out of the country by traders who feared the soldiers but refused to sell at a loss. Hunger began to touch even those who had previously been immune. One Western diplomat later recalled the pathetic gratitude with which a Ghanaian university professor accepted an invitation to an embassy dinner. By the time a chastened Rawlings repented and sought the forgiveness of the international financial community, the Black Star of Africa had joined the ranks of the world's most abjectly impoverished nations.

A CRUSADER'S BITTER PILL

Television was not kind to Gen. Ignatius Acheampong, and maybe that was a reason so few mourned his violent passing. "His oratory was stumbling," wrote one reviewer. "He usually read his speeches, bobbing his eyes distractingly up and down during his television appearances."

Jerry Rawlings, the young pilot who recently overtook his hapless predecessor as Ghana's longest-serving military dictator, labors under no such handicap. His inspired eloquence and telegenic style, honed in frequent whirlwind speaking tours, make him hugely popular in a country where entertainment choices are limited. "Think of Adolf," says a devoted fan with a laugh over beers at a company bar in the dusty mining town of Obuasi. "But only the mannerisms."

Obuasi, sitting on the country's richest gold deposits, attracts more than its share of the flight lieutenant's eloquence. In May, showing up unexpectedly for the unveiling of a new processing plant, he gave a stern lecture on the evils of pilfering and loafing. On previous trips he had hectored the workers about everything from personal hygiene to the importance of not having more children than a miner's paycheck will support.

"Rawlings is a great communicator," says Bill Hussey, the British manager of Ashanti Goldfields Corp. "And he's saying things that people need to hear." One of the company's Ghanaian executives, an educated man with no love for the previous military governments, has a simpler explanation: "Rawlings is God-given."

The dictator and the gold mine have been good to each other. A decade ago, the mine stood at death's door, a victim of the crippling shortages that plagued the economy. Today it is enjoying a dramatic resurrection, thanks to the red carpet the government has rolled out for foreign investors. "Fifteen or 20 percent of Ghana's foreign exchange earnings are coming from right here," says Hussey, sweeping his hand over a map of the tunnels that permeate the surrounding hillsides. "This government has bills to pay, food and fuel to buy. We ship out our product every week, and the money is in the bank by the following Wednesday."

It is another example of the curious alliance between a fire-eating revolutionary and his pro-capitalist bankrollers. Though he is chief cheerleader for his country's economic revival, lauded abroad as a deathbed conversion to capitalism, he neither blames Ghana's problems on socialism nor credits its recovery to capitalism. Ghana's resurrection, he tells his people, is a triumph over "bad men," not bad ideas. "He doesn't look at Ghana's history as the failure of a state-run economy," says Donald I. Ray, a political scientist and author of a study on the Rawlings revolution. "He sees Kwame Nkrumah" — Ghana's first president and the creator of its socialist system — "as having been betrayed by the people around him."

The son of a Scottish druggist and an African mother, Rawlings was educated by missionaries at the elite Achimoto School in Accra and once thought of becoming a priest. Instead, he joined the air force and became a top-notch pilot. Only years later did he rediscover his original calling — while in the dock for plotting a mutiny against the country's military rulers. His courtroom eloquence so inspired his fellow soldiers that they freed him from prison and made him the leader of a moral crusade.

Under the generals, Ghana had become a place where top officers and senior bureaucrats built private mansions with public money, and where young women strode through the ministries exercising "bottom power," the trading of sexual favors for lucrative import licenses. "These mistakes, these rapes, are becoming part of us,"

Rawlings warned, as he executed the generals and returned to barracks. "We are accepting them as the norm."

On the last day of 1981, he made his second coming. Rawlings and a group of soldiers overthrew the scandal-plagued President Hilla Limann after government agents reportedly tried to take Rawlings for a one-way car ride. Tipped off in advance, Rawlings later told a visitor, he had foiled his would-be assassins by declining to escape through an unlocked car door and invite a bullet in the back. The episode convinced him that the moral rot had only worsened under civilian leadership. "You had been manipulated into killing your own moral fiber," he later told his people, "as a result of which justice would suffer and the economic pace would be slow."

At first, Rawlings's strategy for restoring honest stewardship and economic growth consisted of executions and long jail terms, meted out with little concern for judicial niceties. Businessmen, civil servants and traders chewed their nails and scanned the papers each day to see if their names appeared among the lists of those summoned before the kangaroo courts, known officially as defense committees. "They became ghastly vigilante groups," recalls Deborah Pellow, an American anthropologist living in Ghana at the time. "Anybody with money was suspect." Only with the unveiling of the regime's economic recovery program, dictated largely by Western development lenders, did the airman's ax finally strike the roots of corruption. Dangling a billion-dollar carrot, the bankers lured the regime into pruning and disciplining a state run amok.

Money to rebuild the roads and railways and put the country's finances back on an even keel would be doled out only as the regime met targets for cutting the public payroll, trimming back social services and withdrawing subsidies from pampered groups. If past governments met their bills by printing money with wild abandon (and awarding themselves kickbacks for letting out the contract to private printers abroad), the new regime would be taught the value of a cedi, the country's currency. Last year, it paid back 6.7 billion of them, roughly $40 million, to its own central bank.

But nothing did more to purge corruption and restore honesty to government than the abolition of currency controls and most price controls. With the closing of the gaping disparity between the shriveling official economy and the booming illegal one went much of the opportunity for graft. Once again, the change of heart was spurred by the advice, and money, of Ghana's new Western development partners.

The government denies that international lenders were behind its shift from terror to reform. "Our success is not because the IMF and the World Bank have been pumping us with money," says P. V. Obeng, chairman of the Committee of Secretaries and the regime's top bureaucrat. "These steps were seen as necessary by us to introduce discipline into our affairs. Of course, we have welcomed their advice on the extent and timing of the adjustment."

On a crucial question, Ghana has kept its own counsel: the future of the Ghana Cocoa Board, the agency that devastated the country's biggest industry by usurping the profits of growers. To keep the farmers out of harm's way, the World Bank wants the board to disappear. So far, though, the government agrees only to guarantee farmers at least 50 percent of the world price and to divest some of the board's sidelines.

"Cocoa gives Ghana about 60 percent of its foreign exchange," says Kwame Owusu, the board's chief executive. "Should we let the private man decide when he wants to sell his cocoa? How does the Ghana government get the money to let the nation live?"

Yet another collision is brewing over the plan to privatize state corporations. Thanks to the plummeting currency and an International Monetary Fund pact that sharply tightens screws on domestic credit, few Ghanaians may be among those bidding for the first batch of companies. Suspicious of foreign investors and ambivalent about disowning the legacy of Ghana's socialist misadventure, the government is chafing under pressure from the World Bank to get on with the sales.

Despite these discordant notes, the Western-style nostrums have improved Ghana's economy. Production is up sharply across the board, and the economy is surging into its sixth straight year of growth. What is more, the marketplace is delivering on the key plank in Rawlings's revolutionary platform: economic justice for those who work and produce.

In the past, the farmer was plundered to provide city dwellers with cheap food, free education, subsidized water and electricity, and jobs in money-losing factories. Now the balance is shifting, and many of those who fled to the urban areas are drifting back to the farm. Like stick figures in an economics text, they are responding to the new incentives created by the marketplace. But not all of them have a hymn to capitalism in their hearts as they do it. Take the educated son of a diplomat. Normally he would have stepped right into a cozy career in the civil service. "But there are no jobs," he says. "So now I have a little business exporting lobsters to Switzerland."

The once-coveted government jobs are not looking so good either.

Inflation and the regime's hard line on wage increases mean that a bureaucrat's paycheck no longer goes far. "To be frank, I am fed up," says a junior official and 15-year veteran of a ramshackle ministry. "I have a wife and a child, and my money doesn't even last until the end of the week." His dream is to become an exporter of pineapples, the latest fashion fruit on European sideboards. Because his parents are farmers, laying his hands on land is not the problem. What he lacks is capital to buy seedlings, fertilizer and equipment. "I have done a feasibility study," he says. "I can double my investment with my first crop. But where do I get the money?"

Where indeed. "For the first time in years, young people are showing an interest in farming," says Commodore Steve Obimpeh, who left his job as chief of the Ghanaian navy to run the Agriculture Ministry. "The loan requirement is not high, just enough for a few bags of fertilizer, but the banks are unwilling to supply it." The lack of credit hurts not just would-be farmers but the whole range of entrepreneurs. "Private companies are contracting," says James Phillips, chairman of the Ghana Employers' Association. "Many are cutting their payrolls with voluntary retrenchment schemes." That is worrisome to the World Bank, which counts on the private sector to soak up those tossed out of government jobs. "Nobody wants to build a factory with money borrowed at 30 percent," frets Seung Choi, the World Bank's representative in Ghana. "That's a good way to kill yourself."

There are two reasons for the credit crunch. One is an IMF agreement that imposes limits on lending not only in hopes of keeping inflation down but also to cure the banks of some very bad habits. In the past, they were gleeful participants in the general economic riot. Sweetheart loans, sloppy credit analysis and outright fraud were the order of the day. This, coupled with the rapid economic decompression of the early 1980s, saddled them with portfolios that consist of 65 percent bad debt. Instead of building up capital to cover the bum loans, the banks pretended the loans were still performing and used them as the accounting basis for granting still more credit. The IMF-imposed ceilings are meant to encourage the banks to set aside reserves against the bad loans and pursue deadbeats with greater diligence.

Credit is also short because banks have trouble attracting what little savings individuals and businesses are managing to accumulate. One reason is interest rates that are sometimes lower than inflation, but another is loss of faith in the financial system, a legacy of the regime's anticorruption jag of 1982. For example, confidence was badly shaken when Rawlings unexpectedly closed the banks and borders and announced the withdrawal of the 50-cedi note from circulation. The idea was to wipe out the hoards of large denomination bills suspected to be in the hands of illegal traders. "They were trying to get the big guys," recalls Pellow, the anthropologist. "But they ended up screwing the farmers," who could not get to the bank in time to redeem their notes. Worse, from the point of view of many depositors, were the black market witch-hunts. Goon squads were dispatched to rifle through bank files, and people whose balances drew notice were hauled before investigators to explain themselves. Many fled the country, and many others were jailed after they were unable to meet huge bills for back taxes and penalties. The episodes left a deep-rooted suspicion.

But the problem goes beyond distrust of the banks. The private investor and entrepreneur have been regularly vilified ever since Nkrumah hijacked the colony's nascent independence movement in the late Forties from the business leaders and lawyers who had organized it. "Nkrumah distrusted the African entrepreneur," says Phillips, a Cabinet member in Nkrumah's government." He saw him as a political threat. Some of that has lingered."

Rawlings carries a lot of the same baggage. During the trial after the failure of his first coup plot, he laid out a platform that included the expulsion of Lebanese businessmen; and his regime's early assaults on merchants and other traders — many were publicly flogged — suggested an instinctual loathing for private enterprise. Not surprisingly, the investment community has been slow to raise its shell-shocked head. Most investing is still the hit-and-run variety, such as importing and reselling consumer goods. Little money is going into plant and equipment. "I don't see any capitalists in Ghana," observed the late Imoru Egala, an old Nkrumah crony. "They're all living on overdrafts!"

No fan of Western capitalism, Nkrumah still found it useful to deal with foreign investors, who were more likely to remain aloof from local politics and were willing to forward his pet development schemes. Similar ambivalence is apparent in the Rawlings regime. At the prodding of the World Bank, it is cautiously unfurling a welcome mat for investors from overseas.

In 1981, President Limann introduced a bill to liberalize restrictions on foreign investment and then in June trotted off to London to recruit takers. Rawlings accused him of "bending over backwards to satisfy the multinational companies that are out to plunder our resources." Now his own government is undertaking its second revi-

sion of the tax code and other rules in hopes of luring the same foreign money men. It has also labored to clear a heavy backlog of outgoing payments for foreign investors and companies.

Still, the response has been underwhelming. "The foreign investor
is cagey and must be coaxed," says a local consultant. "He has heard
the statement, but he is still waiting to see the deed."

One deed that remains largely undone is the streamlining of procedures. With mail, phones and transportation all notoriously unreliable, jumping through paperwork hoops can absorb more time
than the business is worth. Worse, though, is the feeling that investors
are not really welcome. In a recent edition of the People's Daily
Graphic newspaper, the official in charge of recruiting foreign
money complained that "most Ghanaians view private investment
as exploitive, cheating and not in the interest of the country." This,
he said, was a serious hindrance to getting his job done. His attitude
has not yet filtered through to the rest of the regime. Prominently
featured in the same issue was a high official rattling on in the old
way about "the struggle against neo-colonial domination and the
associated mechanisms of exploitation."

Such rhetoric is the despair of those concerned with lifting the
economy out of the doldrums. But the regime insists that investors
will be protected, and even offers to write its promises into treaties
with other governments. "We have established that we welcome foreign participation," Obeng says. "Of course, there are those who will
only invest when Ghana says there is a free-for-all. We can never
answer the credibility gap for them."

One of the few hardy souls to take up the regime's invitation is
Allan Chou, a Taiwanese businessman who bubbles with confidence
in Ghana's future. While visiting friends five years ago, he decided
that what a poor people living in a tropical climate needed was a very
inexpensive frozen snack, and the Poki was born. Now several
garage-sized factories pump out plastic pouches filled with frozen
fruit juice to the tune of several million units a month. Vendors ped-
dle them on sweltering streets, beaches and at sporting events for the
equivalent of a few pennies each. "It is no money," he says, laughing.
"The children call them *Esi Wano* — In Your Mouth."

Chou is now putting real money where his *wano* is. Like most visitors, he noticed that Ghana is a big graveyard of rusting trucks, tractors and heavy machinery, the legacy of Nkrumah's misbegotten
development schemes. Like few visitors, he bothered to learn that the
locals pay twice the world price for steel. The result is the Wahome
steel mill, a blue and white complex rising above the port city of Tema.

The project will cost about $8 million, raised from several Taiwanese investors, one local businessman and a World Bank affiliate that lends to private industry in developing countries. Before he started, Chou dispatched a team to survey the scrap potential of the countryside. It came back with a figure of 500,000 tons, enough to keep the plant humming around the clock for 10 years. Chou expects to recover his investment in two.

Chou has no qualms about staking his future in Ghana, even though Asian businessmen have been targets of official persecution in other parts of Africa. His wife and children are happy in Ghana, he says, and they look forward to making it their home. He also says the regime has made him feel welcome, though that did not prevent it from expropriating part of the Wahome property. Did it compensate the company? "That's not how this government operates," says a Taiwanese associate.

Such strong-arm tactics are still a regime favorite, especially when domestic critics get too uppity. Though Rawlings sometimes laments what he calls the "culture of silence," it is largely the regime's own doing. In 1978, medical and legal groups were powerful enough to force the military to put Acheampong out to pasture. But since the witch trials of the early Rawlings years, the doctors and lawyers have kept quiet. "Everybody is frightened of the soldiers," says a local executive. "They are still picking on people."

One group that has not been silent is university students. Enthusiastic supporters of the regime in more bloodthirsty times, they became indignant when asked to help out by paying a small part of their tuition, room and board. Few tears were shed by ordinary people when the regime used student protests against the fees as an excuse to shut the universities and send the students packing. "You can't justify subsidies to people who are already privileged to be at university when primary schools in the rural areas don't even have pencils, paper or competent teachers," says a Rawlings adviser.

Only one group remains powerful and independent enough to challenge the regime's policies: the Trade Unions Congress. With almost 700,000 members and shielded by laws in the United States, Britain and West Germany that can make life uncomfortable for governments that suppress labor movements, it has steadily resisted most of the economic reforms.

"The IMF package has brought untold hardship to a sizable figure of our membership," says Acting Secretary General S. O. Nunoo-Quaye. Not only have thousands lost their jobs, but many have seen their standard of living eroded by inflation and devaluation. Since 1985, the purchasing power of the minimum wage has dwindled to about 50 cents a day. Control over wages is one of the few powers the government has not surrendered to the marketplace, and even healthy companies, such as the local branch of Britain's Unilever PLC, are routinely denied permission to raise salaries. Since most workers are still employed in government factories, the regime is eager to smother any hope of higher pay. "Now that they are leaving prices alone," says J. O. Tetteh, head of the union organization's economic and research bureau, "the government is trying to use wages to control inflation."

Urbanites dominate political life in Ghana and the rest of Africa, thanks to their ability to cripple the state with strikes and demonstrations. No such power has been available to peasant farmers. The history of independent Africa is largely a tale of urban freeloaders trying to live it up at the expense of rural producers.

Rawlings makes no bones about his contempt for this past. He describes his own capital city as "parasitic," and he frequently tours the remote farming districts that were largely ignored by his predecessors. "If we say that farmers are the backbone of the country," says Obimpeh, the agriculture secretary, "then they must have a way to contribute their ideas to government."

Democracy is being approached warily by the regime that overthrew Ghana's last elected president. And more democracy does not mean the regime intends to renounce the African habit of making the economy the servant of the state. By balking at the proposal to disband the Cocoa Board, the government gave a clear signal that there are limits to how much economic control it will give up in order to get Western loans.

"Rawlings doesn't want a Reagan-type economy," says Ray. "What he is trying to do is build an infrastructure that he can make use of. The irony of the IMF-World Bank program is that, though by a different route, we are still talking about a government-planned, government-coordinated economy."

Holman Jenkins Jr.

PART 10

ROADS TO RUIN

CHAPTER 33

*Recycled 1970s petrodollars ultimately
turned into a trillion dollars in Third
World debt. By the 1980s, many countries
were saying they were unable to service
their borrowing, let alone make payments
on principal. Why not? In large measure,
as this August 31, 1987, article reported,
because the loans went not for productive
investment, but to finance consumption
and grand but economically preposterous
development projects.*

DEBTORS AND BANKERS
IN A WOEFUL CHORUS

Open, Act 2 of the trillion-dollar Gotterdammerung of Third World debt: In February, Brazil says it will not make interest payments on the $67 billion it owes to foreign banks. Ecuador does likewise. In May, Citicorp, the largest banking company in the United States, boosts its loan-loss reserves from $2 billion to $5 billion, enough cash to cover about a 25 percent loss on its Latin America loans. Other large U.S. banks follow. It is their first open admission that a good chunk of the loans are bad.

By the end of 1985, Brazil's total foreign debt had hit $106 billion. Mexico owed nearly $100 billion. The Philippines, at $26 billion, owed an amount equal to 82 percent of its gross national product. Today, many large debtors are several billion dollars in arrears on interest payments.

The U.S. banks found themselves heavily exposed, as few Latin American governments, deeply indebted to the commercial banks, were able to service their debts. In Africa governments owe money primarily to the international lending agencies — the International Monetary Fund, set up by Western governments after World War II to help countries over short-run financial difficulties, and its sister, the World Bank, which makes loans to aid development. Prospects for the African debtors' self-sufficiency are at best grim. "The situation is getting more difficult as time is going by, partly because time is going by," warns Jean Baneth, director of international economics for the World Bank.

"You know, Fidel Castro is the guy who understands the situation better than anybody," notes Gifford Combs of Pacific Financial Research, an investment consulting firm. "His slogan is, 'The debts can never be repaid and must be forgiven.' That sums it up in a nutshell." Forgiven by whom is the question.

What now appears to have been trillion-dollar madness on the part of creditors and debtors alike had as its trigger the first oil shock, in 1973. When the Organization of Petroleum Exporting Countries suddenly raised prices, enormous wealth poured into the Middle East from consumers all over the world. They suddenly had to spend more on oil and less on everything else. OPEC countries accumulated vast pools of this cash, which came to be known as petrodollars.

The oil countries, neither able nor willing to spend all the money, deposited much of it in safe Western banks. The banks, because they had to pay interest on the new petrodollar deposits, were compelled to lend the petrodollars out to earn interest.

And who better to lend money to than the developing countries of the Third World? The outlook in Latin America appeared bright. Growth was robust, especially compared with the mature economies of the United States and Europe. The developing world was thought to be poised for an industrial revolution.

Even more important, the governments of these countries were eager to borrow. Many, such as Brazil, were also hit by the oil shock. Rather than cut government spending in reaction to higher oil prices, governments borrowed to maintain consumption.

The petrodollar recycling was "a shell game," explains Nick Eberstadt, a visiting fellow at Harvard University's Center for Population Studies. "The banks loaned to the Third World, the Third World bought oil, OPEC got its money and gave it back to the banks. The banks got their fees and interest, OPEC got its price. It looked like manna from heaven."

Bank loan officers roamed the Third World pressing their wares. Walter Wriston, then chairman of Citicorp, assured everyone that sovereign nations could not go bankrupt. And at that time, borrowing simply made sense for one key reason: inflation.

It all started as far back, some say, as the 1960s. President Lyndon Johnson, who printed money to pay for a shooting war in Vietnam and a metaphorical one on poverty, laid the groundwork for an inflationary buildup. President Richard Nixon's policies aggravated those underlying pressures, as did President Jimmy Carter's, until inflation finally exploded with the oil shocks in the 1970s.

That distorted normal price relationships. Prices on inflation-tracking commodities such as minerals and food products, which account for a large share of Third World exports, soared. Servicing the debt would be a breeze. Real interest rates, adjusted for inflation, went negative. If a government could borrow at 8 percent, for example, and inflation was at 10 percent, the real interest rate was minus 2 percent. Loans were like free money. Dollars borrowed today could be paid back tomorrow in cheaper dollars, as inflation ate away their value.

The fact that debtors were in large measure spending the money they borrowed on consumption meant that they were not investing it. And consumption, unlike investment, earns no return that can later service debt. In some respects, the Third World debt picture began to resemble a gigantic international Ponzi scheme, a classic swindle in which early investors are paid off with money provided by later ones who receive the promise that still later investors will take care of them. Nothing productive ever happens. How would these countries service the debt they were accumulating? Perhaps by more borrowing.

What is more, many Third World governments had banned foreign equity investment, in which an investor risks his money in a venture in return for an ownership stake. The equity investor — for example, a stockholder in a U.S. corporation — gets dividends only if the venture succeeds. By banning such investment, these governments had to rely almost exclusively on borrowing to finance development. But loans are risky because, unlike equity funds, a loan accrues interest regardless of the borrower's ability to pay.

Governments grew top-heavy with debt. In Latin America the debt-to-equity ratio grew from a healthy 1-to-1 in the 1960s to a precarious 9-to-1 in the 1970s. Like a business with a skewed balance sheet, the debtors found themselves in trouble when recession hit and their incomes dried up. The interest payments were due, recession or no. "With the blinding clarity of hindsight," wrote Citicorp's Wriston in 1984, "we bankers, along with many others, made a mistake in not recognizing the seriousness of this structural defect, which would become readily apparent at the advent of a worldwide recession."

And recession came. A deep one, deepened by previous inflationary distortions. Prices that had shot upward now plunged. In 1979 the Federal Reserve Board began squeezing out inflation, which was threatening to spiral up out of control. As the Fed throttled money growth, real interest rates turned positive, then soared. The turn-around was astonishing: Debtors went from facing real interest rates of minus 8 percent to facing real rates of positive 16 percent.

The bulk of Third World bank debt carried floating interest rates; unlike fixed rates, floating rates rise and fall with market rates. Debt service costs surged. At the same time, the money to pay them evap-orated: Commodity prices collapsed in the disinflation and for most countries few other sources were available. The result was disaster. In 1981 Poland told its creditors it could not make interest payments. In 1982 Mexico announced the same. The inauspicious Act 1 of the drama was well under way.

Fearing an international bank collapse and a Depression-style worldwide economic contraction, the Federal Reserve infused money into the banking system to help banks maintain reserves. International lending agencies stepped in with emergency loans to Mexico. The commercial banks rescheduled its debt, postponing repayment, so the country could avoid default.

Then the banks rescheduled Argentina's debt and Brazil's debt and Chile's debt and the Philippines' debt and Nigeria's debt and on and on and on at Wagnerian scale. When the debt crisis broke, most everybody hoped it was only temporary — a liquidity problem, a temporary cash squeeze caused by such temporary setbacks as high interest rates and the economic downturn. Over the long haul, the debtors would be able to pay. They just needed a little more money to get back on their feet. Debtor governments promised to make pay-ments and to change economic policies. In return the banks stretched out principal payments, made interest rate concessions and lent more.

As time went on, the banks stretched out not just principal but interest payments. From 1983 to 1986 total reschedulings reached almost $250 billion. Third World debt, in the meantime, swelled to more than $1 trillion.

Nothing seemed to work. Reschedulings failed. Postponing pay-ments got debtors only deeper and deeper in debt as interest on old loans mounted. World economic recovery failed, despite hopes that it would revive debtor nation exports and thus help them make their payments. Interest rates plummeted, but even at the better rates, the debtors remained in trouble.

So did the banks. By the end of 1984 outstanding loans to four Latin American debtors — Argentina, Brazil, Mexico and Venezuela — accounted for 160 percent of Citicorp's reserves and equity.

The relationship of a bank's capital (the amount by which its assets exceed its liabilities) to its total debt is a critical one. Bank assets include loans (because they are money owed the bank), reserves (money on hand) and equity (stockholder investment). Bank liabilities include money owed depositors. If a large enough chunk of the debt is defaulted on, then assets will drop below liabilities. The bank will be insolvent. At Manufacturers Hanover Trust Co., loans to just those four debtors came to 206 percent of bank capital; at Chase Manhattan Corp., 169 percent; at BankAmerica Corp., 145 percent. It was clear that just a couple of defaults could topple the largest U.S. banks.

Hope was kindled by the Baker Plan, a suggestion by Treasury Secretary James A. Baker III that the debtors grow out of their bind — aided by a 50 percent increase in loans from the development agencies and $20 billion more in fresh loans from the banks. But the commercial banks did not cooperate. Instead, they quietly began building up capital, laying the groundwork for moves such as Citicorp's, to boost reserves and so shield themselves from the bad loans.

As it is, nearly all commercial bank loans to the Third World are now made involuntarily, only after much arm-twisting by international agencies and the U.S. government. Big banks coerce smaller banks to join in, because only by making new loans can the banks collect interest on the old loans. But fewer and fewer banks care to go along. Many smaller regional banks have withdrawn. New reschedulings are increasingly difficult to negotiate. The interest rate banks charge has fallen to close to the banks' own cost of money, making the reschedulings unprofitable.

The flow of new money, beyond what debtor countries need to pay interest, has essentially stopped. From a high of $91 billion in 1981, net commercial lending to all developing countries fell to $3 billion last year, according to the International Monetary Fund. As one banker puts it, "Banks, even the bigger ones, just don't want to lend, period." Agency loans cannot fill the gap.

The denouement many people are predicting is this: The debtors, strapped to make interest payments, have little money left to invest. Investment continues to fall and, with it, prospects for economic growth. Poverty deepens. Risk of political upheaval rises, say, in Mexico. The Latin American market for U.S. exports never recovers — there is simply no money there to pay for them — and that costs U.S. jobs. Nervous union leaders and manufacturers agitate for protectionist barriers in the United States. When they spring up, they throttle world trade. The banking system, exposed not only to massive Third World loans but to bankrupt thrift institutions, bad farm debt, bad oil loans, bad real estate loans, heavy consumer debt and corporate debt, teeters. The long world economic expansion ends in a deep contraction.

In a way, Walter Wriston was right. Nations, the sum of their land and people, are by nature ultimately solvent. But what he did not mention was that nations, unlike individuals, don't get hauled off to court if they don't make payments. A bank cannot seize a nation's assets. "Foreign lending has its own special rules," says Carl Campbell, a financial analyst at A.G. Edwards & Sons Inc. of St. Louis. "And if somebody decides to break the rules, there's not much you can do about it."

The banks, it appears, are stuck. "We have a time bomb ticking away out there," contends Rep. Jerry Lewis. "It's a problem that can bring the world economy tumbling down if just a few things go wrong," adds the California Republican. "We've gotten ourselves in the classic position where it's no longer the case where the customer owes the bank $10,000 and so he's in trouble. They owe the bank $10 billion and the bank's in trouble."

A World Bank report cites "serious risk" of a "sustained setback to development in many debtor countries, of a growing breakdown in formal debtor-creditor relations, and of consequent lasting damage to the international financial system and world economy."

Many policymakers are calling for a massive infusion of new loans into the debt-strapped countries by the World Bank, ultimately backed by taxpayers of member countries. James W. Conrow, deputy assistant secretary for developing nations at the U.S. Treasury, says an expansion of World Bank lending of a multibillion-dollar magnitude is needed. Suggested figures have gone as high as $50 billion. "It's not going to be chicken feed," Conrow says. "It's going to be a significant amount of money. Governments are going to have to play their role."

Sen. Bill Bradley thinks the banks should forgive part of the loans to help out the debtors. Then, says the New Jersey Democrat, the debtors would be able to buy U.S. exports, and so boost the U.S. economy.

A proposal by Rep. John L. LaFalce would create a "debt adjustment facility" through the International Monetary Fund. The facility would buy up bank loans at a discount and pass the savings on to the debtors. It might buy a bank loan at a face value of, say, $1 billion for $700 million. The bank would take a $300 million loss and get rid of its loan, and the debtor would owe the facility $700 million.

The New York Democrat's amendment is attached to both the House and Senate trade bills.

The U.N. World Institute for Development Economics Research calls for a "Japanese Marshall Plan" that would "recycle" $125 billion of Japan's trade surplus over five years as new loans to the debtors. The Japanese government would raise the funds and subsidize and guarantee the loans. Japan's Prime Minister Yasuhiro Nakasone himself offered a less ambitious but substantial $20 billion to $30 billion in loans over three years.

There is, however, another school of thought, one that sees the debt problem in a far different light: as a threat not to Latin American democracy but to wasteful state socialism in the Third World, not as the end of development and economic growth but as its only real hope. This view says that the root of the problem is, as one development official puts it, "grotesque political and economic mismanagement" in Third World countries.

Solutions proposed so far have one thing in common, critics charge: throwing good money after bad. Further infusions of money only postpone the chance of sustained Third World growth by permitting the policies that helped create the distress to continue. Debtor governments could go on nationalizing industries, for example, or hyperinflating their economies or spending money on grandiose state projects. More borrowing only makes the ultimately necessary economic adjustments all the more painful, they say.

"You have got to have the right policies in place to grow, and more money is simply going to reinforce the old policies which have already failed," contends Alvin Rabushka, a senior fellow at the Hoover Institution. "Massive amounts of additional new lending from the Western industrial democracies and Japan to the Third World countries are only going to compound the problem they already have by further burdening them with additional debt."

The Citicorp move, carried out under the leadership of Chairman John S. Reed, sets the stage for realism, say the critics. The banks, by showing that they are prepared to accept losses, have less to fear if they refuse to lend new money. Until now, the debtors could retaliate by threatening to default and thus bankrupt the banks. The banks have broken the standoff. Says one banker, "The banks are going to be much, much more careful about the lending." The Citicorp action puts debtors under intense pressure to reform policies so they can again attract voluntary capital.

Further capital infusions provide an escape valve — to Third World governments, by destroying their incentives to reverse past mistakes, and to the banks, by allowing them to rid themselves of their loans. Several questions must be asked. What happened to the money? Billions of dollars of loans, commercial and public, went to the developing world in the 1970s and early 1980s. What did it buy? Finally, what prospects are in store now, for the banks, for the debtors, and for the industrial democracies who many say should foot the bill?

Act 3 begins to unfold.

HOLES IN THEIR POCKETS

Nigeria is building itself a capital, Abuja, from scratch. The cost by some estimates exceeds the nation's total sovereign debt of about $20 billion. Yet Nigeria has trouble making interest payments.

Hundreds of billions of dollars in lending traveled from the industrialized West to the Third World in the 1970s and early 1980s. Even after subtracting the interest portion of the $1 trillion debt, the figure is huge. And much of it consists of "soft" loans from World Bank agencies that — with no interest, a 10-year grace period and a 50-year term — are really more akin to foreign aid. Mexico reaped billions more from oil. Others received massive infusions of direct foreign aid. Today they cannot pay their bills.

Where did the money go?

"In Mexico it was just squandered in a morass of misguided government policies," says one lending agency official. "In the end they have very little to show for it." The same could be said of many debtor governments, of either the middle-income countries of Latin America or the impoverished sub-Saharan nations. "Africa earned its present status not because of an insufficiency of credit," says one commercial banker, "but because of an incapability of governing themselves."

Heavy borrowing bought central economic planning, nationalized industries, deficit spending and roads through uninhabited jungle. It bought national airlines for countries whose citizens travel in ox-drawn carts. It bought synfuel plants to supply depressed oil markets. It bought whole new cities such as Brasilia, built from scratch in the remote Brazilian interior. And a great deal, hundreds of billions of dollars, turned right around and left again through a process called capital flight. As the money came in, citizens and even high government officials sent it back out of the country to escape inflation, high taxes or overvalued exchange rates.

Even the World Bank and the International Monetary Fund concede that much of the spending was wasteful, even destructive. The bank points to a widespread tendency among strapped debtor governments to cut investment and maintenance on critical infrastructures such as roads to permit spending for "government employees, defense and state pensions as well as transfers and subsidies to state enterprises." The IMF notes "a tendency for consumption to be safeguarded at the expense of investment," even though investment is crucial to long-term growth. Beyond perverse spending priorities, the bank lists "a host of measures such as . . . import tariffs and restrictions, export taxes and exchange controls . . . which have a powerful influence on the patterns of domestic production and consumption and thus on efficiency and growth."

The litany of destructive policies includes "high marginal tax rates, compulsory marketing schemes for export crops, minimum wage laws and regulations against layoffs," says the bank. "Nearly all developing countries control interest rates and ration credit according to various 'planning priorities' which stifle the development of the financial sector." During the early 1980s, for example, "about 60 to 70 percent of credit in Mexico was administratively allocated or subsidized . . . [and] channeled to inefficient public enterprises or agriculture programs."

These are all recipes for economic decline, not development. Their underlying framework sprang from what Daniel Patrick Moynihan at the United Nations in 1975 called the British Doctrine, developed at the London School of Economics (and embellished by many leading European and U.S. universities), which equated foreign investment with imperialism, private profit with exploitation.

According to such thinking, public ownership should replace private ownership, and the main economic problem is not how to create wealth but how to redistribute it. Capitalists and landowners had money; whether they might be doing something that generated wealth was irrelevant. The point was to take wealth from them and give it to others or spend it on public projects. When students from the developing world returned home, many assumed influential positions in government, where they vigorously carried out what they had learned. Property rights, the underpinning of an open economy, were ignored. Many nations went on binges of nationalization, Mexico as recently as 1982, when it took over domestic banks. The Mexican government owns some 60 percent of the country's industrial base. Notoriously ill-managed, these nationalized industries require heavy subsidies to stay alive.

Starved for capital and burdened by regulation, private sectors withered. Agriculture was often hard hit by price controls that aid politically powerful city populations at the expense of farmers. Or take the businessman in Peru who filed a request to build a small clothing factory. He spent 289 days lobbying the bureaucracy and met 24 requests for bribes.

Many Third world debtor governments — Brazil, Mexico, Ethiopia, Ghana and Nigeria to list a few — banned private foreign investment on grounds that it was neocolonialist. To a capital-thirsty economy, this meant cutting off its primary source of equity financing. Equity investors risk money in a venture for a claim on ownership. They earn a return only if the venture succeeds. Equity is a basic source of financing for nearly any enterprise.

That route closed, the alternative was to rely almost exclusively on debt to finance development. Debt carries no ownership stake per se, but interest on a loan must be paid regardless of the success or failure of the investment. The borrower rather than the investor assumes the risk, which is why overborrowing is so dangerous. But not only did governments overborrow, they often spent the loan money on current consumption and unprofitable state enterprises that could never generate income to pay the interest. As William Cline of the Institute for International Economics noted in 1983, "Latin America, and Brazil more particularly, had celebrated a festival of nationalism in which extravagant foreign borrowing has replaced what should have been, to a much larger extent, equity financing." By discouraging foreign investment, governments also cut off the transfer of scarce technology and skills that investors bring with them when they put their money in a foreign venture.

As governments sucked up borrowed money and cut off private funds, they choked private enterprise and sent capital fleeing. Black markets became common in many parts of the Third World where it is illegal to change money at anything but an artificially low official rate. Curbside money changers who trade local currency for yen, deutsche marks and dollars at rates far above the official rate vividly display how heavy the losses for residents can be.

By one estimate, citizens of debtor nations may have accumulated about $200 billion in overseas assets by the end of 1985, says the International Monetary Fund. Some say that flight capital from Latin America has at times exceeded the capital left behind. Money hidden abroad is spent abroad.

In stark contrast to the problem debtors are the success stories of the developing world. Hong Kong, now a leading commercial center, has some of the world's most liberal direct investment rules. Thailand has grown rapidly through private agriculture. Said a Thai official, "The private sector will remain the prime engine of growth." South Korea, $43 billion in debt and once devastated by war, is becoming a world-class manufacturer because the money was invested in export industries that are now earning a return.

But for the problem debtors, critics say, the borrowing propped up destructive policies and allowed governments "the luxury of interfering with the private sector," as Alvin Rabushka, a senior fellow at the Hoover Institution, puts it. The loans were cheap and plentiful, and many went directly to governments. "Their economic attitudes were shaped by the perception that this was gift money," says Nick Eberstadt of Harvard University's Center for Population Studies. "Needless to say, when you make unlimited amounts of capital available directly to governments, it changes the balance of power rather dramatically" between the public and private sectors.

Critics say the World Bank and other taxpayer-backed lending agencies, in standing by to lend fresh money when debtors get into trouble, only encourage more bad policy. But what may be the most scathing charge yet leveled against the problem debtor nations is this: They are not unable to service their debts, but unwilling.

It is "rarely asked in polite international society" whether these nations should sell assets to service debt, writes P.T. Bauer, a leading economist at the London School of Economics and a long-standing critic of foreign aid. He points to Pemex, the state-owned Mexican oil monopoly. "Pemex could be conservatively valued (in 1983) at between $35 and $40 billion," he recently wrote. "The sovereign debt of Mexico was then around $80 billion. The sale or pledge of part of Pemex might well have averted the Mexican debt crisis, as it would have shown the readiness of the government to meet its obligation. Much the same applies to most of the other debtors."

Brazil refuses to service its debt because doing so "presumably throttles increases in the standard of living," says Eberstadt. "They say, 'Not only is our current standard of living inviolable, but also we will settle for nothing less than a 6 to 7 percent growth rate in the future, and we will adjust all other promises we've made in the past against this new schedule we've come up with.' What's dramatically unconvincing is the notion that Brazil is unable to pay its debts. You need only look at government ownership of industry and land to realize how preposterous it is. What we're dealing with is a patent unwillingness . . . to honor obligations that they contracted for."

Some nations have begun to change policy, partly because banks have stopped lending to them. Rabushka says the general view in

Africa is that the World Bank will make far fewer amorphous loans to governments to finance consumption. "Out of necessity they're going to have to go for direct foreign investment. They're simply not going to have at their disposal the massive amounts of money made available in the 1960s and 1970s."

But it will be a tough sell. As one U.S. investor said of the Mexican government, "Unless I got some positive guarantee of property rights, I wouldn't trust them. They also play too free and loose with their money. Their devaluations in the past have been catastrophic to foreign investment. To devalue the peso the way they have done is like highway robbery to any investor.

"I look for a country where title is vested in property and deeds are recognized and honored. I don't want anything to do with a country that is prone to just take property." Noting that Indonesia relaxed its investment laws dramatically, gradually lifting bans on foreign ownership, he says, "They realize that people are not going to come over and invest if they can't own property. What's the incentive if you have to give 90 or 95 percent [ownership] to a local to get established in business?"

Other governments take a more resolute stand. The latest instance comes from President Alan Garcia Perez of Peru, who recently announced that his government will nationalize the banks. Garcia also intends to run off Lima's money changers.

Carolyn Lochhead

CHAPTER 34

*Congress's massive 1988 trade act marked
a historic departure in U.S. policy.
Henceforth, the government would single
out countries (notably Japan) for
negotiations on tariffs and other trade
barriers. Rather than aim for free trade,
many of the law's backers wanted to
institute "managed trade," with the
government intervening either to keep out
some foreign products or to secure foreign
markets for American goods. This article
of December 25, 1989, pointed out the
potential flaws of that strategy.*

TRADE NATIONALISTS BANG ON CLOSED DOORS

If U.S. trade relations continue on their present course, Congress in 1990 will watch Super 301, its trade version of the B-1 bomber, drop a payload on Japan, Brazil and India. What will happen next is anyone's guess. Unless President Bush intervenes, or unless the three nations bow to U.S. trade demands, the Super 301 provision of the Omnibus Trade Act of 1988 requires U.S. Trade Representative Carla Hills to start retaliatory action by June 16.

Yet so far, each of these countries has simply refused to negotiate under Super 301, charging that it violates international rules. Most nations appear to be of like mind, accusing the United States of "taking the law into our own hands," says Jagdish Bhagwati, an international economist at Columbia University.

Super 301 is meant as a kind of crowbar to pry open foreign markets to U.S. exports by threatening to close U.S. markets to imports. The hope is that to avoid U.S. restrictions these countries will cease the trade practices Hills cited as unfair in May: Japan by removing barriers against U.S. satellites, supercomputers and lumber; Brazil by easing restrictive import licensing arrangements; and India by lifting barriers to insurance and investment. Hills must also come up with a new list of unfair traders by April 30, to be retaliated against in 1991 unless U.S. demands are met.

Whether any country concedes to any specific U.S. demand, or whether the United States retaliates on any specific product, the implications of Super 301 run far deeper. The provision is a tool of "managed trade," whereby the government would secure export markets for U.S. firms and limit import penetration of the U.S. market. Many in Congress want to see managed trade adopted as policy, believing it would duplicate what they see as the key to Japan's success.

Super 301 represents a striking turn toward economic nationalism, toward a belief that U.S. economic security is under attack and toward the view that America is losing control of its destiny to foreign invaders. "We need to fundamentally rethink our trade policies," says John P. Cregan of the U.S. Business and Industrial Council. "Economic nationalism is the driving force in world trade today, and we are among the last to realize it."

Both the political right and left are beginning to converge around the idea of managed trade. For the left, it closely resembles a government-directed industrial policy. On the right, groups like Cregan's believe Japan and the "little dragons" of East Asia are practicing "turbocharged capitalism," a government-business collaboration to dominate strategic industries. William T. Archey, a vice president at the U.S. Chamber of Commerce, has called Super 301 "a legitimate and long overdue assertion of America's trade rights."

But to many economists, the ideas behind managed trade are old, the analyses flawed and the dangers clear. Pointing to U.S. industrial sectors where government already manages trade — in semiconductors, in textiles and apparel, in steel, in automobiles, in agriculture — they say such policies will damage both U.S. consumers and U.S. industry. If anything, they say, managed trade and its handmaiden, Super 301, will not rescue American living standards but sink them.

" 'Managed trade.' Think of the phrase for a second," says C. Michael Aho, director of economic studies for the Council on Foreign Relations and former adviser to Democratic Sen. Bill Bradley of New Jersey. "Do you think the U.S. could manage managed trade very well?"

Such a policy, say critics, would lead not to Japanese-style success (the basis of which is misunderstood, they contend) but to the government-managed failures so evident around the world — Mexico, Argentina, the Philippines, the East Bloc countries. Such policies also will not reduce the trade deficit, they maintain, because it is driven by savings and investment patterns and federal deficit spending.

"The case for a market-guided, market-coordinated economy does not stop at the water's edge," says Leland Yeager, an international economist at Auburn University. He calls managed trade "a preposterous idea. Do you want to take a model of our agricultural policy, say, or our policy about where to locate Army and Navy bases, as an example of how the government would run the economy?"

While promoted as a tool to open export markets, managed trade and Super 301 are an invitation for companies to lobby Congress for privileged access to foreign markets and protection from foreign competitors. That is "what they're really up to, of course," says Yeager. "You can bet your boots on it." In fact, leading backers of the U.S. Business and Industrial Council belong to the heavily protected steel and textile industries.

Many contend that when firms are protected, they simply become less competitive. Firms also tend to gauge market openness by how much they sell overseas, says Bhagwati. As a result, inefficient U.S. industries tend to drive trade policy. Many Third World countries provide a case in point: Governments often justify protection as a means of generating foreign exchange. "Firms typically run to their governments and say, 'I can save you foreign exchange' " by supplying the domestic market if officials restrict imports, he says. "In this way, governments gradually wind up with heavy protection and sickly industries."

Bhagwati sees a symmetrical development in the United States. American firms, he says, "rush to Congress and say, 'I could export more, but there are other guys not letting me export.' You've got to get the Japanese and Koreans and everybody" to buy the product made by the supplicant firm. U.S. semiconductor policy runs along these lines, demanding that Japan meet certain purchasing targets for U.S. chips. He believes Super 301 reflects a "panic and petulance" growing out of what he calls the "diminished giant syndrome." Although still very much an economic power, the United States has witnessed the erosion of its preeminence as the Far East and Europe have achieved prosperity and success. The competitive challenge was surprising and troubling to a nation that had enjoyed sole domination of the world economic stage.

Congress has high hopes for the Super 301 strategy to save U.S. industry and increase exports. If results are not satisfactory, lawmakers have even stronger measures waiting in the wings. While the full effects of the law will not be visible before the June retaliation

deadline, results from the threat itself have so far been unspectacu-
lar.

A few smaller countries, notably South Korea, have lifted some
barriers in fear of being added to the hit list. But the law has yielded little more than continuing negotiations with it primary targets:
Japan and the European Community. Unlike smaller countries,
these powerful trading partners can retaliate in kind. In fact, the
community was a conspicuous omission from May's list of unfair
traders; European officials had promised a counterstrike against
U.S. exports within 24 hours if community members were named.

The law has generated immense ill will. In effect, the U.S. stance
is, "We are only threatening something illegal, but we are not actually doing something illegal," says Bhagwati. "That's sort of like mobi-
lizing all your troops, calling people to arms, and saying, 'Well, I
haven't actually invaded.'"

Super 301 is a clear violation of international trading rules. In
launching the weapon, Congress embraced unilateralism, calling for
the United States to act on it own against trading partners. This is a
sharp departure from the multilateralism the United States had
championed through the postwar era under the auspices of the General Agreement of Tariffs and Trade, a treaty among 97 nations that
governs world commerce. The United States had led the GATT
effort to liberalize trade and promote economic growth under the
principle of mutual tariff reductions, in which a nation agrees to
remove its barriers if its trading partners remove theirs. Unilateral
retaliation outside of the agreement is illegal.

While critics say GATT is outmoded, its achievements have been
impressive. World tariff levels have fallen in the postwar era, accompanied by a blossoming of trade and economic growth. In the 1970s,
however, countries began adopting nontariff barriers, more subtle
regulations that make it difficult for foreign competitors to penetrate
a market. Several major industries, including agriculture and textiles, also had been excluded from GATT. These areas began to
emerge as a major source of friction.

Trade in the GATT-exempt sectors is distinguished by extensive
barriers, heavy state subsidization and severe economic distortion.
Textile and apparel trade, for one, is "an important empirical example of where managed trade is likely to go," says Thomas Grennes, a
North Carolina State University economist. What began as a simple
temporary quota system during the 1950s to limit cotton textiles
from Japan grew into the monstrously complex Multifiber Arrangement that raises prices to U.S. consumers at least $20 billion a year,

according to William Cline of the Institute for International Economics. Moreover, the quotas severely damage Third World producers, for whom apparel manufacture is a springboard to economic development. By retarding income growth in poorer countries, the trade barriers also stifle other U.S. exports.

In all, U.S. trade barriers cost Americans at least $65 billion a year. They also backfire on industries. Recent increases in U.S. tariffs on ball bearings have raised raw material costs to hundreds of U.S. firms including General Electric Co. and Black & Decker Corp., says Alexander Tabarrok, an adjunct scholar at the Ludwig von Mises Institute, an Austrian economics think tank. The higher costs in turn impede the ability of these firms to compete against foreign producers.

Steel quotas recently helped drive Davis Walker Corp., a Los Angeles producer of steel wire products, into Chapter 11 bankruptcy. The U.S. quotas divide market share for imported steel among some 20 countries, limiting what each can export to the United States. As a result, says Chris Stauffer, vice president for procurement at Davis Walker, "competitive bidding has really been taken out of the picture. Market prices are somehow mysteriously set quarter to quarter, and those are the prices you have to live with."

Davis Walker lost its price competitiveness and imports began eating into its markets. "If you look back," says Stauffer, "every time there's been a quota or a trigger price mechanism" or some other interference, "we've watched our profitability start to slide." The latest round of quotas, implemented in 1984, extends through 1992. "We're facing I think the longest period that we've ever faced now, 7½ years of this," he says. "I don't know how anyone could bear up under that."

By raising prices, trade barriers reduce living standards in each country that uses them, including Japan. Richard McKenzie, an economist at the University of Mississippi, says many Americans would not want to live in Japan "precisely because of some of the management techniques" its government has used to promote exports at the expense of domestic consumption.

But Cregan of the U.S. Business and Industrial Council calls for explicit reductions in the trade deficit with Japan "whatever it takes," including mandated import reductions. What might such techniques mean for U.S. consumers? Sharp supply restrictions and massive price increases on compact disc players, videocassette recorders and automobiles, to name a few items.

Once in place, trade barriers tend to snowball, says Tabarrok, as industries hurt by protection ask for protection themselves, until ultimately "you have a situation where everyone is 'protected,' meaning that everyone is worse off. What one firm gains by protection, it loses by protection that is added for everyone else."

Countries impoverish each other much the same way through destructive barrier building. A close analogy, says Tabarrok, is the dilemma people encounter when watching a parade: "Someone will strain to stand on tiptoe so their view is improved. If one person does this, however, the view of another is obscured. To even the score, this second person will also stand on tiptoe, obscuring the view of a third. Soon everyone is standing on tiptoe yet none has a better view," and all are worse off because standing on tiptoe is uncomfortable.

GATT helps countries overcome similar situations by laying out rules for reciprocal barriers reductions. But Super 301 complicates the U.S. position at the Uruguay round of negotiations under way and scheduled for completion late next year. U.S. officials hope to win concession on areas of critical importance to the United States, including trade in agriculture and services and protection of patents, trademarks and other intellectual property.

Because of the high stakes involved, the GATT, often characterized as weak and ineffective, may emerge as the dominant force shaping U.S. trade policy, at least for now. Super 301 has created a backlash around the world, says Gary Hufbauer, a trade economist at Georgetown University, "but the backlash that counts is Japan and Europe, and they're fed up with being pushed around." In response, he says these countries "have escalated to a principal demand within the Uruguay round that the whole 301 mechanism must be disciplined" by some kind of GATT oversight. "That has become suddenly a very big demand," he says, "and I don't think the Uruguay round will be concluded unless the United States sheathes the sword."

Deep U.S. concern about derailing GATT talks may serve to keep a lid on Super 301. However, when the discipline of ongoing GATT negotiations is lifted, U.S. unilateralism may more fully blossom. Says Aho, "I suspect that in years divisible by four, it's going to be very hard for a sitting president to resist taking on some of these complaints." Certainly Congress has plotted out a number of special targets for Super 301 bombing runs.

Carolyn Lochhead

INDEX

396

communications: Ghana, 363; immigration, 114; Poland, 242
communism vs. capitalism, 218, 225, 227-233, 237, 245-251. SEE ALSO capitalism vs. communism/socialism.
communism: vi, Germany, 175; Poland, 241
Communist Party (Soviet Union), 225
Confederation of Labor Unity, 310
Congress: farm policy, 37-44, 42-44, 46-48, 53; immigration, 109-115; Jackson-Vanik, 288; loan policies, 56-59
Congressional Black Caucus, 114
Connersville, Ind., 32, 39
Conrow, James W., 380
Conservation Reserve Program, 50
Conservative Party: Great Britain, 185, 187, 188, 189, 190-192, 193; South Africa, 337, 340, 345, 347
consumer goods: Ghana, 368; Japan, 265; Nicaragua, 310; Panama, 299; South Africa, 341; Soviet Union, 227
Contra rebels, 308
controversy: European Community, 159, 162; homeless, 92; trade status of China, 285-289; Soviet Union's statistics, 217-221, 228
Cook, Peter, 199
Corps of Engineers (U.S. Army), 302
cotton, 223, 307
Council for Quality Growth (Ga.), 19
Council on Foreign Relations, 388
credit: Ghana, 367; La Paz small businesses, 317-329; South Africa, 338; U.S. government, 56-59
Cregan, John P., 388, 391
Crews, Alton, 20
crime: Ghana, 362; New York City, 71, 76; Newark, 71; Poland, 235; underclass, 75, 82, 87; youth employment, 81
Cuba, 304
currency reform: Germany, 176; Ghana, 353, 365, 367; Israel, 202; Nicaragua, 310
Currey, Fred, 60, 63
Czechoslovakia, 138 (illus.), 176

Danareksa (Indonesia), 291
Dart, Justin, 61
Davignon, Etienne, 161, 165
Davis Walker Corp., 391
daylight saving time, 262
de Gaulle, Charles, 160
de Klerk, Frederik W., 340, 348
de Kock, Gerhard P. C., 341, 344-346
de Mita, Ciriaco, 230
de Villiers, Riaan, 346, 348
DeBoer, Stan, 34
debt: Ghana, 356; Israel, 210; Nicaragua, 307; Panama, 302, 303; South Africa, 341, 346; Third World, 375-386
"deconstructionism," 101
Delors, Jacques, 151, 154, 159, 163, 168-172
Demjan, Sandor, 247
democracy, 26, 239
Democratic Party (South Africa), 346, 348
Deng Xiaoping, 251
Denmark, 161

Depression, 34
Detroit, 12
Dignity Battalions, Panama, 301
"disurbia," 16
Donaldson, Deborah M., 19
Doran, Charles, 198
Doron, Daniel, 202-204, 208, 210, 212
Douglas, William O., 6
Drawicz, Andrzej, 242
drug traffic: Panama, 304; South Africa, 338; Thailand, 129 (illus.); underclass, 82
DSP Financial Consultants (India), 295
du Plessis, Fred, 344
du Plessis, Barend J., 345, 349
Duignan, Peter, 356
Duncan Avenue project (Jersey City), 87
Duque, Carlos, 300
Duran, Marta, 323

earthquakes: Japan, 271; Nicaragua, 308
East Bloc, 132-135 (illus.), 138-139 (illus.), 245-251, 353, 355, 360
East Coast (U.S.), 81
Eberstadt, Nick, 220, 376, 385
Economic Emergency Credit Act, 54
Economic Planning Agency (Japan), 259, 261, 262
economic planning (Agricultural Adjustment Act), 34
Edmonds, John, 187
Edo River district (Tokyo), 263
Edogawa (Tokyo), 259
Education Dept. (U.S.), 56
education: Atlanta, 20-21; Bolivia, 321; Great Britain, 190; Ghana, 370; immigration and education, 109-115; poverty and education, 69, 73; South Africa, 335, 345; underclass, 82
El Alto, Bolivia, 322
El Cocuy, Colombia, 315
elderly persons, 79
elections: Canada, 196; Great Britain, 183, 187, 189; Germany, 177, 180; Gold Coast (Ghana), 357; Israel, 207; Japan, 267, 268; South Africa, 342, 345, 347
Elias, Mike, 93, 96, 99
Ellwood, David T., 78
Elscint Co., 210
emigration, 239: European Community, 161; Israel, 211; Nicaragua, 309; South Africa, 337, 350
employment: Chile, 312; European Community, 157, 162; Great Britain, 192, 193; Germany, 180; Ghana, 359, 371; homeless, 92, 97; immigration, 114; Israel, 211; Japan, 263, 278; job training, 88; Poland, 243; Panama, 305; South Africa, 334, 338, 346; underclass, 75, 80; workplace equality, 101-108
Endara, Guillermo, 302, 304
Ensor, Paul, 293
Environmental Protection Agency, 8
Equal Employment Opportunity Commission, 102, 106
Equal Pay Act, 104
Ernst & Whinney, 232
Erskine, John, 21
Escom (South Africa), 344
Espenshade, Thomas, 113